Body Modification

edited by
Mike Featherstone

SAGE Publications
London · Thousand Oaks · New Delhi

Body Modification is simultaneously published as Volume 5, Numbers 2–3 of *Body & Society*

© Body & Society 2000

First published 2000

Published in association with *Theory, Culture & Society*, Nottingham Trent University

SAGE Publications Ltd
6 Bonhill Street
London EC2A 4PU

SAGE Publications Inc
2455 Teller Road
Thousand Oaks, California 91320

SAGE Publications India Pvt Ltd
32, M-Block Market
Greater Kailash - I
New Delhi 110 048

British Library Cataloguing in Publication data

A catalogue record for this book is available from the British Library

ISBN 0 7619 6795 8
ISBN 0 7619 6796 6 (pbk)

Library of Congress catalog record available

Typeset by Type Study, Scarborough, UK
Printed in Great Britain by The Alden Press, Oxford

Contents

Body Modification: An Introduction

MIKE FEATHERSTONE

Over the last 30 years, there has been a resurgence of interest in body modification in the West. Most noticeable is the increased incidence of tattooing and piercing, evident in the various rings and studs in noses, eyebrows, tongues, navels and other parts of the body. The term 'body modification' refers to a long list of practices which include piercing, tattooing, branding, cutting, binding and inserting implants to alter the appearance and form of the body. The list of these practices could be extended to include gymnastics, bodybuilding, anorexia and fasting – forms in which the body surface is not directly inscribed and altered using instruments to cut, pierce and bind. In these practices, the outer body is transformed through a variety of exercises and dietary regimes, which are generally much slower processes, with the external effects, such as gaining or losing bulk, fat or musculature, only becoming observable over longer periods of time.

In addition, we have to consider the ways in which the body is modified by the use of various forms of prostheses and technological systems. These range from simple prosthetic devices to enhance body motor and sensory functions such as spectacles, to the building of technological environments around the human being, such as the motor car or jet fighter, in which the vehicle's velocity and performance increasingly necessitate the replacement of human sight and motor response by computer-driven vision systems designed to permit greater speed, flexibility and feedback. In the future, it is suggested that increasingly moving vehicles, as well as static vehicles such as home computer multimedia systems, will provide virtual reality environments we will have to learn to inhabit. Alternatively, the technology may be built into the human being in order to replace or augment the functioning of inner organs (heart, kidneys, etc.), body surfaces (skin), senses (hearing, sight, etc.) and limbs. Nanotechnology offers the

Body & Society © 1999 SAGE Publications (London, Thousand Oaks and New Delhi),
Vol. 5(2–3): 1–13
[1357–034X(199906/09)5:2–3;1–13;008851]

potential for further inner body cyborg technological developments, with molecular machines roving the bloodstream to search and destroy viruses. A popular image of the cyborg is that of the powerful male warrior as presented in science fiction films such as *Robocop* (Paul Verhoeven, 1987). While *Robocop*'s body is visibly a human–machine hybrid, the plot of the film *Blade Runner* (Michael Deeley and Ridley Scott, 1982) revolves around the problem of establishing criteria for judging and testing for robotic 'replicants', whose bodies are seemingly indistinguishable from human beings (see the discussions in Holland, 1995; Landsberg, 1995). The ways in which science fiction influences business and research practices, as in the case of William Gibson's (1986) influential descriptions of cyberspace, is a further important process of extending the horizon of expectations of human–machine fusions. Such processes directly and indirectly help to modify our everyday common-sense understandings of how bodies work.

While cyborg imagery modifies the horizons of what a body can be, and points to the fascination with the artificial, existing scientific and medical technologies seek or claim to clarify our perception of the 'natural' body. They effectively define our image of the working of the human body, increasingly through the construction and use of virtual bodies: the three-dimensional computer simulations of the human body such as the Visible Human Project. At the same time, it can be argued that such perspectives which seemingly reproduce the immediate 'visibility' of the body are in fact representations which are already models, especially so in the coming information order when we start to appreciate the code-like quality of digitally generated information systems. This suggests that the lines between nature and culture are inherently blurred and helps us to appreciate Judith Butler's (1990: 7) observation that nature turns out to be culture all along (see Leng, 1996: 45).

Common to many of the accounts of body modification is the sense of taking control over one's body, of making a gesture against the body natural and the tyranny of habitus formation. In his piece on 'Modern Primitivism' in this collection, Christian Klesse cites the following remark, which is typical of many body modifiers:

> I make a statement, I've chosen myself. I am part of a culture but I don't believe in it. My body modifications are my way to say that.

Here we have a sense of control over one's body, that one has somehow taken possession of one's body, which henceforth carries a visible sign of identity. On one level, it can be objected that this is nothing new, that within consumer culture the body has always been presented as an object ready for transformation. The 'makeovers' and 'shapeovers' (the dieting, exercise, cosmetic and fashion regimes) celebrated in the media, advertising and glossy magazines, have a personal transformation rhetoric: with a little money and effort the body can be changed to approximate the youth, fitness and beauty ideals of consumer culture (Featherstone, 1982, 1991). Increasingly, the emphasis within consumer culture has shifted away from disguising the body (hidden and restricted beneath heavy clothing) to the visible contours of the body (lighter clothing and the exposure of flesh). For women, this not only entailed dieting and slimming regimes, but aerobics and bodybuilding, too (Lloyd, 1996; St Martin and Gavey, 1996). Yet, as Bourdieu (1978; see Featherstone, 1987) has argued, rather than seeing people's body work as targeted directly to achieve some singular dominant body form, it is better to consider 'a universe of class bodies' which is structurally differentiated. Hence, transformative practices can go wrong: one can follow the wrong regime and end up with a modified body that sends out the wrong messages to others.

Lee Monaghan, in his piece in this collection, 'Creating the Perfect Body', discusses the pluralities of muscular bodies which can be produced through bodybuilding. This process requires careful judgement and knowledge of the parameters and values of the different forms of body capital which operate in the universe of class bodies which is to be found within a particular society. Because this knowledge of classificatory schemes is rarely articulated and operates below the level of consciousness, it is possible to get things wrong. Hence Monaghan tells us of the sense of surprise and dismay on the part of some male bodybuilders who, after spending considerable time 'working out' to bulk up muscles and develop what they assumed was a desirable form, were dismayed to find that women laughed at them when they paraded their bodies on the beach. As one of Monaghan's informants remarked, he had miscalculated in producing a bulky 'rhino' or 'frog' shape, when he should have been aiming at a more sleek 'tiger' or 'puma' athletic look. One man's reaction here was to go to the beach with his clothes on, but the problems do not necessarily cease here, for to many ordinary people the clothed muscular bodies of bodybuilders seem fat. Hence the need to correct the body from the post-athletic over-bulky look and re-attain a body which looks sleek, muscular and fit – a body like a sprinter or one of the Chippendales. Likewise, Roberta Sassatelli, in her piece on 'Body Culture in Fitness Gyms', argues that it is too simplistic to only regard gym culture as a place where people search for the perfect body. Although participants may have the instrumental aim of body improvement, the gym should also be analysed using Goffman's concept of frame, as a world in itself in which reflexivity is deliberately dampened down. Certainly, it would seem clear that the range of messages read into bodies and the interpretive work necessary to classify them make a structured universe of class bodies much more difficult to construct today. If we consider the case of women bodybuilders, it is hard to locate them in the existing universe of class bodies. As Doug Aoki (1996) has argued, in some instances there is a clear attempt to transgress the normal gender lines. For some women who attain a masculine, muscular, bulked-up body, there is a deliberate attempt to play with gender, by retaining feminine signifiers on their face such as lipstick and earrings. In such instances they can appear to be a strange hybrid, with a female head stuck on a male body, something which Aoki characterizes as 'gender-crossing dressing' (see also St Martin and Gavey, 1996).

The question arises: can such changes be reversed? Can a muscular body builder revert to a 'normal body'? To what extent can such strategies be considered as essentially modern with not only identity, but also the body, seen as plastic and discardable? This question is directly addressed in three articles in this collection: those by Bryan S. Turner, Paul Sweetman and Christian Klesse. In 'The Possibility of Primitiveness: Towards a Sociology of Body Marks in Cool Societies', Bryan Turner contrasts the social framing of body modification in traditional and postmodern societies, arguing that traditional tribalism with its 'thick and hot' solidarities, produced obligatory body markings inscribed in rituals which led to stability of the in-group against outsiders. Today's 'postmodern neo-tribalism', in contrast, favours 'thin and cool' loyalties based upon voluntary membership; hence, body markings are 'optional, decorative, impermanent and narcissistic'. For Turner, the departure lounge is the metaphor which best captures the uncertainties, ennui, anxiety and fragility of modern life. The cool loyalties of its inhabitants, the professional workers and elites, are increasingly found in the new underclass and postmodern youth tribes for whom tattoos, such as the paint-on tattoos worn at football matches, indicate their transferable loyalties.

In his piece 'Anchoring the (Postmodern) Self? Body Modification, Fashion and Identity', Paul Sweetman provides a critique of Turner's position. Sweetman challenges the sharp contrast with traditional societies Turner constructs, arguing that the attraction of body modification practices for many people is that they are permanent and irreversible. In this sense they are to be seen as an attempt to fix and anchor the self by permanently marking the body. Sweetman quotes an American tattooist, Don Ed Hardy, who remarks 'It is on your body, it's permanent; you have to live with it and it hurts'. Some tattoos or piercings can, of course, be removed and can be worn as fashion accessories, as is the case with ear or nose piercings. Permanence and visibility may vary and there is a difference between a man who has his whole body (including face and eyelids) tattooed with leopard spots and someone who has a discrete butterfly tattooed on their buttocks.[1] Here we can refer to the distinction made by Polhemus and Proctor (1978) between fashion and anti-fashion. The latter is characterized by the wearing of uniforms, or scarring or tattooing. For many of the people Sweetman interviewed, body modification was attractive as it resisted the superficiality of consumer culture and the 'carnival of signs'. It was perceived as part of a body project, the construction of a viable self-identity through the body, something which was seen as involving a strong 'commitment to oneself'.

The term 'body project' has been used by Giddens (1991) to suggest that the dissolution of tradition in late modernity is accompanied by ontological insecurity and a reflexive concern with identity and the body.[2] Yet, as Christian Klesse reminds us in his contribution 'Modern Primitivism: Non-Mainstream Body Modification and Racialized Representation', the problem with this notion is that it tends to present identity construction as an option within the reach of all subjects. In contrast to theorists such as Beck (1992; Beck et al., 1994) and Giddens, who present increased reflexivity, individuation, personal design and choice at the centre of the modernization process, others such as Zygmunt Bauman (1991) and Paul Gilroy (1993), for example, argue that anti-semitism and racism still remain at the heart of modernity. Racialized bodies cannot be so easily reconstituted and made into a project; there is always the problem of visibility and passing in which the incorporated history of bodies weighs down the potential for action (Ahmed, 1999; Fraser, 1999; Skeggs, 1997).

For Klesse, most contemporary theories of identity miss the ways in which Western identities depend on a dichotomous concept of the racialized other. This is a mistake not only made by those who discuss the body as a seemingly neutral site for fashion accessories in the form of piercing, tattooing, etc., but also those who reject the reconstitutable body which can be re-commodified to increase its exchange value – those modern primitives who seek to permanently inscribe the body by replicating rituals and traditions. Klesse is critical of the modern primitives for the reproduction of repressive gender and racialized stereotypes. There is the danger that they operate with fixed stereotypes which fetishize other cultures and give no room for agency and cultural mixing for contemporary primitives (see also Eubanks, 1996). One of the famous advocates of Modern Primitivism, Fakir Musafar, is seen by Klesse as idealizing and essentializing primitive culture when he asserts that by collecting photos of the primitives he has 'honored them, envied them and very privately duplicated many of their experiences'. Such identifications are seen by Klesse as entailing a middle-class romanticized and exoticized imagery of the noble savage. They do not take into account the ways in which the early *National Geographic* style material and photographs were produced as part of colonial governability. Klesse argues that we need to question the racialized construction of epistemology around the binaries of primitive/ modern, developed/non-developed, civilized/savage, rational/irrational and enlightenment/ magic. This suggests we should move towards a deconstruction of the strict separation between modernity and primitivism/tradition, especially when the former term is too easily equated with the West and the latter terms with the non-West.

If body modification refers to a standard bodyliness which can be transgressed, the question asked by Margrit Shildrick in her piece in this collection 'The Body which is Not One', is what happens if standard bodyliness is an impossible ideal, something not given, but yet to be achieved. This is the case if the original body is already monstrous, a site of disruption and corporeal ambiguity which resists definition and closure. Normally to be a self is to be distinguished from the other, but Shildrick asks what happens if we inhabit the body of another, or find our bodies shared or invaded by another?[3] The body form of conjoint twins challenges both the distinction between mind and body and body and body. For Shildrick, monsters as entities which do not conform to the normal rules are disturbingly in-between, and demonstrate the fragility of the distinctions between the normal and the other. She comments 'In collapsing the boundaries between the self and the other monsters constitute an indecidable absent presence at the heart of the human being'. Conjoined twins provide an example of a transgressive and indeterminate state in which the other is also the self. Splitting of the twins through surgery does not result in the reconstitution of autonomous subjectivity, but instead produces an effect akin to that of phantom limbs.

Walburga Freitag (1999) has reached similar conclusions about the difficulty of normalizing bodies that have already been modified at birth in her research on thalidomide children. From the perspective of the doctors, the thalidomide bodies were deformed and therefore had to be made normal to help the children adjust. But when this entailed the painful wearing of artificial legs on stunted limbs incapable of bearing the load, there was not a gain but a loss of mobility for the children, who had become agile and adept at moving around the home using their shortened limbs. In effect, the attempted normalization process was for the doctors' benefit and not the children's, for the latter had no problem accepting a body which they had become used to living in since birth. Also interesting in this connection is Roy Boyne's contribution to this collection, 'Citation and Subjectivity: Towards a Return of the Embodied Will'. He discusses the post-operative difficulties of transsexuals, who refuse citational and constructionist notions of identity and any notion of ambiguity and in-betweenness by seeking out fixity. To this end, they seek the support of endocrinal examinations in order to marshal biological evidence, an embodied basis in which to legitimize and anchor their identity space. Hence they seek to escape the alleged postmodern experimentation and shopping for identities through the quest for a permanent transition into an essentialist embodied identity.

One of the most objectionable aspects of body modification, for the wider public, is not just the prospect of a different aesthetic which goes counter to the notion of natural and consumer culture bodies, but the pain and violation of the body associated with cutting. As Victoria Pitts argues in her piece 'Body Modification, Self-Mutilation and Agency in Media Accounts of a Subculture', cutting becomes rapidly pathologized as mutilation by the media. Cutting is generally presented in horror-story terms by mental health experts who seek to recover it into some pathological syndrome, to be placed alongside other forms of self-harm such as anorexia and bulimia. If the body is meant to be the source of pleasure and value in life in the 'if you look good, you feel good' consumer culture philosophy, the disregard and violation of the body generally suggests a threatening lack of respect for the self. In his piece in this collection, 'Tattoos and Heroin', Kevin McCarron disputes this easy equation of the body and the self by arguing that junkies are incapable of seeing the body as anything other than separated from the mind. McCarron suggest that one popular image of the junkie that rings true is that of the methadone clinic full of people with grotesque jailhouse tattoos. People whose tattoos reveal their loathing for the body and its products. The tattoos are a sign of distaste and disgust for the flesh, and at the same time are a sign of the desire to transcend the flesh, to escape the grotesqueness of the body for the mind. In the novel *Trainspotting* by Irvine Walsh (1993), Johnny runs out of veins and starts shooting arteries, and then gets gangrene and has to have his leg amputated. As the addiction gains total mastery, the body becomes irrelevant and disposable.

Cutting the body is central to the development of anatomical science and the understanding of the body in medicine. As Eugene Thacker argues in his article 'Performing the Technoscientific Body', anatomical science sought to visualize the non-visible, to mobilize visualization processes in order to produce new image-bodies. Early anatomical science developed through dissection of the body and systematic observation, to reveal the hidden order of things and construct the universal body of the textbooks. This was the body that was revealed in the 16th-century anatomy theatres, in which dissection turned into disturbing public spectacles. Thacker argues that the recent development of Real Video Surgery, through computer mediated communication using the Internet, represents a further spectacularization of medicine with the penetration of 'cybercasting events' into everyday life. Real Video Surgery, through the use of data streaming, creates a hyperreal simulation of the body that effects our ways of representing bodies. It can be compared to live sex pornography on the Internet: occupying an intermediate place between public spectacle and private voyeurism.

A further stage in this process has been the development of the Visual Human Project, a three-dimensional digital model of the body, which is discussed by Neal Curtis in his article, 'The Body as Outlaw'. In many ways the VHP is the realization of the dreams of anatomical science, because it provides a comprehensive 'atlas' of the body which discloses every vein, muscle, fibre, passage and cavity of the body which, given the three-dimensional formatting, can be scrutinized from any position. While the VHP seeks to represent the universal body, it was derived from the actual body of a 39-year-old convicted murderer, Joseph Jernigan, who agreed to donate his body to science after his execution, so that it could be frozen and dissected into 1mm slices, with each slice digitalized in preparation for its virtual reconstruction (see Waldby, 1997). Curtis draws on the work of Lyotard to argue that the VHP, in its quest for universalism, has silenced the presence of what Lyotard calls *aesthesis*: the singularity, difference and heterogeneity of particular bodies that resist discursive systems such as techno-science. In this sense, the cutting up of Jernigan's body for the purposes of medical science represents a normalization of his body, which is none too different from the normalization of the body through the violence of the law. Here Curtis draws attention to the similarities between the VHP and the 'writing machine' described by Kafka in his short story 'The Penal Colony', in which criminals are subjected to 'the apparatus', a sort of bed and harrow, which uses glass needles to inscribe the crime into the flesh of the convicted over a period of 12 hours.

The work of the performance artists Orlan and Stelarc provide further interesting insights into the relationship between processes of actual body modification and the use of digital information technology. They are both, in their very different ways, concerned with questioning the limits of the body through performance strategies, which explore the possibility of developing 'post-evolutionary bodies'. In her piece in this collection, 'An Order of Pure Decision: Un-Natural Selection in the Work of Stelarc and Orlan', Jane Goodall discusses Orlan's project of challenging the preconceptions of the Western notion of the body. Orlan remarks:

> Like the Australian artist Stelarc, I think that the body is obsolete. It is no longer adequate for the current situation. We mutate at the rate of cockroaches, but we are cockroaches whose memories are in computers, who pilot planes and drive cars that we have conceived, although our bodies are not conceived for these speeds.

Orlan is probably best known for the series of nine operations, 'The Reincarnation of St Orlan'. The operations appropriate Judeo-Christian iconography, including blood and sacrifice, along with elements drawn from Greek mythology, such as the emphasis upon marvellous and grotesque beings. The operations were designed as performances reminiscent of the Renaissance anatomy theatres. The seventh operation was filmed by CNN and aroused a good deal of indignation about whether it could be called art. Such controversies are very much meat and drink to Orlan who, as Robert Ayers tells us in his interview with her, is a seasoned performer who much enjoys the celebrity status and controversy she generates. This is evident in her *conférences*, in which she discusses her sculptured works and video images with an audience. The audiences are generally adoring, with young women especially seeing her as a sort of pop star.

In her interview with Robert Ayers, Orlan restates her aim as being 'To question the status of the body in society and in particular the status of the female body'. This involves an attack on the notion of the classical body and conventional standards of beauty. The later operations in her Reincarnation of St Orlan series involved placing implants in her cheeks and forehead, the latter being the infamous 'Dionysian' horns. The tenth operation is designed to alter the slope of her nose to make it resemble the parrot beak-like nose of King Wapacal; something which will further dramatically alter the cast of her face. Orlan's critique of contemporary Western notions of beauty is based upon an investigation and attempt to replicate some of the different standards of beauty which have existed in different cultures. In her interview she mentions the way in which pre-Columbian Mexican culture found the squint and deformations of the skull beautiful and learned to cultivate them. In advance of the operations Orlan works with a digital artist to morph in the changes on to photographic images of her head and eventually produces large mounted photographs of the intended effects to be achieved by the operations. Orlan does not seek to replace the classical body with the grotesque; rather, she seeks to move beyond such oppositions. As she remarks: 'All my work is based on the notion of "and": the good and the bad, the beautiful and the ugly, the public and the private'.

There are, therefore, a number of senses in which we can agree with Parveen Adams' phrase that 'Orlan is flesh become image', cited by Julie Clark in her piece in this collection. Orlan not only produces photographs of her operations which show her lips exposed and wet with blood trickling down her cheek, alongside grapes, which play off Christian iconography, she also collects and juxtaposes samples of her blood and flesh from the operations in ways which resemble the medieval cult of relics. Orlan explores the disjunctures between identity and the body, she seems to want to remake the body in order to free the body, in particular the face, from fixity and automatic reactions. Julie Clark suggests that here Orlan is influenced by her Lacanian psychoanalyst Eugenie Lemoine-Luccioni who remarks:

> The skin is deceptive ... in life one only has one skin ... there is an error in human relations because one never is what one has. . . . I have an angel's skin but I am a jackal ... a crocodile's skin but I am a puppy, a black skin but I am white; a woman's skin but I am a man; I never have

the skin of what I am. There is no exception to the rule because I am never what I have. (cited in Wilson, 1996: 13)

This is the influential view of the body as a garment, a veil or mask, as something which should be changed and modified to become congruent with changes in the self.[4] Technoscience makes it possible to explore these changes: to produce bodies which escape the fatefulness of both DNA and God, of the notions of destiny and causality associated with religion and science.

If one of Orlan's aims is explore transhuman aesthetics, to deny that human beings have any fixed nature, then much the same can be said of Stelarc. His various prosthetic experiments, such as wearing a third arm, or the exoskeleton in which he experimented with six-legged locomotion, or the planned stretching of the skin of his face to produce a third ear, which will act as a speaker not receiver of sound, are well known. As Stelarc mentions in his piece in this collection, 'Parasitic Visions', and in the interview 'In Dialogue with Posthuman Bodies' with Ross Farrell, he is interested in exploring the ways in which the body does not just become a host for technology through various cyborg fusions, but also the ways in which it can become inhabited by a multiplicity of remote agents. Stelarc wired up his body to the Internet, thus permitting a number of collaborative agents in other parts of the world to activate his muscles and make his body the subject of involuntary movements. As Nicholas Zurbrugg argues in his piece 'Marinetti, Chopin, Stelarc: Auratic Intensities of the Postmodern Techno-Body', Stelarc is trying to show the potential of the technically modified body, by exploring the ways in which technology can help the body to become an evolutionary structure which generates new forms of sensory experience and function without memory and desire.

In his discussion of the techno-cultural artistic avant-gardes, Zurbrugg is critical of those intellectuals and commentators who argue we now live in a post-auratic culture. Rather, for Zurbrugg we live in a '*past*modern' epoch rich in technological revolutions/revelations. Contra Walter Benjamin, he argues that there is strong evidence of the revival of auratic creativity in the work of Marinetti, Chopin and Stelarc. Zurbrugg is interested in Marinetti's desire to explore the extension and education of the senses through technology. He also points to the illusory body modification achievable through using technology in performance art. Henri Chopin's multimedia performances, for example, can be seen in some ways to have fulfilled Marinetti's Futurist vision. In these performances a vast range of superimposed recorded sounds (sounds of the inner body, etc.) are played while Chopin recites his poetry, which produces a strange, partly corporeal and partly technological, auratic energy. Chopin, who is actually a small man, seems to grow to gigantic scale through the complex vocal and non-figurative sounds that are broadcast, until he attains the presence of a 'super-Dracula'.

Paul Virilio and Jean Baudrillard are usually taken to be strong critics of contemporary technological developments. Zurbrugg argues their recent writings show greater ambivalence, with Baudrillard in particular reconsidering the potential of photography as an instrument of magic (see Zurbrugg, 1997). Yet, despite some acknowledgement of the potential of multimedia performance art, Virilio remains a trenchant critic of technology.

According to Virilio, we are on the verge of the third technological revolution: the first involved transport (the steam engine, electric motor, jet engine, etc.); the second involved transmission (radio, television, Internet, etc.); the third involves the miniaturization of objects (the transplant revolution) (see Armitage, 1999). The latter two revolutions have interesting potential effects for modifying the body. They direct us to the ways in which human beings are having to learn new ways of inhabiting technology, in which the world is approached through the mediation of technological environments, on the one hand, and the ways we will have to cope with technology inhabiting us, on the other. Nanotechnology and miniaturization will involve major forms of body modification. This will take us from prosthetic implants such as cardiac simulators, to the introduction of micro-machines which will colonize the body, such as *smart pills* which will be capable of transmitting information on nerve function or blood flow to distant monitoring facilities. For Virilio (1997: 53), this summons up the prospect of 'the technological fuelling of the living body'.

The virtual mobility of the 'last vehicle' (Virilio, 1999; Armitage, 1999), the dominance of the static audio-visual vehicle (television, computer, multimedia) points to the further colonization of the body of what he terms the 'citizen-terminal'. He elaborates:

> The urbanization of real space is this being overtaken by this urbanization of real time which is, at the end of the day, the urbanization of the actual body of the city dweller, this *citizen-terminal* soon to be decked out to the eyeballs with interactive prostheses based on the pathological model of the 'spastic', wired to control his/her domestic environment without having physically to stir: the catastrophic figure of an individual who has lost the capacity for immediate intervention along with natural motricity and who abandons himself for want of anything better, to the capabilities of captors, sensors and other remote control scanners that turn him into a being controlled by the machine with which they say, he talks. (Virilio, 1997: 20)

Virilio emphasizes the convergence between the 'well-equipped disabled person' and the 'over-equipped able-bodied person' in the production of the 'terminal-citizen', whose embodied physical mobility and face-to-face sociability is reduced. If the static vehicle of the terminal permits virtual mobility, through the spatial escape from the confines of the here and now through communication with distant others, then it must be said that temporal escape is a much more difficult proposition. Technology, as yet, has no prospect of mastering time: if we can't escape time, we can't escape the body. We may seek to ignore time, but time as a major form of social synthesis is ultimately grounded in the human body. The finitude of the human life course and lived body time still impose limits on our capacity for technological mastery.

Notes

I would like to thank Roy Boyne, Roger Bromley, Neal Curtis, Owen Gregory, Mike Hepworth, Cressida Miles, Wendy Patterson, Caroline Potter, Justin Reeson, Chris Rojek, Chris Shilling and Bryan S. Turner, who helped in various ways with the organization of the Conference on Body Modification held at the *Theory, Culture & Society* Centre, Nottingham Trent University in June 1996 and in the preparation of the subsequent *Body & Society* special issue.

1. This man, in his 60s, told viewers that he had always felt he was a leopard and had finally undergone the tattooing (BBC1 travel programme on the Scottish Islands, May 1999). An identification which might not be seen as totally strange when considered in the light of the remarks of Orlan's psychoanalyst, quoted below.

2. For a critique of Giddens's view of the body, which presents it as operating with a Cartesian view of the subject steering the body, and thus neglecting the way in which subjectivity is always already embodied and only conceivable through the 'horizons of the flesh', see Shilling and Mellor (1996).

3. The theme of body invasion has been analysed by Andrew Tudor (1995), who provides an interesting discussion of the technology of monsters through contrasting the 1950s movie *The Fly* with the more recent David Cronenberg version.

4. For a discussion of the mask and the disjunction of the body and the self which the ageing process can bring about, albeit from a very different theoretical perspective, see Featherstone and Hepworth, 1991).

References

Ahmed, S. (1999) ' "She'll Wake Up One of These Days and Find She's Turned into a Nigger": Passing through Hybridity', Special Issue on Performativity and Belonging, *Theory, Culture & Society* 16(2): 87–106.

Aoki, Doug (1996) 'Sex and Muscle: The Female Bodybuilder Meets Lacan', *Body & Society* 2(4): 59–74.

Armitage, J. (1999) 'From Modernism to Hypermodernism and Beyond: An Interview with Paul Virilio', Special Issue on Virilio, *Theory, Culture & Society* 16(5): 25–54.

Bauman, Z. (1991) *Modernity and Ambivalence*. Oxford: Polity.

Beck, U. (1992) *Risk Society*. London: Sage.

Beck, U., A. Giddens and S. Lash (eds) (1994) *Reflexive Modernization*. Oxford: Polity.

Bourdieu, P. (1978) 'Sport and Social Class', *Social Science Information* 17(6): 819–40.

Butler, J. (1990) *Gender Trouble: Feminism and The Subversion of Identity*. New York: Routledge.

Eubanks, V. (1996) 'Zones of Dither: Writing the Postmodern Body', *Body & Society* 2(3): 95–105.

Featherstone, M. (1982) 'The Body in Consumer Culture', *Theory, Culture & Society* 1(2): 18–33. (Reprinted in M. Featherstone, M. Hepworth and B.S. Turner [eds] *The Body*. London: Sage, 1991.)

Featherstone, M. (1987) 'Leisure, Symbolic Power and the Life Course', in S. Horne, D. Jary and A. Tomlinson (eds) *Sport, Leisure and Social Relations*. London: Routledge.

Featherstone, M. (1991) *Postmodernism and Consumer Culture*. London: Sage.

Featherstone, M. and M. Hepworth (1991) 'The Mask of Ageing and the Postmodern Life Course', pp. 371–89 in M. Featherstone, M. Hepworth and B.S. Turner (eds) *The Body*. London: Sage.

Fraser, M. (1999) 'Classing Queer: Politics and Competition', Special Issue on Performativity and Belonging, *Theory, Culture & Society* 16(2): 107–133.

Freitag, W. (1999) 'Thalidomide Children's Bodies', paper presented at the *Body & Society* Seminar, Cambridge University.

Gibson. W. (1986) *Neuromancer*. New York: Fantasia Press. (Orig. 1984.)

Giddens, A. (1991) *Modernity and Self Identity*. Oxford: Polity.

Gilroy, P. (1993) *The Black Atlantic*. London: Verso.

Holland, S. (1995) 'Descartes Goes to Hollywood: Mind, Body and Gender in Contemporary Cinema', in M. Featherstone and R. Burrows (eds) *Cyberspace/Cyberbodies/Cyberpunk: Cultures of Technological Embodiment*. London: Sage.

Landsberg, A. (1995) 'Prosthetic Memory: *Blade Runner* and *Total Recall*', in M. Featherstone and R. Burrows (eds) *Cyberspace/Cyberbodies/Cyberpunk: Cultures of Technological Embodiment*. London: Sage.

Leng, Kwok Wei (1996) 'On Menopause and Cyborgs: Or, Towards a Feminist Cyborg Politics of Menopause', *Body & Society* 2(3): 33–51.

Lloyd, Moya (1996) 'Feminism, Aerobics and the Politics of the Body', *Body & Society* 2(2): 79–98.

Polhemus, T. and L. Proctor (1978) *Fashion and Anti-Fashion*. London: Thames and Hudson.

St Martin, Leena and Nicola Gavey (1996) 'Women's Bodybuilding: Feminist Resistance and/or Femininity's Recuperation?', *Body & Society* 2(4): 45–57.

Shilling, Chris and Philip A. Mellor (1996) 'Embodiment, Structuration Theory and Modernity: Mind/Body Dualism and the Repression of Sensuality', *Body & Society* 2(4): 1–15.

Skeggs, B. (1997) *Formations of Class and Gender*. London: Sage.

Tudor, Andrew (1995) 'Unruly Bodies, Unquiet Minds', *Body & Society* 1(1): 25–41.

Virilio, P (1997) *Open Sky*. London: Verso.

Virilio, P (1999) *Polar Inertia*. London: Sage.

Waldby, Catherine (1997) 'Revenants: The Visible Human Project and the Digital Uncanny', *Body & Society* 3(1): 1–16.

Walsh, Irvine (1993) *Trainspotting*. London: Secker and Waburg.

Wilson, S. (1996) *L'histoire d'O, Sacred and Profane, This Is My Body . . . This Is My Software*. London: Black Dog Publishing Limited and the Authors.

Zurbrugg, N. (ed.) (1997) *Jean Baudrillard: Art and Artefact*. London: Sage.

Mike Featherstone is co-editor of *Body & Society* and editor of *Theory, Culture & Society* at Nottingham Trent University. His recent publications include the edited collections: *Love and Eroticism* (1999) and *Spaces of Culture* (with Scott Lash, 1999) both published by Sage, London.

'Modern Primitivism': Non-Mainstream Body Modification and Racialized Representation

CHRISTIAN KLESSE

I make a statement, I've chosen myself. I am a part of this culture but I don't believe in it. My body modifications are my way to say that. (Idexa, in *BP & MPQ* 2(2): 11)

Introduction: Marking the Body and Marking the Problem

A strongly recognizable strand in the development of contemporary subcultural styles in many Western societies is the growing emergence of highly visible body modification practices (Mascia-Lees and Sharpe, 1992; Rubin, 1988; Sanders, 1989). Tattooing, multiple piercing, branding, cutting and scarification are some of the more radical, permanent non-mainstream body modifications in this context (Myers, 1992). 'Modern Primitives' are a subcultural movement in the intersection of the tattoo, piercing, and sado-masochism scenes. The movement originated in the 1970s in California, USA, growing in numbers and significance in the following decades.

The term 'Modern Primitives' applies to people, who 'respond to primal urges' to do '*something*' with their bodies (Fakir Musafar, in Vale and Juno, 1989: 13). Fakir Musafar, the most prominent body modifier within the Modern Primitives movement, who also claims to be its founder, has created the term 'Body Play' for this kind of practice. In his magazine *Body Play and Modern Primitives Quarterly* (*BP & MPQ*), whose analysis has provided the basis for many of the claims made in this article,[1] he defines 'Body Play' as 'the deliberate, ritualized modification of

Body & Society © 1999 SAGE Publications (London, Thousand Oaks and New Delhi),
Vol. 5(2–3): 15–38
[1357–034X(199906/09)5:2–3;15–38;008856]

the human body. It is a deep rooted, universal urge that seemingly transcends time and cultural boundaries' (*BP & MPQ* 1(1): 3).

The broad range of possible variations of Body Play are named in his seven-fold classification of body modification practises.

1. **Body Play by Contortion: 'Bending Bones', 'Distension':**
Gymnastics, contortionism, Yoga exercises and Hindu practises of Sadhus, the 'Scavenger's Daughter', enlargement of piercings, cupping, high heel shoes, foot-binding, stretching part of the body, etc.

2. **Body play by Constriction: 'Compression':**
Bondage, tight ligatures of belts, corsets, tight clothing (like rubber or denim), cords, body presses, etc.

3. **Body Play by Deprivation: 'Shut-Off', 'Frozen':**
Fasting, sleep deprivation, fatigue, restriction of movement, sense isolation in boxes, cages, helmets, body suits, bags, etc.

4. **Body Play by Encumberment: 'Wearing Iron':**
Heavy bracelets, anklets, neck ornamentation, footwear, manacles, encasements, chains, etc.

5. **Body Play by Fire: 'Burn-Out':**
Sun tanning, electricity (constant or shock), steam/heat baths and boxes, the 'pack', branding and burning, as in the Japanese 'okyu' treatment, etc.

6. **Body Play by Penetration: 'Invasion':**
Flagellation, being pierced, punctured, spiked or skewered, tattooing, bed of nails, bed of swords, irritants like hair, cloth or chemical agents, etc.

7. **Body Play by Suspension: 'Hung-Up':**
Hung on a cross, the 'witches cradle', suspended by wrists, thighs, waist, ankles or flesh hooks, suspended by constrictions or multiple piercings, etc. (Fakir Musafar, in Vale and Juno, 1989: 15)

Of course, not everybody who calls himself or herself a Modern Primitive is into all of these things. Many of these practices are part of forms sexuality, labelled with the all-embracing phrase sado-masochism (s/m). Since the 1980s s/m sexuality in the USA has increasingly become coded in terms of spirituality and Modern Primitives can be seen as a rather extreme articulation of this shift (Hart and Dale, 1997: 346; Thompson, 1991). The relationship of Modern Primitivism to s/m sexuality, however, is rather ambiguous. Modern Primitives often stress the spiritual rather than the sexual aspect of their activity. Fakir Musafar, for example, interprets his practices in the first place as 'worship through the body'. The permanent emphasis of body modification as a 'body-first approach' in exploring one's own spirituality and gaining higher consciousness, as rites of passage or a form of tribal bonding can also be understood as a rationalization and de-sexualization of s/m practices (Califa, 1994).

The reasons individual Modern Primitives give for engaging in these activities, however, are highly diverse. Personal motives put forward include spirituality, rites of passage, fun, sexual enhancement, the importance of pain, aesthetics, group affiliation, shock value, etc. (see Myers, 1992: 287–96). Modern Primitives, thus, may best be described as being 'composed of multiple communities' (Torgovnick, 1995), of different (sexual) orientations and persuasions. However, the ethnic background of most of the people involved in Modern Primitive practices is white (Eubanks, 1996; Myers, 1992). Modern Primitives seem to be quite popular within the non-mainstream body modification scene(s) (Myers, 1992), their elaborated philosophies, however, are not shared on a large-scale basis (Sweetman, 1997; Torgovnick, 1995).

One of the most significant characteristics of the Modern Primitives movement is their appropriation of 'primitive rituals'. In their search for radical corporal, psychic and spiritual experiences and their performance of sexual events and encounters, Modern Primitives seek inspiration by so called 'primitive societies' through the adoption of their communal rites and body modification techniques. This aspect has been the prioritized focus of the few academic writings on this subculture (Eubanks, 1996; Torgovnick, 1995; Vale and Juno, 1989).

Vale and Juno's influential book *Re/Search #12: Modern Primitives* (1989) contains few attempts to analyse Modern Primitive practices on a theoretical level. The approach is mostly documentary and the book contains a sample of interviews with people (mainly tattoo artists), who locate themselves within Modern Primitivism. *Re/Search #12*, thus, provides a good source for the study of Modern Primitivism. The analysis of Modern Primitivism's philosophy and practices does not concern Vale and Juno too much.

Torgovnick's (1995) article 'Piercings' is mainly concerned with ethical questions in the context of radical body modification practices in contemporary Western societies. Torgovnick's main issue are the questions of difference and sameness of body modification in 'traditional societies' and in Modern Primitives' appropriations. She clearly rejects any idea of sameness. In particular the fact of genital piercings (and also genital tattooing) has rarely been reported in ethnographic studies on societies, which have engaged in ritual body modification practices. Torgovnick sees the *privatization and erotization* of originally communal and morally approved cultural events as one of the main ethical dilemmas of contemporary piercing in Western societies. Modern Primitivism is located outside of a clearly religious context and presents a form of postmodern eclecticism. Although these claims are valid and justified, Torgovnick's strong emphasis on the 'compulsive transgression' and 'narcissism' of Modern Primitivism has moralistic connotations.

Virginia Eubanks's (1996) discussion of Modern Primitivism, which draws on the analysis of a series of qualitative interviews with Modern Primitives, is theoretically much more elaborated. She engages in a profound and radical critique of the ideology and philosophy of Modern Primitivism. She criticizes the Modern

Primitivist discourse for its naive allegation of affinities with 'primitive' bodies and cultures. According to Eubanks, Modern Primitives' adoption of ritual forms of body modification displays 'a blatant disregard for the history and the context of the symbols and practices involved' (Eubanks, 1996: 74). Modern Primitives' rejection of modern society presents itself as a commitment to sexual freedom and bodily expression, coded in a naive longing for the 'authentic primitive', a profoundly essentialist concept. This involves a variety of problems, such as the reinforcement of the traditional dualism of Western thought (self/other; male/female; nature/culture) and, most importantly: the *denial of cultural difference* in a universalist humanist vision of a 'primal urge'. Eubanks is concerned with a *critique of representation* in the context of Modern Primitives' body modification practices and she provides some important analyses in this context.

I am concerned with similar questions to those posed by Eubanks in this article. However, I think that Eubanks's pleading insistence on a *cultural relativism* in the form of the concept of an *historicized multiculturalism* does not go far enough and, moreover, is in itself problematic (Eubanks, 1996: 87). The dominant notion of multiculturalism can be deployed as just another form of 'othering' and racialization. Furthermore, the problem of power and representation cannot be resolved by simply demanding that we value and accept difference. This is because multiculturalism tends to collapse ethnicity into culture, while at the same time it presents culture as static and essential. Multiculturalism has been profoundly criticized for its theoretical and practical shortcomings (Anthias and Yuval-Davis, 1992; Bhabha, 1990, 1996; Caglar, 1997; Yuval-Davis, 1997). Multiculturalism does not provide a suitable or sufficient basis for the critique of the Modern Primitivist discourse.

Therefore, I take a different angle in this article. I will argue that it is important to deconstruct any idea of '*primitivism*', which has been such a strong and powerful trope within Western thought and discourse (Goldberg, 1993; Torgovnick, 1990). It is by reproducing this 'primitivist discourse', although in a well-meaning and affirmative intention, that Modern Primitivism allies itself with a tradition which played a significant role in the justification of colonial rule and subordination. As a consequence Modern Primitivism reproduces all the inherently repressive gendered stereotypes on racialized people and their sexuality. This describes the limitations of a self-declared radical movement, whose associates perceive of themselves as radical opponents of Western modernity. They remain captured in some of the highly problematic discursive assumptions shaping this modernity.

Establishing the prioritization within Modern Primitivism of body, sexuality, community and spirituality as analytical links, I argue that Modern Primitives' enthusiastic turn towards 'primitivism' represents a particular *identity strategy* within the late modern condition. Recent sociological theory has extensively dealt with the implications of modernity for identity and the body. Some of the insights of this theoretical literature, as I will show, can be deployed usefully for the understanding of Modern Primitive practices of body modification. Most of these grand theories of the body and modernity, however, do not reflect enough on the differentiating histories of colonialism and racialization. Only by drawing on the radical criticism of colonial discourse analysis are we able to show how 'Western' identities have always depended on a dichotomous construction of racialized 'others'. I see Modern Primitives' notion of 'primitivism' as a postcolonial legacy of this tradition of representation.

Modernity, Identity and the Body

Theorists of modernity have emphasized the profound effects of social and economic change, resulting in shifts and breaks within personal processes of identification. Zygmunt Bauman states: 'Though all too often hypothesized as an attribute of a material identity, identity has the ontological status of a project and a postulate' (Bauman, 1996: 19). The experience of fracture has always been at the heart of identity, and identity building has always remained an individual task. Economic and social developments in late modernity have made this task even more difficult. The postmodern condition to a certain degree universalized experiences of alienation, distinctiveness and strangeness (Bauman, 1993).

Anthony Giddens (1990, 1991), too, claims that the maintenance of self-identity has become a particular problem. According to him, late modernity has dissolved most traditional systems of meaning and social order in an unprecedented fashion. As a result individuals are forced to engage in a heightened reflexivity about life and its meaning. In this context of 'ontological insecurity', self-identity has become deliberative. It does not emerge automatically from one's social position. Thus, people are engaged in a permanent re-ordering of identity narratives in which a concern with the body is central.

The Body as an Individual Project
In this condition 'of late modernity . . . we have become responsible for the design of our own bodies', says Anthony Giddens (1991: 102). There has been an unprecedented individualization of the body. Technological developments, among others, allow for the alteration of the body. Shilling (1993) has theorized this development with the concept of '*body projects*'.

In the affluent West there is a tendency for the body to be seen as an entity which is in the process of becoming; a *project* which should be worked at and accomplished as part of an individual's self-identity. (Shilling, 1993: 5)

It is tempting to apply this idea of *body projects* to the phenomenon of non-mainstream body modification and Modern Primitivism. Before I discuss this option, I want to point out some of the difficulties I have with the assumptions about modernity and identity, sketched out above.

I think it is important to be cautious and not to generalize certain experiences which may be of particular relevance for certain groups within Western societies. Identity *has not* turned into a free option for all subjects in all situations and all contexts. Racism as a structural form of oppression within Western societies, for example, operates also as an *enforced imposition of identities* (Anthias and Yuval-Davis, 1992; Solomos and Back, 1996). Ethnic minority people within these societies, therefore, rather have to come to terms with an overdetermination of their identities in the context of this racialization, than with an underdetermination. Grand theories of late modernity often tend to neglect or undertheorize such experiences. This, of course, is not without exception. Writers like Zygmunt Bauman have put their concern with issues of racism and anti-Semitism at the heart of their theories of modernity (Bauman, 1989, 1993).

The theory of *body projects* contains a similar problem of generalization. Although Shilling (1993) acknowledges that these projects have to be theorized as a gendered, ethnicized and class-bound phenomenon, this, in my opinion, is insufficiently elaborated. As a result, the dimensions of choice and personal design appear to be overemphasized, or universalized. The dimension of choice is circumscribed by the complex articulations of gender, ethnicity, ability and class, not to forget location/space. This perspective should be *central* to any theory of the body and identity.

Despite these criticisms, it seems possible to apply this analytical notion to non-mainstream forms of body modification of Modern Primitives. This would emphasize the strong individualism of these modifications, which as Shilling claims mark the difference of modern transformations of the body from the ones in traditional societies (Shilling, 1993: 5, 200). It is not difficult to find statements of Modern Primitives that illustrate such a position. Cliff Diller, for example, praises the uniqueness of his large-scale 'blackwork' back tattoo. He perceives it as an absolute statement of his identity as *difference*:

I am a different person now, and I realize that in many ways, I am not the average guy on the street. On a more public level, my tattoo affirms that difference. It visually sets me apart from the masses. Though it has gained in popularity over the last few years, tattooing of this size will never be mainstream. (*BP & MPQ* 1(2): 11)

The Display of the Body as a Source of Identity in Consumer Capitalism
This statement raises also the question of body representation in consumer culture. People nowadays, Mike Featherstone (1991) claims, are more concerned with their bodies. In particular the *presentation of the body*, emphasizing style, 'looks' and appearance, has been charged with new identity functions. This strong concern with the body is linked to the consumption of commodities or services. Furthermore, in consumer culture the 'display' and the 'performance' of bodily properties and styles has not only become an option, it is *increasingly expected*. In this context the new body images of consumer culture imply a *strong sexualization of the body*. Consumer culture reinforces 'the notion that the body is a vehicle of pleasure and self-expression' (Featherstone, 1991: 170). Self-realization and the self-conscious cultivation of style thus appear as a normative demand of modernism.

Although Modern Primitives rigorously reject the materialism of Western consumer culture, tattooing and piercing, for example, do not escape commodification. In the meantime, small-scale businesses of professional piercers and tattoo artists have been established in all larger cities and definitively establish a profitable market. *Body Play and Modern Primitives Quarterly* is full of adverts for these mushrooming businesses.

The style of Modern Primitives may not serve as an articulation of class status in the same way as many other consumerism-oriented body techniques (Bourdieu, 1996). Modern Primitives might even wish to set themselves apart from mass consumer culture (Vale and Juno, 1989: 5). For many their body modification definitely expresses their individuality and their difference. The value of the body and of the individuality of its owner seems to be enhanced through some body modifications. Many of those, such as tattoos and piercings, increasingly even brandings and scarifications, can be purchased for money like other commodities, too. The growth of these practices has resulted in a new fashion trend and has to be interpreted in the context of an increasingly trendy *aestheticization and commodification of ethnic difference* (see Erel, forthcoming). Sexualization and exoticism, both elements of this broader process, are clearly recognizable in the way genital (and other) piercings and 'primitive' techniques and motives in tattooing are represented within the style of Modern Primitivism.

Modernity, Community, Sociality and the Body

As a distinctive subcultural style, Modern Primitivism raises questions of community, too. The application of Shilling's theory of body projects has put a strong emphasis on individualism as a specific feature of the late modern condition in Western societies. As indicated above, the argument of individualism has been used to state the profound *difference* of modern Western body modification practices from their preceding traditional or 'primitive' models.

The intense individual act of getting tattooed or pierced, however, for Modern Primitives has also the meaning of *creating collectivity*. Princess Cruise states in *BP & MPQ*:

> Among the people I love and respect, whose world views I share in fundamental ways, so many have cut, colored, stretched, compressed, decorated, and otherwise modified their bodies that I even want to do it too. I want to be like them: I want them to know when they see me across a crowded room that I associate myself with them; ... that we are ... family. (*BP & MPQ* 2(3): 5)

The assumption of individualism contradicts the findings of the scarce empirical research on non-mainstream body modification. James Myers (1992) has researched contemporary forms of radical body modification in the San Francisco bay area. He concludes that Modern Primitivism is so popular with contemporary body modifiers because they recognize a need for initiation rituals. People look for *communal rites*, which are perceived as being absent in Western culture. Many of the workshops he participated in as an observer drew a lot of their meaning from the presence of the audience. Myers, thus, prioritizes an understanding of non-mainstream body modification practices in the USA as some kind of *ceremonial event*, close to the traditional rites of passage.

In his recent work Shilling, too, has shifted his perspective away from individualism to forms of sociality. Together with Philip Mellor (Mellor and Shilling, 1997) he analyses the Western history of 'forms of embodiment', i.e. distinctive patterns of making sense of one's experience of the body, in their relationships to different forms of sociality. In the course of the Enlightenment project, he and Mellor claim, Protestant rationality came to present the 'official side of modernity'. Increasing secularization finally undermined Protestantism and new forms of embodied sociality appeared in the course of this continuing 're-formation of the body'. Mellor and Shilling speak of 'sensual solidarities' or 'tribal fealties', which exist along with and construct themselves against 'banal' and rational forms of sociality. The character of these 'sensual socialities', however, remains vague in Mellor and Shilling's account. Their argument is not empirically grounded. I think it is not possible to draw such clear distinction between sensuality and rationality and its corresponding forms of social association as Shilling and Mellor do in their abstract theory. Nonetheless, the term 'sensual sociality' provides a good *metaphor* to illustrate some of Modern Primitives' group characteristics. They represent a strongly body-oriented group which even has adopted the language and philosophy of 'tribalism'. They adhere to a notion of 'primitivism' that is defined as rejection of a rational reductionism of the human existence. Spirituality, or the 'sacred', functions dominantly as a unifying factor within this subculture. Spirituality, community and identity are closely bound up with the discourse on 'primitivism'.

> Community is very important, very important. Having a community, finding your own community where you fit in, gives a sense of belonging. Modern man lost his tribes and other defined communities in the development of what is called the 'global village', but it is a global village of lost souls. We still have this need for a tribe or community, a sense of belonging. So new tribes are forming that are not based on locale [incidental nearness of the members in a geographical location] but on 'likeness'. (Fakir Musafar, in Thompson, 1991: 316)

Modern Primitivism is linked to a revival of tribalism. Within the Modern Primitives movement the spiritual leather and s/m scene groups of friends refer to themselves as a tribe (Thompson, 1991). The kinship-based social model that has been associated with 'primitive' culture seems to offer a stronger promise of belonging than any other form of social association practised in Western industrialized societies. 'Primitivism' offers a broad range of inspiration and possibilities of identification to people, who feel alienated in their contemporary societies.

Alienation, the Crisis of Identity and Primitivism as Identity Space

An increased readiness to work on or to change one's body, the search for new forms of sociality and the emergence of a structural, societal problem of identity have been some of the features of the late modern condition analysed so far. Drawing on arguments similar to those of Bauman and Giddens, Friedman (1994) points out that the development of modernism as a philosophical proposition and a social reality has led to a profound crisis of identification and a widespread *subjective* feeling of *alienation*. Friedman defines alienation as the increasing feeling of separation of individuals from their embeddedness in a world perceived as both meaningful and cohesive. At the same time, a new space has emerged for different possible and optional identity positions, resulting in a historical situation of permanent alterity and personal change.

Friedman (1994) highlights the emergence of a variety of new identification strategies in this context. The dissolution of the faith in the progress of civilization which has been so central to modernity and the dissolution of familiar and secure forms of identity led to an explosion of new cultural movements searching for sources of 'authenticity'. Traditionalism in the form of national and ethnic movements, and also postmodernism, are some of the significant trends, 'Primitivism' is another.

This analysis provides a useful frame for the understanding of Modern Primitivism. The subjective feeling of alienation within and from contemporary Western societies is an important reason for the romanticizing turn of this mainly white subculture to the 'primitive' world. Fakir Musafar, for example, states that he has felt 'like an alien in this culture' since his early childhood (Vale and Juno, 1989: 6).

Colonial discourse analysis and postcolonial theory have provided analytical tools for grasping this 'primitivist' turn. 'Primitivism' as a contemporary identification strategy takes up images and elements which have been integrated in the construction of forms of identity in the 'West' before. Modern Primitives, however, do this in a partly reversed form. 'Western' identity and the Western concept of civilization has never been self-referential, constructed out of itself (Hall, 1992; Nederveen Pieterse, 1994). The 'West' itself, of course, has to be seen as a politically and discursively constructed entity. Central for the development of a 'Western' self-image has been the colonial experience with its binary definitions and counter-definitions that functioned as ascription to the 'Other' or as ascription to the self (Rattansi, 1994; Rutherford 1990). In the self-construction of the 'West', the 'primitive' has functioned as the homogenized notion of the racialized 'other'.

These mechanisms of representation and identification were not without repercussions within their own cultural sphere. They worked as a force of homogenization and constriction also in the cultural context of the 'West', where they originated (Nandy, 1983). What had already been defined as attributes of the subordinated other, could not be an unproblematic property of one's own behaviour. In a more psychoanalytical sense, the 'other', the savage, thus has become the periphery 'out there', but at the same time the repressed and denied 'within' oneself. According to Friedman (1994), the vanishing of the modern identity space and the resulting 'identity crisis consists in the surging to the surface of what is peripherized within us, a closing in of what is peripherized outside of us, a search for meaning and "roots" in the widest sense' (Friedman, 1994: 85).

In particular 'free' sexuality and an 'unconstrained' body have been projected into the 'realm of the Other'. The constituting discourses of Western modernity and most of its social theories have emphasized the need to control and regulate the body and its sexual expressions in order to create civilization (Turner, 1995). In this perception the loss of an immediate, innocent and unrepressed relationship to the body and to sexuality has been the 'price of civilization'. Both, the rational Enlightenment project and Christian codes of morality subordinated the body and, moreover, they subordinated women to men.

The transformation of the discourses on gender and sexuality in the course of modernity have not been unproblematic for the individuals affected by them. It has been argued that in particular in the Romantic vision and in the related colonial discourses European middle classes could work out the contradictions inherent to the changes and disruptions of the period. The feeling of loss and insecurity translated into 'constructions of the medieval and the exotic as imaginary spheres where the conflicts of reason and emotion, of desire and duty, and of competition and harmony could be resolved' (De Groot, 1989: 108). It was in the gendered and sexualized images of the 'sensual oriental', or the 'natural' and 'primitive African', that the ambiguities of the situation of Western men and women were worked through. The colonial imaginary and the colonial context provided the space where uninhibited sexual relationships, based on the idea of an unproblematic and free body, could be fantasized. The Romantic movement, as a response to the Enlightenment rationalism, created the notion of the 'noble savage', an imaginary figure which can clearly be identified in the work of writers such as Rousseau and Diderot (Bloch and Bloch, 1980). The subtleties of sexualization, objectification and subordination are disguised in these *extremely positive depictions and evaluations* of 'primitivism'.

Shifts towards 'primitivism', thus, are no singular phenomenon in history; the ambivalences of the Enlightenment and the naturalism and anti-rationalism of Romanticism were the precedents of contemporary Modern Primitivism. Sexuality and the body have been very significant issues within all these primitivist discourses and they are the predominant features of Modern Primitivism. 'Within Western culture, the idiom "going primitive" is in fact congruent in many ways to the idiom "getting physical"' (Torgovnick, 1990: 228). 'Primitivism' thus has had a long history within the repertoire of colonial fantasy and imagination.

The Ambivalence of Colonial Discourses, Mimicry and the Illusion of Sameness

The ambivalence of colonial discourses has been strikingly analysed in the work of Homi K. Bhabha. He rejects a theory of colonial discourse as *only* intentionally political-ideological in thrust (as in Said, 1979) and is able to integrate in his analysis the undeniable (hidden) fascination and imagination also at play in the colonial relationships. Drawing on a Foucauldian concept of power (decentred, multiple, all-permeating), Bhabha points out the problematic position of the people exerting colonial rule. The 'colonizers' have to be placed *within* the domain of colonial discourse, too. Bhabha breaks down the simple binary colonizer/colonized and opens a space for the theorization of ambivalences, contradictions and hidden feelings. The complex construction of *differences and sameness* in the colonial relationship centrally involves *identification* and also the *crisis of identification.* As a complex, ambivalent and often even contradictory mode of representation of otherness the racist stereotype of the colonial discourse provides a space where scorn and desire can coexist. It leaves space for a 'wide *range* of stereotype, from the loyal servant to Satan, from the loved to the hated; a shifting of subject positions in the circulation of colonial power' (Bhabha, 1983: 31). There is a possibility of simultaneously embracing two contradictory beliefs.

I think this perception helps towards an understanding of 'primitivism' as a strategy of identification. Fantasy, knowledge, power and pleasure in a Foucauldian cocktail, describe the emotional ground for enthusiastically going 'primitive'.

> Who are your role models? Mine are hundreds of anonymous primitives all of whom have undergone some obvious CHANGE-OF-BODY STATE. For fifty years I've *collected* my role models, mostly in libraries, and *captured* their images on photographic film. . . . I *honoured* them, *envied* them and very privately *duplicated* many of *their experiences.* (Fakir Musafar, in *BP & MPQ* 1[3]: 3, my emphasis)

Many Modern Primitives talk about being strongly impressed by early ethnographic material. Old films, photographs, for example from the volumes of the *National Geographic*, a huge range of material is used for inspiration and stimulation (*BP & MPQ* 2[4]: 22; Thompson, 1991: 294; Vale and Juno, 1989: 7). Many Modern Primitives privately collect these products. Moreover, such images have repeatedly been reproduced in an uncritical manner within *BP & MPQ*.

The ambivalences of colonial discourses are particularly obvious in the practice of early ethnographic photography. This photography was part of the project of colonial sciences to construct a generalized notion of 'otherness', to categorize, evaluate, control the colonized 'others' in order to secure their governability (Athanasiou, 1996; Clifford, 1988; Corbey, 1995). On the other hand, this photography coded hidden desire in a language of gender-specific sexualization. This functioned as a further subjugation of the racialized others, silenced and exposed to the 'colonial gaze', the objectifying view of the spectator (see Blackmer, 1998; Corbey, 1995; Lutz and Collins, 1993).

'The colonial discourse produces the colonised as fixed reality which is at once an "other" and yet entirely knowable and visible' says Bhabha in his analysis of the racist stereotype as a fetishized fixation of difference (Bhabha, 1983: 23). I think the meaning of this sentence is brilliantly illustrated by a certain means of representation in *BP & MPQ*. In particular Fakir Musafar, but also other Modern Primitives, like to juxtapose photographs of themselves with temporary body modifications with older ethnographic material that shows their 'primitive' models in the same position (see Figures 1–6).[2] This appears as a reversal of a phenomenon of the colonial context that Bhabha (1984, 1986) termed 'mimicry'.

Figure 1 Fakir Musafar has copied the practice of '*bearing the itiburi*' (a bark belt) from his models, the 'IBITOES' of New Guinea, shown here in an ethnographic photograph. *Source: BP & MPQ* 1(3): 27.

Figure 2 'I was fascinated so I became an Ibitoe, and fell in love with the practice', says Fakir Musafar (in Juno and Vale, 1989: 7). Here he poses with performance artist Ron Athey: 'He not only loves and has some of the most outstanding BLACKWORK tattooing, but he also wants to be an Ibitoe' (Fakir Musafar, *BP & MPQ* 1[3]: 27).

Figure 3 In an article on breast sculpting this old ethnographic photograph is shown with the caption: 'WOMEN OF AFRICA: Above, permanently worn breast band shapes and sculpts breasts' (*BP & MPQ* 2[3]: 9).

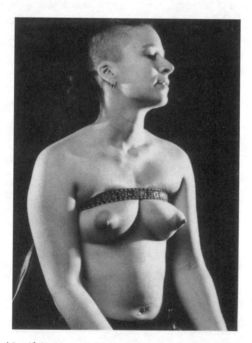

Figure 4 In a no less objectifying manner it is juxtaposed with photographs of the Modern Primitive model Lizard: 'Our beautifully endowed model, Lizard, also tries a decorative breast band. The band creates and emphasizes Lizard's cleavage, and makes her breasts point upward. She said she liked the feeling of the band' (*BP & MPQ* 2[3]: 9).

Figure 5 'Hindu Ball Dancer of South India in the 1930s bears a heavy load of hooked-on limes' (original caption, *BP & MPQ* 1[4]: 19).

Figure 6 'Fakir in 1962 also dances with a heavy load (24 pounds) of 48 hooked-on, half-pound lead weights' (original caption, *BP & MPQ* 1[4]: 19).

'Mimicry' is a metaphor for a process of acculturation and adaptation of imposed cultural concepts and patterns by the colonized. At the same time it is seen as a process both wanted and fuelled in colonialist politics out of a 'desire for a reformed recognisable Other', i.e. a governable, predictable Other (Bhabha, 1986: 198). On another level, Bhabha describes mimicry also as a strategic adaptation by the colonized as a subtle act of resistance. In its effects of doubling, its confusing and contradicting play with sameness and difference, the image of 'mimicry' unfolds the whole ambivalence of the colonial discourse.

In my understanding Bhabha's concept of 'mimicry' serves mainly as a metaphorical explanation of the psychic dimensions and strategies by the colonial people – despite the vice versa effects of acculturation and hybridization which interfere in the identification of both, colonizers and colonized. Because of this, I speak of a 'reversal' of the phenomenon of mimicry.

Duplication and imitation are performed by members of the Western society, in order to cope with the subordinated 'primitive' reality. The desire to experience the same, to be the same is the motor of this kind of mimicry. However, the experience remains in the ambiguous frame of mimicry: 'almost the same, but not quite' (Bhabha, 1986: 199).

An analysis of Modern Primitives' statements about their reasons for engaging in piercing rituals adopted from a Hindu context, for example ('Ball Dance' and 'Taking Kavandi' in Modern Primitives' terminology), clearly shows the syncretism of the spiritual background of the participants. Some of them see this ritual as a way to articulate and work through their pain and grief about the death of friends of AIDS (see *BP & MPQ* 1[4]: 20 and 2[1]: 13–15). These examples show the *eclectic* and also *instrumental* attitude towards societies and practices labelled 'primitive'.

Nonetheless, Modern Primitives claim a universal character for the experiences involved. They are driven by an intense desire to experience, live or be the same as the 'primitive' models. As Eubanks (1996) points out, it is the concept and idea of an *essential, universal 'primal urge'*, which makes possible the sameness of an 'authentic spiritual experience' in the adopted rites. On the basis of this persuasion, differences are denied and sameness is asserted across the boundaries of ethnicity, gender and politics.

Colonial discourses have provided a justification of colonial rule and, on the other hand, they have been at the heart of the contradictory processes of identification of and within the 'West'. Colonial discourses have not been unified in their evaluation of the 'primitive' and the savage, but they are all framed by a strategy of Western hegemony. I suggest an understanding of Modern Primitivism as a 'primitivist' identification in the late modern condition. In the next section I expand on the legacies of historical and contemporary colonial and postcolonial discourses, that play into and are reconstructed within the Modern Primitivist discourse. It is the uncritical reproduction of most of the historical and philosophical assumptions of the 'primitivist discourse' as it emerged in the 18th and 19th centuries, rather than its humanist universalism, that renders Modern Primitivism a highly problematic ideology.

Modern Primitives and the Primitivist Discourse

Modern Primitives are enthusiastically committed to 'primitivism'. This is expressed in their positive reference to 'primitive people', 'primitive societies' and in their adoption of 'primitive' body modification techniques and 'primitive rituals'. In *Re/Search #12* Modern Primitives refer to a long and arbitrary list of societies exclusively because of their traditions of body modification: the Ibitoe of New Guinea, the Sadhus of India, the Masai of Africa, the Maori of New Zealand, the Ndebeli of South Africa, the Padung and the Mayas. Furthermore, Japanese, Thai, Samoan, Native American and Micronesian tattoo techniques are discussed (Vale and Juno, 1989; see also Eubanks 1996).

The 'primitive' in the discourse of Modern Primitivism is a catch-all without any geographical and historical specificity, a homogenizing fantasy. Modern Primitives seem to be more interested in the bodily practices of the 'primitive models' than in a thorough exploration of other societies' philosophies. For them, what is interesting of the 'primitive', is his or her body (modification), and 'marking the body' is seen as the most 'primitive' act (Levi Straus, 1989: 158) .

However, Modern Primitives commonly claim to have further goals and interests. They reject the cultural assumptions of modern Western societies and the associated notion of progress. According to them, the terrible state in which we find our world, can only be superseded by a return to the 'primitive,' or at least by the integration of 'primitive' knowledges, techniques or lifestyles into modern life. 'Modern civilisation could benefit from so much that primitive people know, yet because of cultural arrogance, they miss it' (Fakir Musafar, in Vale and Juno, 1989: 15). Their notion of the 'primitive' in general is shaped by an absolute idealization and romanticization. For example, Fakir Musafar says, in pure, 'primitive' societies there is no cruelty, ugliness, no possessive attitudes, no sexual violence and no transgression (Vale and Juno, 1989: 21; *BP & MPQ* 1[2]: 4).

Eubanks (1996) argues that although Modern Primitives claim to work on changing their contemporary societies, they simply adore an idealized 'primitive' past. Moreover, and even worse, Modern Primitive people have such a deep desire to believe in an imagined pureness, naturalness and authenticity of 'primitive' societies, that every assumed contact of the latter with the 'civilized world' can destabilize or destroy the basis for their appreciation. The enthusiasm for the 'primitive', thus, always remains an abstract idea. Concrete societies can hardly reckon to gain esteem from it. The following quotations demonstrate this drastically.

> Cultures such as the Arabs are not primitive and they're not civilized, so they fall in the worst crack of all. A little bit of civilization is a terrible thing. (Fakir Musafar in Vale and Juno, 1989: 21)

> This happened in Africa, the most desecrated continent in the world. Every culture there that got touched by Western society became extremely cruel and possessive, and all this shit came out. The worst aspects of Western society become assimilated. (Fakir Musafar in Vale and Juno, 1989: 21)

From the latter statement it becomes obvious how colonialism is denied as a reality of power and exploitation. No colonizing perpetrators are visible in this image of two cultures just 'touching' each other. This view obscures real violence and only complains the loss of an imagined pureness of the non-Western cultures.

Modern Primitives' enthusiasm for the 'primitives', finally, articulates itself as a rather ambivalent thing. A brief historical exploration of the discourse on 'primitivism' may show *how the idealization of 'primitivism' always has been integrated in strategies of its subordination.*

'Primitivism' and Anthropology
The word 'primitive' appeared for the first time in the15th century to signify the meaning 'original' or 'ancestor', referring to animals, occasionally even men. The usage of the word spread to a variety of disciplines in the 18th century, always having a connotation of 'pure, 'original', 'simple'. In art history 'primitive' in the beginning referred to all painters before the Renaissance. Later on it included different kinds of early art: ancient, courtly and 'tribal'. The term ceased being used to refer to prehistoric European phenomena. By the 1920s, finally, its meaning was confined to so-called 'tribal' art, originating in the colonized parts of the world (e.g. Native American, Eskimo, African, Oceanic) (Goldberg, 1993; Torgovnick, 1990).

As a 'scientific' idea it crystallized in the philosophical anthropological discussion in the 1860s and 1870s. Modernity has been obsessed with the study of 'primitive lifestyles', 'primitive societies', etc. Ethnography and anthropology have been the scientific disciplines in the forefront of the study of the 'primitive'. Early anthropological writers developed the evolutionist theory of a 'primitive society', drawing on a variety of assumptions which basically constructed 'primitive society' as the *antithesis* or mirror image of modern Western societies.

Although this theory was not based on any historical evidence and early criticism was available, it has not been dropped from anthropological discussion. The 'persistence of this illusion' has to be seen in the ideological suitability of the concept for the West's political claims of superiority (Kuper, 1988). The notion of 'primitivism' has been and still is used as an ideological means for legitimizing colonial and imperial politics.

Anthropology has been very important in the production of profoundly racialized knowledge. Knowledge producers are always set in particular milieus and particular social-historical situations. Anthropological theory, thus, must be understood as power/knowledge configurations of societies involved in expansion and conquest (Athanasiou, 1996; Goldberg, 1993). Within colonial discourse analysis even more radical claims have been made: the production of *all forms of Western knowledge* has been influenced, tinged and impressed by the gross political fact of colonialism (Bernal, 1987; Said, 1979; Young, 1994, 1995).

Evolutionism as Enlightenment Thought and Common-Sense Persuasion
Anthropology has profoundly been an Enlightenment project. Dominant tropes of the Enlightenment discourse have been deployed within anthropological theory in the face of the colonial encounter: the schematization of time as a single progressive narrative as well as the idea of the rational, (allegedly) self-constituting subject. Rationality and morality were conceptualized as the exclusive properties of 'Western' subjectivities and the societies organized by them. These were the categories that marked the threshold between savagery and civilization (Athanasiou, 1996; Goldberg, 1993). Drawing on these tropes of Enlightenment thought modernity has constituted itself with an 'inborn' thrust towards exclusion and subjugation (see Bauman, 1989, 1993). 'Tribalism' and 'primitivism' are discursive assumptions, which emerged out of these internal contradictions and tensions of modernity. The 'West', as an emerging political and economic centre of power, in the course of its colonial enterprises defined itself as the most developed and civilized part of the world. Other regions were downgraded to a peripheral status that correlated with their ascribed lower stage of development (Friedman, 1994).

The imagining of a 'primitive society' as a primal and original form of human association was easily translatable into a simple hierarchy, because of its strong evolutionist connotations. Evolutionist ideas emerged on the discursive agenda from the 16th and 17th centuries. The Renaissance produced the 'temporalization of the great chain of being'. Enlightenment thought developed evolutionism as a coherent and hegemonic world view.

The increasingly *racialized* construction of an epistemology around the binaries modern/primitive, developed/non-developed, civilized/savage, rational/irrational, enlightened/magic, culture/nature (and so on) strengthened the conviction that Western identity is superior to that of all non-Western peoples and cultures (Young, 1995). Originating in anthropological discourses, the notion of 'primitivism' has spread into other disciplines (such as literature, art history, psychology) and into popular culture (advertising, fashions and new media productions). The notions of both 'primitivism' and 'evolutionism' today foundationally inform hegemonic world views within Western societies (Lutz and Collins, 1993: 240). Today a generalized notion of 'primitivism' exists within popular culture bare of geographical and historical specification, simply drawing on suitable generalizations. These multiple and often contradicting myths and persuasions, reproduced over and over again on all levels of Western cultures, according to Torgovnick (1990), inform the various *tropes of a primitivist discourse* which has been foundational to the Western sense of self and Other. As a conceptual order of its own, 'primitivism' has continually underpinned racist assumptions and has become a pillar of racist culture (Goldberg, 1993).

Modern Primitivism as Legacy of Colonialism in Late Imperial Culture

Modern Primitives' celebration of 'primitive societies', in my view, is just another extreme version of this primitivist discourse. Despite its enthusiasm for 'the primitive', this discourse deploys similar assumptions. With a blatant disregard for history and societal and geographic contexts, groups and societies are lumped together in the category of 'primitives'. The dualism between the 'primitive' societies and the 'West' is maintained.

I have suggested understanding the Romantic turn towards primitivism and the elaborations of colonial anthropology as two strands of *one (although ambivalent) primitivist discourse*, held together by a set of common premises. Modern Primitivism, historically rooted in the Romantic movement, represents a particular (postcolonial) strand of this discourse. Even its pro-primitivist stance deploys tropes of a worldview which has been an integral part of colonial discourses, and takes up popular perceptions of 'primitive people'. It modifies some of these assumptions and reinforces others. Modern Primitivism is deeply informed by the ambivalences of stereotyping and racialized representation. The radical critique of the repression of the body and sexuality in 'Western' thought and morality is coded in the celebration of the oversexualized bodies and practices of the 'primitives'. Images and representations of cultures labelled 'primitive' are conjured up in order to exploit them in a personal identification strategy. The dichotomous structure of the 'primitivist discourse' is never upset, not even in attempts to integrate elements of the first into a life in the second. Therefore, it is inevitable that the movement uncritically incorporates evolutionist common-sense perceptions of social reality with all their epistemological ballast.

The contemporary revival of 'primitivism' gives evidence of the fact that the image of the 'primitive' has remained largely unchallenged in popular culture. Worse, this is also true of parts of society that think of themselves as being in *opposition* to this mainstream culture. Most of the explicit academic critique of the concept and the discourse of 'primitivism' has remained faithful to the very parameters of primitivism (Goldberg, 1993). This is also the case with Torgovnick's (1990) critique of the primitivist discourse in anthropology and popular culture. In the end, she does not challenge the 'primitivist discourse' itself, but rather the dominant 'male-centred canonical line of Western primitivism'. 'Going primitive' still appears as a romanticized and idealized possibility of escape from the alienation of industrialized, capitalist, Western societies (Torgovnick, 1990: 246). According to Goldberg (1993), no use of the term 'primitivism', especially when contrasted with concepts such as 'European', 'Western' or 'modern', can escape the value statements intrinsic to the evolutionist frame. The necessary deconstruction of 'primitivism' should entail a deconstruction of most of our conceptualizations of modernity, because one concept is modelled on the other. This should also have implications for contemporary theories of the body and body modification, which have tended to reproduce a juxtaposition between modernity (which is assumed to be Western) and traditionalism (mostly imagined as non-Western) in their historical analysis.

Notes

I wish to thank particularly Umut Erel, Ken Plummer, Chetan Bhatt, Nira Yuval-Davis, Lesley Caldwell and Dan Mahoney, for their help in commenting on earlier drafts of this article. Special thanks to Idexa who has helped me with material on 'Modern Primitivism'.

1. My main sources are the magazine *Body Play and Modern Primitives Quarterly* (vols 1–3, 1992–5), and the book *Re/Search #12. Modern Primitives* (Vale and Juno, 1989).
2. Figures 1 and 2 originally appeared in 'More on Ibitoe', *BP & MPQ* 1(3); Figures 3 and 4 in 'Breasts, Development, Sculpting and Play', *BP & MPQ* 2(3); and Figures 5 and 6 in 'Tantric Hindu Ritual Reveals Deep Secrets to Modern Primitives', *BP & MPQ* 1(4).

References

Anthias, Floya and Nira Yuval-Davis (1992) *Racialised Boundaries: Race, Gender, Colour and Class and the Antiracist Struggle*. London and New York: Routledge.
Athanasiou, Athena (1996) 'Colonial Anthropology: An Enlightenment Legacy? The Lockean Discourse on Nature, Social Order, and Difference', *Common Sense, Journal of the Edinburgh Conference of Socialist Economists* 20: 21–33.

Bauman, Zygmunt (1989) *Modernity and the Holocaust.* Cambridge: Polity Press.

Bauman, Zygmunt (1993) *Modernity and Ambivalence.* Cambridge: Polity Press.

Bauman, Zygmunt (1996) 'From Pilgrim to Tourist – or a Short History of Identity', pp. 18–36 in S. Hall and P. du Gay (eds) *Questions of Cultural Identity.* London: Sage Publications.

Bernal, Martin (1987) *Black Athena: The Afroasiatic Roots of Classical Civilization. Volume I: The Fabrication of Ancient Greece 1785–1985.* London: Free Association Books.

Bhabha, Homi K. (1983) 'The Other Question', *Screen* 24(6): 18–36.

Bhabha, Homi K. (1984) 'Signs Taken for Wonders: Questions of Ambivalence and Authority under a Tree Outside Dehli, May 1817', pp. 89–107 in F. Baker et al. (eds) *Europe and its Others.* Colchester: University of Essex.

Bhabha, Homi K. (1986) 'Of Mimicry and Man: The Ambivalence of Colonial Discourse', pp. 198–205 in J. Donald and S. Hall (eds) *Politics and Identity.* Milton Keynes and Philadelphia: Open University Press.

Bhabha, Homi K. (1990) 'Interview with Homi K. Bhabha: The Third Space', pp. 207–21 in J. Rutherford (ed.) *Identity, Culture, Difference.* London: Lawrence and Wishart.

Bhabha, Homi K.(1996) 'Culture's in-Between', pp. 53–60 in S. Hall and P. du Gay (eds) *Questions of Cultural Identity.* London: Sage Publications.

Blackmer, Corinne E. (1998) 'Ethnoporn, Lesbian Childhood, and Native Maternal Culture: Reading *National Geographic* with Elizabeth Bishop', *GLQ: A Journal of Lesbian and Gay Studies* 4(1): 17–38.

Bloch, Maurice and Jean H. Bloch (1980) 'Women and the Dialectics of Nature in 18th-Century French Thought', pp. 25–41 in P. MacCormack and M. Strathern (eds) *Nature, Culture, and Gender.* Cambridge: Cambridge University Press.

Body Play and Modern Primitives Quarterly vols. 1–3, 1992–5.

Bourdieu, Pierre (1996) *Distinction: A Social Critique of the Judgement of Taste.* London: Routledge.

Caglar, Ayse (1997) 'Hyphenated Identities and the Limits of "Culture"', pp. 169–85 in T. Modood and P. Werbner (eds) *The Politics of Multiculturalism in the New Europe: Racism, Identity and Community.* London and New Jersey: Zed Books.

Califa, Pat (1994) 'Modern Primitives, Latex Shamans, and Ritual S/M', pp. 231–40 in *Public Sex: The Culture of Radical Sex.* Pittsburgh: Cleis Press.

Clifford, James (1988) *The Predicament of Culture: Twentieth-Century Ethnography, Literature, and Art.* Cambridge, MA: Harvard University Press.

Corbey, Raymond (1995) 'Ethnographic Showcases, 1870–1930', pp. 57–80 in J. Nederveen Pieterse and B. Parekh (eds) *The Decolonization of Imagination: Culture, Knowledge and Power.* London: Zed.

De Groot, Joanna (1989) ' "Sex" and "Race": The Construction of Language and Image in the Nineteenth Century', pp. 89–128 in S. Mendus and J. Rendall (eds) *Sexuality and Subordination: Interdisciplinary Study of Gender in the Nineteenth Century.* London and New York: Routledge.

Erel, Umut (forthcoming) 'Grenzüberschreitungen und Kulturelle Mischformen als Antirassistischer Widerstand?'

Eubanks, Virginia (1996) 'Zones of Dither: Writing the Postmodern Body', *Body & Society* 2(3): 73–88.

Featherstone, Mike (1991) 'The Body in Consumer Culture', pp. 170–96 in M. Featherstone, M. Hepworth and B.S. Turner (eds) *The Body: Social Process and Cultural Theory.* London: Sage Publications.

Friedman, Jonathan (1994) *Cultural Identity and Global Process.* London: Sage Publications.

Giddens, Anthony (1990) *The Consequences of Modernity.* Cambridge: Polity Press.

Giddens, Anthony (1991) *Modernity and Self-Identity.* Cambridge: Polity Press.

Goldberg, David T. (1993) *Racist Culture: Philosophy and the Politics of Meaning.* Cambridge: Blackwell.

Hall, Stuart (1992) 'The West and the Rest: Discourse and Power', pp. 275–320 in S. Hall and B. Gieben (eds) *Formations of Modernity.* Cambridge: Blackwell and the Open University.

Hart, Lynda and Joshua Dale (1997) 'Sadomasochism', pp. 341–56 in A. Medhurst and S.R. Munt (eds) *Lesbian and Gay Studies: A Critical Introduction.* London: Cassell.

Kuper, Adam (1988) *The Invention of Primitive Society: Transformations of an Illusion.* London and New York: Routledge.

Levi Straus, David (1989) 'Modern Primitives', pp. 157–8 in V. Vale and A. Juno (eds) *Re/Search #12: Modern Primitives. An Investigation of Contemporary Adornment and Ritual.* San Francisco: Re/Search Publications.

Lutz, Catherine A. and Jane L. Collins (1993) *Reading National Geographic.* Chicago and London: University of Chicago Press.

Mascia-Lees, Francia E. and Patricia Sharpe (eds) (1992) *Tattoo, Torture, Mutilation, and Adornment: The Denaturalization of the Body in Culture and Text.* New York: State University of New York Press.

Mellor, Phillip A. and Chris Shilling (1997) *Re-Forming the Body: Religion, Community and Modernity.* London: Sage Publications.

Myers, James (1992) 'Nonmainstream Body Modification: Genital Piercing, Branding, Burning, and Cutting', *Journal of Contemporary Ethnography* 21(3): 276–306.

Nandy, Ashis (1983) *The Intimate Enemy: Loss and Recovering of Self under Colonialism.* New Dehli: Oxford University Press.

Nederveen Pieterse, Jan (1994) 'Unpacking the West: How European is Europe?', pp. 129–49 in A. Rattansi and S. Westwood (eds) *Racism, Modernity, Identity. On the Western Front.* Cambridge: Polity Press.

Rattansi, Ali (1994) ' "Western" Racisms, Ethnicities and Identities in a Postmodern Frame', pp. 15–86 in A. Rattansi and S. Westwood (eds) *Racism, Modernity, Identity: On the Western Front.* Cambridge: Polity Press.

Rutherford, Jonathan (1990) 'A Place Called Home: Identity and the Cultural Politics of Difference', pp. 9–27 in J. Rutherford (ed.) *Identity, Community, Culture, Difference.* London and New York: Routledge.

Rubin, Arnold (ed.) (1988) *Marks of Civilization: Artistic Transformations of the Human Body.* Los Angeles: Museum of Cultural History, University of California, LA.

Said, Edward (1979) *Orientalism.* London: Routledge and Kegan Paul Ltd.

Sanders, Clinton R. (1989) *Customizing the Body: The Art and Culture of Tattooing.* Philadelphia: Temple University Press.

Shilling, Chris (1993) *The Body and Social Theory.* London: Sage Publications.

Solomos, John and Les Back (1996) *Racism and Society.* London: Macmillan.

Sweetman, Paul (1997) 'Marked Bodies, Oppositional Identities? Tattooing, Piercing and the Ambiguity of Resistance', paper presented at the *Body & Society* Day Conference on Body Modification, Nottingham Trent University, 16 June.

Thompson, Mark (ed.) (1991) *Leatherfolk: Radical Sex, People, Politics and Practice.* Boston: Alyson Publications.

Torgovnick, Marianna (1990) *Gone Primitive: Savage Intellects, Modern Lives.* Chicago and London: University of California Press.

Torgovnick, Marianna (1995) 'Piercings', pp. 197–210 in R. De La Campa, E.A. Kaplan and M. Sprinker (eds) *Late Imperial Culture.* London and New York: Verso.

Turner, Bryan S. (1995) 'Recent Developments in the Theory of the Body', pp. 1–35 in M. Featherstone et al. (eds) *The Body: Social Process and Cultural Theory.* London: Sage Publications.

Vale, V. and A. Juno (eds) (1989) *Re/Search #12: Modern Primitives. An Investigation of Contemporary Adornment and Ritual.* San Francisco: Re/Search Publications.

Young, Robert J.C. (1994) 'Egypt in America: Black Athena, Racism and Colonial Discourse', pp. 150–70 in A. Rattansi and S. Westwood (eds) *Racism, Modernity, Identity: On the Western Front.* Cambridge: Polity Press.

Young, Robert J.C. (1995) *Colonial Desire: Hybridity in Theory, Culture and Race*. London and New York: Routledge.
Yuval-Davis, Nira (1997) 'Ethnicity, Gender Relations and Multiculturalism', pp. 193–209 in T. Modood and P. Werbner (eds) *The Politics of Multiculturalism in the New Europe: Racism, Identity and Community*. London and New Jersey: Zed Books.

Christian Klesse has got academic training in Social and Economic History (at the University of Hamburg, Germany) and in Gender and Ethnic Studies (at the University of Greenwich, London). At present he is doing PhD research on gay and bisexual men in non-monogamous partnerships at the Department of Sociology, University of Essex. His recent academic work has been concerned with issues of sexuality, gender, ethnicity, the body, social movement politics, identity and life historical research.

The Possibility of Primitiveness: Towards a Sociology of Body Marks in Cool Societies

BRYAN S. TURNER

Introduction: Markings

Evidence of tattooing and related practices comes to us from the earliest human societies. For example, Egyptian mummies from the period of the Middle Kingdom have revealed an extensive culture of body marking. In a religious cosmology, the inalienable tattoos of this world could be bartered for spiritual privileges in the next. In these traditional cultures, tattoos generally functioned to guarantee good health and to ward off evil. Throughout the Mediterranean and Middle East, even after the spread of puritanical Islam, tattoos and amulets protected the individual from the evil eye (Hildburgh, 1955). In Hawaii, tattoos were also employed to memorialize deceased relatives and in Indonesia they were indicative of important secular accomplishments (Cohen, 1994). The period of 19th-century colonialism was when social anthropologists became increasingly aware of the relationship between Otherness and tattooing as ethnographic work in the cultures of Melanesia and Polynesia revealed an amazing tradition of body art. Anthropological investigations have uncovered the liminality associated with transitional stages in the life-cycle, where ecstatic experiences were produced by standing outside conventional roles. Tattoos are important in signifying these transitions.

These body marks in pre-literate societies were permanent, collective and largely obligatory. Because they were set within a shared culture of collective meanings, the significance of a tattoo could be read unambiguously. Tattoos in

Body & Society © 1999 SAGE Publications (London, Thousand Oaks and New Delhi), Vol. 5(2–3): 39–50
[1357–034X(199906/09)5:2–3;39–50;008853]

traditional societies were not set within a cultural framework where ironic and simulated interpretations were possible. Following Mary Douglas's orientation to the principles of social membership as expressed through bodily modifications, body marks (which I use as a short-hand for tattooing, piercing, cicatrization, painting and so forth) indicate social membership through the metaphor of the human body as a space where we think about and constitute the body politic (Douglas, 1966). In particular, body marks designate political (specifically gender) identity at certain points in the life-cycle. They are significant in demarcating stages in sexual maturity. The ritual mutilation of the penis in Australian aboriginal communities is a dramatic illustration which designated male identity at a point in the life-cycle where boys crossed over into adulthood (Spencer and Gillen, 1997). Changes in the nature and purpose of tattoos indicate changes in the nature and purpose of social life. By contrast, the contemporary interest in tattoos is no longer confined, as in earlier periods of Western industrialization, to the working-class, youth culture or criminal communities, but extends through the social scale as tattoos are increasingly used to produce an aesthetic enhancement of the body. Tattooing is now more closely related to the commercial exploitation of sexual themes in popular culture than to life-cycle transitions. In short, tattoos have become a regular aspect of consumer culture, where they add cultural capital to the body's surface.

However, the need to imitate the body markings of other and earlier cultures in contemporary primitivism can be taken as further evidence in postmodern cultures of what we might fruitfully term the exhaustion of idiom. Because a culture of simulation does not easily produce, permit or accept 'authenticity', popular idioms are necessarily cliches. Traditional Maori or Japanese signs are woven into global consumerism, where they are endlessly modernized, producing a complex hybridization of signs and messages. Globalization has produced a melange of tattoos which are ironically self-referential and repetitive, and the very hybridity of tattoo genres playfully questions the authenticity of these commercial body marks. This erosion of the compulsory and serious nature of tattooing as a means of cutting social meaning and membership simultaneously into the flesh is a feature of the general secularization of society. It was Emile Durkheim who described religion as 'the serious life' and hence the playful nature of the modern consumerized body mark is an index of the death of God in the contemporary world.

My argument is that we need to understand traditional tattooing within the context of a theory which connects human embodiment to social processes, especially processes of production and reproduction, because tattoos measured the progress of individuals through the life-cycle. The reproduction of bodies (through family formation in households) and the production of wealth (through the economy) are tied together in traditional societies (through laws of inheritance and patriarchy). The meaning of body marks had a certain stability because they were embedded in social processes (sexual and economic production) which were traditional, but in modern societies these social linkages are either broken or at least eroded by transformations in both gender relations and the economy. Love is no longer a prelude to marriage and in this sense romantic passion is a free-floating desire. Body marks no longer need to indicate or to define gender in the life-cycle, and so they become optional, playful and ironic.

It is useful to think about these playful marks as illustrations of the neo-tribalism which is described in Michel Maffesoli's *The Time of the Tribes* (1996) via a reflection on Nietzsche's Dionysus theme. Tattoos and body piercing are no longer functional, but indicate the social construction of traditional patterns of sociability in the modern world. Tattoos operate in a field of Dionysian desire and consumer pleasure, but consumerism has not produced its own (authentic) mythology or consumer theology, and therefore tattoos have no cosmic foundation from which meaning could be derived. Hence they are often parasitic upon the Other and the primitive; they consciously simulate primitive images of sexuality. While Maffesoli's work is suggestive in understanding the creative playfulness of consumer body marks, Nietszche's critique of mass society in the concept of 'the herd' and his commitment to the heroic struggle of the Overman against the modern tribe is hardly compatible with Maffesoli's playful postmodernism.

Drawing somewhat on Marshall McLuhan (1964) I develop a typology of society in terms of two dichotomies – thick and thin solidarity, and cool and hot loyalties. In traditional tribalism, membership was thick/hot and required obligatory body marks. In postmodern neo-tribalism, membership is voluntary (thin/cool) and hence marking is optional. Such a characterization of the division between tradition and modernity rests explicitly on Durkheim, for whom membership of primitive societies often gave rise, through ritual practice, to effervescence. Australian aboriginal society has played an important role in shaping anthropological and sociological views of society. The description of these cultures by B. Spencer and F.J. Gillen (1997) was fundamental in Durkheim's conceptualization of the sacred/profane dichotomy. Certain body modifications in aboriginal society were in fact voluntary. Tooth evulsion, for example, was optional. For the Arunta, tooth evulsion was partly a matter of personal taste and fashion, being performed before marriage. The removal of the tooth represents the arrival of a dark cloud. The tooth is thrown in the direction of the mother's camp but it has no initiatory importance. By contrast, circumcision has a general significance in marking the passage to adulthood and maturity. These rites mark the various points in the life-cycle and hence these body marks are part of a compulsory set of stages in the transition to adult status (Berndt and Berndt, 1964). They indicate forcefully the separation between the collective sphere of sacred objects and experiences, and the everyday profane world of utilitarian actions. They contrast fundamentally with modern tattoos which are optional, decorative, impermanent and narcissistic.

If we were to develop a metaphor to characterize the fleeting and transitory nature of contemporary culture, then we could argue that postmodern society resembles an airport departure lounge where membership is optional (thin/cool) as passengers wait patiently for the next action to unfold through the exit doorway. We are all *flâneurs* when we survey others bodies for playful marks as we consume the surface of other bodies. Gazing at the lifestyles of other passengers becomes a pleasurable pastime, suitable to fill the time prior to departure. Reading body marks is, however, an uncertain form of textual practice because there are no necessary linkages between marks and roles. Body marks are typically narcissistic, being playful signs to the self. They are part of a personal and interior biography, and not an obligatory feature of collective memory.

Metaphors of Traditional and Modern Society

The social sciences operate through and by means of a series of powerful metaphors of society. In late 19th- and early 20th-century sociological imagination, the distinction between community and association played a major part in shaping German academic perspectives on the emergence of industrial society (Liebersohn, 1988). The original intention was to distinguish between two types of consciousness, but the typology has been used mainly to describe two contrasted forms of society and the impact of the process of modernization. Traditional society was defined in terms of the existence of a dense network of solidarity and commonality, a shared culture and system of rituals, and the dominance of collective over individual arrangements. Broadly speaking, traditional societies are rural, tribal, nomadic and politically stationary. By contrast, modern society is urban, industrial, individualistic and dynamic; its culture is, at least formally, secular, individualistic and unstable. This 'ideal type' construction was elaborated by many generations of sociologists through the 20th century in, for example, Durkheim's contrast between mechanical solidarity in traditional society based on shared rituals and organic solidarity in modern society based on the social reciprocity which flows from the division of labour. Max Weber's description of the iron cage of bureaucracy, Theodor Adorno's notion of the 'administered society' and Michel Foucault's concept of the carceral can be interpreted as part of the legacy of the use of *Gesellschaft* as a narrative of modernization. In its essential connotations, *Gesellschaft* is the market place of anonymous strangers who come together to celebrate modernity but under the constraints of personal alienation, moral estrangement and social anomie. The metaphors of modernity in sociology have therefore been primarily nostalgic (Turner, 1987).

We can view the concepts of risk society and McDonaldization as attempts to provide a new understanding of modern society based on the principle of *Gesellschaft*. Modernity is seen by George Ritzer (1993) to be highly regulated and controlled, whereas for Ulrich Beck (1992) reflexive modernity is characterized by unobserved and uninsured risk. However, they both describe a world characterized by the meeting of strangers in an unfamiliar environment where trust is paramount, albeit a form of trust which is more assumed than perceived. We have seen that 'market' was a traditional metaphor for associational relationships which are open and anonymous, but perhaps the best metaphor for such a society, as I have indicated, would be the airport departure lounge. Richard Sennett (1994: 349) observes that the we live in a world 'whose architectural emblem is the airport waiting lounge'. The flight departure lounge is an arena of strangers, nervously but nonchalantly awaiting their turn to depart. They have no commitment to each other or to their place; their social relations are fragmented and fleeting. Because they have no intention to stay or to settle, they are the ultimate 'lonely crowd' (Riesman et al., 1950).

The lounge itself is highly regulated, and yet uncertain and hazardous. Things tend to go wrong despite the confident and simulated charm of the ground staff. Flights are delayed and cancelled; staff may go on strike; there are the routine risks of food poisoning and viral infections from other travellers. There can be more spectacular risks, such as hijacking, international terrorism and mid-flight crashes. In periods of international instability, passenger craft may be shot down by both friendly and enemy fire. Modern international travel involves a mass transport system which is characterized by high risk, and therefore by minute and detailed control and surveillance. The notion that society as a whole could be metaphorically described as an airport departure lounge is useful for this general debate, because airports combine the perspectives of both risk society and McDonaldization. International travel perfectly illustrates Beck's notion of risk because travel is a function of modernization and international travel systems multiply and extend risks. As a result they require heavy regulation and control through Taylorism and Fordism, namely through McDonaldization. The airport can act as a metaphor of the whole because many activities have this quality of individualism, time-out, alienation and pointless leisure – such as channel-hopping in which the passive viewer recklessly (one might say) skips through the imaginary world of television. The couch in the television room can act as the focus of domesticated ennui as one's personal departure lounge.

We can expand this metaphor to begin to develop what I want to term an ironic theory of communication (Turner, 1998). We can initially elaborate the *Gemeinschaft/Gesellschaft* typology along two separate dimensions. Let us first assert that forms of solidarity can be either thick or thin. As I have indicated, thick solidarities perfectly describe the world of the Arunta people of Durkheim's mechanical solidarity in *The Elementary Forms of the Religious Life* (Durkheim, 1912). Their social world involved closed communities, roaming over a virtually unlimited terrain in search of food. Their social relations were solid, permanent, emotive and effervescent. By contrast, modern societies organized around the industrial corporation and the market place are based on thin solidarities as described for example by Georg Simmel (1968) in his account of urban mentalities and the stranger. Modern urban society is the world of the stranger who is geographically mobile and socially transient.

The next theoretical distinction is drawn from McLuhan's notion (1964) of hot and cool communications. In his studies of modern communication systems, McLuhan argued that radio is a hot form of communication whereas the telephone, which offers a unidimensional communication with high definition, is cool. I wish to modify this notion to suggest that we can define social commitments or loyalties as either hot or cool. Strangers have a limited and superficial attachment to local communities; their involvement is always predicated on uncertainty and psychological distance. We can characterize this mode of commitment through the postmodern liberalism of Richard Rorty (1989), who describes postmodern liberalism in terms of systematic doubt about the validity of 'final' vocabularies. An ironist always holds her view of the world in doubt; it is always subject to revision and amendment. In short, the society, or at least our picture of it, is provisional.

Now this culture of ironic reflection appears to describe perfectly the world of postmodernity as characterized by thin solidarities and cool commitments. If modernity involves thick solidarities (nationalism) and hot loyalties (ideological certainty), then the postmodern world is one of shifting or thin solidarities and ironic or cool loyalties. Such a world is described sociologically by the development of the revisable self and the negotiated community of temporary loyalties. Its primary style of communication is ironic, tentative and reflexive; it will eschew ideological hotness and moral certainty, in favour of more relativistic and hesitant opinions and attitudes. Its predominant rhetoric will be couched in terms of questions and provisional statements rather than assertions of irrefutable fact and dogmatic logic. Irony is all too conscious of the risk that what we take to be a confident description of reality today may appear absurd tomorrow.

These theoretical arguments provide us with a useful matrix of social life. As I have argued, cool loyalties/thin solidarities express and describe the world of postmodernism where attachments to social reality are ironic, because they are incompatible with 'grand narratives' (Lyotard, 1987). These reflexive attachments are the exact opposite of political nationalism (hot/thick), where social relations are bifurcated around the contrast between Friend/Enemy. In the language of Carl Schmitt (1976), the political is defined by the violence between insiders/outsiders, a conflict which makes political life moral and meaningful. We can argue that cool/thick relations might be typical of how enthusiastic utopians describe the new Internet communities or virtual groups. Passing enthusiasm for various aspects of popular culture could be described as hot in commitment but thin in terms of forming lasting communities. Because boundaries and borders in contemporary Western societies are not marked by exclusionary body rituals, tattoos become superficial marks.

In a historical context, we can claim that the rise of the nation state from the 17th to the 19th century as the principal administrative unit of modern politics required a more intense pattern of loyalty as the traditional solidarity of religion declined. The new solidarity was nationalism which sought to replace religion as the basis of solidarity in the form of hot commitments and thick solidarities. This period saw the rise of modern citizenship in its nationalistic form as the primary mechanism of hot/thick attachments; it was also the period in which bourgeois civil society as the arena of rational communication was triumphant. This dream of a solidaristic nation-state has been challenged by modern processes of globalization and modernization which drives the political community in the direction of cool/thin modalities of organization. National governments have to presuppose an ethnically homogeneous society, which of course is a state of affairs constantly contradicted by multiculturalism, indigenous people's movements and labour migration.

Tattooing during the period of nation formation was often part of an oppositional culture in which working-class males expressed their class solidarity or occupational solidarity through body marks. State strategies of governmentality interpreted tattoos as part of the culture of the criminal or underclasses. Body-marking was now used for classification and stigmatization. For example, in France criminals were branded with letters to mark their particular crimes (Falk, 1995). In German concentration camps, Jews were branded under National Socialism with numbers as a mark of their expulsion and subordination. These marks were bureaucratically cool, but they also indicated the presence of thick social groups defined by blood and descent into Jews and not-Jews. Branding became part of a routine bureaucratic process of scientific governmentality.

The airport departure lounge captures metaphorically the consequences of globalization for commitment and loyalty, but it also captures the temporary and fleeting nature of modern social relationships. Travellers have multiple commitments, weak affiliations, loose associations and tentative arrangements. Just as flights can be cancelled and re-negotiated, so everyday relations of intimacy are open to negotiation (Beck and Beck-Gernsheim, 1995). Adultery rates could be said to communicate this sense of the temporary nature of commitment. In the postmodern world, flight destinies are open to negotiation and are not permanent or compulsory. Social space, like social relations, can be sampled and tested prior to occupancy. The departure lounge captures the uncertainties of modern life, its ennui, anxiety and fragility. The exit sign offers departure, relief and an escape from boredom and routine. It is an arena of risk and uncertainty, but it is also highly regulated; it offers the promise of regulated and normalized excitement.

We can conceptualize modern societies in terms of different segments of the class structure by reference to their degree of incorporation in the global economy. With the growth of tourism and global travel, larger sections of society adopt personality types which are associated with fleeting, thin and fragmentary relations. The growth of global corporate labour markets has been driven by the emergence of what Robert Reich (1991) has called the 'symbolic analyst'; these professional, white-collar workers include the cluster of professional, business and academic elites who control, develop and manage symbolic, knowledge and information systems. The symbolic analyst is the mental worker of the new global corporation; their loyalties are to international firms and their solidarities are dispersed and fragmented. Because they are ironically cool about social commitments and loyalties, their political orientation may indeed be close to disloyalty. The new lumpenproletariat or underclass who inhabit the unskilled or deskilled casual labour market are neither culturally nor physically mobile in the world economy. Because they are stuck in a sector of the market which is underdeveloped, they are more likely to adopt a neo-tribal mentality which fits their wish for therapeutically thick/hot communities. Gang-land, football clubs, the 'local community', and British pub rock bands are expressions of local solidarity, but they are also partly simulated forms of traditional communalism. Where their neo-tribalism spills over into genuine fascism, their version of belonging can become overtly hostile to the cosmopolitanism of the global market. Tattoos survive in this group as a primary mark of hot/thick loyalties. In traditional working-class occupations, tattoos often unofficially marked occupational membership such as sailor or soldier. Tattoos indicated membership of a male culture of work and hardship. In the modern world of unemployment, tattoos on hands or foreheads which proclaim 'Hate' are indicative of alienation and separation rather than masculine mateship. By contrast, discrete and aesthetic butterflies and flowers on the shoulders and backs of fashion models and middle-class professional women are sexual consumer images; they are removeable adornments.

The Return of Dionysus: Maffesoli's Tribes

The playfulness of sexual imagery in modern society is produced by the separation which has taken place between reproduction, household and economy. In traditional societies, the link between the body and economic wealth was made obvious by laws of inheritance, especially through the principles of primogeniture and patriarchy (Turner, 1997). In feudalism, the social accumulation of landed property within dominant families rested on a system of successful marriage alliances. This pattern of inheritance was backed up by Catholic theological doctrine with its emphasis on female chastity, virginity, filial piety and social duties (of reproduction). Confession of (sexual) guilt functioned as a mechanism of social control to enforce these patterns of reproductive behaviour. In medieval times, monastic celibacy stood alongside and contrasted with domestic debauchery, because marriage was a necessary evil. Even among the refined court of knights, true love in the tradition of the minstrels and Arabic lyric poetry was adulterous love. The Protestant ethic (Weber, 1930) transferred the sexual ideology of the monastery into the domestic sphere, enjoining discipline on all. It was from this historical transition that contemporary theories of Western sex had their origin in a contrast between Dionysian pleasure and Apollonian control, namely in the work of Nietzsche, Weber, Freud and Adorno (Stauth and Turner, 1988). Capitalism required ascetic control and self-discipline, and hence sexual neurosis was manifest in female hysteria, masturbatory insanity and agoraphobia. As a result, women became the principal objects of bourgeois sciences of sexual conduct.

This strict relationship between reproduction and economics has broken down with capitalist industrialization. For example, there is no longer a clear relationship between ownership and management control; the banks play a central role, not families, in providing loans for investment; and family capitalism has been partly replaced by the international corporations. These economic changes provided the background to the transformation of the nuclear family, the rise of the romantic ethos, the sexualization of youth culture and the political emancipation of women. The romantic youth complex brought in a period of sexual experimentation, high rates of adultery, divorce and remarriage, and installed the contemporary fascination with love and intimacy. Youth culture dominates consumer culture to such an extent that there is no clear demarcation of age structures; life-cycle and consumption have no precise relationship. The democratization of love (Giddens, 1992) has followed this great corrosion of the linkage between economic production and sex. The contemporary impermanent 'paint-on' tattoo is indicative of the transferable loyalties of the postmodern passenger.

In metaphorical terms, the airport with its thin/cool relationships contrasts with other possibilities in the matrix of social positions. In modern societies, there is a revival of 'neo-tribalism' (Maffesoli, 1996) and, as aspects of utilitarian individualism are challenged by new versions of subjectivity, emotive communities such as football crowds contrast with the sober discipline of industrialized factories. While modernization brought about both individuation and separation, affective groups survived in everyday society as sites of collective solidarity. These 'little masses' are distinguished by their special clothing, sports and adornments, including tattoos. These emotional communities have resisted the processes of rationalization and bureaucratization which are typical of the public sphere based on the social contract. Maffesoli identifies these neo-tribal groupings – football clubs, working-class gangs, social movements and primary groups in the everyday world – as sites where Dionysian affective and orgiastic experiences are possible.

These neo-tribal configurations might correspond to the survival of hot/thick ensembles of social relationships in a mass society, which are quite different from the thin/cool relations of globalized social communities in the airport. Metaphorically the virtual community (Rheingold,1993) is seen to be a web homestead, where solidarities are possible but through a series of loyalties which remain cool. TV evangelism by contrast has a hot message, but it cannot form the thick solidarities which characterized 19th-century sectarianism. However, one can also argue that these affective relationships are themselves highly simulated and artificial. Working-class football clubs are quickly incorporated into global financial interests, 'communities' are organized by town-planning processes in the interests of protecting 'neighbourhoods', oppositional styles such as Punk become part of the consumer culture of late capitalism, and tattoos are sold as the commercial designs of an aesthetic lifestyle. These elements of cultural commercialism are, however, far removed from Nietzsche's vision of Dionysus as a dangerous and violent god. Nietzsche employed the image of the orgiastic god primarily as a criticism of traditional scholarly views of classical Greek society as orderly and rational, and his sense of a revitalization of culture through music is not compatible with Maffesoli's everyday emotionalism. In any case, contemporary society is 'postemotional' society because individuals no longer respond effectively to the cues and signs of emotion (Mestrovic, 1997); they may be emotionally unable to respond to the neo-tribal habitus.

Conclusion: The World of the Ironic Passenger

The principal theme of this article is the emergence of ironic consumption, the evolution of thin/cool social relationships and the transformation of body marks from compulsory rituals to optional decorations. The modern tattoo is an expression of the growing individualism of contemporary society. The tattoo is simply another sign to be read within consumer culture, but these signs are ironic. They require cool reading, which does not encourage engagement with or contamination by the sign itself. Rational debate within the traditional political space did not encourage irony, parody and bathos. Traditional political and social realities assumed that the social actor was serious and had a capacity for commitment. I have suggested through a discussion of metaphor that if social relations are becoming thin and cool as a result of globalization, then irony and scepticism about grand narratives are produced by the very processes of reflexive modernity which are described in Beck's version of the individualization of risk society. In my terms, the postemotional actor is a member of the airport departure lounge, in the sense that she is blase, indifferent to traditional signs of commitment and remote from the conventional signs of caring. Her tattoos are surface indicators of identity and attachment. Furthermore, the modern tattoo is merely a cliche, borrowing from and adapting Polynesian patterns, Japanese motifs and Chinese military emblems. The aesthetic and sexual tattoo of the middle classes is a product of the thin/cool relationships of a postmodern culture in which there is an exhaustion of idiom. In such a culture, primitiveness must necessarily be simulated and ironic. It is doubtful that being a serious primitive is possible, because committed primitivism is no longer a feasible option.

References

Beck, U. (1992) *Risk Society: Towards a New Modernity*. London: Sage.

Beck, U. and E. Beck-Gernsheim (1995) *The Normal Chaos of Love*. Cambridge: Polity Press.

Berndt, R.M. and C.H. Berndt (1964) *The World of the First Australians*. Sydney: Lansdowne Press.

Cohen, T. (1994) *The Tattoo*. Sydney: Adrian Savvas.

Douglas, M. (1966) *Purity and Danger*. London: Routledge and Kegan Paul.

Durkheim, E. (1912) *The Elementary Forms of the Religious Life*. London: Allen and Unwin.

Falk, P. (1995) 'Written in the Flesh', *Body & Society* 1(1): 95–105.

Giddens, A. (1992) *The Transformation of Intimacy*. Cambridge: Polity Press.

Hildburgh, W.L. (1955) 'Images of the Human Hand as Amulets in Spain', *Journal of the Courtauld and Warburg Institutes* 18: 67–89.

Liebersohn, H. (1988) *Fate and Utopia in German Sociology 1870–1923*. Cambridge, MA: The MIT Press.

Lyotard, J.-F. (1987) *The Postmodern Condition*. Manchester: Manchester University Press.

McLuhan, M. (1964) *Understanding the Media: The Extensions of Man*. Toronto: McGraw-Hill.

Maffesoli, M. (1996) *The Time of the Tribes: The Decline of Individualism in Mass Society*. London: Sage.

Mestrovic, S.G. (1997) *Postemotional Society*. London: Sage.

Reich, R. (1991) *The Work of Nations: Preparing Ourselves for 21st-Century Capitalism*. New York: Random House.

Rheingold, H. (1993) *The Virtual Community: Homesteading on the Electronic Frontier*. New York: Addison-Wesley.

Riesman, D., N. Glazer and R. Denney (1950) *The Lonely Crowd: A Study of the Changing American Character*. New York: Doubleday.

Ritzer, G. (1993) *The McDonaldization of Society: An Investigation into the Changing Character of Contemporary Social Life*. Thousand Oaks, CA: Pine Forge Press.

Rorty, R. (1989) *Contingency, Irony and Solidarity*. Cambridge: Cambridge University Press.

Schmitt, C. (1976) *The Concept of the Political*. New Brunswick, NJ: Rutgers University Press.

Sennett, R. (1994) *The Flesh and the Stone: The Body and the City in Western Civilization*. New York: W.W. Norton.

Simmel, G. (1968) *The Conflict in Modern Culture and Other Essays*. New York: Teachers College Press.

Spencer, B. and F.J. Gillen (1997) *The Northern Tribes of Central Australia*. London: Thoemmes Press.

Stauth, G. and B.S. Turner (1988) *Nietzsche's Dance: Resentment, Reciprocity and Resistance in Social Life*. Oxford: Blackwell.

Turner, B.S. (1987) 'A Note on Nostalgia', *Theory, Culture & Society* 4(1): 147–56.

Turner, B.S. (1997) 'The Body in Western Society: Social Theory and its Perspectives', pp. 15–41 in S. Coakley (ed.) *Religion and the Body*. Cambridge: Cambridge University Press.

Turner, B.S. (1998) 'The Airport Departure Lounge Metaphor: Towards an Ironic Theory of Communication', *Australian Journal of Communication* 25(1): 1–18.

Weber, M. (1930) *The Protestant Ethic and the Spirit of Capitalism*. London: Allen and Unwin.

Bryan S. Turner is Professor of Sociology, University of Cambridge. He has previously held professorial positions in Australia and the Netherlands, and was an Alexander von Humboldt Fellow at Bielefeld University in Germany. He edited (with Chris Rojek) *The Politics of Jean-François Lyotard* (Routledge, 1998).

Anchoring the (Postmodern) Self? Body Modification, Fashion and Identity

PAUL SWEETMAN

Introduction

The last 20 to 30 years have seen a considerable resurgence in the popularity of tattooing and body piercing in the West, a process which has involved not only a remarkable growth in the numbers involved, but also their spread to an ever wider clientele (Armstrong, 1991; Armstrong and Gabriel, 1993; Armstrong et al., 1996; Blanchard, 1994; Curry, 1993; DeMello, 1995a, 1995b; Mercer and Davies, 1991; Myers, 1992; Rubin, 1988; Sanders, 1989). The popular image of the tattooee as young, male and working class is now increasingly outdated, as more and more men *and* women, of various age-groups and socio-economic backgrounds, choose to enter the tattoo studio. Piercing too, though once associated with particular marginal or subcultural groups, is now popular with an increasingly heterogeneous range of enthusiasts (Curry, 1993).[1]

These trends have accelerated since the mid- to late-1980s,[2] a period which has seen increasing numbers of tattooees and piercees become heavily involved with either one or both forms of body modification. Through their high profile in certain key publications, such 'hardcore' body modifiers – some of whom have been termed 'modern primitives' (Curry, 1993; Dery, 1996; Eubanks, 1996; Klesse, 1997; Myers, 1992; Pitts, 1998; Vale and Juno, 1989) – have done much to popularize the new styles of tattoo and piercing which have emerged in recent years. These include a variety of neo-tribal styles and techniques based more or less directly on the indigenous traditions of Polynesia and elsewhere (Curry, 1993: 76; Sanders, 1989: 20).

Body & Society © 1999 SAGE Publications (London, Thousand Oaks and New Delhi),
Vol. 5(2–3): 51–76
[1357–034X(199906/09)5:2–3;51–76;008855]

At the same time, the last ten years have also seen the partial incorporation of both forms of body modification into consumer culture. Numerous celebrities now sport tattoos and piercings, and related imagery is frequently featured in advertising copy, as well as in the work of designers such as Jean-Paul Gaultier (Alford, 1993; Menkes, 1993). Together with their increased popularity, this has led some to dismiss contemporary tattooing and piercing as little more than a superficial trend, one instance among many of the incorporation of 'the exotic' into the fashion system (Craik, 1994: 25; Steele, 1996: 160–1).

Such a position is attractive, not only because of such practices' increasing visibility on the catwalk and in the media, but also because it accords with characterizations of postmodern fashion as an eclectic free-for-all, a 'carnival of signs' (Tseëlon, 1995: 124), where anything and everything is up for grabs in what some have described as the 'supermarket of style' (Polhemus, 1995). It is also, in one sense, largely irrefutable if one accepts the basic tautology that what is fashionable is what is popular, and anything that rapidly increases in popularity can thus be referred to in these terms.

There are, however, several difficulties with characterizing practices such as tattooing and piercing as fashionable per se, in part because of their status as permanent, or 'semi-permanent', modifications to the body (Curry, 1993: 79). Indeed, for writers such as Polhemus, 'any permanent body decoration . . . is as anti-fashion as it is possible to get' (Polhemus, 1995: 13), 'true fashion' being defined as 'a system of continual and perpetual . . . change' (Polhemus and Proctor, 1978: 25).

The following examines both sides of this debate, looking first at the extent to which the resurgence of tattooing and piercing might be seen not only as fashionable, but also as a manifestation of the more or less superficial eclecticism that many argue is a key characteristic of the postmodern scene. Drawing – as throughout – from interviews with a variety of contemporary body modifiers,[3] this section will suggest that for some tattooees and piercees, there is indeed an extent to which their involvement can be described as little more than a fashionable trend. Even among these 'less committed' body modifiers, however, there is also evidence to suggest that their tattoos and piercings are perceived and experienced as more than mere accessories.

The article then goes on to explore these areas in more detail, focusing particularly on the permanence of tattooing and the pain associated with both forms of body modification, before considering whether such practices might instead be characterized as a form of anti-fashion. It is suggested that, for many contemporary body modifiers, an involvement in tattooing or piercing represents not so much an appropriation of the cultural detritus adrift within Baudrillard's 'carnival

of signs', but rather a reaction to such superficiality: an attempt to lend corporeal
solidity to expressions of individuality.

As corporeal expressions of *the self*, tattoos and piercings might thus be seen
as instances of contemporary *body projects* (Shilling, 1993): as attempts to
construct and maintain a coherent and viable sense of self-identity through attention to the body and, more particularly, the body's surface (Featherstone, 1991).
This is explored in the final section of the article, where it is argued that contemporary tattooing and piercing can indeed be interpreted in these terms, as attempts
to anchor or stabilize one's sense of self-identity, in part through the establishment of a coherent personal narrative.

A 'Carnival of Signs'?

As was noted above, certain commentators have dismissed the current popularity
of tattooing and piercing as little more than a fashionable trend. Craik, for
instance, argues that 'the popularity of tattooing has been revived in western
fashion since the 1980s' before going on to suggest that, together, improved techniques of tattoo removal and the introduction of fake (transfer) tattoos, 'have
alleviated some of the stigma attached to tattooing and enabled it to become a
component of high fashion ... that is desirable because of its exotic associations'
(Craik, 1994: 25). Steele, similarly, points out that, '[t]oday tattoos and body
piercing have become increasingly stylish; even fashion models get delicate piercing, and modern bohemians sport pierced lips, cheeks, nipples, tongues, and genitals' (Steele, 1996: 160).

For some, then, tattooing and piercing – as previously 'classed', 'raced' and
gendered practices, associated strongly with specific marginal and subcultural
groups – have now become so 'mainstream' as to almost be considered 'passé'
(Steele, 1996: 161). This arguably accords well with characterizations of contemporary fashion as an eclectic and self-referential system, which freely quotes from
any and every source, transforming the phenomena thus appropriated into more
or less meaningless cultural ephemera: 'floating signifiers' that refer to nothing
but themselves (Falk, 1995: 103).

As Tseëlon points out, for writers such as Baudrillard, postmodern fashion can
be characterized as 'a carnival of signs with no meanings attached' (Tseëlon, 1995:
124), an eclectic mish-mash of once potent styles and devices, desperately appropriated from a variety of sources in a vain attempt to lend authenticity to that
which is no longer imbued with meaning (Tseëlon, 1995: 132; see also Falk, 1995:
103). Postmodern fashion no longer refers to anything but itself, and this lack of
external referentiality means that everything is up for grabs: we can all wear what

we want, with the proviso that what we wear is no longer indexical of anything other than our participation in the fashion system.

There are a number of problems with this position: just because contemporary fashion has accelerated and fragmented, for instance, such increased complexity does not necessarily indicate the *absolute* self-referentiality that Baudrillard's position implies (Tseëlon, 1995: 134). Following Foster, however, Tseëlon distinguishes Baudrillard's 'postmodernism of resistance' from the 'postmodernism of reaction' associated with commentators such as Jameson (Tseëlon, 1995: 132). From the latter perspective, postmodern fashion – however 'playful' and fragmented – retains a definite if tenuous link with an external social reality: it 'still alludes to a reality of signification' (Tseëlon, 1995: 132).

This is important for a number of reasons, not least that it helps to explain the current fascination with all things 'retro', the appropriation of 'bygone styles' representing a vain effort to lend 'historical depth to a world of surface signifiers' (Tseëlon, 1995: 132). Similar arguments apply to the appropriation of 'ethnic' and 'subcultural' styles, and as a system that freely quotes from any and every potential source, contemporary fashion can thus be described as 'a field of stylistic and discursive heterogeneity without a norm' (Jameson, quoted in Wilson, 1990: 223). Indeed, even if one rejects the more extreme theoretical position occupied by writers such as Baudrillard, it is generally accepted that – at the very least – contemporary fashion is characterized by 'a blurring between mainstream and countercultural fashions: all fashion has become "stagey", self-conscious about its own status as discourse' (Wilson, 1990: 222).

Truly 'postmodern' or not, contemporary fashion thus problematizes the notion of sartorial strategies of resistance, as detailed, for instance, in the work of writers associated with the Birmingham Centre for Contemporary Cultural Studies during the 1970s and beyond (see, for example: Hall and Jefferson, 1976; Hebdige, 1988). Quite simply, if everything is 'quotable' and more or less divested of meaning, if there is no dominant dress code or hegemonic standard by which one's sartorial conduct might be judged, then it arguably makes little sense to speak of subcultural or counter-cultural styles of dress (Gamman and Makinen, 1994: 73; Wilson, 1990: 233).

Certain writers within fashion and 'subcultural' theory reject this position, however, suggesting that while contemporary fashion has indeed become increasingly diverse and fragmented, a 'mix & match' of any number of past stylistic devices, this does not necessarily negate the subversive potential of such countercultural or subcultural styles (Gottschalk, 1993; Polhemus, 1995). But while Gottschalk, for instance, argues that American counter-culturalists' appropriation and re-contextualization of 'various historical styles and ethnic traditions'

(Gottschalk, 1993: 367) is both creative and expressive of the 'Freaks'' 'social-psychological and ideological' dispositions (Gottschalk, 1993: 369), he also notes that his interviewees '*recognized that existing deviant styles were cliches that could no longer be adopted to express one's rebellious position*' (Gottschalk, 1993: 366–7, my emphasis; see also Lind and Roach-Higgins, 1985; Polhemus, 1995: 12).

To the extent that everything is now more or less up for grabs, it could thus be argued that Gottschalk's (1993) informants' 'mix & match' strategy represents a last-ditch attempt to retain a sense of subcultural style, a rearguard action which, through a process of *bricolage* (Hebdige, 1988: 102–6), attempts to squeeze the last drops of meaning from what are, in reality, increasingly empty signifiers. In this respect, though indicative of the current validity of subcultural or counter-cultural sartorial strategies, such studies could also be said to signal their impending demise.

To some extent, then, even the arguments put forward by writers such as Gottschalk (1993) and Polhemus (1995) are supportive of the notion that sartorial strategies of resistance are increasingly redundant: that even if one refutes the more extreme argument associated with writers such as Baudrillard, clothing, fashion and appearance are increasingly being absorbed into a *more or less* free-floating 'carnival of signs'. In relation to the increasing popularity of tattooing and piercing, one might then ask whether such forms of body modification should also be seen as all but empty signifiers, once marginal or subcultural devices that have now gone mainstream, thus joining the ranks of the other ephemeral products available in the 'supermarket of style'.

Mere Accessories?

In support of this position, it should be noted that several of the lightly tattooed or pierced[4] informants interviewed for this study appeared – *in at least some respects* – to view their tattoos and piercings as little more than fashion accessories, on a par, for instance, with more standard forms of jewellery or other items intended to enhance a particular 'look'. Lightly tattooed and/or pierced interviewees, in particular, often regarded their own tattoos and piercings in primarily *decorative* terms: 'I thought it would look nice', or words to that effect, being a common response to enquiries regarding their motivation to acquire such forms of body modification.

When asked what she most liked about having her navel pierced, for example, one young interviewee noted the way in which 'we like to change our bodies', before adding, 'all girls like jewellery, don't they, and it's sort of an extension of that I think'. Although she felt that it was 'a bit more special' than necklaces or earrings, for example – thanks to its location 'in an unusual place' – the same interviewee reinforced this sense of treating her piercing as a fashionable accessory by noting her tendency to change the jewellery 'every couple of weeks or so . . . when I get bored with it', and, when asked if she deliberately wore clothes that would show off the piercing, replying: 'Erm, in the summer I do, but . . . I wore skirts that cut below my belly first, and then I had the piercing, to sort of fit with that, rather than the other way round.' The same woman also volunteered that having the piercing done was something of a 'treat': 'a bit like going into a really posh salon and having your hair done'.

More surprisingly, perhaps, certain lightly tattooed interviewees appeared to view their tattoos in similar terms, one young woman with two small designs – one on her back, the other on her ankle – noting: 'it's nice choosing your outfit depending on whether you want to show off your tattoo or whatever, and, I dunno . . . I just think it's kind of like an extra accessory kind of thing'.

At a number of points throughout the interview, the same woman also noted that becoming tattooed was 'not such a big deal', although at one stage she added, 'well I suppose it is kind of, 'cause it's there for the rest of your life, but . . .'. Another young woman, also with two tattoos, noted that both these and her nostril piercing were mainly for show: 'recreating how I want to be on a certain evening or something, whether I've got my nose ring in or not, and whether I'm showing my tattoos or not'. When asked if her decision to become tattooed was a response to fashion, she replied, 'I suppose it is partly', though she subsequently added, '[b]ut I don't think it's something I'll ever think has gone out of fashion and I wish I hadn't got them'.

At the same time as describing their tattoos or piercings as decorative accessories, however, nearly all of the informants in this category *also* regarded tattooing and piercing as 'different', 'original' or 'out of the ordinary': when asked what they most valued about being tattooed or pierced, 'being different' was by far the most common response.

Often expressed rather vaguely, where 'difference' was specified in anything more than very general terms, being tattooed or pierced was seen to distinguish the interviewee either from the bulk of non-tattooed or pierced individuals, or from those within their more immediate peer group. One young male interviewee, for example, saw his nipple piercing as 'a distinction from people who don't have things like that', while a young female tattooee told me, 'it's just nice to be a bit different from my friends'.

Others were a little more cautious, recognizing a degree of tension between their perception of such forms of body modification as a mark of individuality – 'other people are just skin' – and their acknowledgement of tattooing and piercing's increased popularity: 'I do feel a bit different in some ways, but, you're surprised how many people have got tattoos'. Certain interviewees managed this apparent contradiction by referring to the timing of their tattoo(s) or piercing(s), and asserting that this preceded any current trend to which *others* may have been attracted.

In certain cases, such claims were rather questionable, but the extent to which the majority of lightly tattooed or pierced interviewees *perceived* their own tattoos and piercings as 'different' or 'out of the ordinary' arguably militates against a reading of such forms of body modification simply as 'free-floating' fashion accessories, *at least when viewed from the perspective of those involved.* So too does the seriousness with which many lightly tattooed or pierced interviewees appeared to take the decision to modify their bodies in this manner.

One lightly pierced interviewee, for instance, told me that he had 'toyed' with the idea of having his nipple pierced for some months before finally taking the plunge, or, as he put it, a 'massive step into an area I'm afraid of anyway ... and I had no experience or knowledge of'. For him, the act of becoming pierced appears in itself to have been quite profound, his subsequent experience of a fractured shin described as 'nothing' in comparison to having 'a dirty great needle shoved through one of the most sensitive parts of my body'.

While not true of all, a number of the lightly tattooed interviewees similarly told me that they had spent some time building up to having a tattoo, either because they hadn't previously 'had the guts' to go ahead, or because they saw it as a serious step that demanded careful consideration. Thus one young tattooee told me that she had contemplated the decision for a 'couple of years', or long enough 'to really think seriously about it', a process that had also involved reading through several tattoo magazines to find out more about the process itself and the sorts of designs available. As she put it: 'I really wanted to look into it, 'cause its permanent, and I did think about it as a long-term sort of thing.' As will be discussed more fully below, such extensive 'background research' was also common among the more heavily tattooed and pierced interviewees, belying the popular perception of tattoo acquisition, for example, as a universally impulsive and ill-thought-out process (Foster Wallace, 1997: 206–11).

On the one hand, then, the tendency of certain of the more lightly tattooed and/or pierced interviewees to describe their tattoos or piercings as decorative accessories lends support to the notion that such forms of body modification are now just another product in the 'supermarket of style'. At the same time, however, a number of factors appear to contradict such an interpretation, not least the way in which most interviewees regarded their tattoos or piercings as 'different' or 'original', and the seriousness with which many approached the decision to modify their bodies in this manner. Among the tattooees, such caution was in large part thanks to the tattoo's permanence, though both tattooees and piercees also alluded to factors such as the pain involved in the acquisition of such forms of body modification.

Permanence, Planning and Pain

It was noted above that while certain less heavily tattooed or pierced interviewees appeared to regard their tattoos or piercings – to at least some degree – as decorative accessories, factors such as the permanence or 'semi-permanence' of such forms of body modification, and the pain involved in their acquisition, meant that they were also experienced as distinct from other, more ephemeral products in the 'supermarket of style'. Drawing now on interviews with both heavily *and* less heavily tattooed and pierced interviewees – but primarily the former – the following will expand upon these points before considering whether, rather than dismissing contemporary body modification as a superficial trend, it might instead be more appropriately viewed as a form of 'anti-fashion'.

To turn first to the more indelible of the two procedures, the bulk of those interviewed during the course of this study intimated that there was a 'fashionable element' to contemporary body modification, but several also pointed to the permanence of tattooing as problematic in this regard. When asked whether tattooing could be said to be fashionable, for example, one heavily tattooed and pierced female interviewee replied; 'I think it is going that way, but I don't think that's what it's about':

> Because . . . fashion is a passing thing isn't it? What's fashionable at the moment is not gonna be fashionable next year, or in a couple of years' time. So that's totally the wrong reason for having it done.

All of the body modifiers interviewed for this study regarded their tattoos as permanent modifications to the body, however, and while some had had designs re-worked or 'covered up' – and others intended to do so – none referred to the improved techniques of removal which Craik (1994: 25) suggests have contributed to tattooing's increasing popularity. Indeed, several interviewees saw the permanence of their tattoos as a 'very important' element in their overall appeal. A young, heavily tattooed and pierced male interviewee, for instance, argued that '[a] tattoo, whether it's good or bad, is very, very permanent, so it's making a statement of sorts', adding, '[t]hat's why I like them'. Another, lightly tattooed, interviewee distinguished between her tattoo and other modes of self-expression as follows: 'I don't know . . . before, I could express myself in clothes and things like that, but now it's actually something that's permanent and that's definitely me.'

At the same time as regarding the permanence of their tattoos as key to their overall appeal, however, a number of interviewees also noted that this was cause for a degree of caution. As had some of the more lightly tattooed interviewees, several of the more heavily tattooed informants indicated that they had thought for some time before acquiring a tattoo, with one now heavily tattooed and pierced female interviewee telling me:

> I wanted tattoos done ever since I was a kid, but I wanted to leave it until I was old enough to not make a mistake, because I think a lot of people have them done young and . . . regret it.

The same interviewee went on to tell me that in her opinion, the permanence of tattoos 'makes them really special, 'cause you've got be really sure of what you . . . put on yourself'. Another heavily tattooed and pierced interviewee told me that he had 'wanted tattoos' since he was 13 or 14, but though normally 'quite impulsive': 'with tattoos it was very permanent and I thought, "Well", you know, "I'm not gonna get it done unless I actually want the design."'

Like certain of the more lightly tattooed interviewees, several of the more heavily tattooed informants had undertaken a considerable amount of research before going ahead with their first tattoo. One younger male tattooee and piercee told me that he had 'found out' a good deal about the process before going ahead – a tactic which included investigating the various hygiene procedures employed by contemporary tattooists – while another, older interviewee described the way in which he chose his first tattooist as 'a really dull . . . mechanical process', which involved visiting 'fourteen studios within a certain radius of where [he] lived' and scoring them all according to the personality of the tattooist, the quality of the work and the apparent cleanliness of the studio: '[a]nd the one that came out on top in points terms, I went to'.

As one might expect, such 'background work' does not necessarily stop after the first tattoo. While certain tattooists continue to offer a 'walk-in' service, many now work by appointment only, and some are also selective about the sorts of design they will tattoo, the former point necessitating that sessions be booked in advance, and the latter demanding a certain amount of negotiation between tattooist and tattooee. Unless the tattooee prepares the design themselves, or is happy to give the tattooist free rein, *custom* work can also demand a good deal of collaboration between artist and client. Such background work need not be perceived negatively, however. One interviewee told me that he gets 'a lot of enjoyment out of' planning what to do next, and, indeed, out of 'the whole process of booking it, finding a design, going up there, [and] chatting to the artist'. He also noted that he enjoys the healing process, or 'looking after' his new tattoo, and that the procedure as a whole leaves him with a considerable sense of achievement, in part thanks to his necessary involvement at all stages of the creative process.

Planning, collaboration and after-care are not the only factors that can lead to a sense of achievement, however. When asked why she had felt 'proud of herself' after having her tattoos done, for instance, one lightly tattooed and pierced interviewee replied: ''Cause . . . it's quite painful . . . you know . . . it does hurt, and I was like, chuffed that I'd . . . sat there and done it.' To return to the process of being tattooed, then, a further factor which suggests that tattoos should not be viewed as free-floating products in the 'supermarket of style' – and which, in this case, applies to all tattoos, regardless of whether they are carefully planned custom designs, or a 'name' tattooist is employed – is the *pain* involved in their application. As one, heavily tattooed and ex-heavily pierced interviewee put it:

> . . . you can't, well you *can* buy it, but you can't like, go to the shop and try it on and say, 'I'll have one of them', and just walk out with it. You've gotta sit there for hours and put up with the pain. So even if you're really rich, if you can't stand the pain, you can't get tattooed.

In this sense, tattoos differ remarkably from other, sartorial modes of expression:

> . . . people can buy an expensive outfit or, you know . . . a leather jacket, but, you *can* buy a tattoo, but you've still gotta put up with the pain and the process. . . . There's a lot more that goes into it.

As will be elaborated on below, the same could also be said of piercing, but in contrast to tattooing, most interviewees regarded the former as comparatively superficial. When questioned about the relative importance of her tattoos and piercings, for instance, one heavily tattooed but less heavily pierced female interviewee told me that she didn't 'really feel anything about piercing', adding, 'it's not permanent, so I really don't give it that much thought'. The same inter-viewee later described her septum piercing as 'just a fashion accessory'. Such responses were not confined to those with greater involvement in tattooing than piercing. One heavily tattooed *and* pierced interviewee, for instance, noted that his piercings were: 'kind of superfluous, 'cause I can take them out at any time . . . they're a lot less permanent, so they don't mean as much to me.'[5]

That is not to say that all piercings are regarded as equally superficial, however: certain interviewees distinguished between the more popular piercings – eyebrow and navel piercings, for instance – and those that were considered to be more 'extreme' or 'hardcore'. The 'extreme' category tended to include both genital piercing and various forms of 'stretch' piercing, with the former evaluated as distinctive thanks to their location, and the latter because of both the degree of commitment required to achieve the enlarged piercing and the relative permanence of the modification thus acquired. One heavily tattooed and pierced male interviewee, having described how he had stretched one of his genital piercings to thirteen millimetres in diameter, compared the process to becoming tattooed and argued that: 'there's as much validity, probably even more, in achieving that, because you have to do it yourself, you can't get there any other way'.

As a generic term, however, 'piercing' was considered by most to be more superficial than tattooing, thanks primarily to the ease with which most piercings can be discontinued. While the bulk of piercings *are* impermanent, however – and as such may not indicate the same level of commitment as implied by the decision to become tattooed – they still demand that the piercee experience a certain level of pain and/or discomfort while the piercing is applied, and that they indulge in the necessary after-care to ensure that the piercing heals successfully. Although the attendant preparations may take some time, the actual process of *being* pierced is generally over in a few seconds and, in contrast with tattooing, any pain is usually dulled by the use of local anaesthetic. The initial meeting of metal and flesh can still be painful, however, and while the pain associated with tattooing lasts only as long as the tattoo session itself, the pain, discomfort and attendant anxiety associated with piercing can extend well beyond the time one spends in the piercing studio.

One interviewee noted that while he was quite relaxed *prior to* his first genital piercing, things changed somewhat once he was actually in the studio: 'I wasn't too bothered, but . . . once you get in there [you see] all this like, . . . shiny, metal equipment, . . . and you think, "Shit, am I doing the right thing here?" ' However much you read up about things beforehand: 'you don't really appreciate it until you see it done; what's actually involved, and how thick the skin is, or how thick the tissue is. It does take a . . . lot of force to push it through sometimes.'

As well as being a more invasive process than tattooing, piercing is also more likely to lead to short- or long-term complications once one leaves the studio. Referring again to his first genital piercing, the interviewee quoted above also told me that:

> . . . the Prince Albert[6] bled like mad the night I got it done. The anaesthetic wore off, and I woke up about three in the morning absolutely saturated in blood, like all over my boxer shorts, all over the bed, I thought I was dying, you know, it was gushing out. . . . And, that was like, 'Shit, what have I done?' [laughter], you know, 'Fucking outrageous, I've just stuck something through my knob, I'm either gonna get done or it's gonna fall off' [laughter].

Unlike tattoos, then, which generally offer little in the way of physical discomfort following the actual process of application, piercings can be painful – and bleed considerably – for some days after their acquisition. A further contrast lies in the fact that while one can be pretty sure about the time it will take a tattoo to heal – generally around two weeks – piercings can not only take far longer, but the healing time is also more variable, with certain piercings refusing to settle however long one lavishes them with care and attention. Several interviewees told me that they had reluctantly abandoned their navel piercings because, after a period of months, the piercings had refused to settle, and when asked if she had ever removed any of her piercings, one heavily tattooed and pierced interviewee replied: '[n]o . . . [but] the nipple piercings [are] still very sore, and I've had [them] done over a year now . . . I don't regret having them done, but, they do get quite sore.'

Anti-Fashion?

As I hope to have indicated above, tattoos and piercings arguably differ from other 'free-floating' commodities, not only because of their status as permanent or 'semi-permanent' modifications to the body, but also because of the necessary physicality of their production. In respect of the former, several commentators have drawn a distinction between *fashion*, as characterized by continual and systematic change, and those more fixed modes of dress which are relatively static, conservative and resistant to change (Davis, 1985: 22).

Polhemus and Proctor (1978), for instance, distinguish between fashion and *anti-fashion*, noting that the latter term 'refers to all styles of adornment which fall outside the organized system . . . of fashion change' (Polhemus and Proctor, 1978: 16). This definition encompasses 'traditional' forms of dress, as well as uniforms, subcultural styles and so on, all of which are united in their conservatism and opposition to change. While fashion suggests some degree of social mobility, however illusory, anti-fashion is characteristic of relatively 'fixed . . . social environments' (Polhemus and Proctor, 1978: 14), its adoption in a modern social context representing a deliberate attempt 'to symbolically defy . . . change' (Polhemus and Proctor, 1978: 22).

For Polhemus (1995) and Polhemus and Proctor (1978), tattooing, along with other permanent forms of body modification, can be described as 'the ultimate' in anti-fashion (Polhemus and Proctor, 1978: unnumbered), its irreversibility rendering 'change difficult if not impossible' (Polhemus, 1995: 13). As Falk has also noted (Falk, 1995: 102), such *irreversible* body-marking is 'antithetical to the mechanisms of fashion change' (Polhemus and Proctor, 1978: unnumbered), and, for Polhemus and Proctor, tattooing, scarification and the like are thus used to maintain the illusion, if not the reality, 'of social and cultural stability' (Polhemus and Proctor, 1978: 16). This helps to explain not only the widespread use of tattooing in 'traditional' or pre-modern contexts, but also the adoption of such techniques to indicate subcultural allegiances in the West. Tattooing and other forms of permanent body modification are typically employed:

> ... in situations where people feel ... [the] need to preserve their individual and social identities and to advertise ... the would-be permanence of their allegiances, values and beliefs. (Polhemus and Proctor, 1978: unnumbered)

There are, of course, considerable problems with the notion of 'anti-fashion' if one accepts Baudrillard's argument regarding the 'free-floating' nature of contemporary signifiers. In this context, however, it is equally important to note the potential difficulties associated with Polhemus and Proctor's (1978) designation of tattooing as the 'ultimate' in anti-fashion. While it is noted elsewhere that anti-fashions of various sorts are regularly co-opted by the fashion industry (Polhemus and Proctor, 1978: 17–19), the argument surrounding permanent body modification appears to suggest that such practices are so 'antithetical to the mechanisms of fashion change' that they would, or could not be so appropriated. This is certainly the position adopted by Curry (1993), who accepts Polhemus and Proctor's fashion/anti-fashion distinction, and argues that whatever its current popularity, tattooing 'can never be a true fashion ... because tattoos cannot be put on and left off by the season', adding, '[t]he same is true for body piercing ... with the proviso that piercings are semi-permanent rather than permanent' (Curry, 1993: 80).

The key difficulty with this argument – at least in relation to tattooing – is that while the permanence of the tattoo mark may disallow easy revisability in line with the dictates of fashion, this does not imply that the *meaning* of such forms of body modification is also fixed. In other words, Curry (1993) and Polhemus and Proctor (1978) arguably conflate the fixity of the signifier – ink under the skin – with the notion of a permanent signified, but while the tattoo mark *is* more or less irreversible, its external referents can and do change.

This does not mean that Curry's (1993) and Polhemus and Proctor's (1978) argument should be entirely discarded, what it does suggest is that tattoos might become more or less fashionable – signifying, at the connotative level, little more than one's participation in the fashion process – even though this would leave those so motivated to become tattooed in a difficult position once the wheels of fashion had turned. The permanence of tattooing, in other words, means that it is extremely *well-suited* to employment as an anti-fashion device, but it does not imply that its meaning is fixed in these terms.

At the same time, however, a number of other factors intrinsic to both tattooing *and* piercing arguably militate against their full incorporation into

Baudrillard's 'carnival of signs'. Tattoos and piercings are not *only* permanent and/or 'semi-permanent' cultural products, they are also intrusive modifications to the body whose production involves pain, blood and the penetration of the skin in a non-medicalized setting, not to mention varying degrees of planning and 'after-care'.

In contrast to those free-floating signifiers that comprise the bulk of image-based products available in Baudrillard's 'carnival of signs', tattoos and piercings cannot be divorced from the manner of their production. One cannot simply purchase a finished tattoo or piercing in the same way that one might acquire a new sweater, the production and consumption of each form of body modification requiring the tattooee or piercee's active participation in the completion of what is, in effect, a combination of corporeal modification and cultural artefact.

As *corporeal artefacts* then, tattoos and piercings differ remarkably from sartorial accessories: part of the body rather than simply an adjunct to it, 'there is something in [both] which escapes the flow of commodification' (Blanchard, 1994: 292). Even in the case of standardized designs or piercings, 'the replication of the tattoo [or piercing, is] contingent upon its siting on the body of a specific subject' (Blanchard, 1994: 292), and the complete, or healed, tattoo or piercing is as much the work of the tattooee or piercee as it is of the tattooist or body piercer. In this sense, the modified body produces itself. A pair of jeans, or a new pair of training shoes, can be consumed and displayed as 'pure sign', in ignorance of the conditions under which the material product was fabricated. Tattoos and piercings, in contrast, *demand* one's presence as producer, consumer and living frame for the corporeal artefact thus acquired.

The invasive and painful nature of the modificatory process thus suggests that neither tattoos nor piercings can be consumed as 'pure signs'. Equally importantly, however, it also implies that however popular tattooing and piercing become, and however much tattooing and piercing *imagery* is appropriated by the fashion industry, real tattoos and piercings will continue to refer to the manner in which they are produced, and thus to resist full absorption into any free-floating 'carnival of signs'. While Curry (1993) and Polhemus and Proctor (1978) may be wrong to suggest that the permanence or 'semi-permanence' of tattooing and piercing *in and of itself* delimits their wider socio-cultural connotations, factors such as the pain involved in their application mean that, whatever their wider connotations, at the denotative level tattoos and piercings will continue to refer to the manner of their acquisition.

As Gell has pointed out, the underlying 'technical schema' of tattooing – as with body piercing – is 'external to culture as such' (Gell, 1993: 303), and while this may not entirely delimit the socio-cultural connotations of such forms of body modification, it arguably ensures that such practices will retain a particular denotative impact whatever their wider significance. Tattooing's 'invariant processual contour' is such that it can always be broken down into three distinct stages: wounding, healing, and 'the subsequent acquisition of a permanent ... mark' (Gell, 1993: 304). This is not to suggest a universal meaning for tattooing, but 'the integration of this technical schema into any given cultural matrix' (Gell, 1993: 303) acts to *invite* certain readings of the practice, with the dominant reading in any particular context dependent upon which of the three stages is most strongly 'focalized' (Gell, 1993: 304).

According to Gell, the dominant Western reading of tattooing contrasts strongly with the 'core Polynesian reading' (Gell, 1993: 307) in placing exclusive stress on the tattoo as completed artefact (Gell, 1993: 313). In traditional Polynesian settings, by comparison, '[t]he tattoo was significant, not so much as a thing in itself, than as a proof that the tattooing ... had been done' (Gell, 1993: 305–6). As Gell *also* notes, however:

> ... the tattooing process ... is always and everywhere submitted to in its entirety, not bit by bit. Hence differential focalization is always a relative matter; each distinct focalization carries all the others with it.... It is a matter of emphasis, not a complete break. (Gell, 1993: 304)

In other words, while the core Western reading of tattooing may emphasize the tattoo as completed artefact, downgrading the importance of the tattoo process, this is only a matter of *relative* emphasis: the tattoo, as signifying mark, will always refer to the inevitably physical conditions of its production. It can thus be argued that Gell overstates his case when he suggests that the core Western reading represents 'the *complete* triumph of artefactualization' (Gell, 1993: 313, my emphasis): when compared with tattooing in many non-Western contexts, contemporary tattooing in the West may be *relatively* free-floating, but as *corporeal* artefacts even the most playful and ironic of contemporary tattoos retain an echo of the pain involved in their acquisition (Blanchard, 1994: 288). The same is true of body piercing, which also follows an 'invariant processual contour', the key distinction being that the completed body modification is semi-permanent rather than permanent.

That the process of becoming tattooed or pierced remains significant to those involved, however much emphasis is ultimately placed on 'the subsequent acquisition of a permanent [or semi-permanent] ... mark' (Gell, 1993: 304), has already been illustrated above (see also: Sweetman, 1999a). That tattoos and piercings are denotative of the manner of their acquisition to the wider population of non-body modifiers, on the other hand, is evidenced by the standard response offered by those confronted with such forms of body modification. As several interviewees told me, and as has also been pointed out elsewhere (Miles, 1997: 4), one of the questions most frequently asked of contemporary body modifiers by those who have not so modified their bodies is as follows: 'Does [or Did] it hurt?'

Body Projects and Expressive Individualism

While Curry (1993) may be wrong to suggest that the permanence of tattooing and the 'semi-permanence' of piercing in and of themselves mean that such forms of body modification can never become 'a true fashion', the invasive and often painful manner by which such corporeal artefacts are produced adds weight to the argument that it would be misplaced to interpret tattoos and piercings simply as superficial accessories. The comments of several interviewees also suggest that while their meaning may not be entirely fixed in these terms, tattoos in particular are frequently perceived as distinct from other, more 'free-floating' fashion items, as, to a lesser degree, are piercings, thanks to the pain involved in their acquisition. Certain piercings are more permanent than others, but the ease with which most can be discontinued means that they are generally regarded as *relatively* superficial. As with tattoos, however, one cannot simply purchase a complete piercing: 'you've . . . gotta put up with the pain and the process'.

Such comments suggest that both forms of body modification, but tattoos in particular, may be employed by some as a form of 'anti-fashion': that even though their meaning is not fixed in these terms, they may be employed by certain body modifiers as a means of symbolically defying change, 'preserv[ing] their individual and social identities and . . . advertis[ing] . . . the would-be permanence of their . . . values and beliefs' (Polhemus and Proctor, 1978: unnumbered).

To the extent that this is the case, such forms of body modification might be argued to share certain affinities with the subcultural 'uniforms' adopted by skinheads and others in the 1960s and 1970s (Clarke 1976; Cohen, 1997; Hebdige, 1987). In contrast to such subcultural styles, however, contemporary tattoos and piercings appear to act less as markers of group identification, and more as expressions of the self. Few interviewees linked their tattoos or piercings to 'membership' of *specific* subcultural groups, and those who did express an affiliative impact or intention behind their adoption of such forms of body modification tended to refer to this in loosely 'tribal' terms. This was not true of all interviewees, and it should also be noted that 'label-rejection' may have been adopted by some as a strategy to deflect suggestions of 'conformity to a group image' which, as Muggleton notes, 'invites accusations of conventionality by outsiders' (1995: 4; see also Muggleton, 1997: 9).

As discussed further below, however, several interviewees stressed the *personal* nature of their tattoos and piercings, and that both tattooing and piercing are popular among a range of 'subcultural' types, *and among many who appear not to identify with any particular subcultural group*, was confirmed by attendance at several tattoo conventions during the course of this research. Events such as Tattoo Expo and Bodyshow attract an extremely varied crowd, apparently united only by a shared interest in tattooing, piercing or related modificatory practices. Tattoo Expo, in particular – as the largest and longest running annual UK convention – is remarkable for the way in which Hells Angels rub shoulders with rubber-skirted SMers, glamorous fetishists, punks, goths, skinheads and clubbers, not to mention the rest of the international crowd of attendees, most of whom are heavily tattooed or pierced, but the majority of whom are not easily slotted into a particular subcultural group.

Observational data, then, lends tangential support to most interviewees' implicit rejection of specific affiliative intentions, while at the same time supporting arguments that we are witnessing a move 'towards affinity based on heterogeneity', or a form of 'neo-tribalism', which, as Muggleton notes, 'implies an alliance' of sorts, but one that 'can be contrasted with the more sharply defined and strongly collective connotations of "subculture"' (Muggleton, 1995: 8; see also Maffesoli, 1996). A further reason for accepting the majority of interviewees' rejection of any specific affiliative *intention* behind their tattoos or piercings lies with the strong emphasis that many placed on the personal nature of the modifications acquired. Several tattooees told me that they had chosen motifs that were expressive of personal interests or their own biographies, and many noted that they had gone for custom designs in order to ensure that 'no one else would ever have the same tattoos'. As one, lightly tattooed female interviewee put it: 'I saw various designs I liked, but I thought it would be more personal if I had something that was a design of my own.'

A number of interviewees also described their tattoos as 'a sign of [their] personality', but whether or not this was the case, both tattoos and piercings were frequently described as 'very personal' by virtue of their location on, or rather as part of, the body. Several interviewees also stressed that their tattoos or piercings were primarily for their own consumption, and were not intended to be widely displayed. One lightly tattooed and pierced interviewee, for instance, told me that she had chosen to locate her first and only tattoo on her back because she 'didn't particularly care about whether it was ever gonna be seen by anybody else, it was definitely just a personal thing for me'.

To the extent that contemporary tattooing and piercing act as expressions of self rather than as markers of group identification, they might thus be described as a form of 'expressive individualism' (Muggleton, 1997: 11) which, in attending to the body and its appearance, shares considerable affinities with other forms of contemporary 'body project' (Shilling, 1993). Writers such as Shilling (1993) and Giddens (1991) have recently emphasized the increasingly tight relationship between the body and self-identity, as manifest in a growing tendency to treat the body as a 'project' through which a sense of self-identity is constructed and maintained. While in traditional or pre-modern societies identity was relatively fixed, and the size, shape and appearance of the body accepted more or less as given, in late-, high- or postmodernity, identity is *increasingly* fluid, and the body is mobilized as a plastic resource on to which a reflexive sense of self is projected in an attempt to lend solidity to the narrative thus envisaged.

From this perspective, the rise of dieting, 'keep fit', and other corporeally oriented practices reflects the increasing tendency to treat the body as constitutive or expressive of the reflexively constructed self, and the growing popularity of 'non mainstream body modification' (Myers, 1992) might similarly be argued to reflect this trend. Like the forms of 'body project' considered by Shilling, for example, tattooing and piercing have the effect of transforming the exterior surfaces of the body 'in line with the designs of its owner', and can allow a 'wholesale transformation' of the body along these lines (Shilling, 1993: 3). Indeed, as well as regarding their tattoos and piercings as very personal, many interviewees also referred to such forms of body modification as marks of individuality; as 'a way of standing out [and] saying, "Look, I'm me, I'm an individual."' Some also suggested that becoming tattooed or pierced could be seen as an act of 'self-creation'. As one heavily tattooed and ex-heavily pierced interviewee put it:

> ... it makes you feel individual ... you know like, everyone's born with roughly the same bodies, but you've created yours in your own image [in line with] what your imagination wants your body to look like. It's like someone's given you something, and then you've made it your own, so you're not like everyone else any more.

Several interviewees also spoke of increased self-confidence as a result of having become tattooed or pierced, some because of the way in which they had endured the physical process itself, but others, because of the way in which it brought them closer in line with their own self-image. One heavily tattooed interviewee, for instance, told me that he felt 'a better, more rounded, and fuller person for being tattooed', more 'in tune with the person [he] really thought [he] was rather than the ... shy, pleasant, reserved ... kind of individual that [he had previously] portrayed'. Others simply noted that they felt 'more complete'.

On the one hand, then, becoming tattooed or pierced can be seen as an act of 'self-creation', that, through the modification of the body's surface, helps to construct a viable sense of self-identity. As the comments of several interviewees indicated, however, tattooing, in particular, can also assist in the construction of a coherent and *consistent* self-narrative.

Several interviewees told me that their tattoos acted as permanent reminders of particular periods or events, and as one heavily tattooed female interviewee pointed out, tattooing 'has . . . a lot to do with memory' because the tattoo itself 'will always remind you of the time . . . you had it done'. Certain interviewees noted that they had deliberately become tattooed to mark *specific* events such as weddings, while one young female informant, for example, told me that although she had wanted a tattoo for some time, she finally decided to get it done on her 21st birthday, both as a marker of adulthood and as a celebration of the event itself. Her eyebrow piercing was similarly intended to mark and celebrate a specific event, in this case the offer of her first full-time job.

Others noted that tattoos, in particular, served as an indelible connection with specific periods in their lives. As one young tattooee put it: 'It connects me with like, my . . . teenage years really.' Another lightly tattooed interviewee, told me that he regarded the two Native American designs on his upper-arms as 'a commitment to [him]self' and explained that:

> By marking myself I thought I could . . . keep . . . what I felt when I was 18, 19, for the rest of my life, 'cause I'd always remember the time. Because having a tattoo done is such a special thing, there's the pain to begin with, and then there's like the high you get afterwards when you first have it done. . . . But, just looking at them reminds me of that time, and hopefully it will stop me from forgetting who I am, when life starts to get, you know, kick the door in a bit more. The older you get, mortgage, kids, whatever.

In this sense, becoming tattooed might be argued to commit the tattooee to a particular narrative, and at least one interviewee described his own tattoos as a permanent 'diary' that 'no one can take off you'. Others suggested that their tattoos could tell a story, with one heavily tattooed interviewee, for instance, suggesting that once he was completely tattooed, 'the realistic parts of [his] body suit [would] tell some kind of story about [his] view of the world'. The extent to which others would be able to read this text would depend on their ability to 'piece it all together', however, and as another heavily tattooed interviewee pointed out, while 'there's gonna be bits you can pick up', what can be gleaned from another person's tattoos is likely to be fairly limited. For the interviewee in question, tattoos *could* tell a story, but like other forms of diary, this was inherently personal:

> It's like the New Zealand *moko* is the story of the life, isn't it? That sort of thing. Kind of like that. But, I mean, it isn't an outward story of your life, you just remember it because you can see it on yourself, do you know what I mean?

Conclusion

Tattooing and piercing can be seen as postmodern practices in their eclectic appropriation of techniques and imagery from a global scrapbook of design sources and procedures, and it could be argued that their current popularity represents nothing more than the continued incorporation of 'the exotic' into the 'supermarket of style' (Craik, 1994: 25; Steele, 1996: 160–1). As was noted above, tattooing and piercing imagery is increasingly fashionable, and certain of the tattooees and piercees interviewed for this study did appear to regard their respective body modifications as little more than fashionable accessories. From this perspective, the contemporary popularity of tattooing and piercing could be seen not only as supportive of notions of a postmodern shift in a general sense, but also as evidence of the strength of such a shift, the incorporation of such once strongly connotative symbols into a more or less free-floating 'carnival of signs' indicative of the scope of the developments in question.

As was also indicated above, however, factors such as pain and permanence figure strongly in contemporary body modifiers' understandings and experiences of such corporeal artefacts. Despite the tendency of certain lightly tattooed or pierced body modifiers to describe them as accessories, among those involved, tattoos and piercings are not, generally, perceived simply as superficial products in the 'carnival of style'. Indeed, were tattoos and piercings regarded solely as fashionable accessories, then it would be difficult to see why anyone would become tattooed or pierced at all: in this context, stress would lie exclusively with the finished body decoration – as a purely visual signifier – and a tattoo-transfer, or clip-on piercing, would be as meaningful (if not as durable) as the real thing.[7]

To the extent that this is their intended argument, Polhemus and Proctor (1978) and Curry (1993) are arguably wrong to suggest that the permanence of tattooing – and in Curry's case the semi-permanence of piercing – guarantees the 'anti-fashion' status of such forms of body modification: a permanent or 'semi-permanent' signifier does not in and of itself imply a fixed signified. As *corporeal artefacts*, however, tattoos and piercings will arguably continue to refer to the manner of their production, and in this sense to resist full incorporation into Baudrillard's 'carnival of signs', however popular related imagery becomes. The comments of tattooed and pierced interviewees also suggest that whether or not their meaning is fixed in these terms, tattoos, and to a lesser extent piercings, are often employed as a form of 'anti-fashion', or at least valued in terms of their contrast with more superficial, sartorial accessories.

In this sense, such forms of body modification can be argued to share certain affinities with the subcultural uniforms of the 1960s and 1970s, but in contrast with skinhead style, for instance, contemporary body modification appears to serve less as a marker of group identity, and more as an expression of the self. It might thus be argued that while the skinheads' adoption of an exaggeratedly macho style was as a class-specific response to a particular and 'localized' crisis, the growing popularity of tattooing and piercing among an increasingly diverse clientele can instead be seen as a similar, but more diffuse, response to a set of crises and insecurities that are now more felt by a far wider section of the population (Muggleton, 1997: 13; Rubin, 1988: 255). That this is expressed via the adoption of permanent or semi-permanent forms of body modification, rather than, say, a particular clothing style, might in turn be explained by pointing to the increasing redundancy of sartorial markers of identification.

This would accord with the characterization of contemporary tattooing and piercing as 'body projects', as practices dedicated to the construction of a coherent sense of self-identity, and it was noted above that certain interviewees did indeed regard their involvement with such forms of body modification as a form of 'self-creation'. It was also noted that the permanence of tattooing, in particular, meant that it was well-suited to the establishment of a consistent personal narrative.

In conclusion, however, it should be pointed out that while the permanence or 'semi-permanence' of tattoos and piercings, and the pain involved in their acquisition, lends itself well to such a project, it also renders problematic any subsequent attempts to reflexively *revise* one's sense of self through *re*-attention to the body's exterior. As one lightly tattooed interviewee put it: 'you cannot run away from them, you can't stop being a tattooed person'. In this sense, tattooing, and some types of piercing, can be argued to differ from other forms of contemporary body project, their lack of easy revisibility perhaps indicative of a rejection of the ideology of social mobility which practices such as 'keep fit' vigorously pursue. Postmodern practices in that they involve the 'refashioning of personal identities out of cultural materials' (Tseëlon, 1995: 123), tattooing and certain forms of piercing differ from other forms of 'identity project' in representing an attempt to fix, or anchor one's sense of self through the (relative) permanence of the modification thus acquired.[8]

In a recent article on 'body marking', Turner described contemporary tattooing and piercing as 'playful and ironic': 'empty signs' that fail to refer to one's wider social-status, and can instead be read as 'parodic messages to the self' (Turner, 1997, see also Turner, this volume). While it is undoubtedly correct to note that contemporary body modification no longer refers unambiguously to one's class, gender or sexuality, however, the above has indicated that such markings can – on at least two levels – be argued to be less 'empty' than Turner suggests. *Relatively* free-floating, when compared, for instance, with traditional 'marking' in non-Western contexts, contemporary body modification continues to signify at the denotative level, even if its connotative message is increasingly ambiguous. Taken together, factors such as the relative permanence of such forms of body modification, the pain involved in their acquisition, and the active role played by the tattooee or piercee in their completion, also suggest that it would be misleading to label contemporary tattooing and piercing simply as fashionable products in the 'supermarket of style'. As American tattooist Don Ed Hardy points out, while 'there *are* elements of fashion to it' (Hardy, in Vale and Juno, 1989: 58), '[i]t's on your body, it's permanent; you have to live with it; and it hurts' (Hardy, in Vale and Juno, 1989: 61).

Notes

I am grateful to Graham Allan, Kate Reed, Chris Shilling and an anonymous referee for their comments on an earlier version of this paper, and to the Department of Sociology and Social Policy at the University of Southampton for supporting the wider study of which it forms a part. Thanks are also due to the interviewees quoted above, and to the numerous others who have helped with my research in some way, shape or form. The usual disclaimers, of course, apply.

   1. No accurate figures are available, but a number of authors have noted the increasing popularity of tattooing (Armstrong, 1991, Armstrong and Gabriel, 1993; Armstrong et al., 1996; Blanchard, 1994; Curry, 1993; DeMello, 1995a, 1995b; Rubin, 1988; Sanders, 1989) and piercing (Curry, 1993; Myers, 1992), as well as their spread to an increasingly heterogeneous clientele. Several writers have pointed to the growing numbers of middle-class and female tattooees (Armstrong, 1991: 215, 1993: 107–8; Armstrong et al., 1996: 412; Blanchard, 1994: 287; Curry, 1993: 70; DeMello, 1995a: 73, 79, 1995b: 48; Mercer & Davies, 1991: 380; Rubin, 1988: 235; Sanders, 1989: 28–9, 160), while Rubin (1988: 235) has also noted a rise in the number of older clients. Curry (1993: 75) notes that piercing is no longer 'confined to any class, age group or sexual proclivity'.

   These points can be supported by a wealth of circumstantial evidence. During the course of this research, for example, several UK-based tattooists confirmed the increasing popularity of the practice since the late-1970s, as well as an increase in the number of middle-class, female and older clients (see also Dixon, in Bradberry, 1997: 21; 'K', 1995: 49; Knappett, 1997: 29; Papworth, 1998: 12; Potton, 1996: 34; 'Rabbit', 1997: 20–5; Treharne, 1996: 37; Venus, 1996: 45). A number of informants also pointed to an acceleration in these trends since the mid- to late-1980s (see also 'Mark the Wanderer', 1998: 47; 'Annie', in Wainwright, 1996: 2). Similar confirmation was provided in respect of body piercing, with interviewees noting its growth in popularity since the early to mid-1980s, the acceleration of such trends since the late 1980s/early 1990s, and the increasingly diverse nature of the clientele: the practice is no longer confined primarily to those with an interest in the SM or fetish scene, and is popular among a range of age groups and occupational backgrounds (see also Grant, 1995: 15, 18; 'Barry', in Rowlands, 1998: 13).

   The increased incidence of both tattooing and piercing is also indicated by reports of their popularity in the broadcast and print media (see, for example: Bayley, 1996; Bellos, 1996; Brooker, 1994; Garner, 1998; Grant, 1995; Millard, 1995; Moorhead, 1998; Mullen, 1997; Rowlands, 1998; Ryle, 1996; Wallace, 1997; Ward, 1998; Williams, 1996). Many of these articles have called for tighter regulation of body piercing, itself a further indication of the practice's recent rise in popularity: the Local Government (Miscellaneous Provisions) Act 1982 relates only to ear-piercing, reflecting the low incidence of other forms of piercing at the time the legislation was framed (Stokes, 1996). Following a recent Department of Health consultation exercise (Department of Health/Welsh Office, 1996), however, proposals have now been put forward to introduce relevant legislation, albeit alongside the deregulation of other forms of 'skin piercing' (Department of Health, 1998).

2. See note 1, above.

3. The article forms part of a wider study of contemporary body modification, for which in-depth, semi-structured interviews were conducted with 35 tattooed and/or pierced informants, as well as with several professional tattooists, body piercers and other key informants. The study also draws on observation conducted at a number of tattoo conventions and tattoo and/or piercing studios, as well as analysis of the popular literature devoted to the forms of body modification in question.

The 35 core interviewees were recruited in roughly equal numbers at tattoo conventions, through advertisements in a UK-based tattoo magazine and local student publications, and through introductions provided by existing informants, though three were already known to the author. A variety of methods was employed in order to allow contact with a range of contemporary body modifiers. The bulk of the interviews were conducted face-to-face, though seven took place by phone. Interviews were recorded, and ranged in duration from 20 minutes to approximately 3 hours.

Of the 35 tattooees and/or piercees interviewed, 15 were women, and ages ranged from 19 to 40 among the women, and 20 to 60 among the men. The mean ages for each group were 24 and 32 respectively. Occupations ranged from the unemployed and students to credit analysts, local government officers and company directors. Most of the interviewees were white, and while this was not an intentional outcome of the sampling methods employed, it does reflect a lack of ethnic diversity in the tattoo and piercing community. Around 40 percent of the women and 70 percent of the men were heavily tattooed and/or pierced, which generally implies that they had three or more of either form of body modification. This is a fairly loose definition, however: several standard ear-piercings, for example, would not place someone in the heavily pierced category, while someone with a full backpiece as their sole tattoo would certainly be counted as heavily tattooed.

4. See note 3, above.

5. Certain lightly pierced, but non-tattooed informants also offered this as their rationale for choosing the former body modification rather than the latter. When asked if he had ever thought about getting a tattoo done, for instance, one male piercee replied: 'Err, no. Now that was another consideration for getting the piercing done over something like a tattoo, in that if I ever get fed up with it, it just comes out and heals over.'

6. A ring-piercing that enters through the urethra, and exits at the base of the glans. See Myers (1992: 300–1) for illustration and further description.

7. But however realistic their appearance, 'Stick on tattoos are not tattoos' (Curry, 1993: 70), and the very popularity of tattoo-transfers, while indicative of the popularity of tattoo-based *imagery*, also suggests that, for some, a *real* tattoo is simply not an option to be considered. A recent edition of *Tatler* carried an article extolling the merits of small, discrete and *tasteful* tattoos, before going on to suggest that 'temporary-tattoos' were perhaps a wiser option (Green, 1997: 55).

8. As I have suggested elsewhere, there is also an extent to which tattooing and piercing can be said to be resistant of gendered norms of appearance, in part because they move the tattooee or piercee further away from, rather than closer towards, the youthful, slim, and *unmarked* body that is the hegemonic Western ideal (Sweetman, 1999b; see also DeMello, 1995b).

References

Alford, L. (1993) 'Hard Look Story', *Observer Life Magazine* 7 November: 16–17.

Armstrong, M.L. (1991) 'Career-Oriented Women with Tattoos', *Image: Journal of Nursing Scholarship* 23(4): 215–20.

Armstrong, M.L. and D.G. Gabriel (1993) 'Tattoos on Women: Marks of Distinction or Abomination?', *Dermatology Nursing* 5(2): 107–13.

Armstrong, M.L., D.J. Stuppy and D.G. Gabriel (1996) 'Motivation for Tattoo Removal', *Archives of Dermatology* 132(4): 412–16.

Bayley, C. (1996) 'Straight for the Juggler', *Guardian section 2* 26 August: 10–11.

Bellos, A. (1996) 'As British as S&M', *Guardian section 2* 6 November: 7.

Blanchard, M. (1994) 'Post-Bourgeois Tattoo: Reflections on Skin Writing in Late Capitalist Societies', in Lucien Taylor (ed.) *Visualizing Theory: Selected Essays from V.A.R. 1990–1994*. New York and London: Routledge.

Bradberry, G. (1997) 'Branded for Life', *The Times* 20 November: 21.

Brooker, E. (1994) 'He Wears his Scars with Pride', *The Independent Section II*, 11 May.

Clarke, J. (1976) 'The Skinheads and the Magical Recovery of Community', in S. Hall and T. Jefferson (eds) *Resistance through Rituals: Youth Subcultures in Post-War Britain*. London: Harper Collins.

Cohen, P. (1997) 'Subcultural Conflict and Working-Class Community', in K. Gelder and S. Thornton (eds) *The Subcultures Reader*. London: Routledge. (Orig. 1972.)

Craik, J. (1994) *The Face of Fashion: Cultural Studies in Fashion*. London: Routledge.

Curry, D. (1993) 'Decorating the Body Politic', *New Formations* 19: 69–82.

Davis, F. (1985) 'Clothing and Fashion as Communication', in M.R. Solomon (ed.) *The Psychology of Fashion*. Lexington, MA: Lexington Books.

DeMello, M. (1995a) '"Not Just For Bikers Anymore": Popular Representations of American Tattooing', *Journal of Popular Culture* 19(3): 37–52.

DeMello, M. (1995b) 'The Carnivalesque Body: Women and Tattoos', in The Drawing Center, *Pierced Hearts and True Love: A Century of Drawings for Tattoos*. New York/Honolulu: The Drawing Centre/Hardy Marks Publications.

Department of Health/Welsh Office (1996) 'Regulation of Skin Piercing: A Consultation Paper', London: Department of Health/Welsh Office, 3 October.

Department of Health (1998) 'Regulation of Skin Piercing Businesses', London: Department of Health communique, 30 June.

Dery, M. (1996) *Escape Velocity: Cyberculture at the End of the Century*. London: Hodder and Stoughton.

Eubanks, V. (1996) 'Zones of Dither: Writing the Postmodern Body', *Body & Society* 2(3): 73–88.

Falk, P. (1995) 'Written in the Flesh', *Body & Society* 1(1): 95–105.

Featherstone, M. (1991) 'The Body in Consumer Culture', in M. Featherstone, M. Hepworth and B. Turner (eds) *The Body: Social Process and Cultural Theory*. London: Sage.

Foster Wallace, D. (1997) *Infinite Jest*. London: Abacus.

Gamman, L. and M. Makinen (1994) *Female Fetishism: A New Look*. London: Lawrence and Wishart.

Garner, C. (1998) 'There's a Hole in Dad's Argument', *The Independent Monday Review* 15 June: 10.

Gell, A. (1993) *Wrapping in Images: Tattooing in Polynesia*. Oxford: Clarendon Press.

Giddens, A. (1991) *Modernity and Self-Identity: Self and Society in the Late Modern Age*. Cambridge: Polity Press.

Gottschalk, S. (1993) 'Uncomfortably Numb: Countercultural Impulses in the Postmodern Era', *Symbolic Interaction* 16(4): 351–78.

Grant, L. (1995) 'Written on the Body', *Guardian Weekend* 1 April: 12–20.

Green, C. (1997) 'Ink on the Pink', *Tatler* 292(8): 55.

Hall, S. and T. Jefferson (eds) (1976) *Resistance through Rituals: Youth Subcultures in Post-War Britain*. London: Harper Collins.

Hebdige, D. (1988) *Subculture: The Meaning of Style*. London and New York: Routledge. (Orig. 1979.)

'K', B. (1995) 'Tattoo Crazy: Barry K' (interview by P. Callaby), *Skin Deep* 2(2): 44–51.

Klesse, C. (1997) 'The Representation of Primitivism in a Specialised Sexual Subculture', unpublished paper presented at 'Body Modification', a *TCS* conference, Nottingham Trent University, June. (A revised version of this paper appears in this issue.)

Knappett, J. (1997) 'John Knappett: Body Graphics' (interview by P. Callaby), *Skin Deep* 4(6): 28–35.

Lind, C. and M. Roach-Higgins (1985) 'Collective Adoption, Fashion, and the Social-Political Symbolism of Dress', in M. Solomon (ed.) *The Psychology of Fashion*. Lexington, MA: Lexington Books.

'Mark the Wanderer' (1998) 'Mark the Wanderer: A Happy Man' (interview by D. Smith), *Skin Deep* 5(1): 46–9.

Maffesoli, M. (1996) *The Time of the Tribes: The Decline of Individualism in Mass Society*. London: Sage.

Menkes, S. (1993) 'Fetish or Fashion?', *New York Times* 21 November: C1, 9.

Mercer, N. and D. Davies (1991) 'Tattoos: Marked for Life', *British Medical Journal* 303: 380.

Miles, C. (1997) 'Metalmorphosis', unpublished paper presented at 'Body Modification', a *TCS* Conference, Nottingham Trent University, June.

Millard, R. (1995) 'Your Body in the Firing Line for the Latest in Hot Fashion', *The Observer* 22 January: 8.

Moorhead, J. (1998) 'A Lesson in Needlework', *Guardian section 2* 14 January: 7.

Muggleton, D. (1995) 'From "Subculture" to "Neo-Tribe": Identity, Paradox and Postmodernism in "Alternative" Style', unpublished paper presented at 'Shouts from the Street: Culture, Creativity and Change', MIPC Conference on Popular Culture, Manchester Metropolitan University, September.

Muggleton, D. (1997) 'Resistance or Difference? Expressive Individualism, Alienation and Subcultural Disengagement', unpublished paper presented at 'Power/Resistance', BSA Annual Conference, University of York, April.

Mullen, L. (1997) 'The Cutting Edge', *Time Out* 10–17 December: 20–31.

Myers, J. (1992) 'Nonmainstream Body Modification: Genital Piercing, Branding, Burning, and Cutting', *Journal of Contemporary Ethnography* 21(3): 267–306.

Papworth, J. (1998) 'Adventures in the Skin Trade', *Guardian Money* 28 February: 12.

Pitts, V. (1998) 'Provoking the Organic: Representations and Resistance in Extreme Body Marking', unpublished paper presented at 'Making Sense of the Body', BSA Annual Conference, University of Edinburgh, April.

Polhemus, T. (1995) *Streetstyle: From Sidewalk to Catwalk*. London: Thames and Hudson.

Polhemus, T. and L. Proctor (1978) *Fashion and Anti-Fashion*. London: Thames and Hudson.

Potton, S. (1996) 'Steve Potton' (interview by P. Callaby), *Skin Deep* 3(8): 30–7.

'Rabbit' (1997) 'Rabbit: Grin 'n' Wear It' (interview by P. Callaby), *Skin Deep* 4(2): 18–25.

Rowlands, B. (1998) 'There's a Hole in My Navel, My Nipple, My Nose', *The Independent* 1 September: 13.

Rubin, A. (1988) 'The Tattoo Renaissance', in A. Rubin (ed.) *Marks of Civilization: Artistic Transformations of the Human Body*. Los Angeles: Museum of Cultural History/University of California LA.

Ryle, J. (1996) 'Piercing Truths', *Guardian section 2* 15 March: 3.

Sanders, C. (1985) 'Tattoo Consumption: Risk and Regret in the Purchase of a Socially Marginal Service', *Advances in Consumer Research* 12: 17–22.

Sanders, C. (1989) *Customizing the Body: The Art and Culture of Tattooing*. Philadelphia, PA: Temple University Press.

Shilling, C. (1993) *The Body and Social Theory*. London: Sage.

Steele, V. (1996) *Fetish: Fashion, Sex and Power*. New York and Oxford: Oxford University Press.

Stokes, P. (1996) 'Mother Demands New Law on Body Piercing', *The Daily Telegraph* 8 June: 9.

Sweetman, P. (1999a) 'Only Skin Deep? Tattooing, Piercing and the Transgressive Body', in M. Aaron (ed.) *The Body's Perilous Pleasures: Dangerous Desires and Contemporary Culture*. Edinburgh: Edinburgh University Press.

Sweetman, P. (1999b) 'Marked Bodies, Oppositional Identities? Tattooing, Piercing and the Ambiguity of Resistance', in S. Roseneil and J. Seymour (eds) *Practising Identities: Power and Resistance*. Basingstoke: Macmillan.

Treharne, J. (1996) 'John Treharne: Skin Creation' (interview by P. Callaby), *Skin Deep* 3(9): 30–7.

Tseëlon, E. (1995) *The Masque of Femininity: The Representation of Woman in Everyday Life*. London: Sage.

Turner, B. (1997) 'Body Marks: Neo-Tribalism in Cool Societies', unpublished paper presented at 'Body Modification', a *TCS* Conference, Nottingham Trent University, June. (A revised version of this paper appears in this issue.)

Vale, V. and A. Juno (1989) *Re/Search #12: Modern Primitives – An Investigation of Contemporary Adornment and Ritual*. San Francisco: Re/Search Publications.

Venus, J. (1996) 'Johnny Venus' (interview by B. Richmond), *Skin Deep* 3(9): 44–9.

Wainwright, M. (1996) 'Skin-Deep Beauty Treatment Makes a Point', *Guardian* 16 December: 2

Wallace, W. (1997) 'A Skin for Trouble', *Guardian section 2* 9 December: 16.

Ward, S. (1998) 'A Piercing Cry of Anger', *Guardian, Society* 25 February: 2.

Williams, S. (1996) 'Generation Gap', *The Independent Section II* 20 May: 7.

Wilson, E. (1990) 'These New Components of the Spectacle: Fashion and Postmodernism', in R. Boyne and A. Rattansi (eds) *Postmodernism and Society*. Basingstoke: Macmillan.

Paul Sweetman is a lecturer in sociology at the University of Durham. Previously based at the University of Southampton, his research interests centre around the body, identity, fashion and consumption.

This Body Which Is Not One: Dealing with Differences

MARGRIT SHILDRICK

This article is both a series of reflections on the nature of monstrosity in general, and an analysis of some of those categories of corporeal being that are said to reflect the monstrous. The monstrous may of course be the crafted result of techno-organic creation like Haraway's cyborg (1989), or of intentionally transgressive conjunctions and displacements of body parts, as in the novel *Geek Love* (Dunn, 1989), but my interest here is in the epistemological, ontological and indeed ethical status of wholly organic beings whose difference is always already evident. The monstrosity they evidence is not, then, the result of accident, degeneration or disease, nor yet of self-willed modification, but rather the very condition of life. Nonetheless, such congenital monstrosity – particularly as it pertains to my particular focus on conjoined twins – allows us to approach the issue of body modification from a novel direction. As I understand it, the concept of corporeal modification implies reference to a biological given that might be denaturalized, or at the very least to the notion of a standard morphology which might then be altered or transgressed. But if we understand such a standard of bodyliness as an impossible ideal in itself – as something to be achieved rather than as a given – then it makes good sense to take the monstrous as the starting point rather than the end point. I shall be looking, then, at the issue of body modification as an intervention into the always already unstable corpus, whereby what is intended is not the practice of transgression, but is on the contrary a process of normalization, albeit one fraught with anxieties.

During the last decade, both feminist scholarship and postmodernist philosophy have opened up afresh an interest in monstrous corporeality that moves far

Body & Society © 1999 SAGE Publications (London, Thousand Oaks and New Delhi),
Vol. 5(2–3): 77–92
[1357–034X(199906/09)5:2–3;77–92;008852]

beyond a well-established clinical concern – where therapeutic modification is the major issue – to an altogether more discursive analysis. Although the connections are sometimes left implicit in the text, the monster may be read most fruitfully alongside, and supplemental to, the already familiar conjunction of matter and mother through which feminism stages a critique of the dominant forms of Western discourse. All those conditions – mother/matter/monster – are both excessive to, and yet, as feminism has come to recognize, embedded unacknowledged in the structuration of the logos. And it is the very move of excavating that structural function that disrupts and throws into doubt the assumption of a stable, autonomous and singular human subject as the centre of the logos; of a self that is foundational without being embodied; and of a body whose morphological integrity is so unquestioned that it may be forgotten, transcended. Above all it is the corporeal ambiguity and fluidity, the troublesome lack of fixed definition, the refusal to be either one thing or the other, that marks the monstrous as a site of disruption. What is at stake is the fundamental closure of both subjects and bodies that characterizes and propels Western discourse, most particularly in its modernist form. The focus in this article on the phenomenon of conjoined twins points up the more general disturbance that problematizes, as I have put it elsewhere, 'not only the protection of one's own body from encroachments, but a denial of the leakiness between one's self and others' (1997: 178). The issue, then, is one not only of contesting the epistemological and ontological boundaries of bodies of knowledge and bodies of matter, but of reconfiguring the ethics of relationship.

The underlying question of what it is to be a subject, and experience oneself and the world as such, is most usually addressed in either one of two opposing ways: first, the body may be bracketed out, as though it were of no concern. As Descartes puts it in the *Meditations*:

> Although the whole mind seems to be united to the whole body, nevertheless, were a foot or an arm or any other bodily part amputated, I know that nothing would be taken away from the mind. (1990: 443)

Or, second, taking a more phenomenological approach, selfhood may be seen as inseparable from material being-in-the-world. Despite the nature of embodiment being a fundamental component of that approach, the phenomenological perspective assumes, nonetheless, a 'normal' model of corporeal development, and fails to theorize adequately the grossly disordered body. But what if the focus were on the 'abnormal', on the explicitly monstrous? Just as feminist phenomenologists such as Iris Marion Young and Ros Diprose have moved to disrupt the assumption of a gender-neutral, ageless and universalized body as the centre of lived experience, so too we may gain further insights by theorizing non-normative morphology, not as a failure of form (inviting therapeutic modification), but as an-other way of being. I don't mean to suggest, of course, that the phenomenological perspective has not already figured prominently in staging the ontological and epistemological consequences of corporeal anomalies – be they the result of illness, trauma or congenital disorders – but rather that the integrated and fully functioning body remains throughout an implicit standard. Certainly the existence of monstrosity may serve to define by comparison and opposition the delimited corporeality and secure subjectivity of the majority, but what is of more importance is the realization that the standard is not normal but normative.

The question that haunts the Western imagination – 'Who am I?' – has been answered conventionally by reference to a sense of self as the continuing subject of its own experiences that assumes, nonetheless, a transcendent detachment from the material business of the world, or at least an effective, and indeed affective, autonomy within it. To be a self is above all to be distinguished from the other, to be ordered and discrete, secure *within* the well-defined boundaries of the body rather than actually being the body. Although from time to time we may experience ourselves out-of-body, what rarely happens – and then it is defined as a special type of madness – is that we should either inhabit the body of another, or find our own bodies shared – invaded we would say – by another. And while the narcissistic pleasure to be derived from perceiving our image from the outside, most commonly in the mirror, may be accompanied also by the sensation of strangeness and misrecognition, it is the unfamiliarity of the material body itself and the space it occupies that strikes us, not the perception that another subject might occupy that body. In short, though the *integration* of mind and body may be somewhat undermined by a Western discourse of transcendent subjectivity, there are few doubts as to which minds and bodies go together. And though self-identity may always and necessarily be a case of misrecognition in the Lacanian sense, it is precisely the mapping of the boundaries between both singular selves and singular bodies that authorizes our being in the world as subjects. I will merely note in passing that the sovereign 'I', who defines himself against the other, the non-self, describes an intrinsically masculine subject, of which I will say no more, except to mark the inherent exclusivity of such a closure. What concerns me here is to uncover the extent to which the Western notion of subjectivity, and of the body that is one, is, in general, both guaranteed and contested by those who do not, indeed cannot, unproblematically occupy the subject position.

For all that modernist discourse privileges a putative split between mind and body that casts doubt on the ontological status of the body, the result has been neither lack of interest in, nor disengagement from, questions of corporeal being. Contra Descartes, we are obsessed with our bodies. But it is not of course

normative morphology that engages the greatest attention, but those bodily forms
– like conjoined twinning – that most clearly challenge the distinctions both
between mind and body and between body and body. Against an ideal of bodily
perfection that relies on the singular, the unified and the replicable, monstrosity,
in the form of either excess, lack or displacement, offers a gross insult. And
although I am interested here primarily in wholly organic monsters, that should
not be taken as a reiteration of the nature/culture split whereby some monsters
are taken to be more natural than others. On the contrary, it would be more
appropriate to recognize from the outset that *techne* plays a part in the construction of all monsters, indeed all bodies. As Haraway reminds us: 'Biology is
discourse, not the living world itself' (1992: 298).

What I am disputing, then, is the givenness of any body, the sense of a foundational and certain form which then may be compared to an ideal template.
Clearly the developing body is always dynamic, growing and adapting, but I
mean more than that. It is the sense – intended by Judith Butler (1993) – that
bodies, rather than being material and graspable from the start, are materialized
through a set of discursive practices. The so-called normal and natural body is
then an achievement, a model of the proper where everything is in its place and
the chaotic aspects of the natural are banished. It is a body that requires unceas-
ing maintenance and/or modification to hold off the constant threat of disruption:
extra digits are excised at birth, tongues are shortened in Down's Syndrome children, noses are reshaped, warts removed, prosthetic limbs fitted, HRT prescribed.
In short, the normal body is materialized through a set of reiterative practices that
speak to the instability of the singular standard.

In contrast, at the very simplest level, the monster is something beyond the
normative, that resists the values associated with what we choose to call normality, and that is instead a focus of normative anxiety. The transhistorical interest in
teratology, which has taken philosophical, medical, legal and popular forms, has
characteristically defined the monstrous as being intrinsically unnatural, an
affront to the expected that 'throws doubt', as Canguilhem puts it, 'on life's ability
to teach us order' (1964: 27). Nonetheless, the monster is not *outside* nature, but
rather an instance of nature's startling capacity to produce alien forms within. For
the 17th-century cleric, Thomas Bedford, what is demonstrated by 'monstrous
and misfeatured births' is 'that it is a singular mercy of God when the births of
the womb are not misformed, when they receive their fair and perfect feature'
(1635). The simultaneous stress on both the otherness and the incorporation of
the monstrous within the natural is a consistent feature of explanatory and speculative accounts.

The monsters that engage us most, that command intricate explanation, are those which are closest to us, those which display some aspect of our own form, and speak, both literally and metaphorically, a human language. And monsters do always signify. In his sermon on the birth of conjoined twins in his parish, for example, Thomas Bedford characteristically stresses that 'all monstrous and misshapen births, though dead, yet speak for the instruction of the living' (Bedford, 1635). Even when the long-standing belief in the supposedly portentous nature of monstrosity lost favour in the face of the more naturalistic explanations of Enlightenment science, the requirement of interpretation remained. It is true that the purely animal monster may be an object of curiosity or fear, and has a similar history of signalling events to come, of providing a material marker of divine affect or, later, of signifying evolutionary diversity, but it does not thereby unsettle the security of human being. The animal is the other in the comforting guise of outsider, but in its lack of humanity, it is not and cannot be what Kristeva calls the abject. For those that are at least in an ambivalent relationship to humanity, however, the concept of the abject provides an apt descriptor. As Kristeva defines it: 'what disturbs identity, system and order. What does not respect boundaries, positions, rules. The in-between, the ambiguous, the composite' (1982: 4). Human monsters, then, both fulfil the necessary function of the binary opposite that confirms the normality and centrality of the acculturated self, and at the same time threaten to disrupt that binary by being all too human. Although the monstrous may provoke both the fascination and horror accorded the absolute other, that response is never unproblematic, but spills over into the anxiety and repulsion which is occasioned by the violation of internal order. And as Kristeva makes clear, that which is abjected is never completely externalized. It is, then, in their failure to wholly and only occupy the place of the other that such monsters betray the fragility of the distinctions by which the human subject is fixed and maintained as fully present to itself and autonomous. In collapsing the boundaries between self and other, monsters constitute an undecidable absent presence at the heart of human being. Alongside their external manifestation, they leave also a trace embedded within, that, in Derridean terms, operates as the signifier not of difference but of *différance*. What is at stake throughout is the risk of indifferentiation.

I shall turn now to a consideration of conjoined twins, who have warranted comment throughout the socio-history of teratology.[1] The material manifestation of the body which is not one demands a specific epistemological and ontological reflection, in which the issue of the boundaries of subjecthood and, in earlier periods, of a soul, is particularly acute. I will leave aside the very many recorded instances of the supposed conjunction of human and animal bodies, to concentrate on what remains to this day an area of deep-seated fascination. Unlike the hybrid variety, which leaves room for a wholly exclusionary approach, the incidence of corporeal doubling in which both bodies are visibly human is highly disruptive to Western notions of individual agency and personal identity. Rather than such twins being absolutely other to ourselves – and that response as I have said is in any case finally untenable – they are in effect an uncomfortable manifestation of the mirroring process that underlies all identity (Lacan, 1977). Textual evidence suggests that conjoined twins have always counted among the monstrous,[2] though their portentous value was sometimes positive rather than negative. Although most will have undoubtedly died at birth or soon after, they are often portrayed in archival texts as fully formed children or adults, thus throwing up not simply the urgent question of which twin has the soul, but also whether one or both should be considered autonomous persons. Given the necessity of baptism as the prerequisite of salvation, medieval and early modern theologians adopted a kind of fail-safe with regard to that sacrament. The so-called *Ego baptizo* formula carefully required the priest to baptize one head or body, and then turn to the other with the words: 'If you are baptised, I do not baptise you, but if you are not yet baptised, I baptise you' (quoted in Friedman, 1981: 180). It remained unclear how great a degree of separation was required to invoke the formula, but the doubling of limbs alone was not sufficient. Excess is merely monstrous, whereas the conjunction of that which could and should be separate invites and requires discursive normalization.

The significance of morphology, and the relationship between the body and the subject is put centre stage by the wide variety of forms that conjoined twins may take. The simplest from the point of view of understanding them as separate individuals are those whose bodies appear relatively self-complete externally albeit joined by fleshy material and shared circulation, though they might also lack two complete sets of internal organs. The anomaly of conjunction is overridden in these cases by the common-sense judgement that in all other respects such twins *are* two autonomous beings. The famous 19th-century Siamese twins, Chang and Eng, for example, were indeed sufficiently independent of each other to contract marriage to two sisters and to each father several children. The conjunction between Chang and Eng was relatively simple consisting of a 5-inch band of cartilaginous material between their chests with the liver as the only shared internal organ. Although surgical intervention was considered and rejected as too dangerous, it is not surprising that they were each accorded full social and legal identity. Nonetheless, despite such strategies of normalization, the unmodified corporeal excessiveness of the twins' condition labelled them as freaks, who existed only as a unit, and they were frequently exhibited as such. The fascination for the viewing public, and for the wider media who followed Chang and Eng throughout their long life, was the simultaneous possibility of objectifying them as the monstrous other and of identifying with them – in their role of upright citizens – as the same. The twins themselves on the one hand endured conjunction and are known to have insisted on the semblance of autonomy, by maintaining two marital households for example, while on the other they were so identified with one another that the idea of separation is said to have filled them with dread.

The perception that separation is in the best interests of conjoined twins rests on the prior assumption that two distinct persons with distinct identities have, as it were, become trapped in a single morphology. The issue of surgical intervention and modification is taken as settled in principle, and subject only to technical feasibility, as though there is nothing at stake except an inappropriate body. But what that account misses out is the phenomenological sense of being-in-the-world, in which corporeal extension is indivisible from subjecthood and identity. The privileging of singularity and autonomy so evident in Western discourse, and the value accorded bodily self-determination combine to erase any consideration that there might be other ways of being. I am not suggesting that conjoined twins should not be seen as two individuals, but that the question of identity is not so easily settled. The (mis)recognition of the Lacanian mirror stage is in a sense the permanent condition of such twins, with the evident difference that in that moment they may refuse identity in its symbolic sense and choose identification. There is plenty of evidence that monozygotic twins in general habitually blur the boundaries between one and the other – simultaneously thinking the same thoughts, making the same choices, speaking together as one – and it should not be surprising that conjoined twins, who share perforce experiential being, do not make the separations that are commonly taken for granted. If being in the world, and still less identity, is not a given, then might not a different morphology ground other relationships between self and other?

In non-autobiographical accounts of conjoined twins, both modern historical and contemporary, the one consistent factor that overrides differences in morphology is the reiteration of their essential separateness. Clinical understanding is far from decisive, however, and as the *Encyclopaedia Britannica* puts it:

> Such double malformations probably arise following the less than complete separation of the halves of the early embryo, or from partial separation at later stages. (*New Encyclopaedia Britannica*, 1992: vol. 20 Macropaedia, 367)

What this suggests to me is a difference between putative twins who remain unfortunately joined at birth, and a putative singleton whose body has unfortunately begun to divide prenatally. What is at stake with the latter case is perhaps even more ontologically disruptive than the former, and I have yet to see the implications of such specificity addressed. Instead, the question with regard to all conjoined twins is never whether they should be separated, but rather how and how soon. The expected birth of conjoined twins in Manchester in 1996 was, for example, the occasion for a whole spate of articles reviewing similar cases and looking at the prospects of the present pair. Most telling of all were the attempts of the prospective parents to normalize the birth. The father is quoted as saying: 'We have made up our minds to look on the bright side and focus on having two lovely girls who will eventually lead *normal separate* lives' (*Guardian*, 11 October 1996: 5; my emphasis). Quite clearly, and understandably, he and the medical advisers could conceive of the twins' lives only as being on hold until they were separated, stripped as it were of their power to disrupt. So deeply is the ideal of corporeal and mental autonomy written into the Western understanding of what it is to be a person, that any suggestion that the infants could function as a merged unit was swiftly rejected. Even a sympathetic observer such as the attending paediatric surgeon was constrained to find signs of independent personhood: 'They are exploring each other, each touching the other, sparring away with their tiny hands', while a clearly unsympathetic reporter interprets the same behaviour as 'involving struggle, discomfort and distress for each half of this bizarre whole' (*Observer*, 17 October 1996: 12).

I want now to look in some detail at the case of the Irish conjoined twins, Katie and Eilish Holton,[3] whose early childhood and subsequent separation features in two television documentaries. What is at stake throughout for both the parents and the medical team is how best to balance the risk of separation – and it is made clear that the twins' degree of conjunction exceeds any in which surgical intervention has been previously attempted – with the normative desire that each should have a functionally autonomous existence. The issue of corporeal normalization, is, however, clearly distinct from a more complex and contradictory understanding of what constitutes normality in the specific case of the twins. For the parents, Katie and Eilish already operate as two 'normal' children, having individual personalities which they do much to encourage; while for his part, the consultant surgeon is constrained to stress that he cannot promise the twins a 'normal' life if they are separated. The characteristic Western split between mind and body is mirrored in the assumption of an existential normality that is merely obstructed by the abnormal morphology of the children. The voice-over suggestion that 'although we value individuality, they might not value it. They might prefer togetherness' (*Katie and Eilish: Siamese Twins*, Yorkshire TV, 1993) is, then, both a disturbing glimpse of other ways of being, and a reminder of what the normative regime of individuality must repudiate. It is not, I think, that there is any recognition that the concorporation of the twins might speak to new forms of embodied subjectivity, but rather that the ideal of the autonomous subject is contested by the twins' concurrent and co-operative intentionality. Their successful negotitiation of their environment largely depends on their acting as one, even in such small matters as unscrewing a bottle. Nonetheless, the sense that being-in-the-world might imbricate with body and environment is not explored; to those who must decide their future, the discrete subjectivities of the twins is already given and simply awaiting release. Although both parents and doctors are sensitive to the implicitly ethical question of potentially disrupting the twins' current contentment, they are the more concerned with the material risks of surgery. Following a visit to some 'successfully' separated conjoined twins, matters of procedure become paramount. The operation is undertaken with some real confidence, and Katie unexpectedly dies.

The point of turning to this often very moving narrative is not so much to critique the practice of heroic medicine – for in this case the participants, whether detached professionals or closest family, were all properly caring and reflective[4] – but to illustrate the power of ontological anxiety. Against the corporeal excessiveness of Katie and Eilish, the attempt to radically reconstruct their bodies speaks eloquently to the notions of closure and containment assumed to be at the heart of being. What is finally unacceptable about the twins is not the degree of their disability – and indeed it is unclear that a successful outcome would have increased function – but the ambiguity of their concorporation. For all the discursive efforts to normalize their life in terms of assigning dual individuality, it remains undecidable whether they are one or two. In contrast, the conventional understanding of the only proper form of subjectivity requires a clarity of boundaries between self and other, an affective and effective autonomy that is fully realized only by singular embodiment. Despite the death of Katie, then, the father of the twins is constrained to justify the operation by remarking on the surviving twin's enhanced quality of life after separation: 'She's free of being joined to another human being' (Eilish: Life Without Katie, Yorkshire TV, 1995). In fashioning Eilish's body so that she may comply with normative ideals, she is realized as an intelligible subject, and a body that matters. The impossibility of the ideal is made clear, however, in the acknowledgement that for Eilish, body modification must be continued throughout life: her prosthetic leg and body harness must be periodically replaced to ensure scopic normalization. It is ironic that although no-one seems able to articulate the real extent of Eilish's corporeal disruption, the doctor worries that in losing her first prosthesis, she will think some part of her is being taken away. For her own part Eilish renames her new leg 'Katie', in recognition of the absent presence of her self/other.

The phenomenological specificity of concorporate being-in-the-world is addressed by no adult in the films, except perhaps in the psychologist's half recognition that Katie is still incorporated into the life of her surviving twin. At night, Eilish gets what she calls her 'Katie kisses', but even that observation is normalized in the remark that the ritual happens 'in a healthy way, not in any way that is holding Eilish back' (*Eilish*, Yorkshire TV, 1995). That implicit rewriting of the twin relationship as obstructive is reiterated in an interchange between Eilish and her sisters. When asked what she remembers of her sister, Eilish replies: 'She used to bring me round everywhere', only to be interrupted by an older sibling who declares: 'Eilish couldn't go wherever she wanted' (*Eilish*, Yorkshire TV, 1995). What matters to the family is that Eilish should be well-adjusted, and indeed, despite the four months spent in hospital post-operatively in which she is described as traumatized, she does appear happy and talkative in the second documentary shot over the next two years. For her parents, her social and physical recovery is clearly a matter of relief, but it is evident too that for Eilish herself, the splitting of her (subject) body has produced an effect somewhat akin to the phenomenon of the phantom limb. The wound she experiences, unacknowledged, is as much psychical as material, a severe disruption to the unified, albeit imaginary, body map that founds the ego.[5] When Teresa, the elder sister, says of Katie, 'She had freckles', the response from Eilish is both confused and defiant: 'So did I, so do I [pushes Teresa], I still do' (*Eilish*, Yorkshire TV, 1995). Katie both is and isn't there, a shifting body memory and continued inscription on the flesh of her twin.

What these stories emphasize is the persistence of a dominant post-Enlightenment discourse in which our psychic investment in the corporeal is covered over by the illusion that the body is merely instrumental, a source only of impediment or advantage to the subject. The clarity of corporeal boundaries is what grounds existential and moral personhood, while the meeting with the other is premised on bodily self-determination and property rights in one's own body. The conjunction of two consciousnesses is characterized only in terms of a meeting of self and other, properly mediated by contract or by the calculation of individual best interests. But for conjoined twins, the other is also the self – a transgressive and indeterminate state in which corporeal, ontological and ultimately ethical boundaries are distorted and dissolved. What separation surgery attempts then – aside from cases where it is medically indicated to preserve life – is a reconstitution of autonomous subjecthood as the only proper way of being in the world. As Clark and Myser put it, the assumption is 'that conjoined life, precisely because of its imagined phenomenological *un*intelligibility must be intolerable' (1996: 351). And, one might add, intolerable to society rather than to the twins themselves. There is no sense here that corporeality might constitute the subject, only that a somehow foundational subject – or rather two – is thwarted by a monstrous body.

I want finally to look briefly at other forms of conjoined twins whose monstrous bodies do not afford the contemplation, theoretical or practical, of separation into self and other, although less radical modification may be possible. One specific case concerns parasitic twinning where the very naming speaks to a putative insult to an ideal of bodily self-determination; the other concerns the mirroring of heads on a singular body. In both instances the infants involved survived birth and lived for several years in a state of monstrosity. The appearances of the 17th-century Coloredo brothers – that is, the wholly formed Lazarus and his parasitic twin John Baptista – are extremely well documented in popular histories, contemporary ballads and official documents (Figure 1). Although for the most part they were viewed benignly as marvels, the existence of so extraordinary a body raised worrying questions. Here is an account from a pamphlet of 1640 refering to Lazarus, who:

> ... from one of his sides hath a twin brother growing, which was borne with him, and living still; though having sence and feeling, yet destitute of reason and understanding: whence

Figure 1 Lazarus and John Baptista Coloredo – woodcut illustrating 'The Two Inseparable Brothers' (London, 1637)
Source: Rollins (1927: 10)

methinks a disputable question might arise, whether as they have distinct lives, so they are possessed of two souls; or have but one imparted betwixt them both .... (1640 *A Certain Relation of the Hog-faced Gentlewoman*; quoted in Rollins, 1927: 8)

The second case was even more extraordinary, the more so in that the child involved survived until he was 4 years old, when reputedly he was killed by a cobra bite. The so-called Bengali boy was born with two heads – not unusual within the context of conjoined twins, except that the second head grew not from his neck but was attached upside down and back-to-front on the top of the child's scalp (Figure 2). The bone casing of the craniopagus skull, as it was known, was fused where crown met crown and, as a contemporary postmortem report to the Royal Society put it, 'the two brains were ... separate and distinct, having a complete partition between them' (Home, 1790). Moreover, the bodyless head during life was not in itself unusual in appearance, having well-formed facial features, ears and a crop of hair, and separate affect. Nonetheless, the anxiety that such an occurrence might be expected to generate was effaced by regarding the skull, not as the site of contested subjecthood, but merely as an object of bio-medical enquiry. The significance of the craniopagus skull to the British scientific community of the day was not, as it might have been in the past, an occasion for reflection on the notion of maternal imagination – though the initial report from

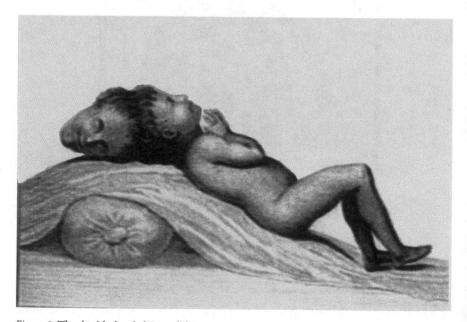

Figure 2 The double-headed Bengali boy
Source: Home (1790)

the East India Company was clearly obliged to assert that the mother had suffered no fright or accident during her pregnancy – but rather as ammunition in a whole medicalized controversy regarding the process of evolutionary development. As Evelleen Richards makes clear in her detailed analysis of that debate:

> ... historical monsters ... may be understood at one and the same time both as anatomical objects and as the embodiments of different strategies of power. (1994: 405)

In her understanding of what she calls 'politial anatomy' Richards is reluctant to pursue a Foucauldian deconstruction of what she sees as 'concrete historical events', but nonetheless her account does point up the discursive construction of the meanings inscribed on the monstrous body. The widespread scientific interest excited by the craniopagus skull, which became and remains a prize exhibit in the Hunterian Museum, indicates too that by the rationalist mid-18th century, monsters were – as before – a primary ground for competing discourses, but stripped now of questions of personal agency. For my own part, however, I want to return to those very questions.

If the issue of subjectivity or identity is at very least problematized in the indistinct corporeality of those conjoined twins with two relatively well-formed bodies, both internal and external, or more remarkably where two heads append the same body, then it is radically challenged by such incomplete instances of doubling as those considered above. In her essay 'Freaks', Liz Grosz remarks:

> ... it is no longer clear that there are two identities, even if the bodily functions of the parasitic twin occur independently of the will or awareness of the other. In such cases, is there one subject or two? (1991: 34)

That question clearly haunts the historical accounts of the cases I have mentioned. Like the distinctive affect of the two heads of the Bengali boy which Everard Home recorded, contemporary descriptions of the Coloredo brothers make frequent reference to the independent physical sensitivity of the parasitic body:

Th' imperfect once the small poxe had
Which made the other brother sad,
but he had never any,
And if you nip it by the arme,
Or do it any little harme,
(this hath beene tride by many)
It like an infant (with voyce weake)
Will cry out though it cannot speake,
as sensible of paine,
Which yet the other feeleth not
(1637, 'The Two Inseparable Brothers', quoted in Rollins, 1927: 13)

What marks a difference between the two cases, however, is that whereas the

Coloredos are always referred to and named as two distinct people, and indeed each was baptized according to report, the Bengali boy is already singular. Although surgical intervention was not a possibility in either case, a discursive normalization of the excessive subject has taken place. That the singularity of all subject bodies is similarly constructed and reiterated by regimes of normalization that defer the slippage of excessive embodiment is obscured by the insistence that monstrosity is radically other, the exceptional case that secures the normative standard.

So what type of subjectivity or identity could fit such a range of differences, and how does the monstrous corporeality of my examples imbricate with the sense of self? Where Liz Grosz, in her paper 'Freaks' (1991), posits a continuum of identity – ranging from the autonomous, self-complete and individuated subject, which Western discourse assumes as the standard for all, to a non-differentiated, quasi-collective subject in which the symbolic moment of distinction between self and other is endlessly deferred – I am inclined to caution. The desire for full self-presence is, I think, never realized, and results only in a phantasmatic structure of subjectivity. As I understand it, monsters both define the limits of the singular embodied subject, and reflect our own ultimately insecure and unstable identities. As Rosi Braidotti puts it: 'the monstrous other is both liminal and structurally central to our perception of normal human subjectivity' (1996: 141). And it is the move to forcibly impose the norm of one body/one mind, the move to erase difference either by exclusion or by processes of normalization, that underlines the instability of the ideal. Where monsters blatantly blur the parameters of being, they invoke in us all – and this seems particularly true of the doubling of twinned bodies – both a nostalgia for identification and the horror of incorporation. They demonstrate that the relation between self and other, as with body and body, is chiasmatic, precisely insofar as corporeality and subjectivity – body and mind – are themselves folded back into each other, overflowing, enmeshed and mutually constitutive.

Though bodily modification may hope to avert the overtly transgressive, its very practice alerts us to the crisis at the boundaries of the body which is never one. As the in-between, as *différance*, the monstrous shows us that neither the one nor the two is proof against deconstruction. Promise and risk lie equally in the move beyond/before – it is undecidable – the one that determines ontological and corporeal unity, and the two that mark difference as opposition, and relationship as the quasi-contractual exchange between autonomous beings. It is the necessarily incomplete abjection of monstrosity that guards against the successful closure of what Derrida has called 'an illegitimately delimited subject' (1991: 108). If, then, such closure is merely a myth of modernity, the attempted limitation of the monstrous body by both surgical and discursive means is doubly doomed to failure. As such I read monsters as hopeful, the potential site of not just a reconceived ontology, but a new form of ethics. To let go of determinacy is to open up the possibility of reconfiguring relational economies. Bearing in mind his naming of the calculable as fundamentally unable to deliver ethical content, I will give Derrida the final word:

> A future that would not be monstrous would not be a future; it would be already a predictable, calculable and programmable tomorrow. All experience open to the future is prepared or prepares itself to welcome the monstrous *arrivant*. (1995: 307)

Notes

1. The 'truth' or otherwise of such accounts is not at issue, and in any case makes appeal to a fixed and given reality which is at odds with my understanding of the construction of all bodies. What matters is the nature of the discursive context in which questions of corporeality figure.

2. Aristotle – whose influence in the medieval and early modern field of teratology was ubiquitous – implies in *De Generatione Animalium* that all twins are monstrous. As Thijssen explains: 'By monsters, Aristotle does not just mean creatures which, due to some pathological process, are misshapen, but, much more generally, all creatures which are out of the ordinary in the sense that they are not the result of the common course of Nature' (1987: 240). Surprisingly, then, the Biddenden Maids reputedly born in Kent in 1100 may be the exception to the rule that conjoined twins are certainly monstrous. Tradition has it that they led an exemplary Christian life, and on their death at the age of 34 endowed a charity for the needy of the parish.

3. The twins' body is merged from the upper thoracic area giving them just two legs and two functioning arms – with two other residual upper limb stumps having been already excised in the expectation of future separation surgery. There are separate hearts and lungs, but other organs are single.

4. For a rather different documentary narrative of medical intervention, in which the concerns of the clinic were overriding, and for which the filming itself realized 'a certain technologized medical gaze', see Clark and Myser's account (1996) of the separation of the Thai conjoined twins, Dao and Duan.

5. In psychoanalytic terms, the mirroring process (both literal and metaphorical), by which the infant comes to see itself as separate and distinct, allows accession to a self-image of corporeal unity that covers over the reality of the fragmentary and uncoordinated motor experiences of the child (Lacan, 1977). As an ego ideal, however, the resultant body map is precarious, having 'a psychical interior, which requires continual stabilization, and a corporeal exterior, which remains labile, open to many meanings' (Grosz, 1994: 43).

References

Bedford, Thomas (1635) *A True and Certain Relation of a Strange Birth which was Born at Stonehouse in the Parish of Plymouth, the 20th of October, 1635*. London: Anne Griffin.

Braidotti, Rosi (1996) 'Signs of Wonder and Traces of Doubt: On Teratology and Embodied Differences', in Nina Lykke and Rosi Braidotti (eds) *Between Monsters, Goddesses and Cyborgs: Feminist Confrontations with Science, Medicine and Cyberspace*. London: Zed Press.

Butler, Judith (1993) *Bodies that Matter: On the Discursive Limits of 'Sex'*. London: Routledge.

Canguilhem, Georges (1964) 'Monstrosity and the Monstrous', *Diogenes* 40: 27–43.

Clark, David L. and Catherine Myser (1996) 'Being Humaned: Medical Documentaries and the

Hyperrealization of Conjoined Twins', in Rosemarie Garland Thomson (ed.) *Freakery: Cultural Spectacles of the Extraordinary Body*. New York: New York University Press.

Derrida, Jacques (1991) ' "Eating Well", or the Calculation of the Subject: An Interview with Jacques Derrida', in Eduardo Cadava, Peter Connor and Jean-Luc Nancy (eds) *Who Comes After the Subject?* London: Routledge.

Derrida, Jacques (1995) 'Passages – From Traumatism to Promise', in *Points . . . Interviews, 1974–1994*, edited by Elisabeth Weber. Stanford, CA: Stanford University Press.

Descartes, René (1990) 'Meditations on the First Philosophy', in S.M. Cahn (ed.) *Classics in Western Philosophy*. Indiapolis, IN: Hackett.

Dunn, Katherine (1989) *Geek Love*. New York: Warner.

Friedman, John Block (1981) *The Monstrous Races in Medieval Art and Thought*. Cambridge, MA: Harvard University Press.

Grosz, Elizabeth (1991) 'Freaks', *Social Semiotics* 1(2): 22–38.

Grosz, Elizabeth (1994) *Volatile Bodies: Toward a Corporeal Feminism*. Bloomington: Indiana University Press.

Haraway, Donna (1989) 'A Manifesto for Cyborgs: Science, Technology and Socialist Feminism in the 1980s', in Elizabeth Weed (ed.) *Coming to Terms*. London: Routledge.

Haraway, Donna (1992) 'The Promises of Monsters: A Regenerative Politics for Inappropriate/d Others', pp. 295–337 in Lawrence Grossberg et al. (eds) *Cultural Studies*. London: Routledge.

Home, Everard (1790) 'An Account of a Child with a Double Head', *Philosophical Transactions of the Royal Society* 80: 296–305.

Kristeva, Julia (1982) *The Powers of Horror: An Essay on Abjection*. New York: Columbia University Press.

Lacan, Jacques (1977) 'The Mirror Stage as Formative of the Function of the I', in *Ecrits: A Selection*, trans. Alan Sheridan. New York: W.W. Norton.

New Encyclopaedia Britannica (1992) 'Biological Growth and Development', in vol. 20 Macropaedia. Chicago: Encyclopaedia Britannica Inc.

Richards, Evelleen (1994) 'A Political Anatomy of Monsters, Hopeful or Otherwise: Teratogeny, Transcendentalism, and Evolutionary Theorising', *Isis* 85: 377–411.

Rollins, Hyder E. (1927) *The Pack of Autolycus*. Cambridge, MA: Harvard University Press.

Shildrick, Margrit (1997) *Leaky Bodies and Boundaries: Feminism, Postmodernism and (Bio)ethics*. London: Routledge.

Thijssen, J.M. (1987) 'Twins as Monsters: Albertus Magnus's Theory of the Generation of Twins and Its Philosophical Context', *Bulletin of the History of Medicine* 61: 237–46.

Margrit Shildrick is SURI Research Fellow at Staffordshire University. She writes extensively on the body, and is the author of *Leaky Bodies and Boundaries* (1997, Routledge), and co-editor with Janet Price of *Vital Signs: Feminist Reconfigurations of the Bio/logical Body* (1998) and *Feminist Theory and the Body: A Reader* (1999, both Edinburgh University Press).

Marinetti, Chopin, Stelarc and the Auratic Intensities of the Postmodern Techno-Body

NICHOLAS ZURBRUGG

It's a strange thing about the 'new'. . . . At first it shocks, even repels, such a man as myself, but in a few days, or a month or a year, we rush to it drooling at the mouth, as if it were a fruit, an apple in winter. (Williams, 1979)

Watching Henri Chopin perform I thought of a powerful vampire, a super-Dracula perhaps, and yet there was nothing malignant about him or his presence. Perhaps it was his power, the erotic vitality of his performing with the microphone, the curious abstraction of his sounds which transcended specific reference but always maintained their intensity. (Higgins, 1992a: 23)

'Anti-Auratic' Theory and Auratic Multimedia Practices

According to theorists such as Lash and Urry, we now inhabit an 'emphatically anti-auratic' culture which 'signals the demise of aesthetic "aura" in a number of ways' (1987: 286). While this reading of 20th-century multimedia culture is widely confirmed by the predominantly negative generalizations of many of the most influential modernist and postmodern media theorists, it is significantly challenged by the finest practices of the modernist and postmodern multimedia avant-gardes.

Indeed, as becomes evident once one examines the century-long tensions between 'anti-auratic' media theory and auratic multimedia practices (discussed here in terms of the increasingly apocalyptic hypotheses of Walter Benjamin, Jean Baudrillard and Paul Virilio, and in terms of the increasingly sophisticated research of artists such as Marinetti, Henri Chopin and Stelarc), the most

Body & Society © 1999 SAGE Publications (London, Thousand Oaks and New Delhi),
Vol. 5(2–3): 93–115
[1357–034X(199906/09)5:2–3;93–115;008863]

momentous postmodern technological mutations of the body devastatingly discredit the myth of postmodern multimedia culture's supposedly post-auratic register.

Put more plainly, new forms of techno-performance such as the French sound poet Henri Chopin's 'vampire'-like projections of pre-recorded and live vocalic 'intensity' and the Australian cybernetic artist Stelarc's equally disturbing explorations of 'electronic voodoo' (Stelarc, 1995: 48) compellingly justify the redefinition of postmodern multimedia culture as a chronologically, technologically and artistically distinct era, alive with inventive energy. Judged in terms of its successive specific practices, postmodern media culture seems as well-served by visionary artists regenerating auratic creativity as it is ill-served by myopic theoretical generalization envisaging the 'postmodern condition' as a whole as a catastrophically distinct era impoverished by the cumulative effects of:

1. the alleged discontinuity and decline between modernist and postmodern cultures (Jameson, 1991);
2. the alleged 'death' of the postmodern avant-garde and 'failure' of the modernist avant-garde (Bürger, 1984);
3. the alleged eradication of 'aura' by modernist and postmodern media culture (Benjamin, 1979).

As these pages will suggest, contemporary cultural theory's and contemporary media theory's most cherished, most seductive and most masochistic master narrative – the myth of postmodern multimedia culture's terminal decay into an era in which 'there are no more masterpieces' (Jameson, 1991: 78) – becomes untenable once one acknowledges that the chronologically distinct mentalities of 'modern' and 'postmodern' culture differ not so much in terms of postmodernism's allegedly irreversible decline and fall, as in terms of the unprecedented ways in which postmodern multimedia practitioners may now both technologically trivialize and technologically revitalize corporeal symptoms of authorial singularity.

Successive technocultural avant-gardes repeatedly celebrate revitalized auratic creativity. For Marinetti's 'Destruction of Syntax-Imagination without Strings-Words-in-Freedom' manifesto of 1913, for example, the early 20th century heralded the age of 'man multiplied by the machine', ushering in a 'New mechanical sense, a fusion of instinct with the efficiency of motors and conquered forces' (1973: 97). For mid-century postmodern techno-poets such as Chopin, early tape-recording technologies inaugurated an 'enormous expansion of human expression' (1982a: 74). Likewise, for late postmodern cybernauts such as Stelarc, 'new sensor technology' and 'computer software' allow artists to construct 'virtual reality environments with intelligent interaction' in a way 'which wasn't really possible . . . in the sixties' (1994: 377).

Constantly refining ever more innovative techno-creativity, the modern and postmodern avant-gardes offer an unbroken lineage of precisely the kind of outstanding multimediated experimentation that Benjamin at his most lucid equates with this century's 'richest energies' (1979: 239). Ironically, modern and postmodern technocultural theory equally persistently overlooks and under-values the originality and authenticity of technocultural creativity by repeatedly diagnosing new mass-mediated practices as symptoms of 'anti-auratic' mass-cultural trivia. Following Benjamin's suggestion in 'The Work of Art in the Age of Mechanical Reproduction' that 'aura . . . vanishes' (1979: 231) from commercial cinema (and by implication, from mass-media culture as a whole), postmodern cultural theorists such as Baudrillard, Virilio, Lash and Urry have tirelessly identified updated traces of endemic 'mass mediatic infantilisation' (Guattari, 1995: 133).

For example, arguing that late postmodern 'automatism' eradicates the alien-ating impact of 19th-century industrial culture (when one could still identify a 'relationship, even if conflictual, between man and machine'), and identifying the demise of the machine/body interface, Baudrillard's essay 'Metamorphoses, Metaphors, Metastases' (1988) provocatively concludes that as 'machine opera-tors' rather than 'actors', we are ourselves new 'kinds of automata'.

> Mechanical machines . . . were still machines with alterity, an other, whereas here it is a huge celibate machine, completely self-referential, and at this point one wonders where the real world is. . . . This kind of artificial world, much more performative than ever before, completely automatized, is also . . . an exclusion of man, of the real world, of all referentiality. (1996: 217–18)

Félix Guattari's *Chaosmosis*, by contrast, identifies a more subtle dichotomy between bankrupt 'mechanic' mass-mediated culture and the salutary aesthetic potential of what he terms 'machinic' production, 'utterly foreign to mechanism' (1995: 108). Insisting that 'Making yourself machinic . . . can become a crucial instrument for subjective resingularisation', and looking forward to new practices facilitating 'the machinic return of orality' (1995: 97) and effecting 'a reinvention of the subject itself' (1995: 31), *Chaosmosis* resolutely concludes:

> Machinic mutations understood in the largest sense . . . should no longer trigger in us defensive reflexes, backward-looking nervous twitches. It is absurd to impute to them the mass media stupefaction which four-fifths of humanity currently experience. . . . Quite the contrary: the junction of informatics, telematics, and the audiovisual will perhaps allow . . . us to escape . . . from the erosion of meaning which is occurring everywhere. (1995: 97)

The alternating currents between Marinetti's, Chopin's, Stelarc's, Baudrillard's,

Virilio's and Guattari's arguments succinctly identify the antithetical ways in which the modern/postmodern interface can be constructed. Viewed, for example, in terms of the discontinuity between Marinetti's early celebration and Benjamin's, Baudrillard's and Virilio's subsequent denigration of technoculture, the postmodern can be seen as an 'anti-modern' era, increasingly distanced from the kind of cultural authenticity generally associated with 'tradition' and 'ritual function' (Benjamin, 1979: 223, 226) or with the 'body of the fable' (Baudrillard, 1998: 45).

Alternatively, viewed in terms of the increasingly refined 'machinic' continuity animating Marinetti's, Chopin's, Stelarc's and Viola's research, the postmodern can be seen as a 'past-modern' epoch, rich in technocultural revolutions and revelations. As Viola and Chopin emphasize, such innovation is often both technologically discontinuous and aesthetically continuous with past cultural tradition. For Viola, 'fascinating relationships between ancient and modern technologies become evident' (1995: 106), and for Chopin, technocultural practices permit an art of 'synthesis', advancing 'towards the future, while at the same time remaining aware of everything that has been written' (1992b: 51).

Viewed from both of these perspectives, postmodern culture is most accurately defined as an epoch at once positively and negatively 'past-modern'. At its poorest and richest extremes, postmodern media culture either desingularizes or resingularizes auratic subjectivity as never before. At their best, postmodern practices explore 'the edge of things, doing something that no one else is doing, putting two ideas together that haven't been put together before' (Viola, 1995: 179). In turn, at its best, postmodern cultural theory similarly refocuses at 'the edge of things', 'putting together' exceptions to its general rules. Implicitly conceding that explicit symptoms of mass-cultural malaise only partially exemplify the complexity of postmodern media culture, Benjamin's, Baudrillard's and Virilio's most perceptive subtexts unexpectedly confirm many of the earlier insights of modern and postmodern avant-garde artists such as Marinetti, Chopin, Stelarc and Viola.

My central argument, then, is that analysis of the divergences between 20th-century media theory and media practice reveals how – across the decades – overgeneralized theory has consistently neglected the auratic intensities of modern and postmodern techno-performance. The following pages preface examination of the modern and postmodern techno-avant-garde's attempts to identify new dimensions of 'tactile sense', 'new ways to educate the handicapped' (Marinetti, 1972b: 111–12) and new strategies for perpetuating 'life in general, and intelligence in particular' (Stelarc, 1995: 49), with examination of those antithetical theoretical strategies claiming that media cultures either presuppose 'no intelligence' (Benjamin, 1979: 240–1) or predispose us to the misfortunes of the 'handicapped'

(Baudrillard, 1988: 51) and the 'spastic' (Virilio, 1997: 20). Those dismayed by panoramic perspectives might recollect William Carlos Williams' advice to readers of Allen Ginsberg's *Howl*: 'Hold back the edges of your gowns, Ladies, we are going through hell' (in Ginsberg, 1966: 8).

Benjamin, Dulac and the 'Richest Energies' of the Cinematic Body

Discussing the seemingly anti-auratic limbo of late modern and early postmodern media culture in 1936, Walter Benjamin introduced his general sense that performative 'aura ... withers in the age of mechanical reproduction' (1979: 223) in terms of Pirandello's claim that in silent film:

> The film actor ... feels ... exiled not only from the stage but also from himself.... he feels inexplicable emptiness: his body loses its corporeality, it evaporates, it is deprived of reality, life, voice.... The projector will play with his shadow before the public, and he himself must be content to play before the camera. (1979: 231)

Sound-film, Benjamin adds, compounds this sense of exile by requiring the actor 'to operate with his whole living person' while at the same time 'forgoing' gestural and vocal interplay before a live audience.

> For aura is tied to his presence; there can be no replica of it. The aura which, on stage, emanates from Macbeth, cannot be separated for the spectators from that of the actor. However, the singularity of the shot in the studio is that the camera is substituted for the public. Consequently, the aura that envelops the actor vanishes, and with it the aura of the figure he portrays. (1979: 231)

But need the film actor and the film audience necessarily be 'exiled' from 'the realm of the "beautiful semblance"' (1979: 232) usually bought about by 'aura which, on stage ... cannot be separated for the spectators from that of the actor' (1979: 231)? Are emanations of performative aura – or what Barthes calls the 'grain' (1977a) of authorial presence – exclusive to live gestures before a live audience? Or can the techno-modified body and voice generate both the 'golem'-like aura that Higgins (1992b: 25) discerns in Henri Chopin's multimedia performances, and the soulful poperatic/poperotic popauratic alchemy that rock aficionados Bergman and Horn identify in Phil Spector's genius for building 'multilayered cakes out of songs by the Ronettes and the Crystals, filling in any cracks in his "wall of sound" with over-dubbed violins, angel choirs, and shaking bells' (1985: 45)?

Benjamin most memorably qualifies his emphasis upon the 'anti-auratic' quality of media culture when remarking that new technologies may well realize past, present and future performative aspirations far more effectively than past ritualistic practices. Insisting that 'One of the foremost tasks of art has always been the creation of a demand which could be fully satisfied only later', he crucially observes:

The history of every art form shows critical epochs in which a certain art form aspires to effects which could be fully obtained only with a changed technical standard, that is to say, in a new art form. The extravagances and crudities of art which thus appear, particularly in the so-called decadent epochs, actually arise from the nucleus of its richest energies. In recent years, such barbarisms were abundant in Dadaism. It is only now that its impulse becomes discernible: Dadaism attempted to create by pictorial – and literary – means the effects which the public today seeks in the film. (1979: 239)

Ironically, these lines both clarify and obscure the significance of Dadaist creativity. On the one hand, they lucidly predict how 'changed technical standards' generate effects surpassing previous technologies and traditions. But, on the other hand, they loosely equate such innovation with the superficial 'effects which the public today seeks in the film', treating Hollywood's and Dada's agendas as one and the same. Rephrased more accurately: Dadaism attempted to create by pictorial – and literary – means the vast array of potentially auratic multimediated visual, textual, sonic and performative artistic effects which the public today only glimpses in commercially correct cinema's predominantly post-auratic practices.

As the modernist film-maker Germaine Dulac points out in 'The Essence of Cinema: The Visual Idea' of 1925, commercial cinematic aesthetics differ considerably from the aspirations of those avant-garde artists who, if 'drawn into making concessions to the taste of the public ... feel they have committed treason' (1987a: 37). Reasoning that cinema 'has not achieved its real place as an intrinsic art' because 'the public, suspicious a priori of every invention, and coming to the support of tradition, has filed it between theatre and literature' (1987a: 39), and noting that whereas 'the industry does not attach itself zealously to the contribution of art; the avant-garde, with its opposite impulse, considers nothing else', Dulac concludes:

We can use the term 'avant-garde' for any film whose technique, employed with a view to a renewed expressiveness of image and sound, breaks with established traditions to search out, in the strictly visual and auditory realm, new emotional chords. . . . The sincere avant-garde film has this fundamental quality of containing, behind a sometimes inaccessible surface, the seeds of the discoveries which are capable of advancing film towards the cinematic form of the future. (Dulac, 1987b: 43–4)

While Dulac suggests that despite its 'inaccessible surface' avant-garde film is most notable for the auratic intensity of its 'new emotional chords', Benjamin rather differently reasons that the immediacy of Dadaist collages strike the spectator 'like a bullet', promoting 'a demand for the film, the distracting element of which is also primarily tactile, being based on changes of place and focus which periodically assail the spectator'; and that in consequence, both avant-garde art and commercial film contribute to a post-auratic culture prohibiting 'contemplation and evaluation', and in the terms of the French writer, Georges Duhamel, requiring 'no concentration' and presupposing 'no intelligence' (1979: 240–1).

To be sure, Benjamin briefly backtracks, noting how slow motion film 'extends our comprehension of the necessities which rule our lives', how enlarged snapshots reveal 'entirely new structural formations of the subject', and how 'The camera introduces us to unconscious optics' (1979: 238–9). Neglecting such affirmative insights, one all too easily equates Benjamin with the negative claims that early media culture simultaneously incites the post-contemplative register of Dadaist art, the post-auratic impact of commercial film and the suicidal 'sense perception' of those Futurist artists anticipating mechanically multiplied destruction 'as an aesthetic pleasure' (1979: 244).

Marinetti's manifesto 'War, the World's Only Hygiene' (1911–15) certainly welcomes both 'the first electric war' (1972a: 107) and the time when Italy will become 'wholly vivified, shaken, and bridled by . . . new electric forces!' (1972a: 104). But as Marinetti adds, such utterance is literary rather than literal, and almost of necessity attacks Italy's '*passéism*' and 'chronic pessimism' with the rhetoric of 'artificial optimism' (1972a: 108). Baudrillard similarly specifies that his speculations should 'not be read as a realist text' (1993a: 132), and defending the 'analytical capacity' of 'Myths' (in Virilio and Lotringer, 1983: 11), Virilio explains:

> I don't like two-and-two-is-four-type writing. . . . I work in staircases . . . I begin a sentence, I work out an idea and when I consider it suggestive enough, I jump to another idea without bothering with the development. . . . I try to reach the tendency. Tendency is the change of level. (1983: 39)

Such speculative 'jumps' often rival Marinetti's most 'artificial' hypotheses, and both artistic and cultural theory frequently wield comparable 'two-and-two-is-five' rhetoric. But whereas effusive artistic polemic is usually demythologized and re-legitimated by its authors' innovative practice, mythological theory frequently remystifies its concerns by refining accounts of the kind of entropic 'Tendency' traced by Baudrillard's ruminations on the 'metastatic' imperfections of the postmodern body and the perfections of 'the body of the fable'.

Baudrillard and the 'Metastatic' Body

Asking 'Where has the body of the fable gone?', Baudrillard's essay 'Metamorphoses, Metaphors, Metastases' introduces its theme as:

> The body of metamorphosis, the one of a pure chain of appearances, of a timeless and sexless fluidity of forms, the ceremonial body brought to life by mythology, or the Peking Opera and

Oriental theatre, as well as by dance: a non-individual body without desire, yet capable of all metamorphoses – a body freed from the mirror of itself, yet given over to all seduction. (1988: 45)

For Baudrillard, the 'power of metamorphosis' lies 'at the root of all seduction', and as 'a body freed from all subjectivity, a body recovering the animal felinity of the pure object', the body of metamorphosis 'knows neither metaphor nor the operation of meaning', and resists 'symbolic order' (1988: 46–7). Subsequently going the way of all flesh, 'pure' metamorphosis deteriorates into an inferior 'metaphoric' register whenever 'a symbolic order appears' and 'the body becomes ... a metaphoric scene of the sexual reality' (1988: 47).

At such points of 'degeneration', the body no longer offers the polyvalent impact of a 'sumptuous theatre of multiple initiatory forms', but evinces 'the scene of a single scenario, the unconscious sexual phantasmatic' that Baudrillard equates with 'the stage of phantasies and the metaphor of the subject' (1988: 48). Worse ensues. 'After the bodies of metamorphosis and metaphor follows the body of metastasis' (1988: 48–9). While the 'body of metaphor' reflects 'meaning in relation to language' (1988: 50), the 'body of metastasis' inhabits the void that Baudrillard equates with a 'deprivation of meaning and territory' and with the 'lobotomy of the body', where there is 'no more soul, no more metaphor of the body' and 'the fable of the unconscious itself has lost most of its resonance' (1988: 50–1).

In Baudrillard's judgement, most of humanity have already dumbed down into this kind of automatized, mechanically metastatic limbo. Locked among the 'cybernetic peripeteia of the body', where all 'passions have disappeared', it would seem that we are all 'mutants' from 'a biological, genetic and cybernetic point of view (1988: 51), and can at best protest:

What has become of seduction today, of passion, of this force which wrests the human being from all localization, from all objective definition; what has become of this fatality, or this superior irony of this evasive aspiration, or this alternative strategy? (1988: 53–4)

Baudrillard offers such searching questions evasive answers. Compared to the 'furious epoch' (1989: 40) of the modernist 1930s when intellectual dinosaurs roamed European capitals, late postmodern culture seems a dead-end in which irony's last embers emerge only 'in a disobedience to behavioural norms, in the failure of programs, in covert dysfunction, in the silence at the horizon of meaning'. 'Transcendence', it seems, 'has drawn its last breath' (1988: 54–5), and since we now confront an increasingly 'altered, inhuman and abnormal universe', our best strategy may well be to observe how the survival strategies of 'the handicapped' apparently 'precede us on the path towards mutation and dehumanization' (1988: 51–2).

Not surprisingly, perhaps, Baudrillard's conclusions reverse gear, echoing the confidence with which the veteran postmodern composer John Cage affirms that life works best 'once one gets one's mind and one's desires out of its way and lets it act of its own accord' (1983: 12), when guardedly identifying the dynamics with which the more or less mythological intervention of the 'exponential' unpredictably resolves the dichotomy between 'connecting and disconnecting', whenever it 'chances upon us, as it does for things when they are left to their own devices' (Baudrillard, 1988: 55–6).

What ultimately happens to the 'body of the fable', Baudrillard implies, is that it becomes even more fabulistic than one ever imagined, be this as a quality of dynamic metamorphosis that degenerates into metaphorical symbolism and into deterritorialized metastasis; as a quality of ceremonial physical fluidity and power whose decline can only be averted by learning from the handicapped; or as a kind of benign otherworldly 'force' that one hopes will always be with one. At this point Baudrillard's conclusions glide light years away from the facts of contemporary practice.

Nevertheless, having 'reconsidered technology in terms of photography', Baudrillard's subsequent reflections on media culture reassess his 'pejorative' tendency to 'typecast' technology as 'a medium of alienation and depersonalization', and outline a 'second' position 'more interested in seeing technology as an instrument of magic' (1997: 38) that at best reveals 'the pataphysical delicacy of the world' in images offering 'stunning clarity' (1993b: 153, 155). Indeed, according to Baudrillard's still more breathtaking conclusions in his introduction to his collected photographs in Car l'illusion ne s'oppose pas à la réalité. . .' (1998), it is precisely by generating this kind of 'magic and dangerous reality', according to 'a principle of condensation diametrically opposed to the principal of dilution and dispersion informing all our images today', that 'photography has refound the aura that it lost with cinema'.

At such moments, Baudrillard suggests, one encounters the auratic presence of the 'Silence of the photograph'; an ideal 'material, objective, autonomy' (rather than subjective autonomy), that he detects in the 'cadaverous immobility' of early photographic subjects, and now finds most evident in his most successful photographic evocations of the dynamic stasis of particular objects. Resisting the 'over sentimental' quality of human subjects, and remarking that 'Only objects have no sexual or sentimental aura', Baudrillard defines the objective aura of 'true immobility' in terms of 'a weight at the end of its pendulum, whose oscillations have almost come to a standstill while still vibrating imperceptibly'.

> It's the immobility of an instant in time – that of photographic 'instantanéité', behind which one always detects a sense of movement, but only a sense of it – the image existing in order to respect this movement, without making it visible and eradicating its illusion. This is the kind

of immobility that things dream about, this is the kind of immobility that we dream about. (1998, my translation)

While Baudrillard's photographs commemorate predominantly objective variants of this kind of 'immobility' (although his more recent photographs, such as *Paris 1996*, the final image in *Car l'illusion ne s'oppose pas à la réalité* [1998], include Giacometti-like standing figures, counterbalanced by right-angled shadows), one discovers their subjective counterpart in images of the partially animated, partially frozen, gestural immanence that French photographer Françoise Janicot captures in such images of contemporary performance artists and performance poets as her marvellous 1980 portrait of Henri Chopin at the Pompidou Centre, when – as Australian poet Ania Walwicz puts it – 'wings lift . . . his arms stretch . . . henri chopin the warrior eagle soars the amazing the glorious in a cathedral of sound he opens his bird eyes he flies his wings in a flight of sound he lifts up now' (1992: 23).

Virilio and the 'Terminal' Body

Like Baudrillard, Virilio predicates his most trenchant critiques of postmodern media culture upon a utopian concept of the authentic body, introduced in terms of 'the wonderful biblical image of Jacob wrestling with the angel'.

> Jacob met his God in the person of an angel and he wrestled with this angel for a whole night and at the end of the night he said to the angel, 'Bless me, because I have fought all night.' What does this symbolize? It means that Jacob did not want to sleep before God. . . . He wanted to remain a man before God . . . he fought rather than just sleeping as though he was before an idol. Technology places us in the same situation. We have to fight against it rather than sleeping before it. (1998)

Virtually asking 'where has the biblical body gone?', Virilio's *Polar Inertia* traces the ways in which the postmodern body enters a state of seemingly incurable metastasis, as animated activity gives way to static, screen-based interactivity, and 'domestic inertia' assumes the *'technical equivalent of the coma'* (1994: 133, 135, my translation). In turn, Virilio's *Open Sky* posits that 'radiotechnologies . . . will shortly turn on their heads not only . . . our *territorial body*, but most importantly, the nature of the individual and their *animal body*' (1997: 11). At this point, Virilio concludes, our situation is 'no different from that experienced by any number of spastics' whom 'the critical force of the circumstance of technology' transform into 'models of the new man' (1997: 17), as 'the super-equipped able-bodied person' becomes 'almost the exact equivalent of the motorized and wired disabled person' (1977: 11).

> Doomed to inertia, the interactive being transfers his natural capacities for movement and displacement to probes and scanners . . . to the detriment of his own faculties of apprehension

of the real, after the example of the para- or quadriplegic who can guide by remote control – teleguide – his environment, his abode. . . . Having been first *mobile*, then *motorized*, man will thus become *motile*, deliberately limiting his body's areas of influence to a few gestures. (1997: 16–17)

Noting how 'the urbanization of the actual body of the city dweller' increasingly introduces the 'catastrophic figure' of the '*citizen-terminal* . . . based on the pathological model of the "spastic" wired to control his/her domestic environment without having physically to stir' (1997: 20), Virilio predicts that once the cybernetically modified body attains 'that point of inertia' at which its weight 'becomes identical to that of a planet' it will become 'the perfect equivalent of a star, an asteroid' (1994: 166, my translation), mutating into a 'weightless *man-planet* whom nothing can now really protect', or what he thinks of as 'a body-without-a-soul, a profane body' at the mercy of 'a science-without-a-conscience' (1995: 113–14).

Like Baudrillard, however, Virilio occasionally identifies significant exceptions to his most monodimensional predictions. For example, while mercilessly denouncing the 'publicity' mentality's indiscriminate claim that 'Multimedia are wonderful!' (1996: 123), Virilio countenances the possibility that more substantial miracles such as Bernadette Soubirous's mystical revelations offer the kind of 'extra-ordinary reality' for which 'you'd give a whole lifetime' (1991: 38–9); concedes that media art may equally convey 'a quality of truth . . . that clearly corresponds to that of the great writers, the great painters (1991: 120); and passionately defends the 'enormous curiosity' (1991: 123) that he associates with affirmative investigation.

> I hope that my remarks . . . haven't led to any kind of misunderstanding. My research is not at all opposed to technology or technological performance. . . . Unfortunately, I realize that many people claim that I am apocalyptic, negative, pessimistic. But all of that is out of date – it doesn't rise to the heights of the situation! (1996: 122–3)

Still more movingly defending those creative insights which rise to the 'heights' of the situation, Dulac stirringly concludes:

> Occasionally, an idea with no precedent springs from a prophetic brain, with no preparation, and we are surprised. We do not understand it and we have difficulty accepting it. Should we not, then, contemplate this idea religiously . . . with a fresh intelligence, stripped of all tradition, avoiding reducing it to our own level of understanding, in order, on the contrary, to raise ourselves up to it and expand our understanding with what it brings us? (1987b: 36)

Huysmans, Marinetti and the Modernist Body

While Baudrillard's and Virilio's most extreme fables drive cultural theory to its lowest depths when equating the future with the 'handicapped' and the 'spastic',

Huysmans' *Against Nature*, of 1884, Marinetti's mid-to-late modernist multi-media experiments, and Chopin's and Stelarc's early-to-late postmodern multi-media research, all discuss the advantages of the technologically enhanced body with a far more 'fresh intelligence'. For example, virtually anticipating virtual reality, Des Esseintes, the hero of Huysmans' symbolist novel *Against Nature*, combines 'ingenious mechanical fishes driven by clockwork', the texture of 'artificial seaweed' and 'the smell of tar' in a domestic environment – or 'installation' – allowing him 'to enjoy . . . all the sensations of a long sea-voyage, without ever leaving home' (Huysmans, 1968: 34–5). Here, he reflects:

> . . . one can enjoy, just as easily as on the material plane, imaginary pleasures similar in all respects to the pleasures of reality. . . . The main thing is to know how to set about it, to be able to concentrate your attention . . . sufficiently to bring about the desired hallucination and so substitute the vision of a reality for the reality itself. (1968: 35–6)

In turn, Marinetti's 'Tactilism' manifesto of 1924 explains how his attempts to both 'educate my tactile sense' and discover 'new ways to educate the handicapped' (1972b: 111–12) begin with the undertakings:

1. to wear gloves for several days, during which time the brain will force the condensation into your hands of a desire for different tactile sensations;
2. to swim underwater in the sea, trying to distinguish interwoven currents and different temperatures tactilistically;
3. every night, in complete darkness, to recognize and enumerate every object in your bedroom. (1972b: 110)

Noting that these exercises revealed categories of 'flat', 'soft' and 'sensual' values, Marinetti describes his subsequent attempt to incorporate these qualities into *Sudan–Paris*, an 'abstract suggestive tactile table', offering the first example of a 'still-embryonic tactile art' (1972b: 110–11).

> In its *Sudan* part this table has spongy material, sandpaper, wool, pig's bristle, and wire bristle. (*Crude, greasy, rough, sharp, burning tactile values, that evoke African visions in the mind of the toucher.*) . . . In the *Paris* part, the table has silk, watered silk, velvet, and large and small feather. (*Soft, very delicate, warm and cool at once, artificial, civilized.*) (1972b: 111)

Both Des Esseintes and Marinetti typify avant-garde experimentation's tendency to begin by exploring unfamiliar realms of tactile sensation and deprivation. Des Esseintes, for example, surrounds himself with 'colours which would appear stronger and clearer in artificial light' (Huysmans, 1968: 28), eats in a 'hermetically sealed' room (1968: 33), attempts to 'exchange' sexual identity with the androgynous 'Miss Urania' (1968: 110–11), and dines upon a 'peptone enema' – the 'ultimate deviation from the norm' (1968: 208).

For its part, Marinetti's 'Tactilism' manifesto speculates that technologically enhanced perceptions may well 'uncover ... many other senses' (1972b: 111), describing how he worked his way through a series of real and imaginary situations, ranging from his initial experiments with gloved hands, underwater swimming and darkness (1972b: 110), to his speculation that in an age of enhanced 'X-ray vision' people will 'see inside their bodies' (1972b: 112). At his most prophetic, Marinetti anticipates the enthusiasm with which the French body artist Orlan's 'Carnal Art' manifesto exclaims: 'I can observe my own body cut open without suffering. . . . I can see to the heart of my lover. . . . Darling, I love your spleen, I love your liver, I adore your pancreas and the line of your femur excites me' (1998: 98). As Orlan notes, her satellite-broadcast surgical-operation-performances attempt to identify and interrogate the almost obscenely auratic intensity of corporeal images that 'force us to close our eyes' and 'make us blind' (1998: 95–6).

While Marinetti predicts the multimediated processes by which – in Orlan's terms – 'the flesh is made word', thereby 'enhancing the body's faculties rather than diminishing them' (1998: 98), Des Esseintes' Baudrillardian strategy of 'disobedience to behavioural norms' (Huysmans, 1968: 54) seems closer to the ritualistic bodily modification practised by a lineage of disaffected 19th- and 20th-century fin-de-siècle 'outsider' artists. While technological avant-garde artists working in the Futurist tradition might claim with some justification to be what Boccioni terms the 'primitives' of a 'completely renovated sensitiveness' (1973: 49), the experiments outlined in Against Nature and in Vale and Juno's survey of Modern Primitives (1989) typify the ceremonial sensibility of successive 'primitives of an old sensitiveness', inspired by what Huysmans calls 'a nostalgic yearning for another age' (1968: 180–1).

Such 'primitive' gestures can either represent the first or last steps towards more contemporary physical and perceptual modification, depending upon their subject's wish to work with or without 20th-century technologies. Marinetti obviously typifies the impulse to work with electronic media, and his 'Futurist Synthetic Theater' manifesto of 1915 characteristically predicts how 'the historical theater, a sickening genre already abandoned by the passéist public' (1972c: 123), will make way for a Futurist theatre enlivened by 'all the electro-mechanical inventions that alone will permit us to realize our most free conceptions on the stage' (1972c: 129).

In turn, Marinetti's 'Futurist Cinema' manifesto of 1916 predicts that cinema encompassing 'Painting + sculpture + plastic dynamism + words-in-freedom + composed noise + architecture + synthetic theater' (1972d: 134) will inaugurate 'a new art, immensely vaster and lighter than all the existing arts' (1972d: 131), and his '*La Radia*' manifesto of 1933 envisages 'A pure organism of radio sensations', allowing the 'amplification and transfiguration' of both 'the vibrations emitted by living beings' and 'the vibrations emitted by matter' (1992: 267).

As Marinetti's prophetic rhetoric suggests, such aspirations all too frequently await comprehensive realization by more advanced technological practitioners. It is precisely such 'advanced' technological postmodern practices as Chopin's and Stelarc's research (as opposed to the tattoos of California's 'modern primitives'), that most forcefully exemplify the auratic originality of the 'research arm' (Viola, 1995: 257) of late 20th-century multimedia performance.

Chopin and the Singularity of the Postmodern Techno-Body

The auratic energies of early postmodern techno-performance are best introduced in terms of the ways in which late 20th-century multimedia artists such as the Americans, Dick Higgins and Ellen Zweig and the Australian, Ania Walwicz, all emphasize the physical and sonic singularity of veteran French sound poet Henri Chopin's performances, likening his presence to that of a 'super-Dracula' (Higgins, 1992a: 23) evincing the 'expansive' spectacle of 'arms raised high and wide ... ready to leap' (Zweig, 1992: 39) into a 'ballet' or 'theatre of sound' (Walwicz, 1992: 23). As Zweig suggests, the live and pre-recorded vocalic and

Henri Chopin, Pompidou Centre, 1980
Source: Photographer: Françoise Janicot. Published by kind permission.

gestural leaps and bounds of Chopin's orchestration of 'the inner landscape of the inaccessible spaces' (1992: 39) manifest an unexpectedly intense partially corporeal and partially technological auratic energy, far outreaching the discourse of 'specific reference' (Higgins, 1992a: 23).

Reflecting upon Chopin's strangely phantasmagoric corporeality in more detail in his article 'The Golem in the Text', Higgins cogently observes:

> The poet uses complex vocal and non-figurative sounds, edited at several levels – electronically manipulating and broadcasting them at top volume – and adding to them in live performance with voice and microphone. . . . Despite his diminutive height, Henri Chopin radiates such an intensity that he seems to grow to a gigantic scale, the gravity of his expression suggesting some kind of vampire or evil spirit. The process by which this spirit emerges on stage can be really terrifying. . . . Because the real process of the work is non-mimetic, deriving from what the artist – in this case Chopin – is actually doing. In other words, the emergence of this spirit is inherent in the live performance of the work. (1992b: 25–6, my translation)

Like Higgins' reflections on Chopin, Barthes' essay on 'The Grain of the Voice' traces an elusive register of performative singularity emanating from 'the body of the man or woman singing or playing', existing 'outside of any law' (1977a: 188), and in consequence, challenging his own antithetical anti-authorial doctrine that:

> . . . a text is not a line of words releasing a single 'theological' meaning (the 'message' of the Author-God) but a multi-dimensional space in which are married and contested a variety of writings, none of them original. (1977b: 146)

Rephrasing and interweaving Barthes' and Higgins' concepts in what Barthes would call a 'tissue of quotations' (1977b: 146), one might more accurately argue that the performative 'grain' or 'golem' arising from the multimediated sonic and corporeal gestures of a techno-artist such as Chopin demonstrates how performance of this calibre reveals a singular 'theological presence' (the 'techno-presence' or 'spirit' of the Author-God), within a multi-dimensional multi-mediated space in which are married and contested a variety of performative energies, many of them profoundly original.

Chopin himself at least partially encourages a spiritual – if not theological – reading of his techno-performances, remarking:

> With the Christian tradition the body was absolutely nothing, but for me the body is of primary importance. I remember that between 1948 and 1949 I studied theology in a seminary, and was furious when people said, 'Only, Christ, Christ'. For me it was absolutely impossible, because the human body is very important. Without the body it is impossible to produce the spirit. (1998)

'Does this mean that your art is a physical revelation of the spirit?', I asked Chopin. 'Of course, of course', he replied, adding, 'It's a great surprise for you!' (1998).

Chopin's comments certainly were a great surprise, given his customary suspicion of religious institutions. But in retrospect it seems clear that Chopin – like Stelarc – typifies the ways in which certain kinds of singular multimediated performance can at times offer an intense quality of authorial 'spirit' reaching beyond what Barthes calls 'the law of culture' (1977a: 188), to the point where 'articulated language is no longer more than approximative and where another language begins'; a point at best 'theoretically locatable but not describable' (1977c: 65); where – as Barthes aptly observes – innovative art is often 'born technologically, occasionally even aesthetically', long before it is 'born theoretically' (1977c: 67).

Outlining his trajectory from initial 'theoretical' dismay before his undistinguished diction, to the technologically 'born' discovery of his voice's unusual abstract energies, Chopin explains:

> I started in '55 with sound . . . the diction with my voice was very bad . . . but I listened to my voice on a tape recorder . . . and my voice is very good . . . the timbre is very good too . . . so I put my finger between the head and the tape on the tape recorder . . . and . . . the sound was different! Distortion! After that I changed with my finger the speed of the tape on a very simple tape recorder and again the speed was different. (1982b: 12)

Following earlier experience 'with the theatre . . . and singers', Chopin's first tape-recorded experiments attempted to synthesize familiar genres and 'produce with one voice ten or fifteen or twenty voices'; a project culminating in his composition *Pêche de Nuit* (1957), made up of '48 superimpositions', recorded at 'six speeds' (1970). Subsequently sampling tactile sounds 'with microphones . . . in the mouth . . . on the ear . . . on the hair too' (1982b: 12), Chopin discovered that 'When I put the microphone into the mouth I have simultaneously five sounds: the air and the liquid in the mouth, the respiration in the nose, the air between each tooth and the respiration in the lungs' (1992a). Further internal explorations of Chopin's body followed: 'In 1974 I put into my stomach a very small microphone and it was a discovery – the body is always like a factory! It never stops – there's no silence!' (1992a).

By the late 1960s, Chopin's definition of his explorations of 'sound poetry, made for and by the tape-recorder', composed of 'vocal micro-particles rather than the Word as we know it', identified a quintessentially technologically born practice, 'more easily codified by machines and electricity . . . than by any means proper to writing' (1967: 11). As he subsequently adds, recent 'new departures' now seem even more distant from the familiar assumptions of 'basic literary ideas'.

> We already have a geometric, computerizable language. But what we still haven't discovered are the ways in which this language will evolve. This is firstly because technology is evolving so

rapidly, and secondly, because whereas computers only have forty or so phonemes, we know that we possess thousands of sonic values. We know that the ear not only receives sounds, but also gives out sounds.

All these discoveries were completely unknown when I began working with sound poetry – I was starting from very basic literary ideas. It's thanks to the new technologies that I've discovered all these new values. In the same way, future technologies will reveal the multiplicity of our auditory and visual cells – the eye, the ear and all our other senses. So while we cannot predict the future, it's certain that new departures have already been made, and that we cannot live without them. (1992b: 51)

A pioneer sound poet orchestrating live and pre-recorded sound; a multimedia theorist defining the mechanically modified body's creative energies; and an internationally acknowledged multimedia *auteur*, Chopin typifies the ways in which first-generation postmodern techno-performance transforms the graphic multiplicity of the Futurist 'running horse' with 'not four legs, but twenty' (Boccioni, 1973: 49) into the sonic multiplicity of '48 superimpositions' recorded at 'six speeds' (Chopin, 1970). In turn, the multimediated sonic multiplicity of Chopin's compositions anticipates the ways in which the techno-corporeal gestures of second-generation postmodern artists such as Stelarc now enter 'an electronic space that connects other limbs, other people, in other places' (1998: 178), identifying and orchestrating traces of the ambiguous 'slippage', 'interface' and 'anxiety' located 'between biology and silicon-chip circuit' (1995: 49).

Stelarc and the 'Split Physiology' of the Cyberbody

Like Marinetti and Dulac, postmoderns such as Chopin and Stelarc insist that the most innovative aspects of their research reach far beyond the poetics of established genres, rituals, ceremonies, fables and conventions. Marinetti stipulates that 'Tactilism' has 'nothing in common with painting or sculpture' (1972b: 111); Dulac defines avant-garde film as the research of artists who are 'Neither writers nor dramatists nor painters nor sculptors nor architects nor musicians' (1987a: 37); Chopin emphasizes that his 'new languages' have 'nothing to do with Dickens or Balzac' (1992b: 50); and Stelarc similarly describes 'a general strategy of extending performance parameters by plugging the body into cyber-systems, technological systems, networks, machines that in some way enable the body to function more precisely or more powerfully' (1995: 46), tracing the origins of his research to discontent with – and disregard for – available performative and artistic conventions.

> It was not a matter of me reacting against theatre, but really coming from the visual arts and not being satisfied with traditional modes of expression like painting and sculpture. And remember that I came at the end of minimal and conceptual art. . . . Conceptual art had played itself out – so then what were you left with? Nothing but your body. (1994: 379)

Explaining that his preoccupation with the 'human/machine interface – the hybridizing of the body with its technologies' (1995: 46) arises from his vision of 'the body as an evolutionary structure' and his fascination for the ways in which 'new media in art' inaugurate 'alternate experiences' (1994: 380), Stelarc notes how his multimedia performances of the 1970s almost wholly abandoned conventional choreographical-musical collaboration in order to explore a kind of one-man fusion of technologically amplified dance, music and performance, to all intents and purposes realizing Marinetti's dream of a 'tactile' art offering multimediated 'modifications of a single keen sense: touch' (1972a: 112) and a 'radiophonic' art amplifying 'vibrations emitted by living beings' (1992: 267).

> When I went to Japan ... I became increasingly interested in connecting body gesture and posture with sound. The idea of amplifying a muscle signal came to mind. Now, if I make a movement, I twist my arm, flick my fingers, contract muscles and electrodes are stuck on the skin, I can pick up the signal, pre-amplify and process it. (1994: 382)

Evoking his early suspension performances as 'a bridge between primal and technological yearnings' and as 'an image of escaping both the planetary pull and by implication, our genetic containment as well' (1994: 383), Stelarc insists upon the essentially 'provisional' and 'speculative' quality of his present experiments.

> [T]here's no blueprint and there's no methodical research directed into any one particular area.... These performances aren't shamanistic displays of human prowess. They're not pseudo-medical scientific research. They're not yogic feats of fine-tuning to attain higher spiritual states. They're none of these things. They're simply works of art, exploring intuitively new realms of aesthetics and images. (1995: 49)

While acknowledging that his suspension performances involving shark hook insertions may 'appear rather primitive and ritualistic' when considered 'out of context' (1994: 383), Stelarc notes how even these works 'were fully amplified performances with laser eyes', and explains that his 'suspensions with insertions into the skin occurred because of a dissatisfaction with all the visual clutter of supporting the body with ropes and harnesses' (1994: 382). Evoking these performances as a kind of postmodern variant upon Léger's concept of the film, 'Ballet Mécanique' (1924), Stelarc specifies how he always envisaged the body as 'a moving projectile ... choreographed by machines' (1994: 383).

Updating Des Esseintes' experiments with sensory deprivation, intensification and 'deviation' (Huysmans, 1968: 208), and Marinetti's analysis of gloved, submerged and darkened sensations, Stelarc's first performances systematically tested the basic 'limits to the body – its genetic repertoire, its structural parameters' (1994: 384).

> I occupied a gallery for a week in Japan. I sewed my lips and eye lids shut with surgical needle and thread. I was tethered to the gallery wall with a pair of cables which connected to two hooks in the back of my body. (1994: 383)

Having made such 'primal' first steps – 'against nature' and 'against sight' – Stelarc's work rapidly assumes a distinctly futuristic register, projecting Marinetti's modernist dream of 'A visual sense . . . born in the fingertips' (1972a: 112) into the postmodern techno-performative reality of a tactile sense, born – so to speak – in the interface between laser eyes and eyelids.

> Initially the laser beams were reflected off small mirrors stuck on the eyes. Later, they were directed by optic fibre cables and collimating lenses. . . . I could scan the space with my laser eyes and, by blinking and moving the muscles of the face, I could actually scribble in space. (1994: 388)

As Stelarc indicates, these eye-constructed images evolved alongside further realization of Marinetti's prediction of the ways in which artists will 'see inside their bodies' (1972a: 112), in techno-physical performances documenting the interface between the camera lens and the intestine.

> At the same time that I was doing laser projections with the eyes, I was making internal probes into the stomach, into the colon, into the lungs. I've filmed three metres of internal space. The events around 1975 were titled events for internal and external probes. This referred specifically to the internal films and the laser eyes. Piercing the space with laser eyes was a metaphor for probing the body itself. (1994: 388)

Like Chopin's ingestion of 'a very small microphone' (1992a), Stelarc's cinematic body probes and his experiments with his 'third arm' – quite literally the 'research arm' of contemporary performance – typify his fascination with the ways in which technological performance research both modifies the body's sounds and images and suggests alternatives to dominant definitions of corporeal identity. Tellingly, Stelarc categorizes his research with 'prosthetic attachments and transplanted organs' as 'experiments in modifying the body', and initiatives prompting the redefinition of 'our roles as human beings' (1994: 388).

As Stelarc further explains, his most recent Internet performances challenge dominant concepts of individuality, identity, agency and autonomy by creating situations in which the body interfaces and interacts with stimulation from a multiplicity of external sources. Considered in Baudrillardian rhetoric, this kind of body incorporates the 'timeless and sexless fluidity of forms' of 'a non-individual body without desire, yet capable of all metamorphoses' (1988: 45). In Stelarc's terms, these performances address the questions, 'Can we consider a body that can function with neither memory nor desire?' and, 'Is it possible to navigate the world, to operate effectively, sense and communicate, in these kind of cool spaces displaced from the cultural spaces . . . of emotion and of personal experience?' (Stelarc, 1998: 176).

Entering such spaces, Stelarc claims, 'your realm of operation goes beyond your biological boundaries and the local space that you function within' to a zone where 'you become an agent that can extrude awareness and action into another body elsewhere'. At this point, he suggests, the artist enters 'the realm of the open, of the divergent rather than the convergent, where what you're creating are contestable futures, not utopian ideals' (1998: 178–9).

Emphasizing that he is primarily interested in 'alternate and possibly augmented experiences' made possible by 'new physical interactions – new kinds of physical intimacies that don't rely on proximity, that are augmented by other sorts of feedback loops' (1998: 186), and resisting both romantic concepts of 'a body with seemingly unbounded free agency' and eugenicist fantasies of 'the body as a total automaton' (1998: 190), Stelarc insists that his body is 'never totally automatic in its operation'.

> It operates with a split physiology, so although the Internet data is controlling my body movements, and inadvertently also constructing the choreography of images and the composition of sounds, electrodes on my abdominal and leg muscles are in fact activating my third hand, so although the Internet controls me, I control my third hand. And so it's a kind of split physiology, voltage in on the left side determining the body's movements, voltage out from the electrodes allowing me to activate my third hand. So the body acts as a more complex entity with a split physiology, interfaced and engaged in a multiplicity of aesthetic tasks. It structures the performance initially through its hardwiring, and of course, it's aware of what's going on during the performance, and it's able to make small adjustments within the flow of activity and images that's occurring. (1998: 193–4)

As Stelarc indicates, his interactive performances all attempt to modify and extend awareness beyond the familiar parameters of cultural convention and individual intention. '[N]ew technologies generate information, and generate new models and paradigms that weren't applicable or possible simply by the imagination alone', and, in turn, 'alternate operational possibilities . . . create new desires and new ways of interfacing with the world' (1998: 201). Aspiring to 'redesign the body to function in this intense information realm of faster and more precise machines' (1995: 47), with the twofold proviso that the technologically modified body should be 'conditioned to perform as an artist' rather than 'as a bureaucrat', and should produce 'multiple possibilities' rather than 'coercive solutions' (1995: 49), Stelarc's explorations of cybernetic technologies evince an inspiringly affirmative logic.

While uncritical technomania may prove as inexpedient and indefensible as uncritical technophobia, the most significant techno-practices of the last decades make it increasingly obvious – as Chopin reminds us – 'that new departures have already been made, and that we cannot live without them' (1992b: 51). Both anticipating and facilitating further 'departures', Stelarc surely carries conviction when he concludes that 'if we're really caring about life in general, and intelligence in particular', it follows that:

> . . . any form of life, whether it be carbon chemistry or silicon-chip circuitry – any form of life that can perpetuate these values in a more durable or a more pervasive form – should be allowed to develop. (1995: 49)

Confronted by ever more momentous examples of the technological reorchestration, resingularization and perpetuation of corporeal performance, the research arm of postmodern cultural theory should surely look beyond fabulistic accounts of the metastatic body, towards those innovative multimedia practices that 'enact' (rather than 'en-text') further instances of the kind of truly fabulous auratic performative energy which – as Baudrillard's most inspired (and inspiring) phrasing puts it – 'wrests the human being from all localization, from all objective definition' (1998: 53–4, my translation).

References

Barthes, Roland (1977a) 'The Grain of the Voice', in *Image–Music–Text*, ed. and trans. Stephen Heath. Glasgow: Collins. (Orig. 1972.)

Barthes, Roland (1977b) 'The Death of the Author', in *Image–Music–Text*, ed. and trans. Stephen Heath. Glasgow: Collins. (Orig. 1968.)

Barthes, Roland (1977c) 'The Third Meaning', in *Image–Music–Text*, ed. and trans. Stephen Heath. Glasgow: Collins. (Orig. 1970.)

Baudrillard, Jean (1988) 'Metamorphoses, Metaphors, Metastases', in *The Ecstasy of Communication*, trans. Bernard and Caroline Schutze. New York: Semiotext(e). (Orig. 1987.)

Baudrillard, Jean (1989) 'The Anorexic Ruins', trans. David Antal, in *Looking Back on the End of the World*, ed. Dietmar Kamper and Christoph Wulf. New York: Semiotext(e).

Baudrillard, Jean (1993a) 'America as Fiction', interview with J. Henric and G. Scarpetta, trans. Nicholas Zurbrugg, in *Baudrillard Live: Selected Interviews*, ed. Mike Gane. London: Routledge. (Orig. 1986.)

Baudrillard, Jean (1993b) *The Transparency of Evil: Essays on Extreme Phenomena*, trans. James Benedict. London: Verso. (Orig. pub. 1990.)

Baudrillard, Jean (1996) 'Endangered Species?', interview with Paul Sutton in 1994, *Angelaki* 2(3): 217–24.

Baudrillard, Jean (1997) 'The Ecastasy of Photography', interview with Nicholas Zurbrugg in 1993, in *Jean Baudrillard: Art and Artefact*, ed. Nicholas Zurbrugg. London: Sage.

Baudrillard, Jean (1998) *Car l'illusion ne s'oppose pas à la réalité. . . .* Paris: Descartes & Cie.

Benjamin, Walter (1979) 'The Work of Art in the Age of Mechanical Reproduction', in *Illuminations*, trans. Harry Zohn. Glasgow: Collins. (Orig. 1936.)

Bergman, Billy and Richard Horn (1985) *Experimental Pop: Frontiers of the Rock Era*. Poole: Blandford.

Boccioni, Umberto (1973) 'The Exhibitors to the Public', trans. anon., in *Futurist Manifestos*, ed. Umbro Apollonio. London: Thames and Hudson. (Orig. 1912.)

Bürger, Peter (1984) *Theory of the Avant-Garde*, trans. Michael Shaw. Manchester: Manchester University Press. (Orig. pub. 1974.)

Cage, John (1983), 'Experimental Music', in *Silence*. Middletown, CT: Wesleyan University Press. (Orig. 1958.)

Chopin, Henri (1967) 'Open Letter to Aphonic Musicians', trans. Jean Ratcliffe-Chopin. *Revue-Disque OU* 33: 11–23.

Chopin, Henri (1970) *Pêche de Nuit*, notes for 45 rpm record in *Le Dernier Roman du Monde*. Wetteren: Editions Cyanuur. (Orig. 1957.)

Chopin, Henri (1982a) Letter of 17 July 1979, *Stereo Headphones* 8–10: 73–4.

Chopin, Henri (1982b) Interview with Lawrence Kucharz, Larry Wendt and Ellen Zweig in 1978, *Stereo Headphones* 8–10: 12–13.

Chopin Henri (1992a) Unpublished interview, ABC Television, Sydney.
Chopin, Henri (1992b) Interview with Nicholas Zurbrugg, in Nicholas Zurbrugg and Marlene Hall, *Henri Chopin*. Brisbane: Queensland College of Art Gallery.
Chopin, Henri (1998) Unpublished interview with Nicholas Zurbrugg.
Dulac, Germaine (1987a) 'The Essence of the Cinema: The Visual Idea', trans. Robert Lamberton, in *The Avant-Garde Film: A Reader of Theory and Criticism*, ed. P. Adams Sitney. New York: Anthology Film Archives. (Orig. 1925.)
Dulac, Germaine (1987b) 'The Avant-Garde Cinema', trans. Robert Lamberton, in *The Avant-Garde Film: A Reader of Theory and Criticism*, ed. P. Adams Sitney. New York: Anthology Film Archives.
Ginsberg, Allen (1966) *Howl and Other Poems*. San Francisco, CA: City Lights. (Orig. 1956.)
Guattari, Félix (1995) *Chaosmosis: An Ethico-Aesthetic Paradigm*, trans. Paul Bains and Julian Pefanis. Sydney: Power Publications. (Orig. 1992.)
Higgins, Dick (1992a) Untitled text, in Nicholas Zurbrugg and Marlene Hall, *Henri Chopin*. Brisbane: Queensland College of Art Gallery.
Higgins, Dick (1992b) 'Le Golem dans le texte', in *Poésies Sonores*, ed. Vincent Barras and Nicholas Zurbrugg. Geneva: Editions Contrechamps.
Huysmans, Joris-Karl (1968) *Against Nature*, trans. Robert Baldick. Harmondsworth: Penguin. (Orig. 1884.)
Jameson, Fredric (1991) *Postmodernism, or, The Cultural Logic of Late Capitalism*. Durham, NC: Duke University Press.
Lash, Scott and J. Urry (1987) *The End of Organized Capitalism*. Cambridge: Polity.
Marinetti, Filippo Tommaso (1972a) 'War, the World's Only Hygiene', in *Marinetti: Selected Writings*, ed. R.W. Flint, trans. R.W. Flint and Arthur A. Coppotelli. London: Secker and Warburg. (Orig. 1911–15.)
Marinetti, Filippo Tommaso (1972b) 'Tactilism', in *Marinetti: Selected Writings*, ed. R.W. Flint, trans. R.W. Flint and Arthur A. Coppotelli. London: Secker and Warburg. (Orig. 1924.)
Marinetti, Filippo Tommaso (1972c) 'The Futurist Synthetic Theater', in *Marinetti: Selected Writings*, ed. R.W. Flint, trans. R.W. Flint and Arthur A. Coppotelli. London: Secker and Warburg. (Orig. 1915.)
Marinetti, Filippo Tommaso (1972d) 'The Futurist Cinema', in *Marinetti: Selected Writings*, ed. R.W. Flint, trans. R.W. Flint and Arthur A. Coppotelli. London: Secker and Warburg. (Orig. 1916.)
Marinetti, Filippo Tommaso (1973) 'Destruction of Syntax-Imagination without Strings-Words-in-Freedom', trans. R.W. Flint, in *Futurist Manifestos*, ed. Umbro Apollonio. London: Thames and Hudson. (Orig. 1913.)
Marinetti, Filippo Tommaso (1992) '*La Radia*', in *Wireless Imagination: Sound Radio and the Avant-Garde*, ed. Douglas Kahn and Gregory Whitehead, trans. Stephen Sartarelli. Cambridge, MA: MIT Press. (Orig. 1933.)
Orlan (1998) 'Carnal Art' Manifesto, website translation of 'L'Art Charnel', in 'Surtout pas sage comme une image', *Quasimodo* 5: 95–101.
Stelarc (1994) 'Just Beaut to Have Three Hands', interview with Martin Thomas, *Continuum* 8(1): 377–93.
Stelarc (1995) 'Electronic Voodoo', interview with Nicholas Zurbrugg, *21.C* 2: 44–9.
Stelarc (1998) 'Telematic Tremors, Telematic Pleasures: Stelarc's Internet Performances', interview with Nicholas Zurbrugg, in *Carnal Pleasures: Desire, Public Space and Contemporary Art*, ed. Anna Novakov. Berkeley, CA: Clamor.
Vale, V. and Andrea Juno (1989) *Modern Primitives: An Investigation of Contemporary Adornment and Ritual*. San Francisco, CA: V/Search.
Viola, Bill (1995) *Reasons for Knocking at an Empty House: Writings 1973–1994*. Cambridge, MA: MIT Press.

Virilio, Paul (1991) *The Aesthetics of Disappearance*, trans. Philip Beitchman. New York: Semiotext(e). (Orig. 1980.)
Virilio, Paul (1994) *L'Inertie polaire*. Paris: Christian Bourgois Editeur. (English translation forthcoming from Sage, London.)
Virilio, Paul (1995) *The Art of the Motor*, trans. Julie Rose. Minneapolis: University of Minnesota Press. (Orig. 1993.)
Virilio, Paul (1996) 'A Century of Hyper-Violence', interview with Nicholas Zurbrugg in 1995 *Economy and Society* 25(1): 111–26.
Virilio, Paul (1997) *Open Sky*, trans. Julie Rose. London: Verso. (Orig. 1995.)
Virilio, Paul (1998) Unpublished interview with Nicholas Zurbrugg.
Virilio, Paul and Sylvère Lotringer (1983) *Pure War*, trans. Mark Polizotti. New York: Semiotext(e).
Walwicz, Ania (1992) Untitled text, in Nicholas Zurbrugg and Marlene Hall, *Henri Chopin*. Brisbane: Queensland College of Art Gallery.
William Carlos Williams (1966) 'Howl for Carl Solomon', in Allen Ginsberg, *Howl and Other Poems*. San Francisco, CA: City Lights.
Williams, William Carlos (1979) Quoted (in text opposite photograph 1) in Jonathan Williams, *Portrait Photographs*. Frankfort, KY: Gnomon.
Zweig, Ellen (1992) Untitled text, in Nicholas Zurbrugg and Marlene Hall, *Henri Chopin*. Brisbane: Queensland College of Art Gallery.

Nicholas Zurbrugg is Professor of English and Cultural Studies, and Director of the Centre for Contemporary Arts, The Faculty of Humanities and Social Sciences, De Montfort University, Leicester. His books include *The Parameters of Postmodernism* (1993), *Jean Baudrillard: Art and Artefact* (1997) and *Critical Vices: The Myths of Postmodern Theory* (G+B Arts, forthcoming 1999).

Parasite Visions: Alternate, Intimate and Involuntary Experiences[1]

STELARC

1. EXOSKELETON: A six-legged, pneumatically powered walking machine has been constructed for the body. The locomotor, with either ripple or tripod gait moves fowards, backwards, sideways and turns on the spot. It can also squat and lift by splaying or contracting its legs. The body is positioned on a rotating turn-table, actuating and controlling the machine legs by by tilt sensors and micro-switches on an exoskeleton housing the upper body and limbs. The left arm is an extended arm with pneumatic manipulator having 11 degrees-of- freedom. It is human-like in form but with additional functions. The fingers open and close , becoming multiple grippers. There is individual flexion of the fingers, with thumb and wrist rotation. The body actuates the walking machine by moving its arms. Different

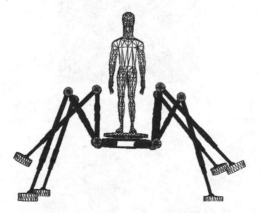

Locomotor Project, Kampnagel, Hamburg 1998. Wire-frame animation still: Steve Middleton. *Source*: Stelarc.

Body & Society © 1999 SAGE Publications (London, Thousand Oaks and New Delhi),
Vol. 5(2–3): 117–127
[1357–034X(199906/09)5:2–3;117–127;008860]

gestures   make different motions-   a   translation of limb to leg   motions. The body's arms   guide   the   choreography of the   locomotor's   movements and thus   compose the   cacophony of   pneumatic   and   mechanical and   sensor   modulated sounds....

2. EXTRA EAR- Having developed a   Third Hand, consider the possibility   of constructing   an extra ear,   positioned next to the   real ear. A laser scan was done to   create a   3D simulation of the   Extra Ear in place. Although the chosen   position is in front of and beside the right ear, this may not be   the surest and safest place   anatomically   to put   it.   A balloon would be inserted under the skin and then   gradually inflated   over a   period of months   until a bubble   of stretched skin   is formed. The balloon is then removed and a cartilage ear shape   is   inserted and pinned inside the bag of excess skin. A cosmetic surgeon would then need to cut and sew the skin over the cartilage structure.

The Third Hand, Tokyo/Nagoya/Yokohama. Photographer: S. Hunter. © Stelarc.

Writing One Word with Three Hands Simultaneously, Maki Gallery, Tokyo. Photographer: K. Oki. © Stelarc.

Rather than the hardware prosthesis of a mechanical hand , the Extra Ear would be a soft augmentation, mimicking the actual ear in shape and structure, but having different functions. Imagine an ear that cannot hear but rather can emit noises. Implanted with a sound chip and a proximity sensor, the ear would speak to anyone who would get close to it. Perhaps, the ultimate aim would be for the Extra Ear to whisper sweet nothings to the other ear. Or imagine the Extra Ear as an Internet antenna able to amplify RealAudio sounds to augment the local sounds heard by the actual ears. The Extra Ear would be a prosthesis made from its own skin. Why an ear? An ear is a beautiful and complex structure. In acupuncture, the ear is the site for the stimulation of body organs. It not only hears but is also the organ of balance. To have an extra ear points to more than visual and anatomical excess....

3. SURFACE AND SELF: THE SHEDDING OF SKIN-

As surface, skin was once the beginning of the world and simultaneously the boundary of the self. But now stretched, pierced and penetrated by technology, the skin is no longer the smooth and sensuous surface of a site or a screen. Skin no longer signifies closure. The rupture of surface and skin means the erasure of inner and outer. An artwork has been inserted inside the body. The Stomach Sculpture- constructed for the Fifth Australian Sculpture Triennale in Melbourne, whose theme was site-specific work- was inserted 40 cm into the stomach cavity. Not as a prosthetic implant but as an aesthetic addition. The body becomes hollow- not the BWO but rather a body with art. The body is experienced as hollow with no meaningful distinctions between public, private and physiological spaces. The hollow body becomes a host, not for a self but simply for a sculpture. As interface, the skin is obsolete. The significance of the cyber may well reside in the act of the body shedding its skin. The clothing of

Stretched Skin/Third Hand, Monorail Station, Ofuna. Photographer: S. Hunter. © Stelarc.

the body with membranes embedded with alternate sensory and input/ output devices creates the possibility of more intimate and enhanced interactivity. Subjectively, the body experiences itself as a more extruded system, rather than an enclosed structure. The self becomes situated beyond the skin. It is partly through this extrusion that the body becomes empty. But this emptiness is not through a lack but from the extrusion and extension of its capabilities, its new sensory antennae and its increasingly remote functioning. . . .

4. FRACTAL FLESH - Consider a body that can extrude its awareness and action into other bodies or bits of bodies in other places. An alternate operational entity that is spatially distributed but electronically connected. A movement that you initiate in Melbourne would be displaced and manifested in another body in Rotterdam. A shifting, sliding awareness that is neither 'all-here' in this body nor 'all-there' in those bodies. This is not about a fragmented body but a multiplicity of bodies and parts of bodies prompting and remotely guiding each other. This is not about master–slave control mechanisms but feedback-loops of alternate awareness, agency and of split physiologies. Imagine one side of your body being remotely guided whilst the other side could collaborate with local agency. You watch a part of your body move but you have neither initiated it nor are you contracting your muscles to produce it. Imagine the consequences and advantages of being a split body with voltage-in, inducing the behaviour of a remote agent and voltage-out of your body to control peripheral devices. This would be a more complex and interesting body- not simply a single entity with one agency but one that would be a host for a multipicity of remote and alien agents. Of different physiologies and in varying locations. Certainly there may be justification, in some situations and for particular actions to tele-operate a human arm rather than a robot manipulator- for if the task is to be performed in a non-hazardous location, then it might be an advantage to use a remote human arm- as it would be attached to another arm and a mobile, intelligent body. Consider a task begun by a body in one place, completed by another body in another place. Or the transmission and conditioning of a skill. The body not as a site of inscription but as a medium for the manifestation of remote agents. This physically split body may have one arm gesturing involuntarily (remotely actuated by an unknown agent), whilst the other arm is enhanced by an exoskeleton

prosthesis to perform with   exquisite   skill   and with   extreme   speed.
A   body   capable of   incorporating movement that   from   moment
t o   moment   would be a pure   machinic   motion   performed
with   neither   memory   nor   desire....

5. STIMBOD - What makes this possible   is a   touch-screen muscle stimulation
system. A method has been   developed that enables   the   body's   movements
to   be programmed by   touching the   muscle   sites   on   the   computer
model. Orange flesh   maps   the possible stimulation sites   whilst   red
flesh   indicates   the actuated muscle(s). The sequence of   motions   can be
replayed   continuously with its   loop   function. As well as
choreography by pressing, it is possible to paste   sequences   together
from a library   of   gesture icons.   The system allows   stimulation
of the   programmed movement for   analysis   and   evaluation
before transmission to actuate the   body. At a   lower stimulation level
it is a   body   prompting   system. At a higher stimulation level   it is a
body   actuation   system . This is not   about remote-control of
the body,   but   rather   of constructing   bodies   with   split physiologies,
operating with multiple   agency.   Was it Wittgenstein who asked   if   in
raising your   arm   you could remove the   intention   of raising it
what   would   remain? Ordinarily, you would   associate intention with
action (except, perhaps in an   instinctual motion- or if you have a pathological
condition like Parkinson's disease). With Stimbod, though,   that   intention
would   be   transmitted   from   another   body   elsewhere.   There
would   be   actions   without   expectations.   A   two-way
tele-Stimbod system   would create a   possessed and possessing body- a
split   physiology   to   collaborate   and perform tasks
remotely   initated and   locally completed-   at   the   same   time   in
the   one   physiology....

6. EXTREME ABSENCE AND THE EXPERIENCE OF THE ALIEN - Such a
Stimbod would be hollow body,   a host body for the   projection   and
performance   of remote agents. Glove Anaesthesia   and   Alien Hand   are
pathological conditions in which   the patient   experiences parts of their
body as not there,   as   not   their   own,   as   not under their own
control- an absence of physiology   on the one hand   and an
absence of agency on the other. In a   Stimbod   not only   would it possess a
split physiology but   it   would experience   parts   of   itself
as   automated,   absent   and   alien. The problem
would   no longer be   possessing   a split personality,   but rather a
split   physicality. In our   Platonic, Cartesian and Freudian   pasts
these might have been considered   pathological   and in our Foucauldian present

we focus on inscription and control of the body. But in the terrain of cyber complexity that we now inhabit the inadequacy and the obsolescence of the ego-agent driven biological body cannot be more apparent. A transition from psycho-body to cybersystem becomes necessary to function effectively and intuitively in remote spaces, speeded-up situations and complex technological terrains. During a Sexuality and Medicine Seminar in Melbourne, Sandy Stone asked me what would be the cyber-sexual implications of the Stimbod system? Not having thought about it before I tried to explain what it might be like. If I was in Melbourne and Sandy was in NY, touching my chest would prompt her to caress her breast. Someone observing her there would see it as an act of self-gratification, as a masturbatory act. She would know though that her hand was remotely and perhaps even divinely guided! Given tactile and force-feedback, I would feel my touch via another person from another place as a secondary and additional sensation. Or, by feeling my chest I can also feel her breast. An intimacy through interface, an intimacy without proximity. Remember that Stimbod is not merely a sensation of touch but an actuation system. Can a body cope with experiences of extreme absence and alien action without becoming overcome by outmoded metaphysical fears and obsessions of individuality and free agency? A Stimbod would thus need to experience its actuality neither all-present-in-this-body, nor all-present-in-that-body, but partly-here and projected-partly-there. An operational system of spatially distributed but electronically interfaced clusters of bodies ebbing and flowing in awareness, augmented by alternate and alien agency....

7. PING BODY / PROTO-PARASITE - In 1995 for Telepolis, people at the Pompidou Centre (Paris), the Media Lab (Helsinki) and the Doors of Perception conference (Amsterdam), were able to remotely access and actuate this body in Luxembourg, using the touch-screen interfaced muscle stimulation system. ISDN Picturetel links allowed the body to see the face of the person who was moving it whilst the programmers could observe their remote choreography. (Although people thought they were merely activating the body's limbs, they were inadvertently composing the sounds that were heard and the images of the body they were seeing- for the body had sensors, electrodes and transducers on its legs, arms and head that triggered sampled body signals and sounds and that also made the body a video switcher and mixer. And although people in other places were performing with the RHS of the body, it could respond by

actuating its   Third   Hand,   voltage-out   from   electrodes positioned on its abdominal and LHS leg muscles. The   Split   Body   then   was   manifesting a combination   of   involuntary - remotely guided,   improvised   and EMG- muscle initiated   motor motions).   In   Ping Body- an Internet Actuated and Uploaded Performance (performed first for Digital Aesthetics in Sydney,   but also for DEAF in Rotterdam in 1996),   instead   of   the   body   being   prompted by other   bodies   in   other places,   Internet activity itself   choreographs and composes   the performance. Random   pinging   to over   30 global Internet domains   produce   values   from   0–2000 milliseconds that are   mapped   to the   deltoid,   biceps,   flexors,   hamstring, and   calf muscles -   0–60 volts initiating   involuntary   movements. The movements of the body   are amplified, with a   midi   interface measuring   position,   proximity   and bending angle of limbs.   Activated by Internet data   the body   is uploaded   as   info and images   to a Web site to be viewed by other people elsewhere.   The body is   telematically scaled-up,   stimulated and stretched   by reverberating   signals   of   an   inflated spatial and electrical system.   The usual relationship with the Internet is   flipped-   instead of the Internet being constructed by the input from people,   the Internet constructs the activity of one body. The body becomes   a   nexus   for   Internet activity- its activity   a statistical construct of   computer   networks. . . . .

8. PARASITE: EVENT FOR INVADED AND INVOLUNTARY BODY- A

customized search engine   has   been   constructed   that scans, selects and displays   images   to   the body- which functions   in   an   interactive video field. Analyses of the JPEG   files   provide data   that is   mapped to the body via   the muscle stimulation   system.   There is optical   and   electrical   input   into the body. The   images   that   you see   are   the   images that move you . Consider   the body's vision,   augmented and adjusted   to a parallel virtuality   which   increases in intensity to   compensate   for the   twilight of the   real world. Imagine the   search engine selecting   images of the body off the   WWW, constructing   a   metabody that   in turn   moves the physical body. Representations of the body   actuate the body's physiology.The resulting motion is mirrored in a   VRML   space at the performance site and   also uploaded   to a Web site as potential and recursive source images   for   body reactivation.   RealAudio sound is inserted into sampled   body   signals and sounds   generated   by   pressure, proximity,   flexion   and   accelerometer   sensors.   The body's physicality provides   feedback   loops of   interactive neurons, nerve endings, muscles,   transducers   and   Third Hand mechanism.   The system   electronically extends the body's optical and   operational   parameters

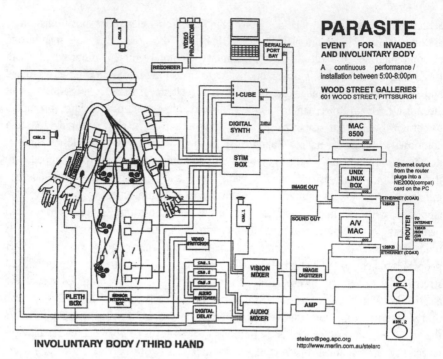

Stelarc, Performance design for *Parasite: Event for Invaded and Involuntary Body*
Credit: Stelarc & Merlin, 1997.

beyond its cyborg augmentation of its Third Hand and other peripheral devices. The prosthesis of the Third Hand is counterpointed by the prosthesis of the search engine software code. Plugged-in, the body becomes a parasite sustained by an extended, external and virtual nervous system. Parasite was first performed for Virtual World Orchestra in Glasgow. It has also been presented for The Studio for Creative Inquiry, Carnegie Mellon University at the Wood Street Galleries in Pittsburgh, Festival Atlantico in Lisbon, NTT- ICC in Tokyo, Ars Electronica in Linz and for the Fukui Biennale. . . .

9. MOVATAR- AN INVERSE MOTION CAPTURE SYSTEM-

Motion Capture allows a body to animate a 3D computer-generated virtual body to perform in computerspace or cyberspace. This is usually done by either markers on the body tracked by cameras, analysed by a computer and the motion mapped onto the virtual actor. Or it can be done using electromagnetic sensors (like Polhemus or Flock-of-Birds) that indicate position/ orientation of limbs and head. Consider though a virtual body or an avatar that can access a physical body, actuating it to perform in the real world.

If the avatar   is   imbued   with   an   artificial intelligence,   becoming
increasingly   autonomous   and unpredictable,   then   it   would   be
an   AL (Artificial Life) entity   performing   with   a   human body   in
physical space.   With an appropriate   visual   software interface
and   muscle stimulation system   this would   be   possible.   The   avatar
would become   a   Movatar.   Its repertoire   of   behaviour   could be
modulated   continuously   by   Ping   signals   and   might   evolve   using
genetic algorithms.   And with   appropriate   feedback   loops   from
the   real   world   it   would   be   able   to   respond   and perform   in
more   complex and   compelling   ways.   The   Movatar   would
be able   not   only to   act ,   but   also   to   express   its emotions by
appropriating   the facial muscles of the   its   physical body.   As a   VRML
entity   it   could   be   logged-into   from   anywhere- to allow your body to be
accessed and   acted   upon.   Or,   from its perspective,   the   Movatar
could   perform   anywhere   in the   real   world,   at anytime   with   as   many
physical bodies   in   diverse   and   spatially   separated   locations. . . .

10. PHANTOM BODIES AND COLLECTIVE STRATEGIES-   Previously
connection and communication with other bodies   on the   Internet   was only textual,
with an   acute absence of   physical presence.   This   was   not   the
experience   of   authentic   evolved   absence
that results in an   effectively operating body   in the real word -   absence of
the body on the Internet   is   an   absence   of   inadequacy, that   is   an
inadequacy of appropriate   feedback-loops.   As   we   hard-wire more
 high-fidelity   image, sound, tactile   and force-feedback   sensation between bodies
then   we   begin to   generate powerful   phantom presences- not
phantom as in phantasmagorical, but phantom as in phantom limb sensation.   The
sensation   of   the   remote   body   sucked onto your   skin   and
nerve   endings,   collapsing   the psychological and spatial   distance
between   bodies   on the Net.   Just as in   the   experience   of a
Phantom   Limb   with the   amputee, bodies will generate   phantom partners ,   not
because   of   a   lack,   but   as   extending   and enhancing   addition to their
physiology.   Your aura will not be your own.   It will only   be   through   the
construction of   phantoms   that   the   equivalent of   our evolved
absence   will be experienced,   as   we   function   increasingly   powerfully
and   with   speed and   intuition   (a successful body operates   automatically).
Bodies must   now perform   in   techno-terrains   and   data-structures   beyond
the   human-scale   where   intention   and   action   collapse
into   accelerated   responses.   Bodies   acting without   expectation,   producing
movements   without   memory.   Can   a   body   act   without
emotion?   Must   a   body continuously   affirm   its   emotional, social and

biological status quo? Or perhaps what is necessary is electronic erasure with new intimate, internalized interfaces to allow for the design of a body with more adequate inputs and outputs for performance and awareness augmented by search engines. Imagine a body remapped and reconfigured- not in genetic memory but rather in electronic circuitry. What of a body that is intimately interfaced to the WWW- and that is stirred and startled by distant whispers and remote promptings of other bodies in other places. A body that is informed by spiders knowbots and phantoms. . . .

11. OPERATIONAL INTERNET/ INTELLIGENT SYSTEM- Consider the Internet structured so that it would scan, select and switch- automatically interfacing clusters of on-line bodies in real-time (the size and expertise of the clusters selected for the task to be performed). Can a body cope with the multiplicity of agents- a fluid and flowing awareness that dims and intensifies as agents are connected and disconnected? Awareness and agency would be shifted and shared in an electronic space of distributed intelligence. The Internet becomes not merely a means of information transmission, but a mode of transduction- affecting physical action between bodies. Electronic space as a realm of action, rather than information. Imagine a body that is open and aware, invaded, augmented and with extended operation. Consider a body whose awareness is extruded by surrogate robots in situations and spaces where no body could go. These machines with arrays of sensors, manipulators and hybrid locomotion would exponentially multiply the operational possibilities- scaling-up the subtlety, speed and complexity of human action. Perhaps what it means to be human is about not retaining our humanity....

Acknowledgements

Stelarc is presently Artist-in-Residence of Hamburg City. He is a Research Consultant at Nottingham/Trent University. In 1997 he became Honorary Professor of Art and Robotics at Carnegie Mellon University. He has received a three-year Fellowship from the Visual Arts/Craft Board, Australia Council. His artwork is solely represented by the Sherman Galleries, in Sydney. Stimbod was developed with the assistance of Troy Innocent at Empire Ridge in Melbourne. The Muscle Stimulation System circuitry was designed by Bio-Electronics, Logitronics and Rainer Linz in Melbourne with the box fabricated with the assistance of Jason Patterson. Tele-Stimbod, Ping Body and Parasite software was developed by Jeffrey Cook, Sam de Silva, Gary Zebbington and Dimitri Aronov from the Merlin group in Sydney. Kampnagel in Hamburg is funding the 6-Legged Locomotor project.

Note

1. The layout and format of this article, and of the accompanying abstract on pages 338–9, are as designed by Stelarc.

Stelarc is an Australian performance artist. He has used medical instruments, prosthetics, robotics, Virtual Reality systems and the Internet to explore, extend and enhance the body's parameters. He has performed with a Third Hand, a Virtual Arm, a Virtual Body and a Stomach Sculpture. He has filmed the inside of his lungs, stomach and colon – approximately two metres of internal space. He has done 25 body suspensions with insertions into the skin, in different positions and varying situations in remote locations. For Fractal Flesh, as part of Telepolis, he developed a touch-screen interfaced Muscle Stimulation System, enabling remote access, actuation and choreography of the body. Performances such as Ping Body and Parasite probe notions of telematic scaling and the engineering of external, extended and virtual nervous systems for the body using the Internet. Recently, for Kampnagel, he completed Exoskeleton – a pneumatically powered 6-legged walking machine actuated by arm gestures. In 1995 Stelarc received a three-year Fellowship from The Visual Arts/Craft Board, The Australia Council. In 1997 he was appointed Honorary Professor of Art and Robotics at Carnegie Mellon University. He is presently Artist-In-Residence for Hamburg City. In 1998 he was appointed a Research Consultant for the Faculty of Art and Design at the Nottingham Trent University. His art is represented by the Sherman Galleries in Sydney.

In Dialogue with 'Posthuman' Bodies: Interview with Stelarc

ROSS FARNELL

For the last three decades the sometimes controversial events of Australian performance artist Stelarc have served as a mediation between the varying discourses of cultural and social theory, science, and the tropes and images of science fiction, translating theoretical, cultural and narrative models of the 'posthuman' into performative parameters of corporeal actualization. His theories are now familiar to many: redesigning the 'obsolete' body, developing new evolutionary strategies, redefining what is human through the 'absent' and 'phantom' body's invasion by technology. Stelarc advocates a 'planetary escape velocity' for the body as a strategy of *fin de millennium* necessity, a proposal for embodied *and* digital alterity that appeals to many proponents of technoculture, from cyberpunk authors to cultural theorists alike. Does this really offer empowered alternative bodies with heightened 'input and output' capabilities, or is it representative of a reductionist objectification of the physical, psychical, political and social body to a *l'art pour l'art* sensibility; subordinating (hyper)reality, theory and ideology to the 'pure' aesthetics of art, image and performance?

Born Stelios Arcadiou in 1946, Stelarc's 'body art' has developed into a unique combination of art and text, praxis and theory, body and technological prosthesis/ symbiosis. His cultural and *theoretical* bricolage elides borders, creating a dialogue with numerous discourses. The tension between Cartesian and phenomenological models of the body are graphically portrayed in the seeming contradictions between his (predominantly Cartesian) performances and (professed phenomeno- logical) theory/rhetoric. Stelarc's proposed transmogrification addresses many of

Body & Society © 1999 SAGE Publications (London, Thousand Oaks and New Delhi), Vol. 5(2–3): 129–147
[1357–034X(199906/09)5:2–3;129–147;008859]

the contemporary issues pertinent to debate surrounding bodies, sexual politics, 'Otherness' and 'becomings'. Whereas today's theorists place an ever-increasing importance on social and cultural context, Stelarc insists on isolating his 'events' within a framework of aesthetics that attempts to repudiate its own ideological basis, and deny the social/cultural consequences that must inevitably arise from such radical posthuman strategies.

While portrayed by some as an exemplary proponent of our putatively optimistic posthuman future, others see Stelarc as being indicative of the apocalyptic dangers of naive and untheorized approaches to incorporating militaristic technologies of control into the body. The following interview with Stelarc attempts to clarify the artist's position on such issues.

RF: Rather than reiterate your theories on the obsolete body and the like,[1] I wanted to talk about the ways in which your work intersects with cultural theory, science and science fiction, and also where it differs. Where does a pragmatist in posthumanism differ from a theorist or a science fiction writer? Are you trying to be the living posthuman today?

Stelarc: Well, not so much that, but certainly to generate situations and simulations of possible modified bodies or of possible future interfaces, but ones that lead to situations where you're coupling expressing an idea with experiencing the consequences of that idea. So you take the physical consequences for what you're doing, and that's always been part of the praxis of what I do, from the suspension events to the internal body sculptures to this new 'Internet Upload' project, where you're remotely activated by others. It's important that it's not purely a fanciful idea or sci-fi speculation, but rather a situation where you plug your body into an extended cyber-system, you try to cope with the precision and the complexity and the speed of this technological terrain, and you ... live with the consequences. [Mutual laughter]

RF: You describe yourself as a performance artist ... [Sure], using your body as the medium of expression: but your work must extend beyond aesthetics, surely there are political, cultural, social consequences, and an ideological grounding to what you're doing?

Stelarc: Even from the late 1960s/early 1970s when I began making art and doing performance, there was a feeling that the artist as a craftsperson was not adequate. I didn't train to be in the business of making beautiful objects, and I was never postmodern in the sense of appropriating cultural archetypical images and generating discourse in that kind of postmodern manner. So the concern was always what does it mean to be an artist but not to make beautiful objects? And then because the body became the central medium through which these performances occurred, there was a general interest in evolution, and how the forms and functions of the body evolved to this point of complexity, and how we might be predisposed to behave or to think in particular ways.

RF: You describe a possible role for the artist as an 'evolutionary alchemist' and 'genetic sculptor', appearing to privilege the role of the artist in any envisaged posthuman future.

Stelarc: Not so much privileging the role of the artist, but simply redefining what it means to be an artist, but in the consequences of what it means to be human and whether it's important any more to have a biological body and a single 'self' that we identify as being contained within the skin. When technology stretches the skin, pierces the body, the skin in effect is erased as a significant . . . Foucauldian site for inscription of the social and of the gendered. It's no longer the boundary of the container of the 'self', and skin is no longer the beginning of the world. It's no longer the site of collapsing the personal and the political if it's no longer there. So for me, to be posthuman means to take up a strategy where one needs to shed one's skin and consider other more deeper and more complex interfaces and inter-connections with the technologies that we've generated.

RF: Jameson, Haraway, Deleuze and Guattari, among others, propose theoreti-cal models of the posthuman as a political being, to re-empower the human in a postmodern inertia. Is there a political agenda to what you're doing?

Stelarc: My feeling is that it's not enough to speak in metaphors or paradigm shifts, or the notion of empowering the human. That suggests the notion of 'the flesh fights back', this idea that, although technology is threatening, we can encompass it and contain it in this very convenient sense of it being simply a means of enhancing the human, a means of perpetuating the biological status quo, and I'm quite concerned about that. [Rather], we should confront and radically question what it means to have a body, whether these forms and functions are adequate, whether we continue to accept a Heideggerian view that existence is only authentic in the face of death.

For me birth and death are evolutionary strategies, and we're in a post-evolu-tionary phase now, so I really question whether birth and death are these funda-mental beginnings and boundaries of existence that define what it means to be alive. [A]ll of a sudden we're confronted with [the technical] possibility that existence is no longer beginning with birth, nor necessarily ending with death, and so to be alive means more to be operational, not this analogue sort of birth, nurturing, maturing, decline that we tend to see it.

RF: It reminds me in some ways of Deleuzean 'becomings', where there's only Milieu.

Stelarc: When I hear that I hear it in the sense of the kind of 'fuzziness' of early consciousness and the ageing procedure which generates malfunctioning memory and inability to perform effectively. It seems to me what Deleuze is doing is centring the meaningfulness of existence in that mid-way point. Whereas I think what I'm saying is fundamentally more radical than that. It literally *means* no beginning or end.

RF: It's actual instead of theoretical.

Stelarc: It's the same with the notion of the 'body without organs', via Artaud. [T]he BwO was a conceptual shock when I read it because it synchronized, in certain ways, with the 'hollow body'. But for me the hollow body was a notion that came out of several experiences. One is the experience of the stretched skin, and the idea that skin becomes erased or becomes shed, where the body is reclothed with a synthetic skin ... that might be much more effective, much more efficient. A synthetic skin would mean radically hollowing out the human body. [T]he complexity, the softness and the wetness of the body would be difficult to sustain off the Earth ... so the strategy for a pan-planetary physiology might be a strategy of hollowing, hardening, and dehydrating the body. So for me the hollow body was a seductive concept because it meant that it was a better 'host' for packing more technology inside.

But also, the experience of a hollow body occurs for me when I amplify the internal signals and functions of the body. [T]hese internalized functions are externalized, the body has an acoustical aura that transforms the container of these functions from this humanoid shape to a cuboid space of the room. [Also], the hollow body came through making three films of the inside of my body, as well as an internal body sculpture. So, the 'body without organs' certainly is something that kind of points to the notion of a 'hollow body'.

RF: Deleuze and Guattari's notion of the BwO is very different to that though, it's desiring machines. . .

Stelarc: Well theirs is a political, social, electronic sort of thing. I find that interesting, and that notion of a 'desiring machine' is a factor within some of the things that I see also.

RF: In what way do you see desire playing a role in your work, is it the desire to 'become-Other'?

Stelarc: Well, simplistically, it's entwined within the agenda of a desire to be an artist. [B]ecause of the focus on the body, it translates in the desire to understand the position of the body in terms of evolutionary development and the notion of what it means to evolve as a species, and so consequently then the desire dissipates from an ego-oriented driven younger body, to one in which you consider the wider ramifications of trying to understand the world. But, that's a kind of reasonably idealistic way of putting it. I think though, that with all of these performances, if one associates desire with that which is elaborated through emotion and spectacle, I would deny that that's an aspect. I've never seen the work in that way, even with the suspension events. I guess it depends on how one positions desire.

RF: How do you resolve the obvious paradox of having to use your body as the 'medium of expression' while simultaneously declaring the body to be 'obsolete'?

Stelarc: It has to do with that questioning of the biological status quo of the body, so I can happily accept that this body has evolved as an absent body, that it's profoundly obsolete, that it's now being invaded, and through technology becomes a phantom body – phantom not as in phantasmagorical, but rather phantom as in phantom limb sensation – a kind of a visual visceral sensation that is still coupled to a physical body. I don't mean a ghost-like body but a sensation of a body that needs to be grounded in the physicality of your body, but in the realm of VR becomes this interactive and operational image.

RF: Has there been a deliberate progression in your work, from initially exploring the body's limits, to prosthesis, extension and now body/technology symbiosis, or just a progression as technology has enabled it?

Stelarc: No. There's never been a deliberate progression, in fact what constantly pleases me is that in creating these unstable situations with the body you generate unexpected outcomes with new interactive possibilities. Whereas once machines were seen as these ponderous entities that were always external to the body and which threatened to encompass and contain the body, now you have with nanotechnology miniaturization the possibility that the body becomes the host for colonies of micro-miniaturized machines that can inhabit the cellular spaces of the body, and whereas the notion of the cyborg was this traumatic tearing away of some organs to be replaced by larger technological parts, you have a situation here where colonies of micro-miniaturized robots might inhabit the body, redesign it, atoms up, inside-out . . . I find that a radical flip in our relationship with machines.

So, with this 'Internet Upload' of the body [a recent event], what it structures for me is some rather unexpected possibilities that I hadn't considered before . . . this muscle stimulation system enables the possibility for the body to become a host for remote and spatially separated agents. Metaphysically and historically we've considered the grounding of our humanity due to the coherence of our individuality. To be individual means to be human, to lose our individuality means to be a machine, to be somehow sub-human. But consider a body with a multiplicity of agents. The pathology of that sort of a body, the pathology of our psycho-social development, might be split personalities, but the pathology of this multiple agency would not be split physicalities, that would be not a pathology but rather a new complexity and multiplicity of choice that one would have.

You would watch a part of your body move, you are not responsible for that

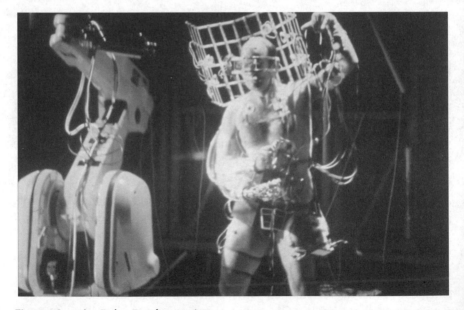

Figure 1 Scanning Robot/Involuntary Arm
Photographer: M. Burton. © Stelarc.

movement. Electronically coupled other bodies are extruding their own agency from one place to another and are being manifested in a part of your body. Not that you're invaded and taken over by an agent, or somehow this results in a kind of an anamorphous Internet collectivity of physical bodies, but rather a physical body with a multiplicity of agents and a new complexity of operation where your awareness will neither be all here, nor all there. [Laughs] And you wouldn't necessarily know the gender, race or location of that (remote) agent. [T]he meaningfulness of the collaboration wouldn't depend on proximity, on affinity to gender, or affinity to cultural ideology.

RF: Theorists like Haraway are trying to reposition the body as an agent instead of a resource, and there's an irony in that you're making the body a resource and removing its agency externally.

Stelarc: It's not so much an erasure of agency, but rather a complexity and multiplicity of operational spaces between bodies and within bodies. Mind you, I do talk about the body being in an erasure zone rather than in a realm of affirmation where it's likely to be no longer merely contained in genetic memory, but rather reconfigured in electronic circuitry, and I'm very intrigued by the possibility of whether a body could function without memory. Now that seems a bizarre and foolish agenda to undertake, but is it possible that a body can function increasingly more in an immediate present and towards speculative possibilities rather than being contained by biological and genetic mappings that to a large degree *pre*-determine its behaviour?

RF: This appears to posit 'the body' as an autonomous agent, which is the opposite to science fictional cyberspace, where 'the mind' is portrayed as a separate agent without a 'meat' body.

Stelarc: Well, as long as we keep reminding ourselves that a body is not necessarily *merely* this biology.

RF: No, it's the phenomenological body of *embodied* knowledge. You assert that your work challenges the notion of Cartesian dualism, however it appears that your events accentuate the notions of splitting mind and body.

Stelarc: No. I think that that's the primary, fundamental misreading of these actions and these ideas. Partly because one is dedicated to using consensual language, and most of this language is coloured and contextual in its cultural comprehension. Therefore, when I talk about the body, I don't talk about it in contradistinction to a mind. I mean this physiological, phenomenological-cerebral package, and when we start making distinctions between persons and bodies and minds and selves and identity, then that's really when we (generate) all sorts of philosophical dilemmas that shouldn't be there.

I sometimes have to resort to referring to this body as 'I', but that's only because of the nature of our language. As long as one remembers that 'I' is this compressed encapsulation of a much larger framework of relationships. 'I' is only meaningful when this body is in the vicinity of another body operating in a social space, communicating in consensual language, at this particular time in history. The problem is that by using language conveniently we are seduced by this compression into a misunderstanding of the actual frame of reference. This is also the dilemma with a lot of science fiction, it postulates a sort of utopian ego-driven future as if this future already exists, whereas I tend to want to function in the way that, at any present moment there's a multiplicity of choices, and an infinity of possibilities. It's that collapsing of those into a situation or an event phenomena that generates the next moment of the present, so in a sense one never arrives at a future, one never escapes from the present.

RF: The perpetual present.

Stelarc: Yes. The problem with us is that we're genetically immersed in the past. So can the trajectory of the body be replotted to minimize its dependence on memory, to enhance the choice and operational complexity of the present and to generate more diverse strategies for any future moment of collapse? If one tries to function in that way I think one perhaps is closer to a posthuman situation.

RF: Despite the differences between what you're doing and SF, there are still many correlations. Do you find it a hindrance that people associate you with SF?

Stelarc: Well, simplistically one can see similar agendas in postulating future bodies or posthuman scenarios, but *accepting* that type of *generalized* similarity, there's a fundamental rupture between what a science fiction writer does and what a performance artist does, especially this one, even if this one is concerned with a post-biological body or a human/machine future. For me, it's inadequate simply to postulate or simply to theorize, or simply to write SF because ... it sounds awfully Marxian in falling back to praxis as a grounding for theory, but for me the authenticity of an idea is made concrete by the constraints *and* unpredictable possibilities of practice.

RF: … of authenticity and actualization.

Stelarc: Yes. Because one might well argue that anything is possible, but what generates actuality is that collapse of possibility into a particular and peculiar interaction.

RF: It has been said that Haraway has 'literalized' the SF metaphor of the cyborg into a theoretical being [Csicsery-Ronay, 1991: 396]. Would you say that you've literalized the SF metaphor of the cyborg into a reality?

Stelarc: I don't know what Haraway's relationship is to SF, [however] I think that when you speak in metaphor and you speak purely in text, then it is a realm of the mind. [N]onetheless, I think that [Haraway's, 1985] 'Manifesto' is very important, the notion of seeing technology as a means of redefining the social role of the female is a very significant one, rather than seeing technology as this patriarchal construct that *purely* perpetuates male power.

The thing that irritates me is the seeming desire to evaluate the status quo of society by referring to its popular culture, like comic books and SF writings and movies. With my work with the third hand, some feminist critique puts it in the realm of a *Terminator 2/RoboCop* sort of dystopian macho-military sci-fi future,

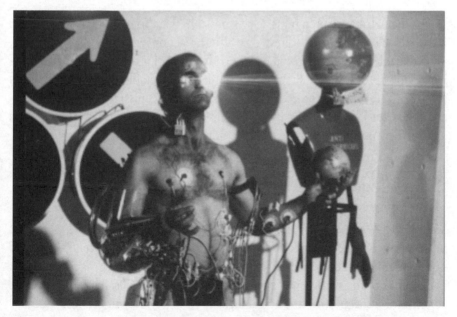

Figure 2 Event for Anti-Copernicus Robot, Newz Gallery, Tokyo, April 1985.
Photographer: Pamela Fernuik. © Stelarc.

whereas when the hand was first made in the early 1980s, those movies weren't around. I'm very uneasy about that strategy, because you're dealing with hype, you're dealing with the simplest of sci-fi scenarios . . . and what's perpetuated in these movies is dystopian futures; a justification of the pathology of the human species. [T]he cold metallic-phallic machines are inhuman and alien, and I just don't see it in those sorts of simplifications.

RF: You appear to have quite an optimism about technology. What reservations might you have?

Stelarc: Well firstly, when I talk technology, I don't necessarily mean '*hardware*' or 'state-of-the-art' technology. I'm well aware of the roots of technology coming from the word '*techne*' meaning 'skills', so for me technologies are merely the contemporary bits of hardware that enable us to undertake alternate strategies. And of course there's hardware technology and there's software technology, and language is a technology, so one has to firstly qualify and clarify what 'technology' means, before one talks about whether it's dystopian or not. Whether I'm optimistic or not, certainly I'm neither naively utopian, because what I say and do is grounded in my experience, so in a sense it's constrained by the limitations of my body and the determinations of the hardware that I'm using and what interfaces are possible.

For me, what's meaningful is what's possible. That's not to deny theory, but rather always trying to manifest theory in an action where, if it's interesting, unpredictable consequences will occur. Art is that business of generating ambivalent, ambiguous zones of slippage where the unpredictable is, and uncertainties are used to restructure and rethink. I'm not naively dismissing the purely theoretical, nor am I wildly and naively optimistic about all these new technologies creating new possibilities; it's a little bit more difficult than that.

RF: How do you feel about having been 'appropriated' by contemporary technoculture?

Stelarc: What is interesting, that has been even more apparent to me, is . . . this proliferation of concern and anxiety about '*the body*', because the centrality of the body, and my constant reference to the body as a structure rather than as a psyche, is indicative of the work I was doing back in the early 1970s. That has been the concern for me right from the beginning, and early critiques of my work focused on the so-called 'reductiveness' of that notion.

RF: So in some ways you feel that the contemporary theories of and focus on the body have now caught up to where you were before?

Stelarc: I'm not claiming that … it's just that for me it was always a discourse about the 'body', not so much a body devoid of social discourse, but certainly a body increasingly seen without the entrapments of what we call a 'mind' or a Platonic 'spirit' or a Cartesian 'split' between mind and brain.

RF: What do you think of Baudrillard's claim that it's no longer necessary to write SF because we've lost all referentiality, we're in 'hyperreality', we are living science-fiction now [Baudrillard, 1988: 36–7]?[2]

Stelarc: Well, I certainly have read Deleuze and Guattari, Baudrillard, Virilio, Lyotard, most of the people that you would be referring to in this sort of question. One would have to say that [Marshall] McLuhan generates the central discourse of technology in the 20th century. Every time I read these people, one is really startled by the diversity and the expansiveness of critique on technology that McLuhan provides. There are certain problems with his discourse and it's obviously clothed in the rhetoric of the 1960s, but for example, the notion of externalizing our nervous central system is for me a central tenet, one that is constantly being manifested in the Internet, in virtual reality technologies. Of course, technology isn't *merely* an extension of the body, but it's certainly a good place to begin the critique.

Coming back to Baudrillard, I think there is a certain factuality about that, and one can then refer back to Virilio's notion of 'speed', that in the technological terrain, technologies, discourse, the body, all of these elements of interactivity are speeded-up, the 'feedback loops' become increasingly invisible because they become increasingly immediate and subliminal. But for me what's interesting is how one could *function* effectively within that, which brings us to the point where we may have to consider the moment in time where we realize that an ergonomic approach to designing technology to match the body becomes superseded by the necessity to redesign the body to match its machines: creating more effective inputs and outputs and interfaces with these new technologies. At the moment, our interfaces are very crude, and I look forward to any unpredictable occurrences in those interfaces. Not necessarily to set the scenario and then to kind of revel in it, as say SF does.

RF: As SF does with the 'interface' of cyberspace perhaps.

Stelarc: Well, of course cyberspace is a consensual, technological interface. Virtual reality is not this hyped-up out-of-body experience, that's just simply a Cartesian extension, or a Platonic desire, or a new age pseudo-spiritual pursuit, which I think is pathological more than meaningful.

RF: Do you agree that we've reached a 'postmodern' era of 'inertia' through information overload, where we need new, possibly posthuman strategies, to enable a type of Jamesonian 'cognitive mapping'?

Stelarc: Well, I think we have. It's not so much the sheer quantity of information that's the problem, but the quality of information. I find it a concern that the information that the body is functioning with is information that it can't subjectively comprehend and sensorily experience. And then we've created a technological terrain of machines that often out-perform the body. That's another reason why the body is obsolete. Another reason is that the body now attains planetary escape velocity ... technology contains and accelerates the body off the Earth, and the body then finds itself in alien environments. For those reasons, the body now has become profoundly obsolete, and we have to query what it means not to be a psyche, but what it means to have this physiology, this structure, this architecture, because by altering or adjusting this architecture, I would suspect we also adjust our awareness to the world. We either have to incorporate this technology within the body so that it becomes part of our subjective sensorial apparatuses, *or* failing that, we have to somehow design more effective inputs and outputs.

RF: Following McLuhan, the 'virus' is a common metaphor for technology, but as such it mostly signifies apocalyptic danger. You have used the same metaphor of the virus *positively* for technology's 'invasion' of the body, saying that it is something that we are not immune to.

Stelarc: Well, I pointed that out in a neutral way, in that, yes we've evolved immunological responses to bacteria and viruses, but technology hasn't been inside the body long enough ... so the body doesn't have any evolutionary raison d'etre to reject it. Whereas once the compatibility of technology depended on the substance of that implant, now it simply depends on its *scale*. If it's bloody small enough, then it's gonna happily be incorporated into the body. The other intriguing thing about the body is that its immunological response doesn't extend to what we consider the most valuable part of the body, the brain. There's only this blood barrier between the body and the brain ... and when the actuality of implanting into the brain is a more viable option than any other part of the body then yes, it is an intriguing possibility.

RF: What is your opinion of the fictional cyberpunk motif of neural jacking?

Stelarc: [It's not] that I don't admire SF writers as textual crafts people that enhance imaginative thoughts, but I think that the metaphor of a neural jack is the cerebral person's transgression that is a biological and sexual day-to-day activity. We in a sense transgress other people's bodies every time we indulge in this intimate sexual act. The neural jack is the cerebral version of that. Is it merely a kind of a 'mind-fuck', or is it something more meaningful? And I suspect in a lot of SF writing, it's not much more than the sexual analogue.

RF: And also often simply a transcendental manoeuvre...

Stelarc: And the dilemma with myself, I mean I can protest until I'm blue in the face, but in reading these performances and actions, the two most common critiques centre around the fact that there're either some pseudo-spiritual pursuit, that there're about transcending the body, or that it's to do with male power – and there's a third one, that it's somehow an inadvertent fascist manifestation of metallic-phallic militaristic sorts. Is it too much to insist on a reading of these performances without that strategy of categorization? Can one evaluate that action *beginning* with the performance rather than *ending* with the performance? By categorizing and comprehending through cultural appropriation of archetypical memories and cultural cliches, one always begins with something else and then finally points to the performance and says: 'that's what it's all about', rather than beginning with the performance and then trying to point to the meaning.

Virilio expresses a concern with the notion of me wanting to incorporate technology into the body, which is a fair enough concern ... [but] I'm totally misquoted by [him], [he]simplifies [my work] into a *Terminator 2* kind of a cyborg.[3] Furthermore, he reports that I also want to *enhance* my sexual prowess ... not to make love to one woman, but to make love to countless women. Now, I don't really talk a lot about sexuality as such, and even in terms of redesigning the body I don't think I've ever talked about sexuality in that way, and the only times that I've spoken about the sensual and sexual possibilities is recently with the 'Internet Upload' of the body. Sandy Stone asked me what this system might mean for cybersex and I said well, I guess touching my chest in Melbourne would result in you caressing your breast in New York, so there is this sort of sexual intimacy possibility with that sort of system.

RF: And there is the 'gender identity' factor that you mentioned previously.

Stelarc: Yeah, I may not be another transsexual, I may not be a man, I may not be a female. I might be an adolescent who's hacked his way or her way on to this web site. . . . So I found [Virilio's interpretation] rather amusing. And then having cited me in these ways he *concludes* that this is the end of art as we know it! . . . that this artist is a prophet of doom! Using his terminology immediately colours the thing into some kind of techno-Shaman, pseudo-mystical, ecstatic non-thinking, non-rational being, right? [H]e reports that I have a naive view of technology. Now that was the thing that I took most umbrage too, because these are ideas that have emanated from interfaces, from direct experiences. One could well say that a theoretician like Virilio might be the one who's naive about technology.

RF: I wanted to ask you about those responses to your work, those who say your just another 'techno jock, toys for the boys, militarism, Eurocentric white male gaze from nowhere', this sort of thing.

Stelarc: Well, isn't there a certain truth to that. But I think that is very simplistic, and the validity and the meaningfulness of feminist critique is undermined if [it] wants to continue with those sorts of simplistic assertions; that technology is simply a construct that perpetuates male power, or that this is all about toys for boys. Certainly the use of technology for me has never been grounded either in that type of technology, nor in that sort of discourse. I think what's more pertinent is to examine the way I've used medical technologies, which is also another happy hunting ground for feminist critique, in that they see medical technologies as another means by which male society has controlled women's bodies.

RF: Yes. Patriarchal appropriation of reproduction. . .

Stelarc: But of course there are different strains of feminism, and one strain of feminism would see the advantage of the [release from the burden of birth]. . .

RF: Yes, Valie Export provides one example of such a point-of-view. Do you see your work addressing racial and gender difference in any way?

Stelarc: Well, not really. Not that it doesn't realize the certain implications. . . . Of course there are some gender distinctions [between the ways males and females utilize technologies], but the other thing that one has to realize in a world of ambiguous gender, in a world of gay and feminist rights, in a world of transgendered operations, gender becomes a blur of lots of shades of subtle distinctions rather than a male and female, a heterosexual or gay, polarization.

RF: Your earlier performances were sometimes banned, whereas now there's quite an acceptance of your work. Does your recent appropriation by mainstream and techno-culture in any way undermine your work, or is it helping to disseminate your ideas? Is it a positive or a negative?

Stelarc: I see it as neither, but what amazes me is the ability of our cultural mechanism to be able to on the one hand generate fringe activities, and on the other, absorb them within years. Now [my early] suspension events are art history fodder for high school kids. It's disconcerting but I guess it also guarantees the generation of other fringe [artists]. . . . The problem with postmodernism is that it becomes incestuous, it becomes self-referential, appropriating cultural archetypes, generating discourse, but then not really proposing new (strategies). What technology does though is *bypass* the ideological rhetoric, and generate alternate strategies, aesthetic possibilities that just weren't applicable or plausible in either modernism or postmodern rhetoric.

RF: You talk about the body as being an essentially automatic process, rather than a free agent, and tied to that was a notion that in this age of information the freedom of expression would no longer be as meaningful as the 'much more fundamental freedom' to manipulate your body. If you don't have freedom of ideas, how do you get a continual process of new form?

Stelarc: I was simply pointing out that in an age of information overload, freedom of ideas becomes less an issue because the access to it is more possible, and what's going to be threatening to political, social, and religious institutions isn't so much whether you have certain information available but rather the more fundamental notion of altering your form and altering your functions, because one can see this Frankensteinian fear; we are frightened by different things with different form, with different functions.

RF: In SF this is referred to as the 'Frankenstein Barrier', where [Mary] Shelley refused to give Frankenstein's creature a bride because that would have meant creating 'difference' as a perpetual Other species [Slusser, 1992]. The posthuman is still generally cast as evil, it's negative rather than desired, and this is the [hubristic] barrier to extrapolation of the 'posthuman condition' that's only just starting to be overcome now.

Stelarc: But I think that there's a problem with both the negation that you spoke of and the desiring, because the desiring then presupposes a particular and peculiar agenda, and we don't want the political and social control of these...

RF: We want diversification, multiplicities. . .

Stelarc: Multiple futures, that's right. The feminist agenda of contesting futures is a valid one in that it guarantees a diversity of outcome and a choice of direction, and that's a really important issue in this.

RF: Talking of multiplicities, Roger Caillois writes about breaking the boundaries of the skin, from a psychoanalytical point of view, as being the metaphorical precondition of a negatively conceived schizophrenia, through changing the body's relationship to its boundaries.[4] Your work has always being concerned with breaking the boundaries of skin and body, relocating yourself spatially and temporally. Does this breaking the boundaries of the skin offer any new valuable multiplicity of perspective to humanity in terms of some *desired* 'Deleuzean' schizophrenic state?

Stelarc: In terms of the person, what's engaging when you're fully extended and plugged in and operational in a performance is that your relationship to your skin and the technology is in a realm of symbiosis where distinctions are not meaningful to be made. Intelligence is extruded into the system of things, it's not just happily located in your body, because if you're functioning within a complexity of 'feedback loops' then your response and the initiation of further actions is not that clearly bounded by a 'self' guiding a body to perform a particular action, and so I would say the realm of symbiosis or the realm of intimate interface and complex feedback loops is almost an anaestheticization of the body, where it has to function in a somewhat different way, one that's not easily spoken about in convenient polarities . . . and I'm not trying to mystify the experience.

McLuhan's notion of technology as being an extension of the body is a kind of one-way extrapolation where the body is the central agent and everything emanates from that, whereas I think what happens now in a post-McLuhan age is that these extensions generate sudden feedback loops and create a different operational experience. [Because I'm not a writer, what I say is really a fairly painful rendering of a lot of actual experiences, it's a very conservative extrapolation of those experiences. It's quite the opposite to the SF kind of play of imaginative possibilities.]

RF: Commodification of the posthuman is a common motif in both cultural theory and SF. All 'technologies' are company owned, and therefore the bodies that they are incorporated into become commodified/compromised. Don't you also have to confront this issue, and a possible elitism in the technological post-human?

Stelarc: Well, the commodification and the elitism of access are both issues that, hey!, I'm up against right now. I can't afford to buy a multimedia, infra-red network Pentium powered [computer]. [It] guarantees a certain uneven dissemination of new technology that's not necessarily unhelpful. All that it guarantees is that the experiments are going to be done on the elite. [Laughs gleefully] If finally you're going to get a heart transplant that works, you're going to probably get it when the bloody thing does really work because they've done experiments on countless others more 'worthy', more financially able people.

RF: You've said this evolution is 'of the Individual, by the Individual', and I was wondering on what basis these 'chosen individuals' would be selected?

Stelarc: What I was trying to point out there is that when I'm talking about redesigning the body, I'm not talking about redesigning the species, or creating a master race. I'm saying that you may decide, either for aesthetic, altruistic or medical reasons to have an implant. It was just to make the distinction between the notion of post-evolution as being more one of choice ... we'd all be suspicious of someone who said, well, 'hey from birth we're gonna completely modify bodies.'

RF: What are your future plans?

Stelarc: There's another version of the 'Internet Upload Event' where there'll be a robot in the system as well. So activating *this* body will also mean interactively controlling this additional robotic device in the loop. Most of my body's movements are controlled by this touch screen interface, but at the same time I'm actuating a virtual body, and trying to avoid a pre-programmed robot, which gets interactively interrupted. The simplicity of my free agency is confronted by programmed robots, involuntary body movements, third hand actuations, remote involvement: how does one cope with all of this? So it's exciting! [More laughter]

Among Stelarc's more recent events is the Ping Body Performance. The following is an edited excerpt from Stelarc's Web page describing the event. More details are available at this site: http://www.merlin.com.au/stelarc

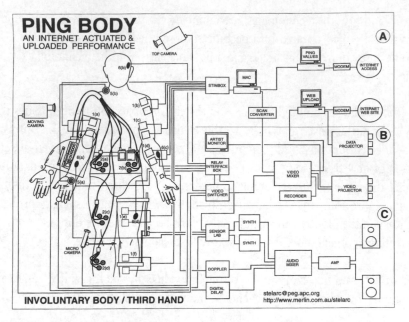

Figure 3 Ping Body: Internet Actuated/Internet Uploaded. © Stelarc.

The Ping Body performance produces a powerful inversion of the usual interface of the body to the Net. Instead of collective bodies determining the operation of the Internet, the collective Internet activity moves the body. By random pinging to Internet domains it is possible to map spatial distance and transmission time to body motion. Thus ping values that indicate spatial and time parameters of the Internet choreograph and compose the performance. The Internet becomes not merely a mode of information transmission, but also a transducer, affecting physical action.

Complementary to the Ping Body are the *ParaSite Performances*. Stelarc attempts to add the body-as-parasite to the digital data streams of the Internet, thus graphically demonstrating the oscillating system of reciprocal extension and influence between body and technology.

> This is not about a fragmented body but a multiplicity of bodies and parts of bodies prompting and remotely guiding each other. This is not about master–slave control mechanisms but feedback-loops of alternate awareness, agency and split physiologies. (Stelarc, 1998, 'ParaSite visions alternate, intimate and involuntary experiences'; available electronically: www.merlin. com.au/stelarc)

Notes

1. Although Stelarc does talk about the obsolete body and related theories in this interview, a more complete extrapolation of these basic ideas is available in his various published writings, such as, Stelarc (1994a, 1994b) and Stelarc and Paffrath (1984). His web site is also a good source of such information [http://www.merlin.com.au/stelarc].

2. This claim is, of course, not limited to Baudrillard. Haraway, for example, states; 'the boundary between science fiction and social reality is . . . [now] an optical illusion' (1985: 66).

3. Stelarc is referring specifically here to an interview with Virilio by Virginia Madsen (1995). Virilio writes about the perceived consequences of Stelarc's body art in many of his own works. See for example *The Art of the Motor* (1995).

4. For a discussion of Roger Caillois' 'Mimicry and Legendary Psychasthenia' as it pertains to the subject's identity and perspective of the world in relation to the space occupied by the body, see Elizabeth Grosz's discussion in *Volatile Bodies* (1994: 46–8).

References

Baudrillard, Jean (1988) 'The Year 2000 Has Already Happened', pp. 35–44 in A. Korker and M. Kroker (eds) *Body Invaders: Sexuality and the Postmodern Condition*. London: Macmillan.

Caillois, Roger (1984) 'Mimicry and Legendary Psychasthenia', *October* 31: 17–32.

Csicsery-Ronay, Istvan, Jr (1991) 'The SF of Theory: Baudrillard and Haraway', *Science Fiction Studies* 18(3): 397–404.

Grosz, Elizabeth (1994) *Volatile Bodies: Toward a Corporeal Feminism*. St Leonards: Allen & Unwin.

Haraway, Donna (1985) 'A Manifesto for Cyborgs: Science, Technology and Social Feminism in the 1980s', *Socialist Review* 15(80): 65–107.

Madsen, Virginia (1995) 'Critical Mass (An Interview with Paul Virilio)', *World Art: The Magazine of Contemporary Visual Arts* 1: 78–82.

Slusser, George (1992) 'The Frankenstein Barrier', pp. 47–71 in T. Shippey and G. Slusser (eds) *Fiction 2000: Cyberpunk and the Future of Narrative*. London: University of Georgia Press.

Stelarc (1994a) 'From Psycho to Cyber Strategies: Prosthetics, Robotics and Remote Existence', [http://www.merlin.com.au/stelarc].

Stelarc (1994b) 'Towards the Post-Human (From Absent to Phantom Bodies)', pp. 20–21, 53 in N. Waterlow (curator) *25 Years of Performance Art in Australia: Performance Art, Performance and Events*. Ivan Dougherty Gallery/ Marrickville NSW: R.F. Jones.

Stelarc and James D. Paffrath (1984) *Obsolete Bodies/ Suspensions/ Stelarc*. Davis, CA: J.B. Publications.

Virilio, Paul (1995) *The Art of the Motor*, trans. Julie Rose. Minneapolis: University of Minnesota Press.

Ross Farnell has recently successfully completed his doctoral thesis at Monash University's Centre for Cultural Studies and Comparative Literature. His thesis is titled: 'Mediations & Becomings: The Posthuman Condition in Contemporary Science Fiction and Cultural Theory'. His prime interests are popular culture, science fiction and contemporary theories of the body. Prior to returning to study, where he completed a first class honours degree in English Literature, he spent a decade as a musician, developing a strong interest in all areas of the arts. His publications include *Bodies That Speak Science Fiction: Stelarc – Performance Artist Becoming Posthuman* (Liverpool University Press, 1997).

An Order of Pure Decision: Un-Natural Selection in the Work of Stelarc and Orlan

JANE GOODALL

'Care to reprogram yourself? Customize your kids? Derail evolution?' (Platt, 1997: 158). This is the opening challenge of a recent *Wired* magazine article on the Human Genome Project. The invitation to speculate about radically enhanced bodies is also an invitation to try on an enlarged idea of human agency and to imagine the potentialities of a human will that has superseded the will of nature. It sounds like a very new fantasy, but also a very old one: the final achievement of human control over human life. What might they be like, the post-evolutionary bodies of the future? In the world of commodities, the finest products of human design combine beauty with functional perfection. In fantasy tradition, from *Frankenstein* to *Blade Runner*, the designer of a new post-natural order of humanity has always at least aimed to achieve this combination. But in our own time, such an aim must inevitably be associated with the troubled history of eugenics. History has proved that the human will is not to be trusted when it tries to take over from the will of nature. Traditional imaginings about the futuristic body may be governed by predetermined ideas, even as they purport to offer entirely new visions of what is in prospect. The human body as a design project situated between the disciplines of aesthetics and engineering is a body interpreted in accordance with long-standing conventions.

This article concerns the work of two artists who, for the last 20 years, have been challenging those conventions. Orlan and Stelarc both work with the body as the primary medium for their art and both, in their very different ways, are

Body & Society © 1999 SAGE Publications (London, Thousand Oaks and New Delhi),
Vol. 5(2–3): 149–170
[1357–034X(199906/09)5:2–3;149–170;008862]

interested in redesigning the body. Their experiments depart radically from popular and traditional ways of imagining enhanced forms of human embodiment and in a climate of intense speculation about the future of the body, their ideas offer some important provocations. The prospect of tampering with natural selection in the human is one heavily invested with cultural anxiety, so that speculation is often overheated and becomes hard to uncouple from its premises. As performance artists, Orlan and Stelarc explore embodiment through enactment in ways that evade the stock formulations of cultural anxiety and open up fundamental questions about the nature and meanings of the human body, questions that are too easily foreclosed by overheated imaginings.

The Extropians, a Los Angeles collective who seek 'to push beyond the merely human stage of evolution' offer a striking example of how futuristic imaginings escalate into exhilaration and paranoia. The Extropian Principles include:

> Seeking more intelligence, wisdom and effectiveness, an unlimited lifespan, and the removal of political, cultural, biological, and psychological limits to self-actualization and self-realization. Perpetually overcoming constraints on our progress and possibilities. Expanding into the universe and advancing without end. (More, 1993: 1)

Such visions can also induce a panic-stricken retreat into what Arthur Kroker calls 'the seduction of domination', which offers 'the promise of limits under the sign of judgement to save us from limitlessness, from an order of existence with no rules, no laws, only excess, only challenge' (1992: 10).

In the late 20th century, the ancient theme of free will versus determinism has found a new crisis, in which it can no longer take its bearings from value systems appealing to the ultimate authorities of God or Nature or Fate. Ethics comes to the fore as the only means by which we can steer a course through 'an order of pure decision' as François Ewald has labelled the human predicament in an era of advanced technology:

> We are irremediably alone, orphaned even by nature. The nature we are confronting today and that we have chosen as our partner is nothing other than our own double. The true speech it is supposed to have taught us and that was to dictate our conduct has never been anything more than we have made it. (1993: 225)

Yet the entry into 'an order of pure decision' involves more than merely dispensing with the stratagem of projecting our own agency onto something called 'nature'. Every decision involves judgement, and where decisions will have social or material consequences, judgement involves ethical analysis of what is at stake. The convention of equating freedom with choice breaks down in a situation where there is no freedom *from* choice. As advances in medical technology are continuously expanding the domain of human decision-making, choice itself is becoming an inescapable obligation in areas from which it was previously excluded. A pregnant woman may be given the choice of whether or not to have amniocentesis but she cannot choose not to choose, nor can she avoid the further decisions that may be consequent upon the initial one. On another level, today's newspaper reports on the signing of the first international ban on human cloning. Thirteen countries have so far decided to commit themselves to the ban and, presumably, some countries will decide not to do so. Either way, the decision must now be made. The elegiac tone of Ewald's pronouncement has a slightly mocking edge. We have taken ourselves too seriously, perhaps, we humans, in thinking of ourselves as cared for by some cosmological agency in the role of parent. We have looked for oracular guidance where there is no guidance to be found other than our own wits. We may allow ourselves the indulgence of a little pathos as we face up to our situation as orphans and ask ourselves just what kinds of creatures 'we' are, or might become, by our own agency.

Alternatively, we can cut the pathos and be blunt:

> Like the Australian artist Stelarc, I think that the body is obsolete. It is no longer adequate for the current situation. We mutate at the rate of cockroaches, but we are cockroaches whose memories are in computers, who pilot planes and drive cars that we have conceived, although our bodies are not conceived for these speeds. (Orlan, 1996: 91)

This is Orlan speaking. She and Stelarc have never worked collaboratively, but their experiments offer significant parallels. The two artists have more in common than a belief that the body is obsolete. They are close in age, both started to produce significant works in the early 1970s, and they are among the few performance artists who have outlasted the performance art vogue of that decade, continuing their challenge to the naturalized body through the 1980s and 1990s. Orlan tests the limits of a new technologically derived freedom to alter the form and appearance of the human body through surgery; Stelarc explores the possibilities of connectivity to a point where he can claim that the body linked up with electronic circuitry has ceased to function as a delimited entity. They are among the few to have put speculation to the test and engaged in the process of actualizing hypotheses. They know what it is to experience certain kinds of organic alteration. Agency emerges as a key issue in the work of both: in the case of Orlan, through engagement with a history of deterministic anxieties in religion, and in the case of Stelarc, through action experiments which problematize the idea of the individualized body as agent.

Despite these parallels, the artists give very different meanings to the experience of inhabiting 'an order of pure decision'. Their approaches present a fundamental contrast in aesthetic and conceptual orientation, and seem to arise from different ontologies. This raises an obvious question about the extent to which gender is a key factor in these differences. Stelarc has been accused of a form of macho narcissism that manifests in an aggressive master/slave attitude to the body (Marsh, 1993: chap. 2). His claim that the body is obsolete, which often forms the theme of his public lectures, is commonly challenged from feminist points of view in question time: isn't this the ultimate patriarchal fantasy, this arrogant denigration of the body, as though there were a self able to declare independence from embodiment? When Orlan endorses Stelarc's most controversial slogan and associates her own feminist project with it, she is making a consciously political gesture. If women are trained to see themselves as totally identified with and determined by their embodiment, perhaps the principle that the body is obsolete has much a more trenchant edge when it is a woman who proposes to act on it. It is also important to recognize, though, that Orlan is implicitly rejecting some of the hard-line feminist critiques of Stelarc's project, and making explicit a commonality of vision and practice. There can surely be no more direct way of confronting the realities of embodiment than to undergo a programme of physical experiences designed to test its limits.

Neither of the two artists has ever shown any inclination to look to nature for true speech. They share a talent for playing the oracle:

> My work is a struggle against: the innate, the inexorable, the programmed, Nature, DNA (which is our direct rival as . . . artists of representation), and God!
> My work is blasphemous. (Orlan, 1996: 92)

> It is time to question whether a bipedal, breathing body with binocular vision and a 1400 cc brain is an adequate biological form. (Stelarc, spoken text in Gruchy, 1996)

Such declarations are clearly designed to provoke. They are in calculated defiance of any form of reverence for the body as a given and are an affront to any residual beliefs that Nature-knows-best. Perhaps Ewald exaggerates in claiming general dependence on such beliefs. Neil Smith offers an alternative perspective, suggesting that the late 20th century 'may well be seen in retrospect as the nadir of a process lasting several centuries in which "western" societies most completely flattered themselves about their autonomy from the natural world' (1996: 39). In this view, the pronouncements of Stelarc and Orlan would be quite uncontroversial: modish contributions, perhaps, to the culture of self-flattery. Ewald, though, is attuned to a more complex Zeitgeist, in which self-flattery is only the other side of an angst produced by the experience of living with perpetual consciousness of risk and nature is in the role of deserting parent, no longer there to focus the ambivalence of rebellion and dependency. This ambivalence is at its most acute with regard to the human body. The notion of autonomy from the natural world can become a threatening prospect when one's own body is potentially implicated. To propose that the human body is entirely negotiable in an order of pure decision is ontologically confronting and strips away most of the historically accumulated responses to the question: 'What does it mean to be human?'

As recent directions in scientific experiment cause this question to be posed with a new urgency and rawness, related experiments by artists may offer a valuable counter-focus. The experimental artist tends to reject institutional identification and sets his or her own terms of operation, often with a deliberately provocative arbitrariness and apparent disregard for how spectators may judge the work as presented. The aim is to destabilize ways of making meaning, rather than to pin them down; to loosen any tenets that promise to become foundational and generally to play the role of *provocateur*, though to do this effectively involves a certain strategic exactness. It may also, as in the cases of both Stelarc and Orlan, involve a sustained commitment at least equivalent to that of the scientist on a long-term research project. While what is done in the laboratory can generate widespread theoretical and fictional speculation, it is not the role of the scientist to respond to ideas arising from the cultural imaginary. The experiments of the artist, on the other hand, can work on the materials of cultural tradition, social formation and generic fantasy by means of procedures carried out on the organic matter of the body and offered to public audience as performance.

Ewald alludes to 'a new generation of risks' created through technological interventions. Both artists have achieved notoriety for taking risks in deliberately spectacular ways. They are creators of *scandal*, in the original sense of the term as σχανδαλον, a trap or stumbling block, metaphorically interpreted as a moral snare causing perplexity and ethical confusion (*OED*). Some forms of risk-taking may be scandalous, but scandal in this sense tests the moral ground and puts morality itself at risk. A scandal arises easily in situations where the social consensus is strong and breaches of it are easily defined. In a postmodern context, a widely publicized scandal will provoke different responses from different pockets of social consensus and, perhaps most interestingly, may generate additional anxiety by seeming to threaten the viability of consensus. Many of the more virulent reactions to the work of Stelarc and Orlan have taken the form of aggressively asserted consensus. By threatening to make a breach in the moral order, a scandal sends shock waves through society, stirring up energies which work to reinforce the ground of common values. If we are entering an order of pure decision, the social impact of this will be immense. Fundamentalist retreats to traditional moral codes are one predictable outcome, but equally predictable is the conflict between such codes on any issue that puts the status of the human body radically in question. A system of moral precepts may be predicated on a principle that serves as supreme arbiter (Midgley, 1991), but a system of ethics may have to negotiate between conflicting systems of morality to arrive at an ultimate principle of arbitration. If formal processes of ethical judgement are going to rise effectively to the new order of challenge posed by late 20th-century technological and scientific breakthroughs, we are all going to have to learn to cope with events that throw our learned principles of judgement into question. A good scandal – one which generates complex confusions around high-intensity issues and cannot be resolved through the simple assertion of precepts – may help to prepare the cultural ground for a quantum leap in the demands on individual and collective decision-making capacities. Stelarc and Orlan offer, among other things, some good scandals.

Orlan overtly courts scandal, and her anarchically experimental attitude to embodiment belongs to a project which is directed against the powerful physical conservatism associated with the Judaeo-Christian belief systems that dominate her cultural heritage. With their practices of bodily purification and discipline, these systems work to promote humility in conjunction with the constant threat of shame. The body becomes a humbling attribute that serves to keep the psyche within bounds and to circumscribe agency. In the Christian monastic tradition, men and women alike are subject to these strictures and the ethic of submission leads to a feminized model of subjecthood for both sexes, as exemplified in the precepts of St Ignatius:

> In the hands of my Superior, I must be a soft wax, a thing from which he is to require whatever pleases him, be it to write or receive letters, to speak or not to speak to such a person, or the like; and I must put all my fervour in executing zealously and exactly what I am ordered. I must consider myself as a corpse which has neither intelligence nor will. (Ignatius of Loyola, quoted in James, 1960: 309)

In secular life, such principles translate conveniently into gender roles. They are applied specifically to the governance of female behaviour and, most particularly, to the management of the body. Social regulations monitor dress, manner and posture in petty detail. If the actions or functions of the body escape discipline, shame is visited upon the subject through a comprehensive repertoire of social enactments. The ungoverned body is a body ostracized from the social and anathema to the body politic. The repression of sexuality, and of female sexuality in particular, is essential to a regime of social control preserved through stringent patriarchal management of all aspects of physical life. Emile Zola's novel *Nana* offers a vivid glimpse of this social world in the 1870s in its portrait of the Comtesse Muffat at home:

> She had no lovers: that was obvious. One had only to look at her beside that daughter of hers, so stiff and insipid on her footstool. That sepulchral drawing room of hers, smelling like a church, revealing plainly enough the iron hand, the austere existence, which weighed upon her. There was no trace of her own personality in the ancient abode, black with damp. It was Muffat

who reigned supreme there, who dominated the household with his devout upbringing, his penances and his fasts. (Zola, 1972: 81)

While the theory of natural selection threatened the theological underpinnings of this disciplinary tradition, it left many of the social and psychological constraints undisturbed, or even served to reinforce them. Fears of the insufficiently governed and socialized body becoming animal, sliding down the evolutionary ladder, heightened the need for social codings of 'good breeding'. (This is one of the major themes of Zola's *Nana*.) The disciplines required to produce the correct indicators of breeding were at their most oppressively anxious among the French bourgeoisie,[1] one of the immediate targets of Orlan's early work. Where Stelarc insists on being a-historical, Orlan acknowledges the potentially determining influences of cultural history in her choice of counter-determining strategies.

In 1971, she created a photographic portrait of herself as 'Saint Orlan'. This was a gesture of both reverence and blasphemy: reverent in its acknowledgement of the potency of Judaeo-Christian iconography, blasphemous in its *detournement* of sacred imagery. In this work, images designed to produce a mixture of spiritual intoxication and physical discipline are turned into sources of physical intoxication and provide the basis for an aesthetic discipline that is profoundly material. Although there is a form of reverence in the adherence to these images, there is no residual adherence to the moral framework which the images have served to create. Orlan worships beauty entirely in its icons and refuses to acknowledge any higher or prior source for it. As her career progresses, she insists that beauty is no longer a goal, merely a stage she has been passing through. The true project is self-determination through designed alterations to her embodiment. There is a deeper blasphemy in the parodic assumption of sainthood together with the refusal of a social identity bestowed, along with the patronym, at christening. Orlan's determination to interfere with her given identity provides the sustaining motivation for her whole oeuvre. In the early works, this interference takes the form of a theatrical game, involving various forms of dressing up and acting out. In *One off Striptease with Trousseau Sheets* (1976), Orlan wound herself in the sheets from her family trousseau to evoke the image of the Madonna, and then unwound them until she was naked. To attempt to transcend one's given social identity by assuming an image to which some special power is attached is a traditional enough stratagem and one endorsed by Catholicism, provided it follows a prescribed pattern. Catholic girls, for instance, may be encouraged to remake themselves in the image of a chosen female saint or martyr, but the goal is self-negation rather than self-advertisement. Orlan's theatrical exhibitionism is an inversion of the ecclesiastically approved practices of veiling and retreat. Her 'sainthood' is a blasphemous violation of the culture of the saintly image, but more than just the image is

Orlan, Occasional Striptease with Trousseau Sheets, 1976
Copyright: Orlan. Reproduced by kind permission.

violated. There is a fundamental offence against doctrines of humility in her exorbitant assertion of self and her commitment to the enlargement of self-will. To an extent, this is specifically a form of 'gender infringement' – a violation of the ethic of meekness inculcated so deeply in women of the bourgeoisie – but Orlan's project goes beyond this. It is a form of Prometheanism that involves feminism, rather than vice versa. She recognizes and exploits the crucial status of the body as that which delimits the self and provides the means by which the overreacher may be humbled (the punishment of Prometheus was a daily reminder that he was embodied and therefore restrainable).

> To interfere with the given form of the body is to invoke divine wrath:
> Psychoanalysis and religion agree in saying: 'One must not attack the body', 'One must accept oneself'. These are primitive, ancestral, anachronistic concepts. We think that the sky will fall on our heads if we touch the body. (1996: 91)

Here Orlan is equating an attack upon the body with refusal to accept 'oneself' as a given. French bourgeois interpretations of psychoanalysis and religion had the effect of reducing female selfhood to embodiment, and this remains a widespread tendency in the women's magazine cultures of the late 20th century. To 'accept yourself' in this culture is to accept the form of your body and face. Magazines will often preach this ethic, recounting inspiring anecdotes and cautionary tales about women who have succeeded or failed in 'accepting themselves', yet interspersing such editorials with uncompromising images of what it means to be 'acceptable' in terms dictated by the beauty industry, and with further editorials offering advice on how to achieve the required image through various disciplines of diet, exercise and purchasing. As Bryan Turner puts it:

> In contemporary society the self is … a representational self, whose value and meaning is ascribed to the individual by the shape and image of their external body, or more precisely, through their body-image. The regulatory control of the body is now exercised through consumerism and the fashion industry rather than through religion. (1996: 23)

Having begun with some attacks at the level of the image, Orlan proceeds to another, more radical stage in her programme of intervention, on the level of corporeal substance and composition. The skin itself may be seen as an expression of the irrational dictatorship of nature, yet also as a plastic medium just waiting for the artist to reveal its design possibilities. Here, she acknowledges as her inspiration a passage by Eugenie Lemoine Luccioni, published in 1983:

> Skin is deceiving … in life, one has only one's skin … there is a bad exchange in human relations because one never is what one has. … I have the skin of an angel but I am a jackal … the skin of a crocodile but I am a poodle, the skin of a black person but I am white, the skin of a woman but I am a man; I never have the skin of what I am. There is no exception to the rule because I am never what I have. (quoted in Orlan, 1996: 88)

Orlan's work was already exploring the lack of fit between identity and image, but here the idea is taken one step further with the invention of an 'I' that refuses to take its identity from its corporeal form. The lack of fit between body and self is made explicit. It would be logical for such an 'I' to seek to choose its own body, so defining itself not by its body, but by its capacity of choice. The idea that identity is fully achieved through the act of making or re-making one's own body according to one's own will is deeply heretical and is powerfully expressed in another of Orlan's favourite texts: Artaud's late poem *To Have Done with the Judgement of God* (first published in 1948). Artaud proposes that in order to restore human being to its proper and free condition, it is necessary to put the body on an autopsy table for a complete anatomical reconstruction. This complex text labels the given body an 'ape' – an imitation human – and proposes that the human proper be restored. In her fascination with the strictly physiological process of achieving a body without organs, Orlan comes closer than Deleuze and Guattari to an interpretation which acknowledges the literal meaning given to the phrase by its context. In a series of works beginning in 1990, she placed herself on the operating table to be reworked, in accordance with her own determination and her own design, and in defiance of the 'organic' or god-given form of her appearance. She planned her series of surgical interventions to include systematic interference with each of the organs of the face. (In French the word *intervention* means 'operation', and Orlan exploits this connotation in her work.) Several of the operations have also involved liposuction on the limbs and torso.

The operations were planned as a series of ten, with the inaugurating title *The*

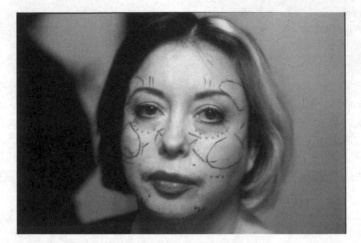

Dessein du dessin (Cibachrome, 1.10m × 1.65m)
Orlan prepared for her operation, 23 November 1993, New York
Source: Copyright Sipa Press, Sydney Freelance. Published by kind permission.

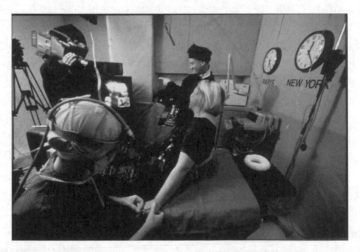

First Contact with the Georges Pompidou Centre via Videophone (Cibachrome, 1.10m × 1.65m)
Orlan in the operating studio during her operation, 23 November 1993, New York
Source: Copyright Sipa Press, Sydney Freelance. Published by kind permission.

Reincarnation of Saint Orlan. Through these works, the concept of reincarnation is stripped of its numinous mystery to be literalized, in the most explicit possible ways, as a programme of alterations to the state of the flesh. The 'works' are not the completed operations, but the operations in process, as performances, with the fully conscious artist being videotaped and photographed through every stage of the procedure. She remains in communication with her remote audience of gallery visitors by talking to them or reading from texts chosen to serve as conceptual commentaries on what is taking place. At the outset, the plan for her transformation was established as a progress through the great mythological images of Western femininity. Orlan would acquire the chin of Venus, the nose of Psyche, the eyes of Diana, the lips of Europa and the brow of the Mona Lisa. The proposed image composite was previewed on computer, a tool which began to have a defining influence on the terms of the project. 'This is my body, this is my software', Orlan proclaimed in 1994, following her penultimate operation. The series has progressed irregularly, with the first and second operation only six days apart in 1990, and the fourth completed before the end of that year. The fifth was in July of the following year, the sixth in February 1992, the seventh (and most significant so far) in 1993, followed by the eight and ninth leading into 1994. She has yet to undergo the final ordeal, which will involve a radical augmentation of the nose. The 'Omnipresence' series – the seventh, eight and ninth interventions – involved implants into the upper cheeks and the sides of the forehead, to give the impression of budding horns. It is with this series that Orlan has made her departure decisively from conventional aesthetic principles for the composition of the face. 'Beauty' is a phase through which she has been passing with her evocation of the goddesses celebrated by the great masters of European painting. It is not, and has never been, her goal, which may rather have been to provoke outrage among the gatekeepers of the art world (a goal she has most certainly achieved) by assuming the equivalence of her own works with those of Leonardo or Boticelli. With the culminating alteration to the shape of her nose at the next operation, yet to be performed, the estrangement of the face will be sufficiently marked to warrant the claim that she has, indeed, transformed her identity. The plan then is to hire an advertising agency to devise a new name for her and to lodge a court application for a new set of identity papers.

This ostentatious interference with the lived body, the social body and the body image has understandably generated strong reactions. It is a rare observer who is so free of inhibitory sensitivities as to be able to watch the surgical performances with equanimity. The seventh operation, first of the 'Omnipresence' series, was relayed live by satellite into the Sandra Gering Gallery in New York, where a packed audience was filmed watching it, and subsequently interviewed about it for

CNN television. The television coverage makes for a strange experience of doubled witness, as the camera shows the face being operated on, interspersed with images of the faces of the audience. As the face on the gallery screen is cut open with a series of incisions at the sides which are then prised wide open for insertions, the faces watching from the gallery painfully contort, or disappear behind shielding arms and hands. Those who manage to watch through this manifest other forms of contortionary reaction when they are interviewed afterwards: indignation that this could be calling itself art; offence at the misuse of medical science and surgical skill; confusion at the apparent pointlessness of the whole exercise.

Interviewed herself, Orlan only adds to the provocation. 'I don't want to be the Barbie Doll', she declares. 'You don't want to be a Barbie Doll?' parrots an incredulous CNN interviewer (whose own Barbie allegiances are very evident). Cindy Jackson, an American talk show celebrity who has undergone over 20 surgical procedures in an attempt to resemble Barbie, is a far less controversial figure than Orlan, and explains herself to interviewers in readily acceptable terms: as an Ohio farm-girl, she longed to get rid of her 'hillbilly image'; she is pleased to have undergone a transition 'from caterpillar to butterfly'; the men who once thought she 'wasn't good enough to buy a drink for' now become nervously syco-phantic when she enters a room. She could not 'accept herself' and accordingly set out to change her body. Orlan is sometimes asked how in re-making herself as an art work she has done something that makes her any different from other plastic surgery addicts. (Michael Jackson is often cited as the example.) Her response is that she is not dictated to by an image culture, but seeks to subvert its tyrannical hold through total control over the design and concept of her own image. She is not trying to conform, but refusing conformity. Unlike Jackson, she has chosen a clinical and programmatic way of enacting non-conformity.

Cindy Jackson may provide a more telling comparison with Orlan than Michael Jackson, for she demonstrates that unnatural selection comes in socially acceptable forms. She and her project get a sympathetic reception from magazine interviewers and talk show hosts, who assist her in emphasizing that the changes she has decided to undergo are prompted not by hubris, but by excessive humility.

> She claims that she was never able to develop self-confidence when she was younger because she couldn't get past what she perceived as her 'ugly' face and body. 'No-one in my family ever told me that I was attractive', she says. 'All I had was a massive insecurity, as a result of which my personality – the "real" me – never had a chance to develop.' (Poitras, 1993: 80)

Jackson's attainment of her 'real' self takes the form of a postmodern martyr-dom to the prescribed image. 'I didn't make the rules – they were already in place when I was growing up . . . I just want to play the game to the best of my ability and come out a winner' (Poitras, 1993: 80). Here, unnatural selection remains attached to the principles of competition and the survival of the fittest. The determination to come out a winner is quite 'natural' in Darwinian terms. What is labelled 'unnatural' may be rejected not for offending against nature, but for breaching culturally determined formations of the subject.

Where experimental art is concerned, according to Rachel Rosenthal, 'Society doesn't enter into the game nor does it know the rules' (1984: 70). The experimental artist seeks a terrain outside the social, where the rules are unknown because they are yet to be made. This is already an order of pure decision before science enters into the picture. The principle of selection may be tenuously linked to the order of the social through some ironic reference, or may appear to float free into pure arbitrariness but, when set in deliberately perverse relation to the principle of natural selection, the choices made by the artist take on a exorbitance that may generate acutely anxious responses. Perhaps what is truly remarkable in Orlan's *oeuvre* is the strength and strangeness of the will that drives it. No-one who has seen a few recent Hollywood movies would find her looks especially strange or hard to take, but she is a strange agent. Where Orlan takes autonomous agency to parodic extremes, Stelarc has begun to undermine the very idea of individuality and of the self as a site of agency:

> The more I've done these performances, the less and less I feel that this body is the repository of a psyche or even a mind. . . . It's necessary for individual bodies to survive in a competitive biological and social world but the more I do and the more I think, I realise that words like 'I' are just a convenient shorthand for a complex interplay of social entities and situations. It's not meaningful to talk about an individual any more. (1994: 388–9)

Where Orlan concentrates on manipulating the form of the body, Stelarc's interest is in exploring functional possibilities. His earliest experiments involved the creation of prosthetic extensions. McLuhan is an obvious reference, and readily acknowledged as such, though there is certainly no evidence of his pronouncements being taken in their intended spirit of warning. 'Any extension whether of skin, hand, or foot, affects the whole psychic and social complex' (1964: 4). This is a contention Stelarc has proved upon himself, turning McLuhan's anxiety-driven speculations into a curiosity-driven exploration of the specific ways in which the psychical implications will manifest themselves.[2]

While still an art student, he experimented with the design of a helmet that could supplement binocular vision with supernumerary perspectives, reflected from outside the edges of the wearer's normal visual field. A much more serious interest, though, was the prospect of creating a third, robotic hand, to be worn continuously as a prosthesis. He moved to Japan, where he could work on this project with robotics specialists at Wasada University and the Tokyo Institute of Technology and began doing public performances with the third hand in the early

1980s. In 1982 at the Maki Gallery in Tokyo, he made the symbolic gesture of writing the word *EVOLUTION* using all three hands simultaneously to form the letters. To achieve this with a fairly high degree of synchronicity and consistency in the letter formations was a significant feat of co-ordination, implying the extension of neural networks to encompass the third hand, whose movements were controlled by muscles in the legs and abdomen. The body's command/control/communications circuitry was further confused in works which involved attaching the left arm to electrodes acting as muscle stimulators, so that its movements were entirely involuntary. In the early third hand performances, the commensurability between body and self was already starting to break down and Stelarc adopted the practice (which he still strictly maintains) of referring to his body in performance as 'the body', never as 'my body'. Marsh (1993) and other feminist critics have viewed this manoeuvre with suspicion, interpreting it as a rejection of embodiment and extending this interpretation to a view of his experiments as a form of abuse of the body prompted by anxieties about its determining role. He is compared unfavourably with female artists whose work celebrates the body. Perhaps Stelarc's rhetoric invites and (to an extent) deserves such responses, but his work tells another story. Every experiment he has performed has involved finely tuning into the capacities of the body in general, and his own body in particular. His art is reliant on multi-dimensional knowledges of the body, all of which are experiential as well as theoretical.

During the five years it took to complete the creation of the robotic hand, he was attracting much more widespread attention with another project, which approached the challenge of extension and connectivity in a starkly different way. This was the series of suspension performances, which began in the mid-1970s and continued during the next 12 years. The suspensions involved no direct electrical or machinic connections to the body and their aesthetic emphasis was often on the relationship between the materials of flesh, stone, wood, water and air. The photographic images in which the events are recorded might easily be taken as belonging to one of the 'back to nature' movements of the time: a naked body hangs from the branches of a large, spreading tree, or sits in mid-air, in the midst of a ring of suspended stones which counterbalance its weight. In a more dramatic and difficult exercise, it is suspended amid the crashing waves of the sea, supported by a structure made from heavy logs wedged among the rocks. More dramatically again, it flies like an oversized bird against a great expanse of sky, 200 feet above the city of Copenhagen, and then is rotated around the sculptured roof of the Theatre Royal on the arm of the crane that has lifted it from the ground. In this and a number of the other suspensions, a machine is used to lift the body but the machine presence seems merely ancillary.

This is not the case with the next series of works exploring 'hybrid human–machine systems'. These draw on a fascination with the NASA project and its research on 'the cyborg'. The term was first used in the *Journal of Astronautics* in 1960, in an article which begins: 'Space travel challenges mankind not only technologically but also spiritually, in that it invites man to take an active part in his own biological evolution' (Clynes and Kline, 1995: 29).[3] In 1978 Stelarc responded to an advertisement calling for scientists, engineers and military specialists to volunteer for mission crews; he proposed that, as an artist, he could make a good case for inclusion as a Mission Specialist. The application was turned down, though NASA showed sufficient interest in the robotic arm to request a demonstration. There are important differences, however, between Stelarc's approach to the cyborg concept and NASA's. A 1963 Cyborg Study commissioned by NASA concentrated on techniques for intercepting negative psychological responses to sensory deprivation, by 'cheating' the senses with artificial stimuli or, ultimately, through modifications of the central nervous system with the goal of obtaining 'the maximum integration of man into a man–machine complex' (Driscoll, 1995: 81). The behaviourist underpinnings of this approach are easy to recognize, as is the residue of Fordism: adapt the organic system by modifying reactions, needs and behaviours which run counter to the operations of the machinic system. Stelarc's own approach to developing hybrid human–machine systems has none of this prescriptive orientation. The focus is on circuitry and feedback loops linking human and machine in a continuous sequence of action, always with the effect of confusing which is the controller and which the controlled. Far from being simply a macho 'control freak', Stelarc minutely explores the phenomenon of control as reversible and even, ultimately, delusory. In *Scan/Signal: Event for Strong Arm and Surveillance Systems* (performed in Kansas, USA in 1993), the body is attached by a harness to the rotating arm of a robot manipulator. The robot (an IRB 2000) has a scale relation to the human body that is equivalent to that of an adult and a child, so that the performer can move within an envelope of space created under its giant arm. As the arm rotates, the body is forced to move with it, apparently offering a model of master/slave relations in which the human is enslaved and deprived of all volition in movement. However, this model is undercut by an arrangement of electronic signalling devices on the floor, which are triggered whenever a foot is placed near them. These signals control the movements of the robot arm, so that body and machine are in fact seamlessly welded into a stimulus/response circuit. In other events, the relation between human and robot bodies is created through more complex and flexible forms of circuitry which leave the body free to move some of its own limbs, thereby triggering movements in the robot, while other limbs are moved involuntarily by muscle stimulators. In such performances, the process of planning and deciding sequences of action becomes an impossibility, and the distinction between moving and being moved is blurred to the point where the site of 'intelligence' can be said to be neither in human nor machine but, as Stelarc puts it 'in the system'.

More recently, the emphasis has shifted from the concept of systemic intelligence to that of systemic agency. A series of Internet-linked performances currently being developed allows the body of the performer to be moved by someone situated remotely and selecting the movements from a body map on a computer screen. In *Parasite: Event for Invaded and Involuntary Body* (1998), the divorce between movement and motivation is completed by the removal of human agency altogether from the choreography. A customized search engine scans the Internet for body images, which are then analysed for patterns indicating gesture and position. This data is then fed into an interactive video field where a 'metabody' moves in accordance with the signals derived from the body images. It could be said that Stelarc is designing the elimination of his own volition, and in this respect his experiments echo those of John Cage who in the 1970s fed computerized sound through algorhithms in order to dislocate it from any compositional intentions. There is something more immediately confronting, though, about Stelarc's experiments with agency because they involve the notion of parasitism. Estranged forms of agency are invited into the body itself. Here is an idea around which paranoid fantasies abound, and yet the experiment and its attendant explanations are apparently entirely free of paranoid anxiety. The idea of the parasite is portrayed as reversible. The body is invaded, but it is also acting as a parasite, drawing its movements from 'an extended, external and virtual nervous system' (Stelarc, 1998: 5). From such experiments, Stelarc spins a wild fabric of hypotheses:

> Imagine a body that can perform an action without memory, a body that can make a motion without knowing that it will carry it out, an action without any expectation.... Consider a body driven by multiple agents, remotely situated and spatially separated.... A problem no longer of having a split personality, but rather a split physicality.... In other words the body becomes a host for another agent. Electronically coupled bodies could then extrude agency from one body to another body in another place. (Stelarc, spoken text in Gruchy, 1996)

Throughout his career, Stelarc has held to a concept of the body as 'empty', as a hollow body that is not a site for a psyche or a self, that can house a sculpture or provide play room for micro-miniaturized robots. Self and agency are thus unhoused, sent wandering in a nebulous space between bodies. There could be no more conceptually potent threat to the concept of individuality.

This, first and foremost, is what differentiates Stelarc from the Extropians,

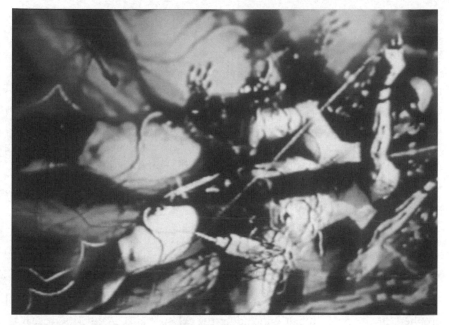

Stelarc, Video still from *Parasite: Event for Invaded and Involuntary Body*
Source: © Stelarc, 1998. Published by kind permission.

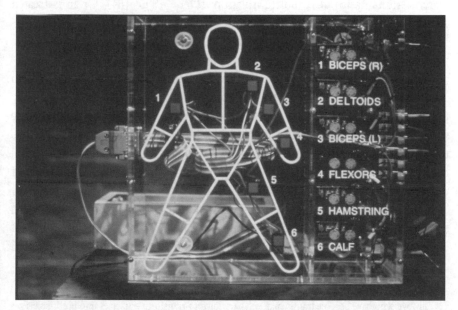

Stelarc, Video still from *Parasite*, 1998
Source: Stelarc, 1998. Published by kind permission.

however closely they seem to echo each other's rhetoric about escaping genetic containment (Dery, 1996: 238). However, as the parallels are so close, it is worth reviewing them. The Extropian project includes 'seeking biological and neurological augmentation' and 'applying science and technology creatively to transcend "natural" limits imposed by our biological heritage, culture and environment'. 'Dynamic optimism', an Extropian principle which 'disallows passively waiting and wishing for tomorrow' and 'propels us exuberantly into immediate activity, confidently confronting today's challenges while generating more potent solutions for our future' (More, 1993) surely has one of its foremost exponents in Stelarc. A decade before the Extropians formulated any principles, Stelarc was proposing:

> The artist can become an evolutionary guide, extrapolating new trajectories; a genetic sculptor, restructuring and hypersensitizing the human body; an architect of internal body space; a primal surgeon, implanting dreams, transplanting desires; an evolutionary alchemist, triggering mutations, transforming the human landscape. (1984: 76)

Mark Dery offers a critique of the Extropians and similarly overexcited prophets of the post-human – including the AI specialist Hans Moravec, R.U. Sirius and Queen Mu (the Editors of *Mondo 2000*) and the Science Fiction writer Vernor Vinge – on the grounds that they naively propose to transcend the complexities of the social. Stelarc is implicated in this critique and accused of 'narcissistic fantasies of complete isolation' (Dery, 1996: 164). Orlan is treated somewhat dismissively as someone who wants 'to be the art world's first post-human celebrity'; her narcissism is taken at face value as an expression of 'the pathologies of a culture drowning in images and obsessed with appearances' (1996: 239, 241). Dery allies himself with Leo Marx, Andrew Ross and Naomi Wolf in an insistence on the social, economic and ecological implications of the post-human craze (or craziness). In an order of pure decision, the cultural critic surely has an important inquisitory role: to ask questions about the assumptions underlying any decisive stance, especially on a topic that is riddled with potential hazards. The spectres of totalitarianism and eugenics hover around the topic of unnatural selection, and there is nothing to allay them in the Extropian vision of 'a polycentric system of distributed power shared among autonomous agents'. In Stelarc's work, agents lose their autonomy. The Extropian vision is composed of empty rhetoric. It is also dangerous rhetoric, driving toward an intoxicated conclusion that is blind to all complexity:

> When technology allows us to reconstitute ourselves physiologically, genetically, and neurologically, we who have become transhuman will be primed to transform ourselves into posthumans – persons of unprecedented physical, intellectual, and psychological capacity, self-programming, potentially immortal, unlimited individuals. (More, 1993)

This is a classic example of what Robins and Levidow interpret as 'a paranoid rationality' which combines 'an omnipotent phantasm of self-control with fear and aggression directed against the emotional and bodily limitations of mere mortals' (1995: 119). Criticism can be sadly ineffective, though, when it comes to dealing with such rhetorical intoxication. The rhetorical provocations of the experimental artist offer more dynamic ways of engaging in the overheated exchanges of post-evolutionary hypotheses.

When the critic does not differentiate between rhetorical intoxication and rhetorical provocation, s/he may be mistaking the antidote for the poison. Intoxication puts judgement to sleep; provocation puts it on the alert. But rhetoric is only one element of what Stelarc and Orlan are presenting, and not the primary element in either case. Dery's charges against both artists are based on too easy a reading of their work, one which approaches their performances through their rhetoric, rather than vice versa. Their work is too difficult, in immediately physical ways, to support the evangelical certainties of vision in which Dery would implicate them. In Orlan's case, the performances are a powerful ironic counterpoint to the artist's presentational rhetoric, so that the rhetoric itself acquires a grotesqueness that is highly effective in distancing its audience from the seduction of glamorized notions of the post-biological. Stelarc, the self-proclaimed 'evolutionary alchemist' and 'architect of internal body space' is prepared to call his own bluff by swallowing a precision engineered stomach sculpture, and in the process experiencing the extremes of the body's reflex resistance to intrusion. This 'work' was as much of an endurance test as the suspensions, and could not have been achieved without exact technical knowledge of the limitations of the organic systems subjected to his intervention. Both artists repeatedly demonstrate that to put the body through any process which involves breaching its natural limits also involves an intensive process of design, planning and selection. The have-it-all rallying cry of the Extropians is a far cry from selection of any kind. It is surely more effectively countered by watching Stelarc choking on his sculpture cable or wide-awake Orlan undergoing a chin implant, than by reading reprimands from sensible critics. Enactments of this kind may actually have a cooling effect on the overheated fantasy life of those who just can't wait to be post-human, and among whom word-mongering about the possible futures of the body has become an inflationary activity.

In areas where cultural obsession has taken hold, we need 'extraordinarily rich resources' to avoid it, as Donna Haraway stresses in an interview with Constance Penley and Andrew Ross (1991: 7). The rhetorical strategies of the critic are not in themselves sufficient. They appeal to ethical intelligence through logical argument, but this has little effect on those who are convinced they have found a higher-order system of values based on a transcendent principle of freedom, and whose own logics are intensively developed. Artists and fiction writers may offer richer resources, especially when they play the *provocateur*, responding to earnestness with facetiousness, literal-mindedness with parody, reverence with blasphemy, anxiety with curiosity. When it comes to dealing with paranoid or exhilarated hypotheses about the future of the body, the body itself needs to enter the discourse. This is where the performance artist taps resources that are not accessed in cultural criticism. 'The beauty of "performance consciousness"', according to Richard Schechner, ' is that it activates alternatives. . . . In ordinary life people live out destinies – everything appears predetermined: there is scant chance to say "Cut, take it again". But performance consciousness is subjunctive, full of alternatives and potentiality' (1987: 6). The subjunctive mood (or as Schechner glosses it, the mood of 'as if') encompasses both the action performed and the self of the actor. 'Like initiations, performances "make" one person into another. Unlike initiations, performances usually see to it that the performer gets his own self back' (1987: 20). The work of Judith Butler complicates this view by exploring the ways in which identity is performative in everyday life, so blurring the distinction Schechner assumes between the acting self and the enacted self. The performance artist will often invert the subjunctive operation Schechner describes, by creating a virtual identity and then proceeding to enact this 'as if' it has the same status as the socially and legally ratified identities of everyday life. With regard to the actions performed, performance art confuses the actual with the hypothetical. The artist begins not with an 'as if' but with a 'what if?', typically attached to a provocative hypothesis concerning the untried possibilities of the body. The 'what if?' is pursued in earnest, in that procedures are exactly designed and are carried out with full awareness of risk of death or injury. Yet there is also a ludic quality. The works of Orlan and Stelarc conform with Schechner's terms in that their declared purpose is to activate alternatives and open up the range of human destinies, though in doing so they put the body on the line in ways that traditional, mimetically based performance avoids.

The principle of unnatural selection is embraced through an anarchic (and sometimes apparently reckless) commitment to the actualization of hypothesis and, in the process, there emerges a highly specific portrayal of agency at work beyond the boundaries of a naturally determined human being. In speculating about the future of the human, we have perhaps been so obsessed about what may become of the body that we have taken the question of agency for granted. The work of these two artists demonstrates, in very different ways, that agency itself changes its meaning as an order of pure decision comes to encompass the function and composition of the human body. Orlan explores extremes of arbitrary individuality, but in doing so she demonstrates the extent to which individuality remains culturally determined, however widely the biological options may be opened up. Agency may be most strictly contingent upon predetermined values just where it seems to be most boldly enlarged. Stelarc throws individuality into question at the level of physiological functioning, so that what he demonstrates is not the 'ultimate individuality' imagined by the Extropians, but rather the condition described by Jonathan Crary and Sandford Kwinter in the introduction to their important essay collection, *Incorporations*.

> Neither human subjects nor . . . [the] objects among which they live are any longer thinkable in their distinctness or separation from the dynamic, correlated, multipart systems within which they arise. Everything, and every individual emerges, evolves and passes away by incorporating and being incorporated into, other emerging, evolving or disintegrating structures that surround and suffuse it. (1992: 15)

Notes

Thanks to Frances Dyson, Christopher Fleming and Bryan Turner for valuable comments on a draft of this article.

1. For a vivid account of the disciplines of costuming and body management practised by the Catholic bourgeoisie in mid-20th-century France, see the first three chapters of Deirdre Bair's *Simone de Beauvoir: A Biography* (1992).
2. Another artist who has interested himself in the the psychical implications of physiological extension is David Tomas, who cites Caillois, and comments: 'Indeed, his description of what it means to occupy "the other side of one's senses" provides a key insight into the bizarre turn that consciousness can take as it is turned inside out of a human skin to find a new home in another and foreign environment. . .' (Tomas 1995a: 257)
3. Clynes's subsequent work manifests a growing interest in the concept of 'participant evolution'. The cyborg is defined as an exercise in unnatural selection with the goal of promoting effective human adaptation to environmental conditions for which the human is not organically designed. Scientists engaged in cyborg research in the 1960s were committed to the enterprise of transporting humans into environmental conditions that challenged every aspect of organic functioning and confounded the whole repertoire of instinctual needs. For a valuable discussion of the influence of these early cybernetic projects on late 20th-century cultures of the body image see Tomas (1995b).

References

Artaud, Antonin (1988) 'To Have Done with the Judgement of God', trans. Helen Weaver, pp. 555–71 in Susan Sontag (ed.) *Antonin Artaud: Selected Writings*. Berkeley: University of California Press.
Bair, Deirdre (1992) *Simone de Beauvoir: A Biography*. New York: Summit Books.
Clynes, Manfred E. and Nathan S. Kline (1995) 'Cyborgs and Space', pp. 29–33 in Chris Hables Gray (ed.) *The Cyborg Handbook*. New York: Routledge.
Crary, Jonathan and Sanford Kwinter (eds) (1992) Foreword to *Incorporations*. New York: Zone.
Dery, Mark (1996) *Escape Velocity: Cyberculture at the End of the Twentieth Century*. London: Hodder and Stoughton.

Driscoll, Robert W. (1995) 'Engineering Man for Space: The Cyborg Study' (final report to NASA, 15 May 1963), pp. 75–81 in Chris Hables Gray (ed.) *The Cyborg Handbook*. New York: Routledge.

Ewald, Francois (1993) 'Two Infinities of Risk', pp. 221–8 in Brian Massumi (ed.) *The Politics of Everyday Fear*. Minneapolis: University of Minnesota Press.

Gruchy, Tim (dir.) (1996) *Stelarc/ Psycho/ Cyber*. Sydney: Sydney Intermedia Network.

James, William (1960) *The Varieties of Religious Experience*. London: Collins.

Kroker, Arthur (1992) *The Possessed Individual: Technology and Postmodernity*. London: Macmillan.

McLuhan, Marshall (1964) *Understanding Media: The Extensions of Man*. London: Ark.

Marsh, Anne (1993) *Body and Self*. Melbourne: Oxford University Press.

Midgley, Mary (1991) 'The Origin of Ethics', in Peter Singer (ed.) *A Companion to Ethics*. Oxford: Blackwell.

More, Max (1993) 'The Extropian Principles' [http://www.nightmare.com/extrop.html].

Orlan (1996) 'Conference', pp. 81–93 in Orlan *This is My Body: This is My Software*. London: Black Dog Publishing.

Penley, Constance and Andrew Ross (1991), 'Cyborgs at Large', interview with Donna Haraway, pp. 1–20 in C. Penley and A. Ross (eds) *Technoculture*. Minneapolis: University of Minnesota Press.

Platt, Charles (1997) 'Evolution Revolution', *Wired*, 5(1): 158–61, 198–204.

Poitras, Diane (1993) ' "I Had Plastic Surgery to Look Like a Barbie Doll" ', *Cleo*, December: 77–80.

Robins, Ken and Les Levidow (1995) 'Socializing the Cyborg Self: the Gulf War and Beyond', pp. 119–25 in Chris Hables Gray (ed.) *The Cyborg Handbook*. New York: Routledge.

Rosenthal, Rachel (1984) 'Stelarc, Performance and Masochism', pp. 69–71 in Stelarc and James D. Paffrath (eds) *Obsolete Body/Suspensions/Stelarc*. Davis, CA: J.P. Publications.

Schechner, Richard (1985) *Between Theatre and Anthropology*. Philadelphia: University of Pennsylvania Press.

Smith, Neil (1996) 'The Production of Nature', pp. 35–54 in George Robertson et al. (eds) *Future Natural*. London: Routledge.

Stelarc (1984) 'Strategies and Trajectories', p. 76 in Stelarc and James D. Paffrath (eds) *Obsolete Body/Suspensions/Stelarc*. Davis, CA: J.P. Publications.

Stelarc (1994) Interviewed by Martin Thomas, pp. 377–93 in Nicholas Zurbrugg (ed.) 'Electronic Arts in Australia', Special Issue of *Continuum* 8(1).

Stelarc (1998) 'Parasite Visions: Alternate, Intimate and Involuntary Experiences', unpublished notes supplied by the artist.

Tomas, David (1995a) 'Art, Psychasthenic Assimilation and the Cybernetic Automaton, pp. 255–66 in Chris Hables Gray (ed.) *The Cyborg Handbook*. New York: Routledge.

Tomas, David (1995b) 'Feedback and Cybernetics: Reimaging the Body in the Age of Cybernetics' in *Body & Society* 1(3–4): 21–43.

Turner, Bryan (1996), *The Body and Society*, 2nd edn. London: Sage.

Zola, Emile (1972) *Nana*, trans. George Holden. Harmondsworth: Penguin. (Orig. 1880, Paris: Charpentier.)

Jane Goodall teaches in a cross-disciplinary Humanities programme at the University of Western Sydney. She is the author of *Artaud and the Gnostic Drama* (Oxford University Press, 1994) and has published widely on experimental drama and performance. She is currently working on a cultural history of performance and evolution.

Serene and Happy and Distant:
An Interview with Orlan[1]

ROBERT AYERS

By Way of an Introduction: Between *Interventions* and *Self-Hybridation*

We now have to regard Orlan as one of the more important artists of the late 20th
century. Her surgical *Interventions* – the works for which she is still best known

Refiguration/Self-Hybridation, 1999, technical help by Pierre Zovilé
(Cibachrome, 1.16m × 1.56m)

Body & Society © 1999 SAGE Publications (London, Thousand Oaks and New Delhi),
Vol. 5(2–3): 171–184
[1357–034X(199906/09)5:2–3;171–184;008861]

– constitute a key feature in the landscape against which a whole subsequent generation of artists concerned with issues around identity, the body, gender and sexuality have worked. Moreover, they force a reconsideration of what actually constitutes *performance* for any of us who seek to work with intelligence in that domain.

As the following interview makes clear, Orlan is now making her most substantial work since then, the digitally manipulated photo-works in the *Self-Hybridation* series. So perhaps it is timely to consider the *Orlan-Conférences*, the activity that took centre stage in Orlan's artistic endeavour between her last surgery and the emergence of the *Self-Hybridations*, if only to ponder the extent to which they provide a link between the *Interventions* and the *Self-Hybridation* series.

On each occasion Orlan submitted herself to surgical procedures, her body underwent considerable physical trauma. She is entirely justified in her assertion: '*I have given my body to art.*' Whatever the wisdom of embarking upon this series of operations in the first place, it is not something that anyone might continue to do indefinitely, and Orlan's decision to turn elsewhere for a *modus operandi* was inevitable.

The *Orlan-Conférence* is the title that she has given to the performance format that had its beginnings, she told me, in her desire to explain and defend the *Interventions* and her other actions – and her taste for declamation, it must be said. For a number of years, however, the *Conférences*, have been the principal situations in which she has appeared before her audience. By accumulation, this is of course a far more numerous audience than that which ever witnessed the *Interventions* either live, or even contemporaneously by the satellite links that she employed towards the end of the series. The majority of that audience will now claim that they have witnessed Orlan in performance and, even if they might concede that what they saw was really more like a lecture than anything else, this – if nothing else – means that they must be regarded as performance works in their own right.

I have witnessed versions of them on half a dozen separate occasions. Their format and content have been pretty constant over the years. While they have almost always included at least a description of the projects that she has been working on at the time that they have been staged – her photographic and video work, for example, or the *Reliquaires* – they have in essence evolved only slowly and, I suspect, more as a pragmatic consequence of the practicalities of the occasion, than any desire on Orlan's part to refocus their content, or – until very recently, at any rate – the opportunities offered by any new technologies.

They tend to take place in a darkened room, auditorium or lecture theatre. Orlan prefers to sit before her audience at a desk. Outside of the Francophone world she is accompanied by a simultaneous translator. She only occasionally stands or leaves

Refiguration/Self-Hybridation No. 38, 1999, technical help by Pierre Zovilé
(Cibachrome, 1.16m × 1.56m)

the desk, and usually only to demonstrate a movement or an action . She reads from
the accumulated text that now also bears the title *Orlan-Conférence* while slide
images of her photo and sculptural works, and – rather more memorably – edited
and manipulated video images of the *Interventions* are projected adjacent to her.
Afterwards, usually after a break, a panel of more or less distinguished speakers –
Orlan prefers them to be drawn from spheres of professional or scholarly expertise outwith the arts – will offer opinions on her work, ask her questions, and a
discussion among them and the audience and Orlan herself – still interpreted by
her translator – will ensue.

I suspect that, apart from their reactions to the videotapes – which are often
less violent than one might expect – the strongest impressions taken away from
the *Conférences* by most people will be of Orlan's personality and what I can only
call her stage presence. Despite her black lipstick and remarkable hairstyle – half
jet black, half lemon yellow – she comes over as nothing so much as a middle-
aged, middle-class French academic, with a delightful self-deprecating sense of
humour. Her script may comprise radical, iconoclastic, politicized stuff, but she
spices it with pressure-relieving jokey asides. She routinely begins with a gag
about having been unable to buy the batteries to power the automatic translation
implants that she says she wears in her temple-bumps, and – as the audience

respond with unease to the more gruesome moments in the videos – she suggests that flirting with the person in the next seat might provide the excuse to turn away from the projection screen.

Her audience, on each of the occasions that I have been there, has been sympathetic, sycophantic, adoring, with young women in particular responding to her like some pop music role model. It has to be said that she appears to adore this. She indulges her fans to an extent that other lesser celebrities might do well to imitate: she will have her photograph taken by or with anyone who asks, and she signs autographs equally enthusiastically. As I have said, this comes as something as a surprise to many who experience it, regardless of how playful, how mischievous she comes over in those videotaped operating theatres, all carnival and pantomime. It certainly caught me off guard the first time I witnessed it, and for a while I had to be satisfied with the rationalization that this was another of those dualities that she is so happy to have exist in her work (and which she talks about towards the conclusion of this interview). I now understand that this presence is essential to the significance of the *Conférences* in Orlan's oeuvre and to what they tell us about the rest of it.

Whatever else has been asserted for them, Orlan's *Interventions* are, I would suggest, important primarily for the simplicity and profundity with which they breathe life into the old cliche of performance art analysis, that in them she uses her body as her artistic material. In many, indeed most, of the cases where this expression is employed, it carries a degree of not always acknowledged metaphor within it. The number of artists of whom it can be meant as literally as in Orlan's case is minute. (Of her generation I can call to mind only Annie Sprinkle who has concentrated so exclusively upon her own flesh as a medium, though for her this has meant display and manipulation rather than surgery.) This is of course why she is so significant to artists like Ron Athey, who have chosen to employ wounded flesh to rather different, more narrative ends, and younger artists like Franko B and Kira O'Reilly whose own bodies are the irreplaceable location for, material of and – most remarkably – the *meaning* of their performance art. At a rather different level, it is why she is also so special in the estimation of a whole generation for whom piercing, tattooing and other body modifications are so central to their sense of chic.

Of course, the sort of claim that I am making for them only holds good while the *Interventions* were actually being made, or at least for as long as they were ongoing. (In the interview that follows I ask her about further surgery. To my ear, her response seems more or less to push such possibilities into the realm of fantasy.) As an ironic consequence of the operations' brutal radicality, 'mere' photographs or videotapes of them – no matter how unpleasant they are to look

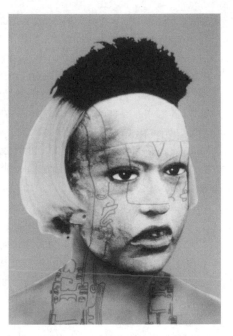

Refiguration/Self-Hybridation, 1999, technical help by Pierre Zovilé
(Cibachrome, 1.16m × 1.56m)

at – only serve to exaggerate their own distance from the physical activity that was the art's actual substance. They have indeed, in my experience, not only rendered their spectators *un*sympathetic to Orlan's endeavours, but made them seem less radical than those of artists who are actually working in far more traditional modes of performance. But put the living, declaiming, joking, Orlan back alongside them, with her glittery *bosses* and her willingness to have people touch them, and the intensified corporeality that is the *Interventions*' most pressing characteristic, and which is at the heart of their power to move us, is once again revivified.

For by being there, another human being in our presence, while the image of her own sliced open flesh is projected behind her, she causes us to ponder this intensified corporeality of her work: a corporeality which on the one hand neither her intelligence nor her will has any control over (they are not her gloved hands that delve into the gory recesses of her body, she cannot *act* her own bleeding) and which on the other is so intensified that it invites, or rather obliges (for in the face of it, it is as though we too are stripped of will) empathic participation in the spectator. Which is to say that, by literally making her performance out of herself, or out of aspects of herself that are physically common to all of us – her punctured and scraped flesh and her trickling blood – and by focusing, and forcing us to focus so exclusively upon them, she is making an art which (once again filling a cliche with meaning) is as universal as it is, because it is, individual.

Once an artist has travelled this far, it as though there is no middle ground that can be occupied with integrity. Once her body has been employed so literally as the material and subject of her art, the possibility of performing, and thus employing it more metaphorically, is going to seem like a withdrawal to audiences still gripped by a neo-modernist sense of the edge. This is the realization that renders the entirely non-performative *Self-Hybridations* the inevitable successors to the *Interventions* at the centre of Orlan's art-making. For unlike the video- and photo-works, that take the *Interventions* as their 'subject matter', or even the sculptural *Reliquaires* with their little flasks of Orlan's fat, these cross-fertilizations with the art of Pre-Columbian America are not compromised in their audiences' minds by their failure to be surgery themselves. Particularly as their making is, as she explains below, so entirely dependent upon the digital devices of virtuality, rather than upon anything closer to the more traditional physicality of the artist's studio. (Her main collaborator works, significantly enough, on the other side of the Atlantic!)

And thus the success and importance of the *Conférences*. For while they ostensibly perform the function of lecture or discussion or, literally, conference, which is to say they apparently exist at a level once removed from actual art works, and while their performative character seems to slip in around their edges or, more accurately, at their beginning and end while Orlan basks in the warmth of her audience's adoration, or through the device of having her own words reinterpreted on their way to their audience's ears, then her continuing to be a performer at all is, somewhat ironically, still possible.

Serene and Happy and Distant – An Interview with Orlan

Robert Ayers: Orlan, I wonder if we could begin by talking about the work in your present exhibition here at the Espace d'Art Yvonamor Palix. For anyone who knows your work primarily through the surgical *Interventions* – and I suppose that means the majority of people – these digitally manipulated photo-works seem like quite a departure.

Orlan: You could say that they continue the work that I did in my surgical operations, but in a different way – just as those surgical performance works were the continuation of the work I'd been doing previously, but in a more radical form. The thread that runs through all of them is that my approach has always been to question the status of the body in society, and in particular the status of the female body.

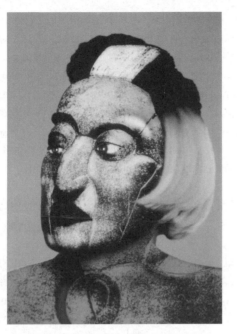

Refiguration/Self-Hybridation No. 10, 1998, technical help by Pierre Zovilé
(Cibachrome, 1.16m × 1.56m)

Robert Ayers: That much is obvious, but in terms of how we look at them, these are more traditional, while technically, they are highly innovative.

Orlan: After the surgical operations, which focused on the real, I've been working on the virtual, and the idea of undertaking a world tour of standards of beauty in other cultures, civilizations and epochs. Here I've started with the Pre-Columbian civilizations, which have a relationship with the body which is particularly disturbing for us, which completely challenges us and which is very intense – whether that be because of their human sacrifices, or because of things which I'm very interested in, like the god who's always represented in sculpture by the figure of a priest who is wearing the skin of his victims, which had been prepared in a specific way, for about 20 days. This is the idea of entering into the skin of the other. These civilizations have standards of beauty which are completely different to ours. For example, the squint. For them, a squint was the guarantee of great beauty, to such an extent that they cultivated it by putting a ball of wax or earth in between the baby's eyes to train them to squint. Similarly (although this isn't something that's specific to their culture, because it's been discovered in Egypt and Africa, and I've even been told that it happened in Albi, here in France) there was the tradition of deforming the skull. They deformed the skull, and always in the same way by clamping bits of wood around the baby's head for three years until the skull bones set and it took on a completely different appearance. What's of interest and worth noting about these skull deformations is that they were practised on men and women, and by members of all social castes. It wasn't a question of money, nor religion for that matter; it was really an issue of beauty. The images that I've been working on are digitally generated and are taken from sculptures which represent these standards of beauty and my own face, which is supposed to represent the standards of beauty of my own time. Except, because of these two bumps, it has an appearance which is alien to our customs and civilization.

Robert Ayers: And, if I can just risk a suggestion, once again there's this bringing together of opposites, which – I've come to understand – is so basic to your work.

Orlan: Well, I tried to create a sort of hybrid (and of course the exhibition is called *Self-Hybridation*) and so I produced a work using Photoshop. I should point out that this work was done with a technician in Montreal: I sent him the scanned images and, following my directions, he did the work that takes a bit of time (because I hardly have any) and then he sent them back by email. I corrected them, sent him the colour palettes, reworked the images and sent them back with a certain number of instructions; he worked on them and once the work was completed he sent it back to me; I said whether I agreed with it or not, and we reworked until the image was considered finished.

Robert Ayers: And technically, how are the finished works produced?

Orlan: These are cibachromes, which are mounted on aluminium, behind plexiglass, and then framed. They are a series of large photos – 1.10 metres by 1.60. You can take this one as an example: that's the nose of the King of Wapacal, with the skull deformation and scarification. In this one, it's using an Olmec mask where there is also a skull deformation and drawings on the face which are a type of – well, not really a tattoo – but rather lines like fine scars on the face which follow the shape of a 'U' or a 'V', which – for a certain category of person who had power in society – were symbols for ceremonies. All of the images that you see here are photos produced in this way. These aren't screen-printed images. We developed the image without keeping any trace at all of the computer production. In fact, in order to distort Photoshop, I did a few things like these textured effects for example, which weren't done by computer, but were in fact produced because I sent very bad photocopies by fax. So, instead of working with a really good photo of my face, or the sculptures, we worked from images

Refiguration/Self-Hybridation No. 22, 1999, technical help by Pierre Zovilé
(Cibachrome, 1.16m × 1.56m)

that were already blurred, images which had already been worked on, or which had already been exposed to the elements, as it were. That's something else that appeals to me.

Robert Ayers: So, does the fact that it's computers – or new technology as it still gets called – that's being used to mediate the images, does that have any significance for you at all?

Orlan: People ask me, 'What would you like computers to do? How could they be improved?' I say that I couldn't care less. What counts is that I can distort these things and rework them differently. The images aren't geared to new technology for its own sake, because I'm not fascinated by new technology. It simply exists, it's part of the time I live in, I use it as I'd use anything else, with the same desire to subvert it, as I would any other technique: to play with it, and not be taken in by it.

Robert Ayers: But to return to the content of the work, which is probably much more interesting, to what extent are these pieces to do with appearance, and to what extent are they concerned with identity?

Orlan: Here we're quite a long way from the problem of identity. These are images that I put before the public, which could find takers in our society, and which, in the end, present themselves as being 'acceptable' as a type of face that doesn't, strictly speaking, refer to identity. Of course there's an inference in relation to what *I* am, but no, this isn't work concerned with identity. You could put it like this: it's simply the idea of saying that beauty can take on an appearance that is not usually thought of as beautiful.

Robert Ayers: But I'm thinking in more general terms. Very often, when people have been thinking and talking about your work, they have very quickly attempted to relate your interest in appearance with an interest in identity – particularly in female identity.

Orlan: That's just a fraction of my work. What's difficult in my work is that it's uncomfortable in every sense. So far as the operations are concerned, it is physically uncomfortable for me and for those who look at the images. But it is also uncomfortable to make sense of it. It is difficult to discuss it, because describing it takes an enormous amount of writing. So, because we are all people who are extremely pressed for time, who live in an age of communication, we tend to go with the quickest, fastest way. So each person tends to look at only one aspect of the work, and this is extremely reductive because there are many facets to my work. My work can be read psychoanalytically; or in terms of art history (and all of the references that my work makes have been related to art history, because as everyone knows – and to flog a dead horse, somewhat – all supposedly new images are a product of the images that precede them; and so there is the old and the new which come together in the same space). My work can be talked about in philosophical, sociological or in feminist terms, or again it can be discussed in terms of my relationship with the media, for example, which has always been extremely significant and conflictual, and which has caused a great deal of problems. There are many different ways: you could even talk from a purely aesthetic point of view. At the moment, people even talk about it from a fashion perspective, since the fashion industry has now caught up with me. My work appeals to many fashion designers. One in particular uses it in a very literal way – perhaps you saw it in his catalogues? – and there is one who pays tribute to my work by making up his models with the same bumps as me.

Robert Ayers: Yes, I find this fascinating, the way that popular culture is gradually reassimilating your work. But I suspect you must find it enormously irritating, because, rather than the passage of time seeing the better understanding of

Refiguration/Self-Hybridation No. 15, 1998, technical help by Pierre Zovilé
(Cibachrome, 1.16m × 1.56m)

what your work is about, it's as though misunderstanding is simply being piled
upon misunderstanding.

Orlan: Well, here's an example: in New York a collector bought a piece of my
work and he told me that if I came to San Francisco he'd organize a big party. And
he did, on the day when I had the exhibition opening and the *Conférence*. And at
the end of the evening he told me that some friends were waiting in the next room,
and he invited me to go and see them. I went to see his friends – 30 or so sado-
masochistic homosexuals, all clad in leather with chains and zips, tattoos and lots
of body piercing. There was one who spoke very good French, and he said to me,
'We think that you are the most important artist of our time and so we'd like to pay
a tribute to you: we'd like to pay you to organize our surgical operations. You can
do whatever you like in the operating theatre, with music, texts, and sound,
etcetera. We'd like to get your surgeon from New York to come and create the same
bumps that you've got, because we're going to start a new trend: after body piercing we're going to start "bumping" and very quickly, in a few years or so, it'll catch
on in Europe'! Well, I was furious and I told him he'd offended my sensibilities. I
said, 'But this is unthinkable! Impossible! I can't make money from this, when
that's precisely the principle that I'm working against.' I'm certainly not in favour

of fashion and its dictates. In fact, I explained to them that I wasn't surprised to be imitated by people who have body piercing and tattoos. I'm not against these things, but it's quite obvious that the majority of people who are into those things believe that they are liberating themselves from the dictates of a certain society, but in fact it all boils down to the same thing because they are conforming to the dictates of a smaller, mini-society. So I left it there. What's interesting is that someone told me they'd recently seen a San Francisco group on TV who had put bolts and plaques on their heads, as well as needles. They were just like punks, or they might as well have been. It might be them. Maybe they understood that I didn't want models, and so it was up to them to do it for themselves.

Robert Ayers: Well, yes, that must have been disconcerting, to say the least. It seems to me that people get themselves caught up with particular aspects of your work, and that almost prevents them from comprehending how it's developing. There's one particular thing that I suppose we should get straight: have you now completely finished with surgery as a means of working?

Orlan: No, there are still two surgical operations that I'd like to do. There's one which is quite involved and the other is lighter, more poetic, but I'd like these to be the apotheosis of all my operations. I want to get all the medical, artistic and financial arrangements in place, and that takes a lot of time to arrange. If I don't manage it, well, bad luck! I think that I'm an artist who's given a lot, physically and intellectually and psychologically as much as financially, and so if I can't do these operations under good conditions, I won't do them. It won't matter too much. Still, I'll tell you about these operations. I'd like to construct an operating theatre for one of them which will be a huge sculpture, 8 metres by 6, and it will look like an egg, or a diamond cut regularly. It'll be something made in colourless ice so as to look like a peep show. I've got the idea that, depending on how it's lit, the museum public will be able to see the operation. Inside there'll be a surgical operation – not plastic surgery, but something that is intended to change my appearance much less, but which is intended to heighten my faculties. I can't say exactly what, but it's a first in the medical world. And the other one simply consists of opening up the body to produce images like the one [*Rire de plaisir en voyant mon corps ouvert*, 1993] on the front of the *Collection Iconotexte* book: of my body opened up with me at the same time having a completely relaxed and serene expression as I watch these images being transmitted by satellite with my surgeon. I'll be able to answer any questions asked. It'll be 'opening up and closing the body' and it will be a perfect illustration of my manifesto of body art which, in particular, denounces pain. I'm not at all in favour of pain. I don't consider it made for my

Refiguration/Self-Hybridation No. 5, 1998, technical help by Pierre Zovilé
(Cibachrome, 1.16m × 1.56m)

redemption or purification or whatever. The celebrated giving birth in pain is completely ridiculous in our day and age, when we have epidurals and a whole pharmacopoeia which allows us not to have to suffer if we don't want to.

In my work, the first deal I have with the surgeon is, 'no pain'. I wanted to show this body, opened up, and to produce it with lots of photographs of me there, laughing, playing, reading etcetera, while the body is opened up. And then I'm open to any other suggestions that are made in the laboratory, whether that be in terms of robotics, or biotechnology or genetics. It's still the same: I want to remain serene and happy and distant. I don't want it to be something suicidal or difficult, beyond the level that I've already set myself for these operations. Of course, for these operations there is a price to be paid: I don't suffer but I am aware that my body suffers, which are two very different things. If the body is in pain, that's one thing, but if I am not suffering, I can talk, I can do other things. If I am in pain, I can no longer do anything – I'm forced to suffer.

Robert Ayers: You know, the way that you're talking now seems to me central to your whole attitude to your work. You're identifying a self that is, on the one hand, independent of your body, but which on the other is intimately tied up with it. Isn't there a sort of contradiction there?

Orlan: No, it's like I've said to you before about the terms that people use to talk about the exhibition: there's something I'd like to say about 'and' and 'or'. At the moment I've moved on to the virtual, but that doesn't mean to say that I won't do any more operations in the future, given the right conditions, which will be carried out in real life. What I wanted to say was that, effectively, our whole culture is based on the notion of 'or' – for example, good or bad, private or public, new technology or painting, etcetera, etcetera. This forces us to condemn one element and to choose the other. All of my work is based on the notion of 'and': the good and the bad, the beautiful and the ugly, the living and the artificial, the public and the private – because during my operations images of me are transmitted by satellite, so you've got them both there at the same time. There are also the drawings made in the operating theatre: I draw with my fingers and my blood. It's extremely primitive, but this doesn't stop these same operations from being transmitted by satellite, in a totally different way. Its always based on the notion of 'and' and I think that that's something interesting and important, with regards to our epoch.

Notes

The transcribed interview with Orlan was conducted by Robert Ayers at the Espace d'Art Yvonamor Palix, Paris, 8 January 1999, while Orlan was exhibiting the new digitally manipulated photo-works that form her *Self-Hybridation* series. All transcription, interpretation and translation was by Francine Morgan, CPEDERF, Paris. An edited version of fragments of this conversation appear as *Live Art Letters* 4, March 1999, *The Special and the Unusual – Listening to Orlan*, ISSN 1361-3731.

1. The photographs in this article are reproduced by Orlan's kind permission. The copyright belongs to her. The computer technician who collaborated with Orlan to modify the images is Pierre Zovilé.

Robert Ayers has been making performances of one sort or another for 27 years, and writing and talking about them for almost as long. He is Artistic Director and Professor of the Contemporary Arts at the Nottingham Trent University. He is project champion for the Nottingham Future Factory project – a collaboration between university, city and other partners to found an international centre for new creativity in Nottingham, which will open in 2002. He travels widely in the pursuit of his profession and his recent publications have involved him working with artists such as Stelarc, Orlan, Annie Sprinkle, Marina Abramovi, Franko B, Meg Stuart and Jim Dine. Last year he acted as the first ever guest curator to the [British] National Review of Live Art. He was a member of the Drama, Dance and Performing Arts panel for the 1996 Research Assessment Exercise and is a member of the Music and Performing Arts postgraduate panel of the Arts and Humanities Research Board.

The Sacrificial Body of Orlan

JULIE CLARKE

The Body Electric

As we approach the 21st century, there appears to be a general consensus among critics of new technologies that the human body is being distanced from its material and visceral nature, particularly through the use of computer imaging programs[1] which posit the human body as digital information which may be enhanced, manipulated and altered. This practice is reflected in cosmetic surgery and genetic engineering, and is acutely evident in the Visible Human Project.[2]

Developments in medical and perception technologies – television (broadcast and cable), video and the Internet, have elevated the emphasis on the scopic and contributed to the construction and perception of new body images, which include the diseased body of the AIDS sufferer, the augmented (prosthetic) body and the spectacular cybernetic body. The discovery of HIV in 1982 placed more emphasis on DNA and was one of the motivating factors for the instigation of the Human Genome Project, which sought to sequence the genetic map or code of the human species.[3] Consequently, genetic engineering was further promoted as a strategy against disease and undesirable human characteristics; and difference, which was once seen as pertaining to the body exterior, was displaced by indicators gleaned from the unseen body interior.

We are living at a time in which the perceived boundaries between genders, the self and its image, real and virtual, synthetic and organic, interior and exterior, public and private space, past and future have been all but erased. In this technological culture body images appear to be infinitely mutable, yet still linked to existing iconographic and ideological systems.

More and more our identity is linked to image, and that image is inherently linked with technology. In this environment we are forced to ask ourselves such

Body & Society © 1999 SAGE Publications (London, Thousand Oaks and New Delhi),
Vol. 5(2–3): 185–207
[1357–034X(199906/09)5:2–3;185–207;008864]

Figure 1 Poster for St Orlan et les objets du culte (1983)

questions as: how does an individual operate within an environment which on one hand makes image important, but simultaneously determines body status based on what is unseen? To what extent is our present state of being determined by current computer technologies? Are we our image?

In the midst of the polemics surrounding the status of the body in technology, the French performance artist, Orlan, began a project in 1990 called *The Reincarnation of Saint Orlan*.[4] The project is a series of nine operation/performances to redesign her face and body with cosmetic surgery.[5] Using the facial features of women from Renaissance art, she created a prototype with the aid of computer technology.[6]

Superficially, it seemed that Orlan was intent on becoming the epitome of all beautiful women throughout Art History, and on displaying in a very public way the process of plastic surgery and the construction of woman. I intend to show that Orlan's project is about self-image and identity within technological culture, and one which challenges white Western notions of homogeneity by engaging with aberrant body forms and the abject. She performs this by appropriating Judeo-Christian iconography, including blood and its associative notions of sacrifice and transformation, Greek mythology, with its emphasis on marvellous and grotesque beings, and French literature. There is not enough space here to draw on the breadth of psychoanalytic theory that may be applied to Orlan's oeuvre, however, the readers attention can be drawn to an excellent essay by Parveen Adams (1996) on Orlan's operation/performance.

Aesthetic

Orlan's more recent performance aesthetic is dissection, recalling the spectacle of autopsy theatres in Europe during the Renaissance. She is an *echorcée*, reminiscent of Enlightenment anatomical studies, in which the flayed body, looking very much alive, displays the splendour of internal body viscera. Jonathan Sawday argues that 'as a theatrical performance indeed, the anatomy demonstration rivalled the stage for the hold it exerted . . .' (1995: 269). This is true today, for to witness an operation on a human body is an experience like no other. No dramatization of war or horror can surpass the knowledge that what is being observed in the operating theatre is a body that while simultaneously alive, expresses the stasis and bodily mutilation associated with traumatic death. Orlan's facial surgery displays a different theatre of spectacle, one which is linked not only with autopsy and the medical technologies of surveillance but also with the greedy consumption of fashion. According to Glenda Nalder, a 'characteristic of recent feminist work in performance and machine art has been its use of the viscera to rupture and to seep through the boundaries at the human/machine interface' (1993: 22). Orlan does this to reveal the media's reliance on surface images and to inject the dry virtual space of computer imaging with images of wet body material. Orlan's photographs of the inside of her face, show that even the sinews and muscles of the face are surfaces that fix the eye and seduce us into the realm of the abject. She reveals that all bodily images no matter how beautiful or horrific are reduced to pure surface by technological imaging.

Image

While our self is more than our face, it is our face that greets the world. To change our face is to change our identity and the way that we communicate in society. When Orlan consciously decided to transform her facial features, she sacrificed the old self in favour of a new one that had been evolving since the 1970s, and one which questioned the status of the body. Although Orlan was in the state of becoming through her *Reincarnation of Saint Orlan*, it was also a return for her to issues that she considered important in her early years of performance. In 1978 she used her body to measure the streets of France and the Georges Pompidou Centre. She knocked on doors requesting soap and water to wash her dirty clothes, then emptied the residue into bottles (Bronson and Gale, 1979). The dirty water became a relic and trace of her performance and enabled her to speak about body containment and dispersal.

Orlan's 'reincarnation' highlights corporeality at a time when body status is defined by electronic imaging. There is a stress on DNA code; the face, retina and fingerprints may be scanned in electronic transactions to authenticate identity. As such, Orlan's operation/performances could be seen as an extreme example of body inscription, in which she uses the surface of her flesh as an indicator of a culture disintegrating into its images. However, Orlan does not just reveal the surface of her face and body creating more images to be consumed; she shows the abject, bloodied subcutaneous layers beneath the skin that signify the organic and the imminence of death.

> The body interior speaks directly of our mortality. Hence the sight of these hidden contours has traditionally been denied us since they are usually encountered only at the risk of enduring great pain and quite possibly death. (Sawday, 1995: 12)

The gaping, fleshy wounds of surgery on Orlan's face challenge media images of beautiful body forms, which are more attractive to a viewing audience, because they are linked with concepts of transcendence.

Elizabeth Grosz, in support of Kristeva's thesis on the abject, states that:

Abjection involves the paradoxically necessary but impossible desire to transcend corporeality. It is a refusal of the defiling, impure, uncontrollable materiality of a subject's embodied existence. (1989: 72)

Through her performance Orlan asks that the audience interrogate the image of her reconstructed face and the way it relates to notions of identity in a technological culture. In a spectacular representation she offers her body as meat and pre-packages her photographic image for consumption by the art community. Her face prior to surgery is marked up with black lines, like a carcass ready for the butcher's cut. These raw images of her surgery are continually played out against images of her intact and healed face, and the organic body is revealed as remodelled and reincarnated by technological intervention. Orlan consistently contrasts the 'natural' woman, untouched by cosmetic surgery, with the cultural impact of technological and medical intervention.

Orlan is not against plastic surgery, but 'against the standards of beauty, against the dictates of dominant ideology that impress themselves more and more on feminine and masculine flesh' (Armstrong, 1995b: 13). She uses medical and computer technologies to enter into a dialogue with the abject and as a vehicle to transcend the body which is tied to its DNA.

In a photograph, *Imaginary Generic No. 31: Successful Operations(s)*, 1990, [7] Orlan is standing in front of a large canvas which portrays black and white reproductions of candidates for her facial prototype. Red transparent rectangles frame the selected features, and red arrows denote the new characteristics on the completed face. It is not only the naming of the photograph which stresses the word generic (genesis – coming into being; eugenic – well-born; genus – kind/class), that points to Orlan's interest in genetic engineering. It is also in the deliberate selection of particular characteristics that are considered desirable, as opposed to undesirable ones that may be eradicated, that points to genetic restructuring – revealing perhaps that beauty is equated with health, whereas unattractive and unwanted characteristics are aligned with disease.[8]

Orlan has said: 'My work and its ideas incarnated in my flesh pose questions about the status of the body in our society and its evolution in future generations via new technologies and upcoming genetic manipulations' (Armstrong, 1996b: 9).

Style

Mary Russo, in her discussion of carnival and theory states that:

The grotesque body is the open, protruding, extended, secreting body, the body of becoming, process, and change. The grotesque body is opposed to the classical body, which is monumental, static, closed, and sleek, corresponding to the aspirations of bourgeois individualism; the grotesque body is connected to the rest of the world. (1997: 325)

When we look at Orlan's face, the constructed portrait reveals a self colonized by technological invasion, and a physical body being displaced by image. Her deviant face, with high forehead and small horns is the mutant offspring of surgical intervention, enabling Orlan to embrace images of the carnival and of the grotesque. As Russo asserts:

Making a spectacle out of oneself seemed a specifically feminine danger.... For a woman, making a spectacle out of herself had more to do with a kind of inadvertency and loss of boundaries: the possessors of large, aging, and dimpled thighs displayed at the public beach, of overly rouged cheeks, of a voice shrill in laughter, or of a sliding bra strap – a loose, dingy bra strap especially – were at once caught out by fate and blameworthy. (1997: 318)

Although women scrutinize themselves in the mirror before they go into public, what they see is their double. What they don't see is the image of the self as seen by others. Self-portraiture in some ways deals with the nuances of the inner notion of self-identity represented by the mirror.

By restructuring her face, Orlan creates a woman that is obtainable only by technological intervention, and one who is continually constructed through media images. By assaulting the vision of the spectator through the abject, she not only shocks the viewer, but also challenges their perceptions of beauty, for she is not beautiful; her new face is too smooth, controlled and expressionless. By engaging with and embracing notions of the grotesque, she transgresses standards set by the beauty industry.

Mirror (Mirabula – Miraculous)

In Orlan's *Bride of Frankenstein* photograph, she is a Siamese twin.[9] Joined at the shoulders and at the top of her hair, she is a twin, a double and mirror image of herself. The blue Gothic swirls in her otherwise black hair, spiral towards one another. Like an un-stranded double helix of DNA, she is a human cell still linked, yet not completely divided self from self. She evokes miraculous associations with the mirror and calls into question the concept of the original and simulacrum. A Siamese twin is suggested, as separation is required for the individuals to function as distinct units. Historically they were not separated because of the possibility of death. It is in this photograph that Orlan directly addresses the carnivalesque, as conjoined twins were often exhibited as aberrant creatures, which challenged accepted concepts of normality.

Orlan also plays with the imaginary mythical figure of the hermaphrodite, a combination of Hermes and Aprodite, producing a double-sexed individual or blurring of self.

The notion that there is an internal imaginary body that differs from the external body identity is addressed by Orlan in her appropriation of the Medusa myth, and the performance acts as a cleansing of the old body in favour of the new. 'Although the ego is formed through a recognition of its body in the mirror phase, it recoils from the idea of being tied to or limited by the body's form' (Grosz, 1989: 77). The imaginary body, as a construct of the mind, posits a mind/body split.

'At the sight of the vulva, the devil himself flees' (Wilson, 1996: 11) is the text that Orlan distributed after exhibiting her genital area in her 1978 performance *A Documentary Study: The Head of the Medusa*. The Medusa, a mythic being haloed by serpent hair, was said to turn men to stone. Orlan's recent surgery on her face wound is the revisited Medusa's head, the uterus, the interior female body, the place of life or death.

According to Greek mythology:

> Perseus approached Medusa while she slept, and taking care not to look directly at her, but guided by her image reflected in the bright shield which he bore, he cut off her head. (Bulfinch, 1969: 152)

It seems to me that the Medusa's head was fragmented from her body by the shield, which functioned like a mirror. The sword acts out what the mirror already achieved. In Orlan's operations, the scalpel is the instrument which produced the Medusa head, an opened wound on which no one wants to look, even though it was viewed via the screen (the mirror). The mirror, which removes the power of the real body, also replaces it with the power of the fragmented image, which carries our own fears about what lies outside of the frame. For the most part, images of mutilated bodies are images that precede the moment of tragic death.

The Sacrificial Body

Orlan uses Judeo-Christian symbolism to speak about the history of body fragmentation and relics, and posits the body as sacrificial. The body has to be sacrificed in order for it to be transcended. According to Georges Bataille:

> It is the common business of sacrifice to bring life and death into harmony, to give death the upsurge of life, life the momentousness and the vertigo of death opening on to the unknown. Here life is mingled with death, but simultaneously death is a sign of life, a way into the infinite. Nowadays sacrifice is outside the field of our experience and imagination must do duty for the real thing. (1987: 91)

Orlan speaks about sacrifice, through her use of Judeo-Christian iconography and Greek mythology. Grapes, blood, crosses, skulls, horns, pitchforks, music, text and costume are used as essential elements in her operation/performances.

In her *Mouth for Grapes* photograph, the surgery on her lips is juxtaposed with a bowl of grapes.[10] Thematically this photograph is similar to documentation of

Meret Oppenheim's *Spring Feast* (1959), in which she presented a naked girl with a gilded face whose body was covered in fruit. The relationship between the female body and nurture, and the face as commodity is addressed in each of these presentations. Whereas in Orlan's photo-documentation it is the costumes that provide the glitz and glitter associated with things considered decorative or precious, in the Oppenheim piece it is the gilded face which loads it with significance. Although the woman's body is offered as a delicacy alongside other fruit, the object of desire is the mask.

In this photograph Orlan's lips, exposed and wet are like purple grapes with their thin membrane peeled. Blood from the wound, which trickles slowly down her cheek renders the mouth passive. In this way she draws attention to preconceived notions of femininity. The mouth need not speak; the lips only need to be perfectly shaped, reiterating perhaps that women who are beautiful are not expected to be articulate. The blood-cut on Orlan's mouth, hints not only of childbirth and the episiotomy (a small incision made by the surgeon, so that the vagina will not tear), but also the lips and mouth as areas of eroticism, may be related to the mouth of the newborn child (a new identity), who cannot yet articulate desire through language.[11] Orlan, who has not paid her 'tribute to nature, in experiencing the pains of childbirth' (1996: 92), gives birth to her new self via the opened, bleeding wound. Ash explains that 'The agonising pain of the crucifixion, the suffering of Christ in his passion, was the suffering, the "passion" of a woman giving birth' (Ash, 1990: 86).

Reincarnation

Parveen Adams, in her excellent psychoanalytic discussion of Orlan's operation/performance *Omnipresence*, said that Orlan 'claims to be flesh become image' (1996: 144). Christ too was flesh become image. According to Richard Sennett, during the Middle Ages the Crucifixion 'was increasingly portrayed, and increasingly realistic' (1994: 161), so that the common person could show their care for another's suffering by associating with, or imitating the suffering of Christ. During the 13th century Sennett claims that 'surgery revealed the physical reality of Christ's Passion and Crucifixion, teaching the lesson of moral arousal through suffering' (1994: 166).

This is My Body . . . This is My Software is the title of Orlan's first exhibition in the United Kingdom in 1996, which highlighted photographic images of Orlan's seventh operation/performance, *Omnipresence*. The title reveals two things, first, that Orlan views the body as 'software' – information that can be modified, and, second, that she is playing on the words of Christ at the Last Supper.

In 1971 when she named herself Saint Orlan, it was a cynical attack on Christianity, and her pseudo-canonization was a strategy to align herself and her actions with the heroic aspects ascribed to sainthood.[12] She draped robes around her body (*Saint Orlan*, 1971) and (*Drapery – the Baroque*, 1979), defiled, slashed and remade them into collage (*A Documentary Study: The Head of the Medusa*, 1978; *1001 Reasons Not to Sleep*, 1979). Robes are significant as clothing that establishes identity or status within culture, and in the *Reincarnation of Saint Orlan*, skin is the literal costume of the body and face. The soft fabric, as outer surface of her head is cut, reconfigured and sewn into a new garment for her identity. Like Buffalo Bill, the transvestite serial killer in the *Silence of the Lambs*, whose fantasy was to wear the body of a female; Orlan's metamorphosis also involves the notion of becoming other through the reconfiguration of flesh.[13]

Before each performance Orlan reads from an essay written about her by a Lacanian psychoanalyst, Eugénie Lemoine-Luccioni:

> The skin is deceptive ... in life one only has one's skin ... there is an error in human relations because one never is what one has ... I have an angel's skin but I am a jackal ... a crocodile's skin but I am a puppy, a black skin but I am white; a woman's skin but I am a man; I never have the skin of what I am. There is no exception to the rule because I am never what I have. (Wilson, 1996: 13)

In fact, it was the text of *La Robe: Essai psychanalytique du vêtement*, which Orlan had read by 1983 that gave her the idea of putting words into action – using surgery to create an external image that more closely matched her internal self-identity – 'a move from reading to the carrying out of the act' (Orlan, 1996: 88). The book, which contained sections about 'cutting, the nude, the mask, the veil, the second skin' (Wilson, 1996: 13), was obviously an immense influence on Orlan's future performances, given that she was already using the robe and her body to speak about religious iconography and the human body.

In a brief discussion about the reading aloud of texts in Orlan's work, Parveen Adams remarks 'that the reading is a resolute turning away from the body at the moment when it is critically involved in surgery' (1996: 165). But this is not body denial, it is instead, an engagement with text and the ideas generated by them.

In an interview Orlan said: 'I also use a lot of Artaud, because I am interested in the concept that the body is obsolete' (Sas, 1995: 110). Orlan said that she liked a piece of Artaud's writing, 'that famous passage when he says that you shit so many times in your life, you pee so many times, you sleep and pick your teeth so many times, and for all that a poet might only produce fifty pages of poetry' (Sas, 1995: 110). She draws on these ideas to contrast involuntary bodily functions necessary for survival with conscious or voluntary acts of human creation. Both

Artaud and Orlan struggle with the notion of an imaginary body, one that was not tied to the flesh, and the tangible manifestations of its production.

Antonin Artaud's most famous book *The Theatre and its Double* (1970) was a great influence on performance artists. However, Orlan is referring to part of his 1947 radio play *To Have with the Judgement of God*, and to concepts which inform the French theorists Gilles Deleuze and Felix Guattari (1987), who reconfigure much of Artaud's notions of the body. The BwO (body without organs) which they refer to in their seminal text of 1987, has become a potent metaphor in current discussions that circulate around virtual bodies.

Susan Sontag has observed of Artaud that:

> Far from being disembodied, his consciousness is one whose martyrdom results from its seamless relation to the body. In his struggle against all hierarchical or merely dualistic notions of consciousness, Artaud constantly treats his mind as if it were a kind of body. (1988: xxiv)

In a way, Artaud attempts in his writing to give form to thought, creating an imaginary body that does not possess organs. When he wrote:

> For the great lie has been to make man an organism,
> ingestion,
> assimilation,
> incubation,
> excretion,
> thus creating a whole order of hidden functions
> which are outside the realm of the
> deliberative will. (Sontag, 1988: 515)

he desired a body not hindered by the function of the organism, nor fettered to disease, deterioration and decay; but free to become whatever form it wanted. He wanted to free thought from the constraints of physicality and untie it from the original body form and matter, predetermined by the organism (DNA). He attacked the concept of God, order and the body organism when he said:

> When you have made him a body without organs, then you will have delivered him from all his automatic reactions and restored him to his freedom. (Sontag, 1988: 571)

He saw the organs as separate body parts all functioning in different ways, a machine, which worked against the unity of the body. According to Artaud, the only way to rid oneself of the pain of being human, is by placing man 'on the autopsy table to remake his anatomy' (Sontag, 1988: 570).

Orlan cites Artaud as an early influence in relation to obsolete bodies, and Stelarc has been stating that the body is obsolete since 1976; a message that he reiterates constantly. 'The body is obsolete. We are at the end of philosophy and human physiology' (Stelarc, 1991: 591); a notion appropriated by Orlan when she said 'The body is Obsolete. I fight against God and DNA' (Armstrong, 1995b: xiv).

There is certainly a relationship between Artaud's ideas and those adopted by Orlan, for to 'fight against God and DNA' is to fight against Religion and Science: two major paradigms that have mediated and defined the human body. They are also entities that are unseen and outside of our usual realm of experience. To deny DNA is to deny that bodies can be reduced to code, a strategy to escape from the biological, destined-to-die body, to the post-biological, technologically enhanced body, in which life may be extended.

On the one hand Orlan stresses corporeality and its associations with the sacrificial, its diseases and inadequacies; on the other hand she recreates her body as text, which situates her back within a discourse that historically ascribes to women the source of monsters and grotesque births. Consequently Orlan's reconfigured face is a screen on which we project our hidden fears of disfigurement, disease and abnormality. Furthermore, although she engages with the notion of surface difference, she reveals that the inside of the body is the exact location in which difference is defined. By displaying her body interior, another monster is produced by the scalpel, which insinuates a possibly more sinister side of medical technologies, such as genetic engineering.

The notion of Other, as something distinctly different from us, is replaced here with death as Other; as though all the Others already produced by society have become invisible. Jean Baudrillard says that the 'Other is no longer an object of passion but an object of production ... we can only remember that seduction lies in not reconciling with the Other and in salvaging the strangeness of the Other' (1995: http://www.ctheory.com/). Orlan salvages the Other partly to alert us to genetic engineering, which would reconfigure human DNA, and produce homogeneity within the body in-terior, as cosmetic surgery has in standardizing Western ideals of exterior beauty.

Ritual

The use of grapes in Orlan's photograph is not only a decorative element, but one which points to Dionysus and the ritual of Sparagmos, and Christ's blood as the transformed wine (grapes).[14] Orlan evokes the erotic nature of blood, and the taboos and rituals associated with it. It's almost as if she wants to break through to an inner experience that may only be obtained through the transgressive act of opening up her skin. Surgeon and cadaver, she is both self and Other strangely associated with, but detached from, her body. Murder, sacrifice, trauma, rape, scream from the opened wounds on her face which appears cannibalistic, eating away at human flesh, until the new contours appear. The blood trickling down her cheek is like water nourishing arid land, providing a relationship between blood and nurture, and the Christian concept of transubstantiation.[15] 'Take this and eat, for this is my body; take this and drink, for this is my blood', said Christ at the Last Supper. The bread is transformed miraculously and the body as flesh is ingested as concept and substance.

Blood is not only the life force, carrying within it the substance of mankind, it is also a potent symbol of life. Its appearance creates both repulsion and attraction. We desire what challenges us, we desire to experience anything outside our usual realm of experience. Hence the strange seduction of Orlan's images and their powerful associations with transformation. However, in the current AIDS crisis the mixing of blood or its spillage on to another person is seen as violent and dangerous because of possible viral transmission. The act of penetration, whether by intravenous injection or sexually, is also perceived as violent. Now, as in medieval times all bodily fluids are equated with blood (Bynum, 1992: 82). Blood is the link between life, death and the sacrificial, through the subject's desire to assimilate the abject.

Orlan's mouth, eyes and wound are interchangeable as metaphors. As doorways to the self, they are empty receivers of images, screens and theatrical space. She said, 'it seems to me your eyes become black holes, and the images come into those holes down into the body where it hurts' (Orlan, 1996: 9). Openings in the body allow the outside world in and the wound as point of entry testifies to the fact that injury has occurred. As erotic zones they are also producers and receptacles of mucous, secretions, excrement. Sites that remind us that we are finite beings. However, the absence of these signifiers of normal body functioning points to a deterioration of the mechanism, so the presence of the abject may be seen as life embracing.

Reliquaries

Emile Durkheim remarked: 'there is no religious ceremony where blood does not have a part to play'. Some of these ways were 'the anointing of men with the blood of others, sacred images being drawn in blood soaked ground, and streams of blood being poured upon rock, and entry into and with the sacred' (1915: 137). For Orlan, blood is a link with the sacrificial; a way to speak about life, death and transformation, no longer enabled by religion, but by science and technology.

As Orlan remarks:

The vision of my body being opened painlessly was extremely seductive aesthetically ... I found it similar to the light coming through the windows of a church illuminating the religious imagery inside. (in Gale, 1995: 31)

Here she is aligned with mystical and religious women of medieval times such as 'Mary of Oignies (13th century) who hacked off pieces of her own flesh while immersed in a vision of the Crucifixion' (Ash, 1990: 94).

Ash proposes that:

> The ascetic practices of the religious woman, her mystical experiences, constituted the radical refusal of her own 'self' as the 'patriarchal female' and a reconstruction of subjectivity and sexuality beyond the strictures of the Law. And this constituted her own 'inquiry into femininity', her attempt to locate a different 'self' a bodily being beyond the Name/No of the Father. (1990: 95, 96)

At the Sydney Biennale in Australia in December 1992, Orlan included phials containing samples of her liquefied flesh and blood drained off during the 'body sculpting' part of the operations and at the Sandra Deering Gallery in New York other relics, blood and fat procured via liposuction were exhibited (Rose, 1993: 85).

Aligning herself with Catholicism and Saints through the use of robing and veiling, and her exhibition of reliquaries, further positions this part of Orlan's project within the cult of relics and within a discourse that invests power in the body, even in fragmentation. Orlan offers not only the supposed link with transformation of matter that the relic provides, but also the commodification of body parts, linked in this culture with the female body.

Orlan is not the first performance artist to exhibit relics. Hermann Nitsch, one of the Viennese Actionists, also engaged with Judeo-Christian symbolism and exhibited 'relics' after his actions. His performances (called 'actions') were a displacement of the Christian Mass and involved the use of sheep and cows and their blood.[16] Orlan, however, is the first performance artist to exhibit relics that are remnants of her body sculpting.

The implantation of small pieces of cartilage into Orlan's forehead in November 1993 is not only Orlan's way of assimilating the forehead of the Mona Lisa, but are small horns that link her with the Greek God Dionysus. Represented in Greek mythology as satyr, Dionysus was associated with joyful orgiastic dance and excessive activity. Wine and religious dance were the main components in Dionysian and Bacchanalian ecstatic religions, which were considered to be cathartic. *Dionysos-Botrys, the Deified Grape*, an image of Dionysus from the 1st century, shows him covered totally by grapes, revealing not the Christian doctrine of transubstantiation, but a transfiguration – that his divinity had been in the grape all along (see Campbell, 1975: 249). Orlan's new self was also always within her. In Christian mythology Christ was often represented as grapes, and wine, while Dionysus, as horned satyr, became the image of the beast (the devil).

In the display and sale of her relics[17] Orlan raises important issues in regard to the commodification of the human body, particularly in relation to genetic engineering, donor organs and foetal experimentation. However, it is more importantly a remnant of her former self, a casting off of the old, which is transformed into the new self-identity. Current ideas about virtual bodies and virtual selves spilling out into the mediascape continue the debate about original or compensatory bodies; and with new technologies such as the Internet, personas may be created that have nothing to do with an original physical body.

The relationship between the body and its double, real and virtual bodies and technological body images is addressed by Orlan in her reliquary *Blood and Phototransfer on Gauze*. The original relic from her *Omnipresence* performance (1993) shows Orlan's bloodied facial imprint impregnated into the cloth; the trace of her lips and the marks of incision are clearly seen as the surgeon removes it from her face.[18] The image is a bloody trace of her skeletal facial structure. However, the image reproduced in *Art and Text* (Moos, 1996) has a phototransfer of Orlan's face fused into the final relic. In this image produced by surgical intervention and imaging technologies, she meshes past with future, blurring foreground and background together in a total immersion of surface and texture. The imprint, like a psychological blot test, spills upwards revealing the head of a goat, with small horns protruding from the forehead. The image is of the satyr, or devil; imagery that is echoed in the triptych of the operation in which Orlan brandishes a pitchfork and a human skull is depicted with horns.[19] In this depiction Orlan plays with distinct binaries: human/animal, sacred/profane, normal/pathological, perfection/abjection, life and death.

According to John Lash: 'Twinning is rampant in the Christ Mythos, where mimesis and substitution, sacrifice, scapegoating and transference multiply in a dazzling display of motifs' (1993: 22). Orlan's 'sacrificial body' might also be viewed as a scapegoat, for Lash also proposes that: 'In the Biblical scapegoat, the animal is splattered with blood, invested with the sins of the community, and driven into the wilderness. Scapegoating is the most perfect mechanism of expurgation known to humanity' (1993: 80).

This particular reliquary is reminiscent of the facial section of the Shroud of Turin, which is posited as holding the image of Christ, after the crucifixion.[20] Housed in Turin, France since 1532, the shroud is historically linked with the Mandylion cloth 'a picture of Christ not made by human hands' (Kersten and Gruber, 1994: 110). Originally located in Edessa, the Mandylion cloth had been highly revered since the 6th century, it was 'so important that many copies were prepared, and all were claimed to be the original' (Kersten and Gruber, 1994: 110). The Shroud of Turin is believed to be either the original or copy of this cloth.

Commercially available holographic cards of Christ are constructed from

phototransfers of a painted depiction of Christ's visage which overlays a reproduction of the facial imprint on the shroud, linking the constructed image with an
image assumed to be Christ's body traces.

When cloth is wrapped around a corpse, various substances are expelled into
the material, leaving traces of corporeal matter. In some ways the cloth becomes
a body of evidence which attests to Christ's death and resurrection, but more
importantly that Christ has risen unified and intact. Orlan's relic survives as testa-
ment that she has sacrificed her self-identity to Art and the technologies that
enable body modification. And this is what incites negative criticism, for society
in general is not opposed to cosmetic surgery, it is however opposed to deliberate
body mutilation.

Body unity was, and still is important for identity. Historically fragmented
body parts were perceived as miraculous or evil, and tampering with the body was
considered transgressive. After death, relics (fragments) of the bodies of Saints
enshrined by the Catholic Church, were considered sacred and were desired for
their magical quality. However, to many people fragmented body parts were
conceptualized as living decay, because they were associated with diseases such as
leprosy.

During the Renaissance:

> The most perfect male body was that of Christ, who, despite the mortification endured during
> the passion, and his depiction as the broken and passive object of contemplation in the number-
> less images of the pieta, nevertheless preserved his essential spiritual and aesthetic unity.
> (Sawday, 1995: 217)

The face on Orlan's 'relic' is the perfectly constructed female face working against
the notion of perfection attained through Christianity. Orlan subverts the Christ
face by replacing her face, as signifier of the sacrificial and alerts us to how much
faith is engendered by Science and in the images that we hold sacred.

By constructing this phototransfer on gauze, Orlan asks us to question the
authenticity surrounding the relic; the original and simulacrum. She provokes us
with the question 'Is self identity our body or our image?' – a potent question in
light of the current rhetoric that surrounds the body in cyberspace interactions.
Questions also arise about the sacrificial body posited through Christ's crucifixion and suffering – he who gave his earthly body for his father, and Orlan, who
has 'given her body to Art'. 'J'ai donné mon corps à l'art' is the text that accom-
panies a photograph of Orlan after her *Omnipresence* operation. In the postcard
she looks like a woman who has been bashed, her hair is dishevelled and her eyes
are bloodshot.[21]

The title of Orlan's operation/performance, *Omnipresence*, refers directly to
the Christian God, who is present in all places simultaneously. In the current

Figure 2 Manipulation of the white cross and the black cross for the fifth plastic surgery operation performance (8 December 1990) (Cibachrome, 1.10m × 1.65m) Published by courtesy of Sipa Press.

ethos of technological interface, omnipresence is Orlan's way of referring to 'telepresence', as her performance was linked, in real time, to several galleries across the world, with the help of interactive communications equipment.

Crosses feature prominently in many of Orlan's photographs. A white transparent cross overlays a close up of Orlan's lips being injected for the 8 December 1990 – *Lips of Europa*, operation performance. Photographs of her, prior to and during this same operation, show her holding both upright and inverted, black and white crosses.[22] In *Orlan, Successful Operation No. 1: Death Head, 1991*, her central head and torso are overlaid with the shape of a white lengthwise cross; on either side are mirror images of skulls (see Orlan, 1996: 44). This image speaks more literally of transformation, death and resurrection, for Christ was crucified at Golgotha (Latin: Calvary) 'the place of a skull' (Matthew 2: 33) and while most people would not be aware of this association, Orlan uses it metaphorically.

In *Cruciform* she stares out from within a dark shaped cross. The photograph is reminiscent of paintings of the High Renaissance. Illuminated from a dark background, her face is bandaged, mummified; the gauze which is pulled tight across her cheekbones renders her face wrinkled and malleable, as if wrapped in polythene. The sacrificial body anointed and preserved, ready for resurrection.

In a video still from Orlan's operation/performance *The Mouth of Europa and the Figure of Venus*, Orlan's face is shown from four different viewpoints.[23] The framing of the screen and close-up of her face render it mask-like and fragmented from the rest of her body and its surroundings. Her eyes have disappeared into the dark background. The piece, entitled *A Little While Longer and You Will See Me No More ... A Little While Longer ... You Will See Me*, depicts a face obscured from view that appears as through a glass darkly, to have suddenly entered our vision. Orlan said that she used the words of Christ before the passion and projected the words on to the ceiling 'because the spectators would be obliged to feel uncomfortable while watching a body in discomfort' (1995: 109).

Nature/Culture

In recent photo-documentation Orlan has either one or both breasts exposed. Barbara Rose suggests that Orlan's exposure of one breast aligns her with the Virgin Mary, who is often represented exposing only one breast and 'to differentiate Saint Orlan from a topless pin-up' (1993: 84). As the identity of Saint Orlan developed during Orlan's performances in the 1980s 'her trademark became this single exposed breast jutting out irreverently through virginal fabrics' (Lovelace, 1995: 23). According to Jennifer Ash, 'the bleeding body of Christ crucified can be recognized as maternal in function, the bleeding wound in Christ's side functions as a lactating breast' (1990: 86), a statement supported by Sawday when he said that 'there also existed a tradition of Christ represented as a nurturing female body' (1995: 217).

While Orlan's exposed breast may refer to breast feeding, it is more likely that the reference is to Christ's wound which was assimilated as 'the later bleeding of the Cross to the earlier bleeding of the circumcised infant' (Bynum, 1992: 87). Bynum states that 'Renaissance sermons often emphasised the bleeding of Christ's penis at the circumcision of a special proof of his true – that is, his fleshy – humanity' (1992: 84), a concept supported by Ash when she said: 'The fleshy matter of incarnated Divinity was inherited from His mother Mary. Christ's flesh was Mary's flesh, was quite literally feminine fleshiness' (1990: 90). It may be that Orlan also refers to the Renaissance *'Anatomia'*, which sought to uncover the mysteries of the female body through dissection of the uterus, and to more recent surgical intervention into the female body, such as breast reduction, silicon implants, reconstructive surgery and the commodification of the female breast in the media.

I am reminded of Marcel Duchamp's *Prière de toucher* (*Please Touch*, 1947) which represents a dismembered breast on a background of black velvet. Fragmented like this from the woman that it represents, it becomes a bizarre trophy, an object of desire to be touched, as though the breast itself is making the invitation. However, the sexual/sensual connotations ascribed to the female breast is lost, and Duchamp creates an analogy between the breast and death. There is a sense of voyeurism and sadomasochism attached to the dismembered breast. *Please Touch* is similar to another of Duchamp's works, *Etants Donnés*, which shows a 'mysterious crack in a barn-like door, [through which] one is treated to what seems at first a romantic nocturnal scene – until one notices what lies in the middle, the splayed body of woman who looks like she has just been raped' (Lovelace, 1995: 20).

Orlan, although seduced by the rhetoric of technology, has turned to excess as a strategy against the benign and controlled nature of the screen, and the homogenization of body images. Her new identity, although not extreme, is a site of resistance in a society bent on eliminating forms that threaten the status quo. By linking her performances with Judeo-Christian iconography she establishes her work as sacrificial. More importantly she is involved with what may be called trans-human aesthetics which circulates around experimentation and investigation of the human form as a strategy to uncover what is human. The aesthetic is a cross-over from the idea that the body is contained, immutable, bounded, restrained by natural forces and sacred. Its philosophy denies that the human has any fixed nature, and instead looks to mutation and differentiation to expand the repertoire of human interaction and invention. It is concerned with asking vital questions about man's relationship to the machines and technology invented. According to Ansell Pearson, 'being, is a becoming, nothing other than becoming, becoming as invention'; and 'the transhuman condition is about man's self-overcoming in order to discover or reinvent what is human' (1997: 15).

Notes

1. Computer tomography, combined with other computer imaging systems EEG, PET, MRI and CAT scans present the human body as image and code, rather than flesh and blood. False-colour scanning electron micrographs, which enlarge and isolate human bone and tissue, render the body as pure surface, alienated from the social body.

2. The Visible Human Project was instigated in 1991 at the University of Colorado Health Sciences Center in Denver. A Denver man (Joseph Paul Jerigan), who had to represent an average human in good health at the time of death, was scanned with MRI and x-rays, and then sliced into millimetres from head to toe. Photographs of these slices were then digitized and stored on 70 CD Roms. This electronic cadaver is the first complete body image to inhabit the Internet.

3. Human Genome Project instigated at the University of Colorado in Santa Cruz in 1985. See O'Neil (1990: 42).

4. 30 May 1990, in Newcastle, England.

5. She has undergone seven operations, beginning on 27 July 1990, when she had a chin prosthesis inserted by Dr Cherif Sahar. The September and 8 December 1990 operation – *The Lips of Europa* – was performed by Dr Bernard Cornette de Saint-Cyr. *The Mouth of Europa and the Figure of Venus* operation was performed in July 1991. The February 1992 operation/performance was carried out at the Performance Festival in Liège. In February 1993 the *Omnipresence* performance occurred. In November 1993 she had implants inserted in her temples by Dr Marjorie Cramer. 'There have also been three attempts to put a cleft in her chin' (Norris, 1996: 40).

6. The prototype was made from the chin of Botticelli's *Venus*, the nose of Gerôme's *Psyche*, a Fontainbleau *Diana*'s eyes, the lips of Gustave Moreau's *Europa*, and the brow of Leonardo's *Mona Lisa*.

7. See photograph by Alain Dbome in Sas (1995: 111).

8. I am reminded of Barbara Kruger's *Untitled, 1989* photosilkscreen/vinyl image which depicts a black and white image of a woman's face. Divided in the centre, the right hand side of the face is the negative image which perhaps reveals another separate identity. The textual overlay is achieved by large red rectangles which contain the words YOUR BODY IS A BATTLEGROUND. The total image not only suggests binaries, but focuses on the war of images and image-making in regards to women's' faces.

9. Photo by F. Leveque, photoshop manipulation by Hi Dee Pholi, in Sas (1995: 108).

10. 8 December 1990 operation, photograph by Joel Nicolas in Rose (1993: 86).

11. Gina Pane, a French performance artist of the 1960s also dealt with issues surrounding the commodification of the female face, the relationship of the mouth to language and the taboos related to blood and other bodily fluids.

12. Orlan was born Mireille Porte in 1947 (Lovelace, 1995: 15).

13. *Silence of the Lambs*, 1991, Dir. Jonathan Demme, Orion. He intended to construct the garment from pieces of flesh cut from his victims.

14. Sparagmos is an ancient Dionysiac ritual in which a live animal was torn apart and eaten. This ritual was against the Orphic religion that did not believe in the spilling of blood, as it was considered to be a carrier of infections. See E.R. Dodds, *The Greeks and the Irrational* (1968: 154).

15. In Catholic doctrine 'transubstantiation' is the belief that the wine and bread (host), that are offered in communion are transformed into the blood and the body of Christ.

16. The Viennese Actionists are Hermann Nitsch, Otto Muel, Gunter Brus and Rudolf Schwarkkogler.

They were influenced by the writings of Freud, the philosophy of Nietzsche and Greek mythology, and were involved in the displacement of Judeo-Christian rituals through their Orgy/Mystery Theatre performances. See Brus (1988). The 'relics' were the blood stained cloth or the clothing that he wore during the actions.

17. The relic, through history, has been a source of hope and spiritual peace and a material link to idea of immortality. More than this, it is a potent sign of transformation from this life to an afterlife, as promoted by Catholicism.

18. See photographs of the cloth in Armstrong (1995a: 61) and in Orlan, *This is My Body. . . This is My Software* (1996: 77).

19. *Triptyque opération – opéra 5ème dite à la tête de mort* (1993) in Orlan, *This is My Body. . . .* (1996: 44).

20. In 1988, at the order of the Vatican, three groups of experts, using the so called radiocarbon method, dated the linen cloth to the 14th century. See preface to Kersten and Gruber (1994).

21. Parisian postcard, cARTed 14, Pasca Pithois, 16 ave. de Normandie, 50130 Octeville, France (1995).

22. For other 'blasphemous' uses of the cross, see Man Ray's *Homage to D.A.F. de Sade* (1933), reproduced in ACT (1993: 139).

23. From the fifth operation in July 1991 – Sydney Biennale, photo Stephen Auriach in Rose (1993: 87).

Bibliography

ACT (1993) *Surrealism, Revolution by Night*, exhibition catalogue. Canberra: National Gallery of Australia.

Adams, Parveen (1996) 'Operation Orlan' pp. 141–59 in *The Emptiness of the Image: Psychoanalysis and Sexual Difference*. London and New York: Routledge.

Ansell Pearson, Keith (1997) *Viroid Life: Perspectives on Nietzsche and the Transhuman Condition*, London and New York: Routledge.

Anzieu, Didier (1989) *The Skin Ego*, trans. Chris Turner. New Haven, CT and London: Yale University Press.

Armstrong, Neil (1996) 'Skin Deep', *The Crack* (Newcastle, UK) April 1996: 11–13.

Armstrong, Rachel (1995a) 'Post-Human Evolution', *Artiface* (London) 2: 53–63.

Armstrong, Rachel (1995b) 'Orlan, Mute', *Digital Art Critique* 1 (spring): xiv.

Armstrong, Rachel (1996a) 'Carnal Art', for *'Digital Aesthetics One'* conference, April, Sydney, Australia.

Armstrong, Rachel (1996b) 'Cut Along the Dotted Line', *Dazed and Confused* 17.

Ash, Jennifer (1990) 'The Discursive Construction of Christ's Body in the later Middle Ages: Resistance and Autonomy', in T. Threadgold and A. Cranny-Francis (eds) *Feminine, Masculine and Representation*. Sydney: Allen and Unwin.

Artaud, Antonin (1970) *The Theatre & its Double*. London: Calder. [Orig. 1938.]

Balsamo, Anne (1994) 'On the Cutting Edge: Cosmetic Surgery and the Technological Production of the Gendered Body', in Camera Obscura Collective (ed.) *Imaging Technologies, Inscribing Science*. Berkeley, CA: Camera Obscura.

Balsamo, Anne (1996) *Technologies of the Gendered Body: Reading Cyborg Women*. Durham, NC and London: Duke University Press.

Barker, Francis (1995) *The Tremulous Private Body: Essays on Subjection*. Ann Arbor: University of Michigan Press.

Bataille, Georges (1987) *Eroticism: Death and Sensuality*, trans. Mary Dalwood. London: Marion Boyars.

Baudrillard, Jean (1983) *Simulations*, trans. P. Foss, P. Patton and P. Beitchman. New York: Semiotext(e).

Baudrillard, Jean (1993a) 'The Hell of the Same', in *The Transparency of Evil: Essays on Extreme Phenomena*, trans. J. Benedikt. London and New York: Verso.

Baudrillard, Jean (1993b) 'Plastic Surgery for the Other', trans. F. Debrix, *Ctheory: Theory, Technology and Culture* 19(1–2): 3.

Beckett, Andy (1996) 'Suffering for her Art', *Independent on Sunday*, 14 April: 18–21.

Bond, Anthony (1993) 'Orlan – France', *9th Biennale of Sydney Catalogue*. Sydney, Australia.

Braidotti, Rosi (1989) 'Organs without Bodies', *Differences* 1(1): 147–61.

Bronson, A.A. and P. Gale (1979) *Performance by Artists*. Toronto: Art Metropole.

Brus, Gunter (1988) *Von der Aktionsmelerei Zom Aktionism: Wein, 1960–1963*. Klosenfurt: Ritter.

Bryant, Gay (1995) 'What Price Beauty?', *Marie Claire Australia*, premier issue (Sept.): 199, 201–2.

Bulfinch, Thomas (1969) *The Age of Fable or Beauties of Mythology*. London: Dent.

Bynum, Caroline W. (1992) *Fragmentation and Redemption – Essays on Gender and the Human Body in Medieval Religion*. New York: Zone.

Campbell, Joseph (1975) *The Mythic Image*. Princeton, NJ: Princeton University Press.

Creed, Barbara (1993) *The Monstrous Feminine: Film, Feminism, Psychoanalysis*. London and New York: Routledge.

Crimp, Douglas (1981) 'The Photographic Activity of Postmodernism', *October* (spring): 91–102.

Deleuze, G. and F. Guattari (1987) 'Bodies without Organs', in *A Thousand Plateaus: Capitalism and Schizophrenia*, trans. Brian Massumi. Minneappolis: University of Minnesota Press.

Dodds, E.R. (1968) *The Greeks and the Irrational*. Berkeley and Los Angeles: University of California Press.

Durkheim, Emile (1915) *The Elementary Forms of The Religious Life*, trans. Joseph Ward Dwain. London: George Allen and Unwin Limited.

Ebbs, Geoff (1995) 'Humanitarian Bounds', *Informationage* Feb.: 7–21.

Foucault, Michel (1977) *Discipline and Punish: The Birth of the Prison*, trans. Alan Sheridan. London: Allen Lane.

Frueh, Joanna (1989) 'Has the Body Lost its Mind?', *High Performance* (summer): 44–7.

Gale, David (1995) 'Knife Work', *Gentlemen's Quarterly* (London) February: 31.

Goodall, Jane (1997) 'Whose Body? Ethics and Experiment in Art', *Artlink* 15(17): 2, 10–15.

Gray, Louise (1996) 'Me, My Surgeon and My Art', *Independent*.

Griffin, Annie (1996) 'Facial Figurations', *New Statesman and Society* 12 April: 30.

Griffin, Michelle, 'No Pain, No Fame', *Melbourne Weekly* 17: 12–13.

Grosz, Elizabeth (1989) 'Julia Kristeva: Abjection, Motherhood and Love', in *Sexual Subversions: Three French Feminists*. Sydney: Allen and Unwin.

Grosz, Elizabeth (1994) *Volatile Bodies: Towards a Corporeal Feminism*. St Leonards, NSW: Allen and Unwin.

Jones, Amelia (1996) *Postmodernism and the Engendering of Marcel Duchamp*. Cambridge, New York, Australia: Cambridge University Press.

Kersten, Holger and Elmar R. Gruber (1994) *The Jesus Conspiracy: The Turin Shroud and the truth about the Resurrection*. Shaftesbury, Dorset, Rockport, MA, Brisbane, Queensland: Element Books.

Lash, John (1993) *Twins and the Double*. London: Thames and Hudson.

Le Goff, Jacques (1985) 'Head or Heart? The Political Use of Body Metaphors in the Middle Ages', in M. Feher (ed.) *Fragments for a History of the Human Body*. New York: Zone Books.

Lifton, Robert Jay (1993), *The Protean Self: Human Resilience in an Age of Fragmentation*. New York: Basic Books.

Lovelace, Carey (1995) 'Orlan: Offensive Acts', *Performing Arts Journal* (Johns Hopkins University Press), 17(1): 13–25.

Marsh, Anne (1993) *Body and Self: Performance Art in Australia, 1969–92*. Melbourne, Australia: Oxford University Press.

Mirzoeff, Nicholas (1995) *Bodyscape: Art, Modernity and the Ideal Figure*. London and New York: Routledge.

Moos, Michel (1996) 'Memories of Being', *Art and Text* 54 (May): 69.

Nalder, Glenda (1993) 'Under the VR Spell', *Eyeline 21* (Australia) Autumn.

Nietzsche, Friedrich (1984) *Twilight of the Idols* and *The Anti-Christ*, trans. R.J. Hollingdale. Harmondsworth: Penguin Books.

Nitsch, Herman (1969) *Orgien Mysterien Theatre*. Munich.

Norris, M. (1996) 'This Woman Has Surgery to Distort Her', *Marie Claire Health and Beauty*. (London) April.

O'Neil, Graeme (1990) 'Human DNA: Cracking the Code', *ZIC* summer 90/91: 39–44.

Orlan (1994) *Conference paper*, France.

Orlan (1995) 'Intervention – Orlan', trans. Michel Moos and Tanya Ausbeurg, USA.

Orlan (1996) *Orlan: Ceci est mon corps . . . Ceci est mon logiciel. . ./This is My Body . . . This is My Software*, ed. D. McConquodale. London: Black Dog Publishing Limited and the Authors.

Osborne, Barbara (1992) 'Is it Technology, or is it Just Bad Art?', *High Performance* (spring): 38.

Palmer, Judith (1996a) 'Corporal Punishment', *Independent* 26 April: section 2, p. 5.

Palmer, Judith (1996b) 'Theatre, Orlan, ICA', *Independent*, May, London.

Porter, Mark (1996) 'The Face of an Artful Bodger', *Sunday Express* 17 March: 45.

Price, Anna (1995) 'Orlan', *Artiface* (London) 2: 46–51.

Reiser, Stanley Joel (1978) *Medicine and the Reign of Technology*. Cambridge: Cambridge University Press.

Rose, Barbara (1993) 'Is It Art?', *Art in America* February: 82–7, 105.

Russo, Mary (1997) 'Female Grotesques: Carnival and Theory', pp. 318–36 in K. Conboy, M. Medine and S. Stanbury (eds) *Writing on the Body*. New York: Columbia University Press. (Orig. 1986 in *Feminist Issues/Critical Issues*, 1986.)

Sas, Miryam (1995) 'The Doyenne of Divasection', *MONDO 2000* 13: 106–11.

Sawday, Jonathan (1995) *The Body Emblazoned: Dissection and the Human Body in Renaissance Culture*. London: Routledge.

Scarry, Elaine (1985) *The Body in Pain: The Making and Unmaking of the World*. Oxford and New York: Oxford University Press.

Sennett, Richard (1994) *Flesh and Stone: The Body and the City in Western Civilization*. New York: W.W. Norton.

Seward, Keith (1993) 'Orlan – Penine Hart Gallery', *Artforum* 32: 90–91.

Smith, Caroline (1995) 'Beyond Flesh and Blood', *New Scientist* 28–9.

Sontag, Susan (ed.) (1988) *Antonin Artaud: Selected Writings*. Berkeley and Los Angeles: University of California Press.

Stelarc (1991) 'Prosthetics, Robotics and Remote Existence: Postevolutionary Strategies', SISEA, Groningen, The Netherlands, *Leonardo* 24(5).

Stone, Allucquere Rosanne (1995)*The War of Desire and Technology at the Close of the Mechanical Age*, Cambridge, MA and London: The MIT Press.

Stone, Allucquere Rosanne (1996) 'Speaking of the Medium: Marshall McLuhan Interviews', pp. 43–51 in Orlan, *This is My Body . . . This is My Software*, ed. D. McConquodale. London: Black Dog Publishing and the Authors.

Turner, Victor (1962) *The Forest of Symbols: Aspects of Ndembu Rituals*. Ithaca, NY: Cornell University Press.

Wilson, Sarah (1996) 'L'Historie d'O, sacrée et profane/L'Histoire d'O, Sacred and Profane', in *Orlan: This is My Body . . . This is My Software*, ed. D. McConquodale. London: Black Dog Publishing Limited and the Authors.

Young, Robert J.C. (1995) *Colonial Desire: Hybridity in Theory, Culture and Race*. London and New York: Routledge.

Julie Clarke is an exhibiting artist/writer who completed a BA in Fine Arts at the RMIT University (1992); a Postgraduate Diploma in Art History at the University of Melbourne (1994) and a Master of Arts in Fine Arts (Art History) by research thesis at the University of Melbourne (1997). The thesis title was 'Transhuman Aesthetics: Performance Artists and Cyberculture'. She is currently undertaking a part-time, Master of Arts by research project in Multimedia Arts with RMIT University, which will focus on identity. She recently shared the inaugural Faulding Literary Award for writing for multimedia at the Adelaide Festival of the Arts in April for the CD Rom, *Flightpaths – Writing Journeys*, which was later exhibited at Love Bits, Stafford, England in May 1998. She is currently the Assistant Manager, Multimedia Environments at the Interactive Information Institute at RMIT.

Citation and Subjectivity:
Towards a Return of the Embodied Will

ROY BOYNE

A Recent Rupture in the History of the Self

Has there been a recent break in the representation of identity within late modernity? Up until very recent times, perhaps up to the beginning of the 1980s, our understanding of personal identity, it might have been thought, was built on a notion of inner being which was typically hidden, shielded behind surface appearances which required demystification and penetration in order to allow uncertain access to an inner subjectivity. This was not a Cartesian condition. The subject revealed by hermeneutic exploration was rarely taken to be some simple and fixed kernel of incorporeal selfhood, although Sartrean existentialism perhaps came close to this with its terminal notion of a nauseous being, crowded upon by the viscosity of events. Mostly the imagined world of the inner self was taken to be quite a complex affair, generally with a high capacity connection to the even more complex arena of social power. The Freudian model is paradigmatic, the control functions of its hydraulic system being imported through ego and super-ego. What Freud and the post-Freudians, from Klein to Lacan, share is a revealed view of the inner self as a complex but relatively regular dynamic structure, but a structure generally concealed from casual view.

It is well known that postmodernism became defined in opposition to meta-narratives, psychoanalysis being one example, which appear to dictate ontological structure. It is not therefore surprising that the postmodern approach to inner being was to see it as fluid, even fragmented, and this is typified by the rhizomatic philosophy of Gilles Deleuze, and by the fracture paintings of the German artist Georg Baselitz, who spoke of pandemonium and painted broken foresters and

Body & Society © 1999 SAGE Publications (London, Thousand Oaks and New Delhi),
Vol. 5(2–3): 209–225
[1357–034X(199906/09)5:2–3;209–225;008865]

exploded dogs (Baselitz, 1992; Boyne, 1995). A longer-standing opponent to the Freudian view about the workings of the inner self is, however, the phenomenological model in which the inner impulses of the self are never to be seen apart from their outside target objects, and are at least in part defined by them. As Husserl put it:

> The phenomenologically reduced ego is . . . nothing peculiar, floating above many experiences: it is simply identical with their own interconnected unity. In the nature of its contents, and the laws they obey, certain forms of connection are grounded. They run in diverse fashions from content to content, from complex of contents to complex of contents, till in the end a unified sum total of content is constituted, which does not differ from the phenomenologically reduced ego itself. (1970: 541)

From the phenomenology of the ego through existential psychology to Searle's essays in the philosophy of mind, intentionality, the property of mental states 'by which they are directed at or about or of objects and states of affairs in the world' (Searle, 1983: 1), is the crucial assumed characteristic of inner being, within this problematic. When, as is often the case in some contemporary analyses of embodied conditions such as anorexia nervosa (Baerveldt and Voestermans, 1998) or invasive disease (Spence, 1995), one of the crucial external references is the person's own self, we can see that the unhinging of structure and the confusion of reference points creates a picture which is every bit as complex as a typical case study from *The Interpretation of Dreams* or from the Freudian annals of surrealist art. Indeed understructured reflexive intentionality has been the main alternative to psychoanalysis as the key approach to the understanding of identity in late modernity, underscoring for example the moral reading of the contemporary self that we find in the work of Charles Taylor (1989).

Both phenomenological and Freudian frameworks allow a strong role for the forces of social reproduction, but both also concede the possibility of a minimally autonomous core self: in Freud this is the territory of the *id* ('the ego is that part of the *id* which has been modified by direct influence of the external world', Freud, 1984: 363); in Lacan, the possibility exists within the realm of the real; for the phenomenological approach, the concession is made clear in different ways: in terms of the traditional concept of free will, by the very possibility of underdetermination,[1] and by the theoretical possibility of phenomenological reduction to its essence, such as we find in Bataille's investigations of inner experience. In contradistinction, and logically, the reduction and final eradication of a core self entails a corresponding increase in the power of forces exterior to the self, especially the social. If we were still unequivocally in the Freudian (or even the Husserlian) century, with identity and selfhood understood, however hazily, to be a matter of socio-historical events linked through the dynamic but ultimately uncertain energies in some dark core, then we could quite possibly look at all of the socio-logical aspects of identity as secondary (but far from unimportant) matters. So, there may be a gain, at least for the strong proponents of the hugely important area of the social, in moving away from any residue of core self: the social could then take absolutely centre stage without fear of challenge. One version of that gain would be the possible establishment of particular identities as prime: gendered identities as a prime focus within feminism and queer theory, tribal identities flowing from contemporary disindividuation (Maffesoli, 1996), cultic identities emerging from and dissolving into liminal conditions (Turner, 1982), to take three examples. However, any such gain might appear somewhat regional, and, for whichever sector, might be more apparent than real. For any given identities within a resolutely anti-essentialist culture enter into fierce competition with all other potential sources for citation: tribal, national, racial, religious, economic, culture-capital, to name but some of the more obvious ones. Thus it may be that to refuse even to entertain the occasional primacy of the flows within the core may be to shift from uncertain ground to no ground at all. But perhaps this is a call too late.

We are tempted now with the thought that we no longer have to assume anything about inner being, about what might lie behind the screen. Critiques of Freud abound from such writers as Stanley Fish (1998), arguing that the analytical session is where the therapist exerts power over the patient, and Frederick Crews (1998), who attempts to demonstrate that Freudianism is a scientific fraud which has had some notably pernicious social consequences, such as false memory syndrome. Powerful systems of sociological thought find all that can be known about social action in the properties of actant networks or in fields of power. So, we have now moved, it might appear, to a culture of citation, to the verification of identity through, and to the exhaustion of identity in, the citation of sources, rather than through some form of depth hermeneutical revelation of self. As Judith Butler has pointed out, this situation is inherent in the deconstructionist critique of the very idea of the origin. Yet even at the time of writing *Bodies that Matter*, in the early 1990s, it is not clear that she grasped the extent of the change. She still wrote, at the time, of citational practice that might remain unmarked:

> To what extent does discourse gain the authority to bring about what it names through citing the conventions of authority? And does a subject appear as the author of its discursive effects to the extent that the citational practice by which he/she is conditioned and mobilized remains unmarked? Indeed, could it be that the production of the subject as originator of his/her effects is precisely a consequence of this dissimulated citationality? (1993: 13)

It is possible that this view of the subject as dissimulation incarnate, as plagiarist, whether artful or hapless, has been surpassed. Late modernity has encouraged us to simulate and stimulate our selves and shop for our identities in cults, through films and at chain fashion stores. As identities are constructed statement by statement, performance by performance, we are made and confronted by cut and paste, with citations impeccably and publicly correct, and with discursive reaffirmations of sources providing guarantees of presence. The paradigm case is Brett Easton Ellis, *American Psycho*. This is a typical passage:

> I take a hot shower and afterwards use a new facial scrub by Caswell-Massey and a body wash by Greune, then a body moisturiser by Lubriderm and a Neutrogena facial cream. I debate between two outfits. One is a wool-crepe suit by Bill Robinson I bought at Saks with this cotton jacquard shirt from Charivari and an Armani tie. Or a wool and cashmere sport coat with blue plaid, a cotton shirt and pleated wool trousers by Alexander Julian, with a polka-dot silk tie by Bill Blass. The Julian might be a little too warm for May but if Patricia's wearing this outfit by Karl Lagerfeld that I *think* she's going to, then maybe I *will* go with the Julian, because it would go well with *her* suit. The shoes are crocodile loafers by A. Testoni. (1991: 76)

Identity in the consumer society is secured by footnotes, but there is no core text to which they refer. Beyond the citation of sources, there is, to use Brett Easton Ellis's phrase, '*Less than Zero*'.

The movement from the self as *arcanum* to the citational self has, effectively, been welcomed, particularly in the work of Judith Butler, but also in the archetypal sociology of Pierre Bourdieu. There is a powerful logic behind this approbation. When self-identity is no longer seen as, even minimally, a fixed essence, this does not mean that the forces of identity formation can therefore easily be resisted, but it does mean that the necessity for incessant repetition of identity formation by the forces of a disciplinary society creates major opportunities for subversion and appropriation. In the repeated semi-permanences of the citational self, there is more than a little scope for counter-performances marked, for example, by irony and contempt. As Butler puts it, 'it is precisely the *expropriability* of the dominant, 'authorized' discourse that constitutes one potential site of its subversive resignification' (1997: 157). Let us be clear, it is not here suggested that both Judith Butler and Pierre Bourdieu agree that contemporary consumer society is populated by emptied out footnote selves, nor that they would necessarily accept the characterization of identity in the 20th century as post-Cartesian in the way described above. But it is asserted that her work on performance and the self, and Bourdieu's conceptualization of field and agency, are compatible with a view of late modern identity as coreless and citational. This has some implications, in particular, with regard to essentialism.

The Hidden Self

By constructing two quasi-hypothetical narratives about transsexualism, one before and one after a conjectured ruptural moment in the recent history of the self, it can be shown that there is a complicity between essentialism and citation-alism, and that the sources for resistance and reconstruction for selves citationally defined may actually be much less secure than might be thought.

The first narrative may represent the last breaths of the Freudian century.[2] It concerns the case of Agnes and, what was at the time, a quite stunning deception which she practised on a team of medical specialists, whom she persuaded that she had been born with the wrong sexual anatomy. When Agnes turned up at the UCLA Psychiatry Department in 1958 she wanted a surgical solution to her physical misconstruction.[3] Agnes was a woman whose hormonal system had malfunctioned causing her to have male sexual organs. She wanted this mistake of nature corrected. While Agnes had a penis and scrotum, she also had well-formed breasts and a tapered waist. Her skin was soft and she had long, fine hair. The natural mistake here was that she did not have vagina, labia and clitoris, and, furthermore, an abdominal laparotomy performed in 1956 had revealed that she was anatomically male with no internal signs whatsoever of being female.

Her case history was relatively straightforward. Her primary and secondary socialization had been into the male role. However, while she had been raised as a boy, she claimed that she had always realized that she was female. She had hated 'rough' games, and as a young boy was 'more or less considered a sissy' (Garfinkel, 1967: 128). In her early teens, with the onset of puberty, her bodily development began to alter, and a set of subordinate female sex characteristics began to emerge. Agnes found this to be entirely natural, and a source of immense relief. An earlier mistake of nature was in the process of being exposed for what it was, an error that needed, if possible, to be corrected. Agnes had come to the Medical Centre at UCLA to get something done about this. She demonstrated a sophisticated awareness of what it was and what it would continue to take to live as a woman, and she very clearly distinguished herself from any form of sexual deviance. She had a boyfriend, and despite a certain reticence about their sexual relations, presented herself in this context as a subjectively 'normal' woman with an 'objective' problem which her boyfriend knew about, and which both she and he wanted to be resolved.

Garfinkel referred to Agnes's social condition as 'passing', saying:

> Each of a great variety of structurally different instances required vigilance, resourcefulness, stamina, sustained motivation, preplanning.... Passing was not a matter of Agnes's desire. It was necessary for her. Whether she liked it or not she had to pass. She enjoyed her successes and feared and hated her failures. (1967: 137)

For Garfinkel, if Agnes was performing, she was doing so no more than every-body else does. It was just that her role was spectacularly difficult, largely because 'Agnes was unable to exercise the assumption that her circumstances, as they appeared to her would appear in a more or less identical way to her interactional partners, were they to exchange places' (1967: 126). Garfinkel suggests, then, that in the case of Agnes's passing, Schutzian 'reciprocity of perspectives' as precondition of routine social interaction would not apply. This would be so for two reasons. First, Agnes assumed that if others knew the full story they would not be able to exchange perspectives since what they would be facing would be so far outside their experience. Second, since she did assume that, then reciprocity could not take place because the open condition of identity required for Schutzian reciprocity did not obtain. Therefore, Agnes could not 'normalize' her life, and enter into Schutz's phenomenological version of the social contract until the mistake of nature had been corrected. For Agnes, physical and social normalization amounted to one and the same thing. Agnes' passing was not deception as much as anticipation, and the UCLA Department of Psychiatry 'validated Agnes' claim to her status' (1967: 128) despite the lack of evidence relating to any specific physiological cause of her symptoms, and agreed to surgical intervention. They categorized her as suffering from 'testicular feminization syndrome', a hypothetical condition in which the testes produce oestrogen. This hormone production was treated as responsible for the emergence of Agnes's feminine characteristics, but also, in some sense, as the true chemical seat of Agnes' being. Her penis and testicles were surgically removed, with the skin of the penis used to create a vagina, and part of her scrotum made into labia. She was then prescribed oestrogen replacement therapy to deal with the spontaneous postoperative emergence of menopausal symptoms. The medical team treated Agnes as a female and sought to correct the physio-chemical mistakes of nature, and to put Agnes into her natural anatomo-biochemical category.

In Judith Butler's oblique discussion of passing in her *Bodies that Matter*, we find a tropically equivalent case. Clare is a character in Nella Larsen's *Passing*. Clare passes as white, 'not merely on occasion, but in her life' (Butler, 1993: 169). She does this not, as in Agnes's case due to a mistake of nature, but rather as an individual will set against an error of culture, the error that we might describe as injustice, prejudice and discrimination. Clare's 'changeableness signifies a certain freedom, a class mobility afforded by whiteness' (1993: 170). The story of Agnes's passing appears to close with her operation. An elderly aunt treats her as 'a real female after all' following her operation. Clare's passing is also terminated, but in a different way. Her racist husband discovers her in compromising circumstances which can only mean that she has been passing as white when she was in fact not. The next moment, Clare is dead, lying on the sidewalk below the upstairs window. Both the story of Agnes and the story of Clare seem to point to a world where passing conceals something beneath the surface. In the case of Agnes, what lies below is precisely what 'she' will not reveal. In the case of Clare, as discussed by Butler, there are depths of eroticism and the forbidden other, metonymically exposed when, with Clare, no longer white, falling through the window, the husband shouts, using a term which had previously been playfully and affectionately erotic, 'Nig! My God! Nig!' (1993: 172).

Perhaps it is possible to imagine that Clare might have continued to pass as white with her husband's connivance. But that is not how the story continued. Agnes could have continued her life as a woman, no longer driven by any desire or necessity to pass. In this case also, however, the narrative does not proceed in that way. We find ourselves here, then, at the point of rupture. For Agnes makes a full confession to Robert Stoller over seven years after the operation. Doctors, psychiatrists, sociologist had been deceived. Agnes admitted that, since she had been 12 years old and specifically at the time that her voice began to deepen, she had been stealing and taking her mother's Stilbestrol (prescribed for her after a hysterectomy), a drug which invariably causes impotence and gynaecomastia if taken by males. So her feminization was not caused by testicular production of oestrogen after all. Agnes had successfully simulated a female identity and an intersexual identity, and while her simulation concealed the sources of her being, her confession appears to reveal them, and so there appear to be two consecutive 'truths' about Agnes. First we find Agnes 'passing' as a woman, simulating a female identity which is overlaid upon a hidden self. Agnes' first 'true' self was buried below her performances: a paradigmatically Freudian case.[4] The second 'truth' of the story is, however, in important part, a biochemical matter. Agnes becomes Stilbestrol, she exemplifies the overwriting of her chromosomal masculinity. Her cited sources fill her identity-space, the hidden identity of the passing actor replaced by a definitively referenced construct: a movement from the self-conscious awareness of alienation to the submersion of self in documented history.[5] Clare was to die rather than give up her secrets, but Agnes eventually revealed what was below.

What Judith Butler learned from Derrida was that the performance of identity is not traced back to some original self, but is rather rooted to the repeatable models of selfhood and identity which are already vested with social authority. These models are drawn upon to create a mirage of originating subjecthood. As she puts it:

> Freud argues that 'the ego is first and foremost a bodily ego' that this ego is, further, 'a projection of a surface,' what we might redescribe as an imaginary morphology. Moreover, I would argue, this imaginary morphology is not a presocial or presymbolic operation, but is itself orchestrated through regulatory schemas that produce intelligible morphological possibilities. These regulatory schemas are not timeless structures, but historically revisable criteria of intelligibility... (1993: 13–14)

While it might be possible to take issue over this interpretation of the ego (which, for the Freud of *The Ego and the Id*, is part of a domain which is far from entirely determined by exterior regulatory schemas), Butler's formulation does allow Agnes's condition to be framed, if we concede that Agnes's use of the appropriate regulatory schema was quite intentional, and also was deceitful. Both the intention and the deceit can be further subsumed under the regulatory schema which was emerging within the field of transsexualism. As Bernice Hausman's careful working through of transsexual autobiographies makes clear, 'the autobiographies of those transsexuals who have successfully maneuvered within the strict protocols of the gender clinics constitute guide-books of no mean proportion' (Hausman, 1995: 143). We must, at this point, be careful, however, that we are not allowing a relatively uncertain and emerging body of experience to function as an unalloyed 'regulatory schema'. Overall, it would seem that the early experience of transsexuals is a significant counter-instance to the thesis of coreless subjects dissimulating within a culture of citationality. There was a point in this history at which the experience was being made rather than cited. It is, then, the concept of dissimulation that makes it difficult to go all the way with the total deconstruction of the subject. At the very least, a historically informed economic geography of regulatory schemas is required, a theorization which will attend to their variable power in different contexts and at different times. This does, however, allow some further scope for some level of residual subjectivity as a strategic function within a complex socioscape. There is, however, a further twist in the story.

The Citational Self

Deception may be a cue if not a precondition for recognition of an uncertain, but nevertheless abiding, inner core of self. We may, however, have entered a time when this is becoming increasingly unthinkable. There are two reasons which we can point to in the case of Agnes. Since the beginning of the 1990s, there has been an irruption into the field of identity of biological-chemical-genetic definitions of selfhood (Strathern, 1995) which become a necessary set of cited references in certain circumstances. Second, as noted above, the emergence of these new definitions occurs within a culture where citation of sources has become the rule. The effect is that Agnes just could not exist inside this new chapter in the history of identity. The gender clinics have become much wiser to the transsexual subculture of dissimulation, and transsexuals themselves have begun to say, 'most transsexuals would rather there were a biological reason for their situation than that they had just screwed up somewhere'.[6] Agnes shopped for her identity but (against the current trends within consumer society) would not cite her sources. She was (at least in the field of sexual identity) the last plagiarist; she lied about her sources; her performance was dishonest. Now, in the citational context, lies and dishonesty in the presentation of self become transmuted into dramatic ineptitude and partial performance. Perhaps for the first time, late modern culture may be described in terms of the increasing necessity of the open reciprocity of perspectives of which Schutz spoke. Thus, the scenario which Butler sketches (and with which Bourdieu's work is complicit) comes to appear accurate, with just one adjustment: the concept of dissimulation is lost from the framework.

If, since the time of Agnes, we have witnessed a shift from the helpless concealment of the particular sources of our being in which Freud would have us believe, towards a much more open, even coreless, culture of citational identity, what might this mean? What are the implications of representing identity in this kind of way? Source-cited identities might seem to bespeak heightened control, but they may be a sign of a model of identity in which by definition self-control is taken even further away than in the Freudian model. As Johnny in Ian McEwan's *Enduring Love* put it, 'it's a big deal when you point a gun at someone. Basically you're giving them permission to kill you' (1998: 206). The situation is the same for the self, for our individual identities, in an age of citation. Pointing our citational sources to someone may invite our dismissal as minor constructions, as nothing more than happenstance assemblage whose value resides in what we represent rather than what we are. The project of an ethics for this time has not even been started, and the fixity of the structures of inequality within such a context has yet to be dreamed of.

To consider this further, we must turn to the sources, and we find that some of the key authorities being used to authenticate the cited self are bio-genetic. The potential power of the bio-genetic over both the will and the social (in the form of the law) is illustrated by the 1990 case of the father cleared of a charge of incest when DNA testing showed that he was not genetically related to the child. The man was freed on appeal, despite having previously pleaded guilty to unlawful intercourse with his daughter (Strathern, 1995: 103). Marilyn Strathern's careful discussion of genetic essentialism, and her search for a set of metaphors which might be used to retain the social determination of identity as a continuing possibility despite the arrogations of science, also led her to the US Supreme Court case of *Johnson v. Calvert*, in which there was a dispute over the custody of a child conceived through *in vitro* fertilization. The Calverts provided both egg and sperm, and the fertilized ovum was implanted in Johnson's uterus. The Calverts had a contract with the surrogate mother, who was going to carry Mrs Calvert's baby because she was unable to do this herself. After the birth of Christopher, the surrogate mother refused to relinquish the child. When DNA tests revealed that the Calverts were almost certainly Christopher's genetic origin, the legal process worked to grant them custody, with no custody rights at all given to the embodied mother – an object lesson in the sociology of levels of determining embodiment. What both examples indicate is that when it comes to citation, there is an order of priorities, with scientifically established credentials appearing toward the top.

Further examples point to increasing importance of genetic definitions of selfhood and identity, and indicate an increasing reliance on hard evidence, on citability and a lessening of importance of social definitions of self, let alone the kind of personal definition which the existentialist might champion. Behavioural psychologists can easily make male rats perform lordosis (the kind of crouching behaviour shown by a four-legged female animal during copulation) and female rats attempt to take the male reproductive role. In a classic experiment, a female rat was perinatally treated with testosterone propionate and a male was castrated neonatally and treated with androgen during adulthood. A totally sex-hormone dependent inversion of sexual behaviour was thereby demonstrated, with the female attempting to mount the male, and with the male crouching to receive the metamorphosed female rat (Ruse, 1995). Michael Ruse uses this experiment as part of an enquiry into sexual identity, concluding at the end of his article that, 'the important thing is . . . to work for a society where people can feel free to work out their identities as they will' (Ruse, 1995: 98). However, his scrupulous argumentation against simple solutions, and for the idea that sexual identity is *both* reality and construct, is no match for his earlier comment, following his account of the inverted sexual behaviour of the rats, that 'hormones in like manner affect the sexually dimorphic behaviour in humans, and thus one has an explanation of alternative sexual orientations' (Ruse, 1995: 87). Take also the example of the International Olympic Committee which introduced the buccal smear sex chromatin test (cells from the interior of the cheek are stained and examined) for female athletes in the 1968 summer games in Mexico City (Hausman, 1995; Hood-Williams, 1995). Earlier in the 1960s, female athletes were required to parade naked in front of a panel of judges, or to submit to a pelvic exam, in order to verify their sex status. Sex chromatin testing establishes chromosomal sex status (it was just such a test that established Agnes to be chromosomally male). The theory behind the test is simply that males and females exhibit a different genetic pattern. Normally, humans have 46 chromosomes, two of which determine sex. In the female, these two chromosomes are similar, and have an 'X' shape. Males, on the other hand, are styled the 'heterogametic' sex, and have one which is 'X' shaped and one which is 'Y' shaped. It is this difference between 'XX' and 'XY' which is the usual genetic signifier of sexual difference. The cultural variation of gender behaviour constitutes an elegant 'proof' of the deconstructionist thesis that there is no fixed connection between signifier and signified, but this lack of direct connection also allows the genetic signifier to function as the determinant principle. The role of the 'Y' chromosome as the determining signifier of difference is emphasized in the somewhat perverse terminology of the 'Adam principle' (Ruse, 1995: 67) which refers to the bio-genetic theory that the emergent human foetus will tend to grow into a female: the presence of the 'Y' chromosome causes the production of two hormones, one of which (androgen) is responsible for the growth of the male sex organs, while the other (Mullerian-inhibiting factor) prevents the default emergence of female organs. This structure explains the phenomenon of women who are (chromosomally speaking) androgen insensitive males (Ruse, 1995: 70).[7] From all outward signs, such people are female, and will mature into women with breasts, vagina, and all the other outward physical and cultural characteristics that signify women in the society concerned (with the exception that such women are sterile). The International Olympic Committee's buccal smear test would, however, tend[8] to determine them as male, something incidentally (and without meaning to imply any approval of the practice) the parade ritual in earlier Games would not have done.[9] What we can see is that, in the field of identity, genetic essentialism is unthreatened by the movement to citational identity. It may even be strengthened by it since the genetic sources of citational identity emerge from the extraordinarily powerful field of scientific objectivity, the marginal deconstructions of which by cultural theorists do not yet greatly reduce its power to arouse and define.

These examples of the way in which the citational self appears to be under the control of others, by definition subject to alien expert logics, may, however, be contradicted by what has happened within the transsexual realm. One of the first major responses to transsexualism from within feminism was Janice Raymond's *The Transsexual Empire* (1980), and the position of that book, written twenty years ago, was that transsexual women are deviant males. She condemned the fact that a whole apparatus of psychiatrists, psychologists, councillors and surgeons had been built on the false attempt to deny this. A more recent illustration of fixed-natural-category essentialism concerns the astrophysicist Rachel Padman, elected in 1996 as a Fellow of Newnham College, the one remaining women-only College of Cambridge University. When Germaine Greer, who is reported as regarding sex-change operations as mutilations (Longrigg, 1997), sought to challenge the propriety of Newnham's decision to admit Dr Padman, who had a sex change in 1982, both students and staff of the College defended both the College and Dr Padman. Lisa Jardine's comment, 'Think of the damage this is doing to that woman' (Longrigg, 1997) was typical of the generally protective response to Germaine Greer's attempt to disable the College's naturalistic discourse and to replace it with another set of natural certainties. Both Raymond and Greer stand for a feminist politics predicated on primeval certainties. For Raymond, writing in 1994, citational culture in the form of displayed transgendering 'has encouraged a *style* rather than a *politics* of resistance, in which an expressive individualism has taken the place of collective political challenges to power'.[10] Greer, similarly, has a strong sense of feminine particularity and potential, scorning, for example, the aesthetic universalism of Elizabeth Barrett Browning (although it is surely coincidental that Barrett Browning used to dress up as a page, in homage to Byron, as a young girl), and asserting that women will typically care more for the exigencies of real life than for the ethereal aspirations of art (or political theories?).[11]

The new engineers of gender identity, with their medico-genetic transformative practices, are not as certain of the situation as Raymond and Greer appear to be. They were well aware that the process began within the 'hidden self' paradigm. As Billings and Urban say (1996: 108), 'transsexualism is initially self-diagnosed and because there are no organic indications of the disease, physicians are dependent upon the accuracy and honesty of patients' statements for diagnosis. . .'. The initial experiments with trust did not work out too well. What was discovered was that patients often did not tell the truth, that they regularly presented a well-rehearsed case history that fitted with the ideal requirements of a case requiring sex-reassignment surgery. Patients began to admit having researched the role and studied the part in order to deceive the sex-reassignment team. What is more the deceptions continued post-operatively. Kate Bornstein, a transsexual male-to-female performance artist said, for example:

> At voice lessons I was taught to speak in a very high-pitched, very breathy, very sing-song voice and to tag questions on to the end of each sentence. And I was supposed to smile all the time when I was talking. . . . All therapists, as good and noble as they might be, counsel transsexuals to tell a little lie. . . . People are going to ask you about when you were a little girl and you are going to say, 'When I was a little girl'. . . . Every transsexual is counselled not to reveal their transsexuality, but to devise a past for themselves. (Bell, 1993: 112–13)

The pre-operative deceptions began to come to light as the extraordinary range of post-operative complications became clear. A list of these complications compiled in 1982, included:

> breast cancer in hormonally-treated males; the need for surgical reduction of bloated limbs resulting from hormones; repeated reconstruction of vaginal openings; infections of the urinary system and rectum; haemorrhaging; loss of skin grafts; post-operative suicides and suicide attempts; . . . depression, psychosis and phobia; sexual dysfunctions; pre- and post-operative prostitution often necessitated by the high cost of treatment. (Billings and Urban, 1996: 108)

The experience of some of these post-operative difficulties not only brought out amendments to the pre-operative histories, they also led to law suits and threatened violence against plastic surgeons who were accused of developing a subspeciality purely for profit.

In the light of such developments, it is not surprising that the protocols for dealing with transsexuals underwent revision. So also did the underlying egology. Although the term transsexual remained in use the underlying theorization came to refer to gender dysphoria syndrome – a clinical condition of mismatch between gender and sexuality, between behaviour and the body – which widened the field of which transsexuals were a part (to include transvestism, for example) and which attempted to turn the assessment and diagnosis focus more fully on to the behavioural syndrome. The citational self, fully complicit with the theorization of the self in positivist behaviourism, supported by the scaffolding of endocrinological examination, having become the clear focus, questions of interiority and motivation fade into the background. The principal criteria become intimately associated with demeanour in the public sphere. Concealment is grounds for removal from a gender reassignment programme; hidden motivations, by definition, come not to exist. Transsexuals become public property, propelled into a welcoming culture already well-populated by citational, footnoted selves, powered there by a causally efficient history of distrust and disaster attached to the now jettisoned depth egology. This condition makes the most important question about transgendered identity, 'How are they made?' It is not surprising, since it turns out that they are regarded as made on the intersecting vectors of psychiatric, endocrinological, and behavioural invariants, a field of forces which surely deserve to be labelled essentialist, that some transsexuals are returning to an essentialism of their own bodies as a way of reclaiming a space of identity over which they themselves have some rights.

The theorizing of transgender recently authored by Ekins and King specifies four logically inclusive categories. They refer to oscillation across the gender divide, negation of the original natal sex designation, migration from one category to the other and a transcending movement to a new category (Ekins and King, 1998). It is likely that a powerful practical anti-essentialism, if it is to be found at all, will be associated with negation and transcendence, the categories of migration and oscillation being too attached to the essentialist heritage for things to be otherwise. Ekins and King find that cases that might fall into the category of negation are extremely rare, but they do point to the history of the eunuch, and also to the category of the male submissive. The anti-essentialism of the lived experience in both of these cases has yet to be assessed, but it seems likely that the traditional sexual dualism remains a crucial reference point, as logically it must in any case of pure negation. We are then left with the category of transcendence, and here there is no shortage of case studies of transsexuals who define themselves as transcendent of the traditional sex dichotomy. A sharp recent example is that of Jay Prosser, who writes:

> Transsexuals, now refusing to pass through transsexuality, are speaking en masse as transsexuals, forming activist groups, academic networks, transgender 'nations.' No longer typically ending transition, transsexuals are overtly rewriting the narrative of transsexuality . . . as open-ended. (Prosser, 1998: 11)

Prosser embraces the reading of transsexuality found in Feinberg's *Stone Butch Blues* (1993), which Janice Raymond, from her essentialist position, found to be reactionary precisely because it did not turn toward the feminine, but turned toward something 'other'. As support for this emerging discourse of transsexual otherness, we also find Prosser emphasizing the importance of body narratives. Not, as he found Hausman's usage to be, as a way of affirming the inextricable link between transsexualism and medico-psychiatric apparatus, but as a way of making two simultaneous and only apparently contradictory moves. The first of these moves is to resist the subordination of personal transsexual narratives to a programmatic and ultimately essentialist discourse of transsexualism. The second move is, and this is presented precisely as non-contradictory, to link the experience of transsexualism with the essential materiality and corporeality of the permanent transition. This is a doubly effective answer to the critique of citationalism, and also a compelling critique of Butler's constructionist anti-existentialism. If citational culture is characterized as a general invitation to inauthenticate its members who are only what their references point to, Prosser's response is that autobiographical citation avoids that and that such citation establishes a variable distance between the subject and the forces that have at least partly caused it to become what it is.

The nascent critique of Butler that emerges from Prosser's grappling with transsexual subjectivity opens a third chapter in the story of Butler's concept of performance. The first chapter is constituted by an unscrupulous reading of *Gender Trouble*, which finds that gender performativity might equal gender theatricality, and is unscrupulous because Butler had made it quite clear, especially in her discussion of the residual subject in Foucault, that there was no ontological place from which a decision to be one sex or the other might be made. The second chapter is constituted by Butler's reframing of performativity in terms of citation, and has been the prime focus of this article, which has wondered if citation might mean a quite vicious return of essentialism, in lots of guises, but particularly in the form of genetic essentialism. This third chapter, opened by Jay Prosser, seems now to question the overdetermination of the subject by discourse and social process in Butler's work, since this is precisely what other-referenced transsexualism and what the self-direction inherent in narratives of the embodied self may reject.

Notes

1. Elspeth Probyn's formulation is illustrative of this combination of intentionality and underdetermination: 'We must consider anorexia as a local practice used against the exigencies of place, time, gender, biography, age, family, etc. . . . This approach, therefore, considers the articulation of selves, subjectivities, biographies as inscribed and lived across a local body' (1988: 210).

2. Recently obituarized by Andrew Scull in these terms: 'Psychoanalysis emerged in the early decades of this century as a powerful challenge to a biologically reductionist psychiatry that was at once deaf to the psychological dimensions of madness and wedded to a failed therapeutics and a degenerationist metaphysic of despair. Freud's invention reaches the millennium in a sadly reduced state, its hopes of establishing itself as the foundation of the psychiatric enterprise apparently permanently dashed. It survives instead by virtue of its appeal as a source of "discursive practices" and "theory" to a set of ideologues and anti-humanist humanists' (1998: 10).

3. Harold Garfinkel published his account of the case some nine years later: he had been researching with the small team who had been researching on cases of problematic sexual identity (Garfinkel, 1967).

4. A second example of a 'hidden' self asserting that it is other than its footnotes tell us, again drawing from the field of transsexualism, is Terri Webb. She was born an apparently normal male child but remembers transgender feelings from the age of 6. She underwent medical treatment leading to sex-reassignment when aged 40. She worked for many years as a housing officer in Southwark, and was a councillor in Lambeth. She is now a continental truck driver. This is what she has recently said: 'I am other than I pretend to be. I believe this is not a matter peculiar to me. I am convinced that it applies to each and every male-to-female transsexual that I have ever met. . . . We pretend to be other than we are . . . without any doubt we are men, albeit men with a desperate need to be women. . .' (Webb, 1996: 190).

5. The difficulties of passing are well explored by Julie Inness who observes that passing entails 'a logic of escalating estrangement' (1995: 220) which she contrasts against the forging of friendship through the reciprocity of gifted trust.

6. Rachel Padman, cited in Baty (1997: 21).

7. Although Ruse concentrates on this particular type, it should be noted that XX males occur at an estimated frequency of 1 in 20,000, and that more complex variations such as XXY and XYY are possible (Hood-Williams, 1995: 5–6).

8. There is a debate within athletics about such cases. 'In Britain, Dr. Elizabeth Ferris, medical officer to the Modern Pentathlon Association and former Olympic diving medallist, argues that women are not advantaged by the presence of Y chromosomes' (Hood-Williams, 1995: 5).

9. The taking up of 'genetic references' in such circumstances seems to have something in common with the journalistic exploration of the private lives of public figures. If we are all denied meaningful interiority within citation culture, there is no axiological bar upon any kind of identity parade. Indeed, participation in such parades comes to be defined as a sign of honesty, and as such is widely approved.

10. Raymond (1996: 222). It should be noted that Raymond's analysis of Leslie Feinberg's *Stone Butch Blues*, in this article, condemns Feinberg for moving beyond the male–female dichotomy, so that 'Jess's final transformation is *from being woman-identified to being other-identified*' (1996: 220), but then condemns transgenderism for failing to move beyond traditional sex-roles: 'What good is a gender outlaw who is still abiding by the law of gender?' (1996: 223).

11. Greer writes, 'Women's creativity does not demand the right to build monuments that will loom in the minds of people yet unborn. Women's art is potentially biodegradable' (1995).

References

Baerveldt, C. and P. Voestermans (1998) 'The Body as a Selfing Device: The Case of Anorexia Nervosa', in Henderikus J. Stam (ed.) *The Body and Psychology*. London: Sage.

Baselitz, G. (1992) 'Pandemonium Manifestoes', in Charles Harrison and Paul Wood (eds) *Art in Theory: 1900–1990*. Oxford: Basil Blackwell. (Orig. 1961).

Baty, P. (1997) 'The Essential Guide to Sexuality', *The Times Higher Educational Supplement*. 18 July.

Bell, S. (1993) 'Kate Bornstein: A Transgender Transsexual Postmodern Tiresias', in Arthur Kroker and Marilouise Kroker (eds) *The Last Sex*. London: Macmillan.

Bilings, Dwight B. and Thomas Urban (1996) 'The Socio-Medical Construction of Transsexualism', in Richard Ekins and Dave King (eds), *Blending Genders*. London: Routledge.

Boyne, R. (1995) 'Fractured Subjectivity', *History of the Human Sciences* 8(2): 51–68.

Butler, J. (1993) *Bodies that Matter*. London: Routledge.

Butler, J. (1997) *Excitable Speech*. New York: Routledge.

Crews, F. (ed.) (1998) *Unauthorized Freud*. New York: Viking.

Ekins, R. and D. King (1998) 'Towards a Sociology of Transgendered Bodies', paper presented at the British Sociological Association Annual Conference, Edinburgh.

Ellis, Brett Easton (1991) *American Psycho*. London: Pan.

Feinberg, L. (1993) *Stone Butch Blues*. Ithaca, NY: Firebrand.

Fish, S. (1998) 'The Primal Scene of Persuasion', in F. Crews (ed.) *Unauthorized Freud*. New York: Viking.

Freud, S. (1984) *The Ego and the Id*, in *The Pelican Freud Library*, vol. 11, *On Metapsychology: The Theory of Psychoanalysis*, ed. Angela Richards. Harmondsworth: Penguin. (Orig. 1923.)

Garfinkel, H. (1967) *Studies in Ethnomethodology*. Englewood Cliffs, NJ: Prentice-Hall.

Greer, G. (1995) 'A Biodegradable Art', *Times Literary Supplement* 30 June.

Hausman, B. (1995) *Changing Sex: Transsexualism, Technology and the Idea of Gender*. Durham, NC: Duke University Press.

Hood-Williams, J. (1995) 'Is the Genetic Sexing of Humans Tautological?', *Social Biology and Human Affairs* 60(2): 3–9.

Husserl, E. (1970) *Logical Investigations*, vol. 2. London: Routledge.

Inness, J. (1995) 'Passing in *Europa, Europa*', in Cynthia Freeland and Thomas Wartenberg (eds) *Philosophy and Film*. London: Routledge.

Longrigg, C. (1997) 'A Sister with no Fellow Feeling', *Guardian* 25 June: G2, 6–7.

McEwan, I. (1998) *Enduring Love*. London: Vintage.

Maffesoli, M. (1996) *The Time of the Tribes*. London: Sage.

Probyn, E. (1988) 'The Anorexic Body', in Arthur Kroker and Marilouise Kroker (eds) *Body Invaders: Sexuality and the Postmodern Condition*. London: Macmillan.

Prosser, J. (1998) *Second Skins: The Body Narratives of Transsexuality*. New York: Columbia University Press.

Raymond, J. (1980) *The Transsexual Empire*. London: The Women's Press.

Raymond, J. (1996) 'The Politics of Transgenderism', in Richard Ekins and Dave King (eds) *Blending Genders*. London: Routledge.

Ruse, M. (1995) 'Sexual Identity: Reality or Construction?', in Henry Harris (ed.) *Identity*. Oxford: Oxford University Press.

Scull, A. (1998) 'The End of Freud?', *Times Literary Supplement* 30 October.

Searle, J. (1983) *Intentionality*. Cambridge: Cambridge University Press.

Spence, J. (1995) *Cultural Sniping*. London: Routledge.
Strathern, M. (1995) 'Nostalgia and the New Genetics', in Deborah Battaglia (ed.) *Rhetorics of Self-Making*. Berkeley: University of California Press.
Taylor, C. (1989) *Sources of the Self*. Cambridge: Cambridge University Press.
Turner, V. (1982) *From Ritual to Theater: The Human Seriousness of Play*. New York: Performing Arts Journal Publications.
Webb, T. (1996) 'Autobiographical Fragments from a Transsexual activist', in Richard Ekins and Dave King (eds) *Blending Genders*. London: Routledge.

Roy Boyne is professor of sociology at the University of Durham, where he teaches courses on surveillance and film. His recent publications deal with Kieslowski, Derrida, Serres and Cronenberg. He is in the final stages of completing a book on subjectivity to be published by Sage.

Interaction Order and Beyond:
A Field Analysis of Body Culture
within Fitness Gyms

ROBERTA SASSATELLI

With the same divine faculty which is of children to take seriously their games, we bestow our magic on the things we play with and then we let them bewitch us. It is no longer a game, but a marvellous reality . . . another reality, far away from yours and still so ephemeral and fleeting, where one does not need to think. Here we live of this. Without anything, but with all the time for us: illegible richness, boistering of chimeras. (Luigi Pirandello, *The Giants of the Mountain*)

The lithe and energetic body, tight and slim, with its firm and toned-up boundaries is a powerful image of contemporary culture, especially as articulated in advertising and consumer culture. Not only has the toned body become a commercial icon, but also the gym has become highly visible as the site where this body is produced. Gym scenes are increasingly portrayed and glamourized in an ever widening range of adverts. There is thus the temptation to understand what happens in the gym as the direct result of consumer culture, as the obvious response to normative injunctions which have been described as inviting individuals to joyfully take responsibility for their bodies, to work on them as plastic matter and to invest in body presentation for their self-constitution (Amir, 1987; Bordo, 1993; Featherstone, 1982; Frank, 1991; Le Breton, 1990: 125–45; O'Neill, 1985: 91–117; Synnott, 1993: 22–37; Wolf, 1991). This article, however, takes a different perspective. It looks at the keep-fit culture not as a series of commercial images nor as the product of broader cultural values, but as a set of situated body practices, that is, practices taking place within specific institutions where these values are not just reproduced but translated and, to some extent, filtered.

One such institution is indeed the fitness gym. As I shall show, the fitness gym

Body & Society © 1999 SAGE Publications (London, Thousand Oaks and New Delhi),
Vol. 5(2–3): 227–248
[1357–034X(199906/09)5:2–3;227–248;008869]

is experienced not simply as an ingredient in the search for a perfect body, but as a place which has its own rules and where a vast array of meanings and identities are negotiated. Wider cultural values, the ideals of the fit, toned and slender body, coded as both a conspicuous sign of personal worth and a matter of individual choice, are indeed mediated and reinterpreted in locally prescribed ways. My article thus tries to look at the fitness gym from the inside, from the specificity of its microphysics. This has required a detailed analysis of *how* the gym realizes its ascribed cultural goals by focusing on the interaction arrangements which are locally sustained without reifying the discontinuity of the gym from everyday reality.

To do so I have adopted a Goffmanesque view of interaction. According to Erving Goffman, interaction is a domain of social, face-to-face action which is 'loosely coupled' with the cultural order (1982: 11), but characterized by its own forms of fragile and yet indispensable 'procedural order' or 'working consensus' (1959: 173). The interaction order comprises 'the conditions and constraints placed upon the manner in which ends are sought or activity carried out' as well as 'patterned adaptations associated with these pursuings', rather than the 'choice of ends or the manner in which these ends may be integrated into a single system of activity' (Goffman, 1971: x–xi, see also 1963a: 7–8, 1982). A Goffmanesque approach to the gym may thus help to overcome some of the shortcomings of macro-analyses concerned with either social stratification or commercial representation. An exclusive emphasis on stratification discounts the fact that the multiplication of exercise opportunities within the gym, each appealing to different social groups, is a means by which fitness exercise is spreading beyond the new service classes that originally endorsed it (Bessy, 1987).[1] Like the approaches which rely on commercial images it runs the risk of losing sight of the role played by the local organization of resources as well as the meanings that participants actively negotiate in their practices.

Based on an ethnographic study of gym environments, this article describes how gyms are organized and how their internal organization acquires meaning for clients. I will consider how time and space are locally orchestrated, how interaction during training is managed and how these arrangements both promote and rely on specific forms of relation with oneself and one's own body. The findings here presented refer to fieldwork conducted in two Italian gyms, suitably renamed 'Shape' and 'BodyMove'. These two cases constituted the extreme poles of fitness supply within the same middle-class neighbourhood thus helping to focus more persuasively on what is typical of the interaction rules within gym environments. For my analysis I have drawn on four different sources: participant observation, semi-structured interviews with clients, informal interviews with trainers and managers, and specialized publications such as fitness manuals and periodicals.[2] Shape and BodyMove thus offered empirical settings, allowing for a consideration of interaction, subjective meanings and institutional discourses. This in turn has facilitated a bottom–up approach, whereby the meanings of the gym are traced back to its constitutive organization of resources and meanings.

The Gym as a World in Itself

Colonizing contemporary urban environments, the fitness gym is a commercial institution which offers the consumer exercise opportunities ranging from traditional aerobics and body building to the latest combinations of dance, yoga and martial arts. In this sense the gym epitomizes the spreading of disciplinary body techniques, previously confined to disciplinary institutions or production organizations, into leisure environments (Ewen, 1988; Foucault, 1975; Turner, 1987; Weber, 1946). It also exemplifies the replacement of public concerns with individual choice as a rhetoric of institutional legitimation (Defrance, 1976, 1981; Green, 1986; Grover, 1989; Hargreaves, 1987; Vigarello, 1978, 1988). As a commercial institution the fitness gym is typically open to everyone who has the cultural competence and the economic capital to act as a consumer. Yet, its market openness contrasts with the protected nature of the practices included within. Fitness gyms are relatively separated from everyday reality as specialized spaces. Here people who occupy very different social roles overtly care for their bodies and forcibly display postures and movements which would normally be conceived of and felt as weird – if not indecent – outside them. Fitness gyms are thus both open and protected, both separated and connected to everyday life: they are regions where the body may be prepared for different daily routines and yet they operate on the basis of local rules which translate, negotiate and filter the relevances of these very situations.

Entering the front door of a gym, as the noise of the streets recedes, the newcomer encounters a contained and protected space. Via the use of space, light and decoration, every gym organizes its own distinctive ways of marking passage from the everyday world to the exercise world. Shape is a well-known and fashionable gym. By impersonal signals of architectural details and lights, the wide and sporty hall with its stylish reception and glamorous windows under-score the transition to the two-storey training areas. This creates a space which is, in the words of many clients, 'very well-known as one of the best gyms in town'. Such perceptions are fostered by the gym staff: while helping me to get on with my training, Mark, one of the four machine trainers, maintains that Shape 'has been designed to be an enjoyable place, where clients can find professional services of high quality'. Compared to the professional, impersonal and high-tech environment of Shape, BodyMove is for many reasons a very different place. Its architecture has a somehow improvised and understated character and clients describe it as a 'pretty much improvised', 'tiny and cheaply set up' environment, also speaking of 'a sense of familiarity'. The passage to the gym consists of a simple glass door opening to a minuscule corridor from which the aerobics areas are immediately visible and accessible. Marked by the unavoidable presence of photographs of the trainers, BodyMove's passage from the external world largely relies on the promotion of a sense of communality with the instructors. Louise, the director of the gym and one of its most popular trainers, insists that the 'simplicity' of BodyMove is one its assets: 'the trainers are competent, they provide a personal relation with people, a family atmosphere'.

It is clear that different modalities of passage from the outside world, both spatial and symbolic, set the official style or tone of each gym. Gym environments are nevertheless all constructed as specialized places relatively separated from the external reality. This is evident when we consider how gym environments organize time and space within their boundaries and how this organization accounts for their specificity and separation. Although embodying opposite modalities of fitness provision, Shape and BodyMove are remarkably similar in their internal organization. Rather than concentrating on their differences – which are certainly relevant for a comparative perspective on their relative history, success and target groups – this article focuses on what they have in common. The aim is to single out the specific characteristics of these spaces which constitute a particular type of social environment.

The fitness gym is a compound and complex environment. Within the gym body practices are sorted in functionally differentiated areas. This environment offers different and distinct spaces for exercise of the body, besides spaces where the body is prepared for the exercise and for the return to everyday reality. Certain body practices, such as undressing and direct body care, which are usually powerful signs of a private situation, are exclusively and rigidly confined to the changing-rooms. The specific characteristics of changing-rooms surely contribute to the particular tone of each gym, those of Shape being more comfortable, aseptic and impersonal as compared to BodyMove's tiny, improvised and informal ones. However, the separation of similar spaces says something about the internal organization of gym environments in general. The specificity of the gym is not simply due to its physical separation from external reality, but is more fundamentally negotiated through changing-room practices. Within its boundaries the gym offers a space to facilitate shifting, both inwards – into the world of training – and outwards – back to different external realities. The changing-room is thus a remarkably complex space. Due to the simultaneous presence of clients who enter and exit the world of training, the changing-room is a 'liminoid' space where the cultural de-classification typical of passage rituals is lived individually, each client being asked to manage the specificity of his or her own shifting requirements.[3] However, shifting inwards is more symbolically supported than shifting outwards, the symbols participants require to go back to their different social roles being beyond the official definition of the gym. Changing-rooms are indeed organized to facilitate an institutional passage, marshalling symbols to support a switch to exercise as the activity which defines the gym.

Functioning first and foremost as symbolic keys for exercise, changing-rooms help clients to enter its spirit, sustaining its specificity and suspending other relevances. The change from everyday costumes for a purpose-made, gym-specific outfit is, for example, not simply a material requirement of training. It is also a fundamental symbol of having entered the gym, of tuning in, of being in the right spirit to work out, recognizing the specificity of the work on the body that is to be done. Despite the very different routines that clients may follow within changing-rooms, these practices are always important for them. Describing their typical day in the gym, clients recall small details of their changing-room practices as both necessary and meaningful. Charles, a middle-aged surgeon for years committed to fitness work-out at Shape, illustrates the symbolic potentialities of the changing-room, underlining, for example, that it responds to 'the need to cut off from the external world': 'when I arrive here and take off my clothes I am already getting away; I then put my shorts and my belt on and there I am, ready for the gym'. Lilly, a middle-aged clerk who, on and off, attends a training programme at BodyMove, says that it is necessary to be in the right frame of mind to 'enter the spirit' of the gym: 'I take it easy, a free afternoon, and I like to go [to the gym] on foot . . . and then undress slowly, get out my outfit, my shoes, dress up, as if to get ready for the work I'll have to do.'

Changing-rooms thus index training situations, reducing their potential equivocality, bestowing the exclusivity of a fitness session on practices which could be easily classified otherwise. They operate as a 'segmentation mark', something which is particularly important for social actors when the activities to be undertaken conflict with the normal expectations of everyday life (Giddens, 1984: 377–9; Goffman, 1963a: 39–41, 1974: 560–76). Changing-rooms are thus meant to strip individuals of their external identities, filtering out social attributes which could interfere with training and making their bodies equally into an object to be moulded by a serial and yet personalized training. Their sexual division along the duality male–female, for example, openly reproduces patterns accepted in the wider culture only to block their relevance during exercise. Thus, on the part of clients and trainers, there's a tendency to portray men and women's bodies as equivalent with respect to their exercise potential, inclinations and capabilities, as if the training body were a-gendered.[4]

As the changing-room allows clients to switch to the realm of exercise, to its rules and its meanings, so the division between different work-out areas facilitates training by responding to the specific demands of different training modalities. Within both Shape and BodyMove there is a more or less marked spatial separation between gymnastic exercise – including aerobics, step-aerobics, callanetics, stretching, soft yoga, etc. and machine training – either with vascular or weight-lifting equipment. Gymnastic exercise is based on an active cooperation between participants who openly share the focus of attention. They are all asked to look at the trainer, imitating her movements and following her instructions. Through the simultaneous reproduction of movements, the time of training is collectivized and the space is all invested by exercise. With machine training, by contrast, time is individualized and the training space constituted by reciprocal civil inattention. The continuation of the exercise relies on the capacity of each client to isolate from others and to focus on a personal sequence of movements.

In both modalities of training, exercise is the officially prescribed focal point. Participants' involvement, however, follows different expressive modalities. Involvement requires a shared focus of attention during gymnastic exercise and asks for an exclusive and personal focus during machine training. These are clearly incompatible demands whose respective strength and coherence is enhanced by the specialized nature of work-out spaces. By segregating incompatible demands, the separation of machine training from gymnastic exercise allows participants to enter expressive contexts which stimulate concentration on the exercise as officially prescribed. A gathering overtly sharing the same lesson in the machine area would distract other participants from their individual training no less than a client working on his or her own personal abdominal sequence during an aerobics class. The separation of these two modalities of training is thus fundamental to avoid uncertainty and distractions, to keep interaction ordered and unambiguous, geared to the accomplishment of training.

As shown, the organization of local resources plays a fundamental role in the construction of the gym as a structuring context where some specific and exclusive patterns of social interaction take place. It is certainly true that the gym's perimeters are sustained by wider cultural goals which reach beyond contingent locality. The care and transformation of the body towards an ideal of fitness and well-being are their specific legitimating objectives. These objectives are also promoted by the growing wealth of specialized manuals and magazines and resonate within instructors' claims and clients' narratives of motives. Different discourses thus contribute to define the purpose of the gym as 'improving one's own body' and 'shaping it up', at 'taking care of the body' and 'feeling good'. However, the gym is first of all a 'social occasion', 'bounded in regard to place and time' and 'facilitated by fixed equipment' (Goffman, 1963a: 18). The way in which the environment is organized is thus important in its own right. In particular, the configuration of the gym as a compound environment works to maintain its unity and specificity.

In effect, it is through the shifting parameters of meaning which cut across the gym that training is sustained. Careful organization of space and time is essential to create a milieu where individuals are able to concentrate on training, and forget their normal duties and everyday social roles.[5] It is precisely thanks to the consistently supported relevance of exercise as specifically prescribed that not only is training sustained but also the gym as a whole may be perceived as a relatively straightforward social experience. Through a spatio-temporal organization which works at the work of the body, the gym is thus constructed as a world in itself, a domain of action which has its own rules and meanings. As Christine, a professional in her 30s, says, in the gym 'one immediately knows what is going on, there are no misunderstandings', 'distracting ideas' have to be 'forgotten' because everyone 'is somehow forced to work out'; 'there isn't much else' to do but training as required by the different work-out spaces and/or sessions.

Expressive Behaviour during Training

The gym is constituted as a world in itself to the extent that the client is pushed and pulled to concentrate on body work-out. This circumstance is both simple and fundamental. Training within fitness gyms has in fact the characteristic of a world-building activity. In this, it is a similar form of social action to play and, although the gym is a relatively serious and purposive affair, like play fitness training generates meanings which are exclusive to it. It allows experiences that are perceived as part of a set of meanings different from all others except the ones deployed when the same game is played at other times (Goffman, 1972).

This happens not only through the organization of different spaces within the gym, but also thanks to specific patterns of interaction during training. Expressive behaviour – a basic dimension of interaction comprised of both verbal and bodily signals aimed at underlining participants' involvement in the ongoing interaction and their reciprocal positions – plays a crucial role. Training within fitness gyms not only promotes an official and clear focus of attention, the exercise, but also requires a nearly continuous involvement in it. In a typical training scene, participants appear as entirely engrossed in the exercise. In such circumstances their postures, glances, facial expressions underline that what they are doing is indeed just and only training.

As suggested, within gymnastic exercise this requires the bodily demonstration of a continuous attention to the trainer, reproducing his or her movements and following his or her directions. Trainers continuously stress the exercise, ceaselessly underscoring the process of training by counting repetitions, giving instructions about sequences and highlighting difficult passages. Witnessing an aerobic class, for example, one cannot avoid noticing the trainer's stream of directions matched by participants' displayed collaboration in simultaneously reproducing his or her movements. Each of these signals works within the exercise as an indication of what is punctually to be done while, summoned up as a complete show, they encapsulate the exercise, making clear that what is happening is actually a training session. A similar double function is accomplished within the machine areas by the built-in characteristics of the machines, that is their ever more sophisticated devices for quantifying and analysing performances, as well as by certain forms of 'self-talk' such as each individual's strained grunts (Goffman, 1981: 78–123). Individual body demeanour is particularly important in machine areas because, unlike in gymnastic exercise, trainers do not dictate the official focus, but introduce each client to the activity by means of a personalized induction. Clients' facial expressions, their capacity to express and mobilize their own involvement, thereby become fundamental to confirm their own individual sequences as the officially prescribed focus. During relaxation intervals between exercises which could easily give way to distracting or disruptive episodes, participants' continued self-absorption is typically underlined by an expressionless, absent face. While remaining on their machine or moving toward the next one, clients may glance around focusing on anything in particular, and they assume inexpressive, or even hostile, expressions or cast a distracted smile, avoiding eye contact.

Both during machine and gymnastic forms of exercise, when distracting episodes take place they tend to be short or located at the margins of the workout spaces and they may even be directly monitored by trainers. In both modalities of training, trainers and gym staff have the authority to enforce appropriate behaviour, and may even ask participants to leave the training scene. A direct disciplinary intervention is, however, exceptional within the fitness gym, and would clearly be defined as an unfortunate incident. The exercise interaction arrangements are in fact essentially based on the tacit, continuous cooperation of participants, on their endorsement of a specific form of expressive behaviour and on their reciprocal surveillance.

Expressive behaviour is thus crucial as it encapsulates the exercise situation: to use an expression made famous by Goffman, it helps to 'frame' the activities taking place within work-out spaces as fitness training. The notion of 'frame' is important here. Goffman used this concept to indicate the 'principles of organization which govern events – at least social ones – and our subjective involvement in them' (1974: 10–11).[6] Frame is thus a set of 'organizational premises – sustained both in mind and in activity' (1974: 247), a 'context of understanding' and a 'membrane' which orientates our perceptions within it (1974: 39, 1972: 71). As a framed activity, training is not only the product of the local availability of specialized spaces which facilitate its accomplishment, but also of 'transformation rules' which define what is proper and must be given weight within a training session (1972: 27ff). The rules of expressive behaviour during training in fact operate as transformation rules which block, select and transform some properties of everyday interaction and some attributes of individuals. Establishing what is relevant and what is not, these rules try to ensure that during training individuals are clients, ceremonially equivalent and formally equal. They shape expectations so that each client is expected and expects to concentrate on the exercise of his or her own body, moving it, observing it, exposing it to the gaze of others as prescribed by the demands of the exercise.

Transformation rules have important cognitive and affective functions, something which has been underlined by Gregory Bateson (1954), an acknowledged source of inspiration for Goffman. Bateson considered 'framed activities' as domains of actions marked by 'meta-communicative' messages: a message which 'explicitly or implicitly defines a frame' in fact 'gives the receiver instructions or aids in his attempts to understand the messages included within the frame' (Bateson, 1954: 161). A meta-communicative message thus guides the evaluation of the messages contained within the picture it has encapsulated. Participants' involvement in the official focus of attention during training, their strained grunts, their concentration on the trainer's movements, their tense faces and sweaty outfits, all contribute to reinforce the message, 'this is a training session'. The properly expressed involvement of a participant in the official focus of cognitive and visual attention is thus a signal of the reality of training: it tells 'others what he is and what his intentions are, adding to the security of the others in his presence'; it also confirms 'the reality of the world' inside, and 'the unreality of other potential worlds' which might be obtruding (Goffman, 1972: 37). Furthermore, as Goffman also recognizes (1974: 345 ff), frame organizes more than meaning; it organizes involvement, too.[7] Thus, if clients become involved in the focus of attention as prescribed by training, they typically feel natural and at ease, submerged in the reality of the exercise. Especially after training, it is commonplace to hear clients making comments on body work-out as producing a valuable sort of experience.

This experience is defined as 'concentration' on the physical activities, a heightened perception of one's own body as defined by the exercise and a liberation from all external pressures. Training is described by assiduous clients as furnishing a sort of protected recreation of oneself, a worthwhile moment 'rescued' from the normal demands of everyday life when one 'can and must only think of moving one's own body' according to the demands of the exercise. Training is thus a domain of action where clients may be brought to concentrate on their own movements with very little need to address them reflexively. In Bateson's words, we may say that the working of expressive behaviour as a meta-communicative device creates a relatively clear communicative space, freed of the need for communication on the nature and relevance of the actual exchange. The exercise frame is organized so that participants can sustain training without the need to question what is going on and, as I shall show, with only limited departures from it, the importance of which lies in the way they help reinforce the frame.

The implicit meta-communicative value of the organization of expressive behaviour is crucial not only for participants' actual experience of training, but also for their longer-term capacity to continue a work-out programme. Clients' capacity to trust and endorse the rules of expressive behaviour which operate during training partially accounts for their concrete participation in the exercise. Enthusiastic and assiduous clients reconstruct their successful initiation to training as a process of re-framing which led to a deeper sense of involvement in the activity and to a more sustained participation. Barbara, for example, a young university student who has followed a regular step-aerobics programme for more than six months, is able to put her story in eloquent terms. She explains that during her first days of training she did not feel engrossed: she felt 'useless', she 'really could not follow' and kept 'losing concentration'; while 'everyone looked so good', she just felt 'out of place'. She comments on her initial difficulty of leaving aside normal, outside expectations, both related to body ideals and to her local performance. To this she now imputes some of her initial flaws: 'at the beginning I tried much less, instead of thinking of the exercise I just tried to hide . . . as if people were there to look at me rather than looking at training'. In some measure, this alienated her from the action, making it difficult to endorse it, producing embarrassment and shame instead of involvement. In order to enter the exercise she needed to take seriously, trust and endorse the continuous indexing of the activities in the exercise area as a 'training session'. Also, thanks to the encouragement of Patty, a lively step-aerobics instructor, Barbara has 'thrown' herself 'into' the proceeding of the exercise: 'I said to myself: "come on", now I look at the mirror, I want to see if my movements are fine, I follow each step of the trainer, I do just everything, I sweat, I really put myself into it!' As other assiduous clients have also reckoned, Barbara is convinced that it is this chance to 'be involved' which has 'helped' her to 'train regularly'.

Together with the 'benefits' and the 'results' which they obtain for their bodies in the long run, all regular clients stress the importance of the actual 'context' of training for sustained participation. They prize 'concerned' trainers who are 'able to convey enthusiasm', they appreciate a gym where other participants 'do not want to play silly', they relish training for its 'relaxed' and yet 'serious' and 'concentrated' atmosphere. All these features contribute to make fitness training engaging in itself, a genuine 'diversion', something which draws participants into its own rules and relevances and then allows them to forget, partially and momentarily, other external relevances. The clients who tell stories of successful initiation to training both at Shape and at BodyMove thus seem to have understood different signals framing the exercise, making it into a relatively distinct, clear, safe and absorbing domain of action. In particular, they have learned to reinterpret glances at the body as related to training. As Amy, an articulate mature student, says, the perfect gym for her is one where she 'can sweat without feeling ugly' and where there is no need to mark one's own social position by 'showing off labelled clothes'.

Body Definitions and Local Identities

In reinterpreting glances at the training bodies as connected to the process of exercise, clients master a complex set of practical and implicit rules of glance management. By glance management I refer to how glances are passed and exchanged, as well as how they are handled when resorting to verbal justifications. The rules of glance management operating during training help the neighbouring bodies to be filtered out, defined by the exercise and, to some extent, made neutral and innocuous. These rules are loaded with meanings: they help to sort out body definitions, prescribing how the body must be properly understood during training, which attributes and qualities have to be blocked out, which can be left in the background as still of use to the exercise itself. In order to understand which body definitions are sustained and how this contributes to training, it is thus important to look in some detail at the rules of glance management at work.

During aerobics classes, which are often crowded both at Shape and BodyMove, it is evident that training itself requires a continuous attention to the body postures and movements proposed by the instructor. Clients stress that it is important to pay attention to the instructor's body and conceive of this as a 'normal' demand of training, as part of the officially prescribed exercise arrangements. Thus James prefers BodyMove 'when there are less people' since 'it's easier to follow the trainer's movements', 'keep[ing] one's eyes on her' and thus 'concentrat[ing] on body movements much better'. When an overcrowded class makes this difficult, it is another client who is looked at. Glenys, also a keen customer of BodyMove, maintains that 'instructors always ask [you] to watch them', yet 'if there are lots of people' it is 'necessary to look at those [clients] in the first row'. Clients also look very often at their own bodies in the surrounding mirrors. This is again felt and promoted as an officially prescribed glance. Jane, one of the most popular trainers at BodyMove, during her step-aerobics lessons never forgets to encourage the group, suggesting that 'it's important to do even the smallest movement with precision and the mirror is there for this, it helps you to understand what you're doing with your body!' Although it may happen that some individuals do not feel at ease with it – like Eleanor who prefers 'to avoid looking' at herself in the mirror because she would feel 'vain' – at least at the interaction level this modality of glance is prescribed and does not require any particular justification.

On the other hand, when following their neighbours' movements, clients may find themselves coming across their reciprocal glances. When eyes repeatedly meet, participants tend to rapidly divert their eyes, or they exchange a signal of mutual support and even openly justify their behaviour. Similar expressive routines underline that looking at another client is not a straightforward and indisputably permitted modality of glance. Being not explicitly entailed by the exercise, this is an equivocal glance which can refer to external notions of the body. George, an athletic shop manager, after having repeatedly met the eyes of one of the two young newcomers during his favourite body-sculpt class, turns to the trainer and comments 'you can tell that there are new people, but they are good! When I started, I didn't keep your pace'. Similar justification strategies are not only meant to re-establish a threatened ceremonial order, they may also be actively sought after in order to stress the cooperation between participants. Andrew, a pensioner who has recently joined Shape, usually takes a central position in the stretching group and pursues eye contact with his neighbour which he then justifies with comments such as, 'Oh, goodness me, I just cannot any more, how can you go on? This is impossible, I always lose my balance!' The exercise is thus confirmed as the working of participants' ceaseless cooperation, something which, as suggested, is even more evident in machine training areas. During machine training, no less than in the gymnastic areas, participants are prone to justification when eyes repeatedly meet. Here as well they mention training, by furnishing or asking for advice, or by commenting on their own performance, thus reclassifying the meaning of their glancing at others' bodies.

The justification strategies enacted during training, when customers' eyes meet, reveal that glances at the body can and must be justified with reference to the exercise. The definition of the situation is precisely one of 'physical exercise' and it is the exercise which has to be confirmed if the specific interaction is to go on. Distractions from the focus of attention prescribed by the exercise frame may only be tolerated if rapidly drawn inside its boundaries, if and when the body which is looked at is confirmed as defined by the ongoing physical activity. The ambiguity of the glance at the body during training, however, underlines a pressure from external body definitions. The justifications adopted in fact testify to clients' capacity to recognize the definition of the body within the exercise as distinct from other definitions. The analysis of similar justification strategies thus says something of the body definitions at work during training, of both those definitions which are prescribed by the exercise frame and those which are kept outside it.

When justifying their glances at the others, clients contribute to specifying which body characteristics are considered as relevant during the ongoing activity. While working out, the body may not be adequate to the task, it may not 'have enough energy' nor 'keep in rhythm', its movements may 'not be coordinated'. A similar notion of the body is sustained not only by expressive ceremonies, but also by trainers' advice and by clients' explicit narratives of motives. Both Shape and BodyMove trainers usually refer to the body as a machine, 'something which has to be kept oiled' and a series of 'levers' linked to a composite external 'shell'. Similarly, clients, such as Charles for example, maintain that everyone 'has' to go to the gym, because the 'body is like a scaffolding with muscle layers: if you train regularly, your muscles are always ready to perform appropriately in whatever situation'.

The specificity of the exercise body as a tool and a machine is first obtained by neutralizing the body of the changing-room, confining the organic body within it. Instead of 'making mistakes' as the training body indeed does, the body of the changing-room may be obscene or polluting. While shifting, clients comment on their physical sensations, the 'ache' felt after all their 'efforts', the 'pleasure' of finding oneself 'with relaxed nerves'. The body of the changing-room is of organic matter, clean or dirty, made of sweat, pain and pleasure, its shortcomings being those of an undisciplined organism.[8]

From a perspective internal to the gym, the exercise body offers to the individual a possibility of control, while the changing-room body highlights the limits of such control. During training participants are asked to work on their bodies as an instrument of the self. Contradictory notions of the body, whereby the body is a measure of the self, its organic source and worth, must be kept at bay as they would offset the definition of the situation. However, changing-rooms also contain other body definitions. While shifting, clients are in fact much closer to their external social realities than they are supposed to be during training. The organic body, prepared to return to everyday reality, yields to the individuals' social bodies. By washing themselves, dressing up, doing their hair, individuals demonstrate their cultural competence to return to their social roles. In their specificity, these practices say something about each individual's social body, about their own specific embodied roles and body presentation requirements. Thus, George comments on the 'necessity of taking a shower if one has to go back to the office' and Glenys maintains that she 'prefer[s] to come in the evening' since she does 'not need to dress up' to go back to her 'family'. I have already suggested that, as opposed to inwards shifting, outwards shifting finds space but not much symbolic support in the changing-room, in that a particularly conspicuous dress can obtrude excessively in the preparation for the exercise with the actor risking ceremonial exposure. Outwards shifting practices remain personal and multifaced preparatory activities supported by personal external anchorages. These external anchorages are not completely anonymous though, they re-emerge in the form of projected social roles during training. Here the individual social body may function as a tension release mechanism which helps interaction to proceed smoothly.

Indeed, the implicit rules of glance management during training not only block out body definitions incompatible with the demands of the exercise, they also reintroduce external notions of the body in specific patterned ways. They translate external body notions for a temporary relaxation of what is strictly prescribed by the exercise frame, for a pause which is authorized within it. What is interesting to notice here is a leap beyond the order of interaction which is negotiated and ultimately contained within such order. Notions of the body external to the exercise which refer to one's own social body are supported by individuals when they consider that they may become the object of a surplus of attention, perceiving they have made a mistake while engaging in training. Patricia and Joanne are both BodyMove clients of some years standing and have met up at the same aerobics morning classes. During training they both remark on their effort to follow what they consider to be a 'difficult series of movements'. This attracts the curiosity of the other participants and the two friends are stimulated to justify themselves even more: 'Gosh! I really cannot follow this one, I am just not a professional dancer', says Joanne, supported by Patricia who laughs and alludes to how her friend will 'impress everyone at home'.

These limited exchanges are typically allowed and even approved of by trainers and other participants with smiles and supportive glances. They are managed as forms of informality considered as proper during physical activities in the gym. The exercise's body definitions as well as its demands on participants may thus be perceived as stringent, but not coercive or oppressive. In a situation where participants are asked to concentrate their attention and emotions on to their objectified bodies, to make them work out as neutral tools and perfectible machines, respect for their selves as not contained by the crudity of the situation may be crucial. Informality, in fact, allows for what Goffman famously defined as 'role-distance' (Goffman, 1972: 85–152). The reintroduction of external notions of the body helps the individual to gain 'distance' from his or her 'role' as defined by training, to project a self beyond the locally attributed identity. Translated as informality, reference to external definitions of the body thus helps participants to ease tension during training. The deployment of such definitions is governed by the exercise frame, and can reinforce its continuity and strength and furnish a perspective on the participants' negotiation of meanings for the local preservation of projected selves.

The availability, in the background, of external definitions of the body is in fact both cooperatively managed by participants as a tension-release mechanism, and actively pursued by individuals as a risk management strategy meant to control ceremonial risks during interaction (Goffman, 1959, 1963a, 1967: 168–239). Irony, often in the form of consciously out-of-frame reference to a different, even contrasting, external body may be used as a means to avoid annihilating oneself completely within the exercise, confining oneself to the identity which is thus locally attributed. When, as noticed, Joanne says half-joking that the aerobic sequence is too much for anyone but a professional dancer, she shows her competence to recognize what is required within the exercise as a docile body, and she is detaching herself from her local performance, refusing to reduce herself to it and her body to a pure instrument of training.

As an individual strategy irony is not only used to gain distance from the local identities attributed during training, but also from the body ideals which training is geared to, from the toned, tight and slim body which exercise is deemed to produce. As the idealized final goals and the conspicuous outcomes of training, these body ideals are obviously linked to the docile mechanical body of the exercise. Nevertheless, they are not coextensive with it. The exercise body is a pure instrument, a neutral machine made of energy beyond any distinction or specification but those strictly necessary for carrying out the prescribed movements. It is a pure and universal utility which is thereby layered with a wealth of meanings as soon as training gives way to other social situations. The fit and toned body as portrayed in advertising and the media is in fact typically and conspicuously gendered, charged with racial and sexual connotations, indexed to a set of prized social roles (Bordo, 1993; Cash and Pruzinsky, 1990; O'Neill, 1985; Wolf, 1991). All these external appreciations are instead officially filtered out during training as they may upset the definition of the situation, and distract clients from involvement in the ongoing activity. Irony also functions as a relativizing recognition of the body ideals which, from an external viewpoint, sustain training. It neutralizes clients' own inadequacy with respect to culturally defined body ideals, which are obviously associated with fitness work-out, by means of their re-introduction within the exercise as important but locally irrelevant.

This is well exemplified by a machine training episode where Wendy and Mary, two middle-aged women who typically spend a couple of hours a week in the gym, engage in a brief dialogue. Wendy asks Mary: 'Do you need this machine now? ... It's really good for a slim waist and against those hip bulges'; and Mary answers, 'Yes, yes, but how many shall I do, uh?! ... working hard, working hard.' Mary intervenes not so much to protect her physical appearance as to stress her mastery of the body ideals which culturally sustain the exercise while discounting them as somehow suspended during training: she is ready to take responsibility for her exercise performance as well as her capacity to work on her body, but not for her embodied qualities. And so does Amy, who, by similarly joking about her physical appearance, actively contributes to make the gym into a place where people can work on their objectified bodies without feeling exposed. When, during a stretching class, the instructor asks participants to turn their torsos far enough to see their posteriors, she cannot help whispering to the complaisant neighbours: 'Indeed, I always see mine!'

The flexibility of the exercise frame, its relatively high degree of informality, allows participants to deploy irony as a risk management strategy. The maintenance of cooperation during exercise thus implies both taking the exercise seriously and discounting such seriousness as peculiar to the contingent framed reality. Exercise is indexed to other external realities, social roles and cultural values about the body, that are present even if recognized as locally irrelevant. Discounted as part of an encapsulated activity, the definition of the body within exercise and the relative local identities attributed to clients become nevertheless real. Thus indexed they may be considered by participants as less threatening for their own projected self, and may be endorsed more easily.

While different body definitions are managed by the fitness gym as part of its organization, their selection, variation and combination also underpin the creation of local identities, those identities which are attributed to participants during physical activities in the gym. Abstracting from all those parts of themselves which do not fit with the exercise, playing down the body requirements of their social roles, looking at their body as a pure instrument of training, knowing what to do and what is next, participants subjectively endorse the local identity attributed to them. Involvement within training authenticates the reality of the exercise and validates the competence of the actor. Regular clients' descriptive narratives, in effect, show that training fosters sensations of body control as well as power, strength, agility, harmony, expressivity. These are all feelings of accomplishment which are easily classified as confirmation of one's own competence. Nancy, for example, maintains that when she gets 'concentrated' and 'works out seriously', it 'feels great to be able to follow', a sensation which puts her 'in the right mood all day long'. The confirmation of local identities thus reverberates outside gym environments. In the long run, what has been singled out as relevant within the exercise frame tends to have effects on external relevances. In particular, local identities as well as the notion of the body which is so poignantly appropriated fuel personal identities, becoming relevant for the individual as a biographical unity.

Precisely because it requires similar identity plays, training may prove to be a risky business, whereby inadequacy as opposed to competence is experienced. It is thus an important feature of the exercise frame that it allows for some elements of informality in the form of partial detachment from the exercise, from its local demands and its cultural goals.[9] Regular clients learn to modulate their local identities with limited and typically half-joking allusions to their social roles and the corresponding body requirements. Notions of the body referring to clients' social roles may thus intervene to facilitate the endorsement of local identities, such as when, after a mistake, participants in a fitness session allude to their external body requirements while striving to resume training. At the same time, these very local identities, the necessity and capacity of clients to concentrate only on training a neutral and machine-like body, filter out the wider body ideals which the exercise is geared to.

Although linked to the exercise body, ideals of the fit and toned body as portrayed in the wider culture are not coextensive with it; they could therefore conflict dangerously with training and need appropriate managing during it. This complex game of meanings shows that what happens in the gym is not simply directly produced by broader cultural values which are imposed on individuals. Cultural values, distinctions and body ideals exist as situated practices, they are crucial only insofar as they are negotiated through locally specific interaction rules which require the active contribution of all participants.

Concluding Remarks

Training within the gym is sustained by the local organization of resources, time and space management in particular, and by a host of implicit interaction rules which help to frame the exercise. The exercise frame facilitates participants' cognitive and affective concentration on training and it is thanks to this that the gym may be experienced as an obvious, meaningful and relatively separated reality. The body is thus not only the material object of training, but also the fundamental symbolic device for participants to implicitly agree on the definition of the situation. The rules of interaction in fact sustain a particular definition of the body as relevant within training and translate external definitions in prescribed and locally specific ways. The situatedness of fitness training is crucial: the local organization of resources, interaction and meanings filter out the ideal of the fit body from its wider, typically gender- and class-specific charges, transforms it into the exercise body, a pure instrument of training bearing little resemblance to the organic body confined inside the changing-rooms, an objectified utility which is beyond any social role specification. Social roles and their body requirements are both important for individual clients' structural chances to join the gym and locally neutralized or reduced to tension-release mechanisms. Similarly, the cultural ideals of a fit, toned and slender body contribute to the legitimation of the fitness gym; yet the actual capacity to train is less the result of the direct grip of culture, than the outcome of clients' dynamic and, to some extent, always highly contingent adjustment to an articulated set of local rules of interaction.

Body definitions are not simply embodied by the gym nor reproduced by its clients, but continuously and actively negotiated and transformed. Clients are, in fact, asked and allowed to play a particular game of involvement with and detachment from the mechanistic and abstract exercise body. The docility of the body and its correlative plasticity are, for example, all but total within fitness exercise. This is so not only because instructors continuously limit such plasticity to the exercise itself as opposed to other techniques of body transformation available on the market, but also because the docile objectivity of the exercise body is tempered by a series of identity mechanisms which allow clients not to be reduced to it. The informality of the work-out scene facilitates training by allowing for limited pauses whereby clients are able to negotiate some room for their projected selves as existing beyond the contingent locality, its body requirements and its ascribed body ideals. The docility of the body is thus enacted, as opposed to being imposed on or chosen by the participants. Participants are able to approach and impersonate such a body only by partially detaching themselves from it. It is thus through a series of personal adjustments regulated by the local organization of interaction that the exercise body is transformed and indexed to one's own personal reality. Thus negotiated, it can be subjectively appropriated as a fit body, layered with meanings rooted in different social situations and experiences, a body which indeed is felt and deployed as a conspicuous sign of personal worth.

Acknowledgements

An earlier version of this paper has been presented at the Conference 'Body Modification', Nottingham, June 1997. I would like to thank all the participants for their comments as well as Robin Bunton, Pier Paolo Giglioli, Emilio Santoro, Alan Scott, Barbara Steward, John Street and an anonymous referee for their helpful suggestions. A special acknowledgement is due to the clients, instructors and managers of the gyms examined for without their precious time, concern and consent this study would not have been possible.

Notes

1. Some of the most recent studies on the specificity of various exercise techniques are also pointing in this direction. See Aoki (1996), Courtine (1991), Ewen (1988), Mansfield and McGinn (1993) and St Martin and Gavey (1996) on body building; Lloyd (1996) and Metoudi (1987) on aerobics; Blouin Le Baron (1981), Perrin (1985) and Thirion (1987) on new 'soft' and 'expressive' gymnastics.

2. The fieldwork, which is part of a larger study on the commercialization of body discipline, was conducted in Florence during 1994 and 1995. Shape and BodyMove differed with respect to size, facilities, type and variety of fitness activities, number and socio-economic background of clients, number of trainers and cost. I participated as a client in the activities of both gyms for more than six months for several hours a day at different times, following all the different training programmes and instructors. Clients to be interviewed were selected on the basis of a theoretical sampling covering different participation profiles within the gyms. The actual names of the clients, instructors, managers and gyms concerned have been changed to protect confidentiality. Words or phrases in quotes are drawn from interviews and conversations with clients and trainers or from gym scenes. For more details on the method and context of this research see Sassatelli (1996: 212–87).

3. The notion of the 'liminoid' is borrowed from Victor Turner. Turner developed it to describe how 'liminal' spaces get transformed in modern societies, becoming less predetermined and more subjective (Turner, 1969, 1982). The changing-room shows very well what I would call the individualization of liminality, the fact that individuals are asked to continually negotiate the social understanding of passage symbols. On this and on how the changing-room manages intermediary tensions between the meanings of the gym and of everyday life see Sassatelli (1999).

4. If there still seems to be a certain preference among men for machines and among women for aerobics, this is by no means a sharp divide (Dechevanne, 1981; Mandard, 1987; Mansfield and McGinn, 1993). Fitness gyms are not only sexually mixed environments, they are also structured as to allow for a switch from aerobic to anaerobic work-out and vice versa, pushing clients to pursue their own personalized routines combining different exercise techniques. Nevertheless, it is evident that the suspension of traditional gender divisions is very selective. The relevance of gender is blocked within training and reintroduced within the unfocused interactions and acquaintanceships scattered around it. The latter thus tend to become overcharged with aesthetic and sexual concerns related to seduction.

5. These observations may be seen as developing toward interactionist concerns, a perspective which considers both consumer and leisure spaces in commercial modernity as contained spheres of ordered disorder (Elias and Dunning, 1986; Featherstone, 1991; Turner, 1969; Urry, 1995).

6. Developing Bateson's idea that play illustrates our capacity to make sense of situations on the basis of a message or a frame of meaning which guide our orientation within them (Bateson, 1954), Goffman deployed the notion of frame in his own work on games (1972) and later elaborated it in *Frame Analysis* (1974) considering the experience of social actors as the enmeshing oscillation of a multiplicity of everyday life frames. The notion of frame has been appropriated by a host of disciplines which have placed a number of different emphases on it (Tannen, 1993). For a critical discussion of Goffman's notion of frame see Giglioli (1990); Gonos (1977); Verhoeven (1985); and Wootton and Drew (1988).

7. Goffman understood that some psychobiological implications may be derived from this notion: 'when an individual becomes engaged in an activity, whether shared or not, it is possible for him to become caught up by it, carried away by it, engrossed in it' (1972: 35, see also 1974: 346–7). The emphasis that I have placed on the notion of meta-communication, requiring only a minimal anthropology, is in this sense meant to address involvement from a sociological perspective as related to the local organization of experience (Sassatelli, 1997). On these issues, see Burns (1992); Giglioli (1990) and, for a socio-psychological application, see Csikszentmihalyi (1982).

8. Within the vast scholarship on the development of ideas about the body in modernity, several authors have underlined the progressive relevance of the body-machine imagery especially within institutional contexts (Ewen, 1988; Foucault, 1975; Le Breton, 1990; Synnott, 1993; Turner, 1987; Vigarello, 1978). Others have underlined the importance that a notion of the body-organic has maintained both as a backstage counter-image and as a ritual tool (Douglas, 1966; Elias, 1939; Falk, 1994; Goffman, 1963b).

9. A similar emotional structure is fundamental for fitness training precisely because it is organized as an interaction domain with a very limited and strictly prescribed focus of attention and as a highly consequential set of activities, i.e. the exercise is deemed to obtain objectives which are crucial in everyday life. Informality is particularly important for those categories of people which are structurally more likely to participate in fitness due to the importance that body capital has for them, i.e. women and young people (Bourdieu, 1978; Shilling, 1993), or to a wide gap between their own body characteristics and body ideals (Markland and Hardy, 1993). The possibility of locally filtering body ideals while pursuing activities which are aimed at their accomplishment is decisive in protecting individuals from a dangerous exposure of their inadequacies. Informality thus helps clients to govern the paradox by which the more important the body projects pursued by training, the less individuals are able to concentrate in actually doing it.

References

Amir, Gisèle (1987) 'Au menu de *Vital*: un concentre d'idéologie de rapport aux sport', *Sport et change-ment social. Actes des premières journées d'études*. Bourdeaux: Maison des sciences de l'homme d'Aquitaine.

Aoki, Doug (1996) 'Sex and Muscle: The Female Bodybuilder Meets Lacan', *Body & Society* 2(4): 59–74.

Bateson, Gregory (1954) 'A Theory of Play and Phantasy', *APA Psychiatric Research Report*, reprinted in Gregory Bateson *Steps to an Ecology of Mind*, New York: Chandler, 1972.

Bessy, Olivier (1987) 'Les salles de gymnastique: un marché du corps et de la forme. Le nouvel age du sport', *Esprit* IV: 79–94.

Blouin Le Baron, Jacqueline (1981) 'Expression corporelle: le flou et la forme', in C. Pociello (ed.) *Sport et société. Approche socio-culturelle des pratiques*. Paris: Vigot.

Bordo, Susan (1993) *Unbearable Weight: Feminism, Western Culture and the Body*. Berkeley: University of California Press.

Bourdieu, Pierre (1978) 'Sport and Social Class', *Social Science Information* 17(6): 819–40.

Burns, Tom (1992) *Erving Goffman*. London: Routledge.

Cash, T.F. and T. Pruzinsky (1990) *Body Images: Development, Deviance and Change*. New York: Guilford Press.

Courtine, Jean-Jacques (1991) 'Les stakhanovistes du narcissisme', *Le Gouvernament du Corps, Communication* 56: 225–45.

Csikszentmihalyi, Mihaly (1982) *Beyond Boredom and Anxiety*. New York: Jossey-Bass.

Dechevanne, Nichole (1981) 'La division sexuelle du travail gymnique', in C. Pociello (ed.) *Sports et société. Approche socio-culturelle des pratiques*. Paris: Vigot.

Defrance, Jacques (1976) 'Esquisse d'une histoire sociale de la gymnastique', *Actes de la Recherche en Sciences Sociales* 6.

Defrance, Jacques (1981) 'Se fortifier pour se soumettre?', in C. Pociello (ed.) *Sport et société. Approche socio-culturelle de pratiques.* Paris: Vigot.

Douglas, Mary (1966) *Purity and Danger: An Analysis of Concepts of Pollution and Taboo.* London: Routledge.

Elias, Norbert (1939) *Uber der Prozess der Zivilisation, II: Wandlungen der Gesellschaft. Entwurf zu einer Theorie der Zivilisation.* Basel: Hans zum Falken. (English trans. Oxford: Blackwell, 1982.)

Elias, Norbert and Eric Dunning (1986) *Quest for Excitement: Sport and Leisure in the Civilizing Process.* London: Basil Blackwell.

Ewen, Stuart (1988) *All-Consuming Images: The Politics of Style in Contemporary Culture.* New York: Basic Books.

Falk, Pasi (1994) *The Consuming Body.* London: Sage.

Featherstone, Mike (1982) 'The Body in Consumer Culture', *Theory, Culture & Society* 1(2): 18–33.

Featherstone, Mike (1991) *Consumer Culture and Postmodernism.* London: Sage.

Foucault, Michel (1975) *Survelleir et punir. Naissance de la prison.* Paris: Gallimard (English trans. *Discipline and Punish,* London: Penguin, 1979.)

Frank, Arthur (1991) 'For a Sociology of the Body: An Analytical Review', in M. Featherstone, M. Hepworth and B.S. Turner (eds) *The Body: Social Processes and Cultural Theory.* London: Sage.

Giddens, Anthony (1984) 'Corpo, riflessività, riproduzione sociale: Erving Goffman e la teoria sociale', *Rassegna Italiana di Sociologia* 25(3): 369–400.

Giglioli, Pier Paolo (1990) *Rituale, interazione, vita quotidiana. Saggi su Goffman e Garfinkel.* Bologna: Clueb.

Goffman, Erving (1959) *The Presentation of the Self in Everyday Life.* New York: Doubleday Anchor.

Goffman, Erving (1963a) *Behaviour in Public Places: Notes on the Social Organization of Gatherings.* New York: The Free Press.

Goffman, Erving (1963b) *Stigma: Notes on the Management of Spoiled Identities.* Englewood Cliffs, NJ: Prentice-Hall.

Goffman, Erving (1967) *Interaction Rituals: Essays on Face-to-Face Behavior.* New York: Pantheon.

Goffman, Erving (1971) *Relations in Public: Microstudies of the Public Order.* New York: Basic Books.

Goffman, Erving (1972) *Encounters: Two Studies in the Sociology of Interaction.* London: Penguin. (Orig. 1961.)

Goffman, Erving (1974) *Frame Analysis: An Essay on the Organization of Experience.* New York: Harper and Row.

Goffman, Erving (1981) *Forms of Talk.* Philadelphia: University of Pennsylvania Press.

Goffman, Erving (1982) 'The Interaction Order', *American Sociological Review* 48: 1–17.

Gonos, G. (1977) 'Situation vs. Frame: The Interactionist and the Structuralist Analysis of Everyday Life', *American Sociological Review* 42: 854–67.

Green, H. (1986) *Fit for America: Health, Fitness, Sport and American Society.* Baltimore, MD: Johns Hopkins University Press.

Grover, K. (ed.) (1989) *Fitness in American Culture: Images of the Health, Sport, and the Body 1830–1940.* Amherst: The University of Massachussets Press.

Hargreaves, John (1987) 'The Body, Sport and Power Relations', in J. Horne, D. Jary and A. Tomlinson (eds) *Sport Leisure and Social Relations,* Sociological Review Monograph 33. London: Routledge.

Le Breton, David (1990) *Anthropologie du corps et Modernité.* Paris: PUF.

Lloyd, Moya (1996) 'Feminism, Aerobics and the Politics of the Body', *Body & Society* 2(2): 79–98.

Mandard, Gisèle (1987) 'Un nouveau modele de pratique sportive feminine', in *Sport et changement social. Actes des premières journées d'études.* Bourdeaux: Maison des sciences de l'homme d'Aquitaine.

Mansfield, Alan and Barbara McGinn (1993) 'Pumping Irony: The Muscular and the Feminine', in S. Scott and D. Morgan (eds) *Body Matters: Essays on the Sociology of the Body*. London: Falmer Press.

Markland, D. and Hardy, L. (1993) 'The Exercise Motivations Inventory', *Personality and Individual Differences* 15(3): 289–96.

Metoudi, Michèle (1987) 'De nouveaux usages pour les sports d'hier', *Esprit* 125: 42–52.

O'Neill, John (1985) *Five Bodies: The Human Shape of Modern Society*. Ithaca, NY: Cornell University Press.

Perrin, Eliane (1985) *Les cultes du corps. Enquete sur les nouvelles pratiques corporelles*. Lausanne: Favre.

Pociello, Chistian (ed.) (1981) *Sports et société. Approche socio-culturelle des pratiques*. Paris: Vigot.

St Martin, Leena and Nicola Gavey (1996) 'Women's Bodybuilding: Feminist Resistance and/or Femininity's Recuperation', *Body & Society* 2(4): 45–58.

Sassatelli, Roberta (1996) 'Pratiche ed esperienze di consumo. Palestra, disciplina e cultura del corpo', PhD thesis, Florence: European University Institute.

Sassatelli, Roberta (1997) 'Space and Time Regulation within Fitness Gyms: Territories of the Body, Territories of the Self', paper commended in the International Sociological Association Young Sociologists Worldwide Competition 1995–1997.

Sassatelli, Roberta (1999) *Anatomia della palestra. Cultura commerciale e disciplina del corpo*. Bologna: Il Mulino.

Shilling, Chris (1993) *The Body and Social Theory*. London: Sage.

Scott, Sue and David Morgan (eds) (1993) *Body Matters: Essays on the Sociology of the Body*. London: Falmer Press.

Synnott, Anthony (1993) *The Body Social: Symbolism, Self and Society*. London: Routledge.

Tannen, Deborah (ed.) (1993) *Framing in Discourse*. Oxford: Oxford University Press.

Thirion, Jean-François (1987) 'Les nouvelles pratiques et la notion de developpment personnel', in *Sport et changement social. Actes des premières journées d'études*, Bourdeaux: Maison des sciences de l'homme d'Aquitaine.

Turner, Bryan S. (1987) 'The Rationalization of the Body: Reflections on Modernity and Discipline', in S. Whimster and S. Lash (eds) *Max Weber, Rationality and Modernity*. London: Allen and Unwin.

Turner, Victor (1969) *The Ritual Process: Structure and Anti-Structure*. London: Routledge.

Turner, Victor (1982) *From Ritual to Theatre: The Human Seriousness of Play*. New York: Performing Arts Journal Publications.

Urry, John (1995) *Consuming Places*. London: Routledge.

Verhoeven, Jef (1985)'Goffman's Frame Analysis and Modern Micro-Sociological Paradigms', in S.N. Eisenstadt and J. Helle (eds) *Micro-Sociological Theory*. Sage, London.

Vigarello, George (1978) *Le corps redressé: Histoire d'un pouvoir pédagogique*. Paris: Delarge.

Vigarello, George (1988) *Un histoire culturelle du sport: techniques d'hier et d'aujourd'hui*. Paris: Revue EPS.

Weber, Max (1946) 'The Meaning of Discipline', in H. Gerth and C. Wright Mills (eds) *From Max Weber*. Oxford: Oxford University Press.

Wolf, Naomi (1991) *The Beauty Myth: How Images of Beauty Are Used Against Women*. London: Vintage.

Wootton, Anthony and Paul Drew (eds) (1988) *Erving Goffman: Exploring the Interaction Order*. Cambridge: Polity Press.

Roberta Sassatelli is a lecturer in Sociology at the School of Economic and Social Studies, University of East Anglia, Norwich.

The Body as Outlaw: Lyotard, Kafka and the Visible Human Project

NEAL CURTIS

Introduction

The aim of this article is to use the Visible Human Project (VHP) – a digitized simulation of the human body set up by the National Library of Medicine, Maryland, USA, and currently on view on the Internet – to illustrate the relation between the body and the law, or the body and the discursive practices inscribed upon it. I will employ the writings of Jean-François Lyotard, in particular his interpretation (1993b) of Kafka's short story 'In the Penal Colony' as a theoretical tool for understanding this relation. It will also facilitate thinking the body as heterogeneous to the law, without recourse to a fundamentally 'natural' body in opposition to the 'cultured' body of inscription. To do this Lyotard conceived of the heterogeneity of the body in terms of the *bodily mode* of *aesthesis*, an openness and receptivity prior to the law. It is this bodily mode which I will discuss in this article and which, I argue, is refused, or excised, in the 'complete' body of the VHP.

The purpose of the VHP was 'to create a digital atlas of the human anatomy' (Lorensen, 1997: 1). The simulation was made from a series of digital cross-sections of a cadaver producing the most sophisticated computer model yet. The body was scanned and imaged using Computer Tomography (CT) and Magnetic Resonance Imaging (MRI) producing 'fresh' data, before the body was frozen in gelatine at $-70°C$. When solid, the body was put into a laser dissection device called a cryomatrome, which shaved 1mm thick slices from the frozen body. Each slice was then digitized, and further CT scan and MRI images were made. Obviously, what is missing from this 'complete' digital human body is the body itself, the flesh and blood, the fact that it is no longer alive. But what is of interest to me

Body & Society © 1999 SAGE Publications (London, Thousand Oaks and New Delhi),
Vol. 5(2–3): 249–266
[1357–034X(199906/09)5:2–3;249–266;008866]

is not the materiality of this absent flesh, but its quality as a surface receptive to sensation and affect, a receptivity heterogeneous and prior to the ordered rules and codings of inscription.

In Franz Kafka's short story, where the method of executing criminals in the penal colony is a writing machine which cuts the sentence into the body of the condemned prisoner, engraving the body to its death, the similarities between the ever deepening wounds on the body of Kafka's criminal and the slicing of the body in the VHP, which Catherine Waldby has called 'the violence of cryosection' (1997: 5), are evocative. However, I do not intend to suggest that the one has its analogue in the other. Instead, the focus of this article is to think the (in)significance of the body with regard to the law and the modificatory practices which always attempt to subsume the body within it. Using Lyotard's essay to think through the excision of the bodily mode of aesthesis in the VHP, this article intends to bear witness to the wrong instituted there.

I argue that the VHP institutes a wrong in that it attempts to hide a differend. The differend, which for Lyotard appears 'when the "settlement" of the conflict that opposes [two parties] appears in the idiom of one of them while the tort from which the other suffers cannot signify itself in this idiom' (Lyotard, 1993c: 9), takes the form of an ordering of the body according to the discursive practices of medical science to which the body is irreducible. This article will, therefore, explore this irreducibility by examining precisely what is meant by Lyotard when he argues that the body is prior to the law, and how this priority might give us a conception of the body incommensurate to the discursive orderings and body modificatory practices through which the law is inscribed.

To continue this brief qualification of terms, I will deploy the term 'law' in three ways: first, to signify the normative procedures through which the body is brought within the rules of a culture or community; second, as the discursive practices which manage these procedures of inclusion and exclusion; and, third, in a more extended way, I will deploy the term 'law' to signify the conceptual rules by which the body and the sensible world are conceptually ordered and brought within the realm of the understanding. The term 'law' will, therefore, be used generically, as rules through which the sensible is made intelligible, and rules through which the ends of discursive practices (juridical, techno-scientific, medical, etc.) are secured.

The Violence of the Law

In 'Prescription', Lyotard writes that '[w]ithout deliberation or warranted judgement the sacrificial execution [of the law] must be repeated automatically each time a criminal birth occurs' (1993b: 181). But, before considering why the body, from birth, is always already an outlaw, it is useful to examine why Lyotard reads Kafka's story as an allegory of such a preordained criminality. In the Kafka story, a traveller has been asked by the New Commandant of the colony to oversee the execution of a prisoner by an officer devoted to the Old Commandant and his methods of punishment. The criminal is placed within a device known only as 'the apparatus', which executes the law and the prisoner simultaneously by writing the crime in the flesh of the criminal over a period of 12 hours. At which time, if the criminal is not already dead, the apparatus forces a large metal needle through the head of the accused, and then dumps him in a pit. The apparatus comprises 'the bed' on which the criminal lies, 'the harrow' – a set of fine glass needles which 'correspond to the human form' in order to inscribe the crime into the flesh, and 'the designer' which takes the scripts written by the Old Commandant and etches the punishment according to their design. Although the apparatus operates with great 'artistry', its violence is brought to the fore by a few small details in its construction: the numerous straps that hold the criminal secure, and the stub of felt which the criminal must insert into his mouth to prevent him screaming and biting his tongue – a stub on which numerous other men have agonizingly chewed before him – and the layer of cotton-wool which 'rolls and turns the body slowly on to its side, to give the harrow a fresh area to work on' (Kafka, 1992: 136).

Despite the harrow's artistry 'the most important thing' is the 'designer' which controls the 'harrow' and sets or directs the machinery according to the drawing representing the sentence to be passed. There are seven such designs completed by the former Commandant. The officer shows them to the traveller – although he is not allowed to touch them, as they are the officer's 'most precious possession' – but the traveller cannot read them, he is bemused by 'a maze of criss-cross lines which covered the paper so closely that it was difficult to make out the blank spaces between them' (1992: 135). The officer concludes by informing the traveller that it 'isn't easy to decipher the script with one's eyes; but our man deciphers it with his wounds' (1992: 137).

The force of the law is also developed in two other features of both 'designer' and 'harrow'. First, the inscription of the text denoting the crime is reserved, we are told, for a 'narrow band running round the body; the rest of the body is set aside for the embellishments' (1992: 136). Why embellishments? Why decoration? We are never really told, save for the rather functional comment that the inscription is not intended to kill the criminal straightaway but only after a period of 12 hours, once he has had time to consider it. Second, the glass needles, although presenting problems during installation in the machine due to their delicacy, are an extremely important feature because, as the officer announces, 'now anyone can observe through the glass how the inscription on the body takes place' (1992: 134). Also, the necessary visibility of the law's inscription is highlighted by the inclusion of small water jets next to the glass needles, which ensure that as the script is written deeper and deeper, the blood is continually washed away. Even in death – and this is one way in which a similarity may be drawn between Kafka's story and the National Library of Medicine's representation – the body must not obscure the clarity of the law, it must be at all times open to public view. This clarity is also made explicit earlier in the story where, to the amazement of the visitor, the accused has not been told of his crime nor even that he has been sentenced and, consequently, he has had no chance to defend himself. Lyotard's claim that 'without deliberation or warranted judgement the sacrificial execution must be repeated automatically each time a criminal birth occurs', echoes the officer's statement that: 'The principle on which I base my decisions is this, *guilt is always beyond question*' (1992: 132; emphasis added).

Kafka's story, however, is not simply about the authority and violence of the law, for it also problematizes such a simple representation of the relationship between the law and the body. Although much of the story is given over to the body's inscription, a strange twist in the story offers some sense of the body's resistance. At a key point in the story, when the officer realizes that the traveller is not convinced by the apparatus and will no doubt give a bad report to the New Commandant who will in turn put an end to the practice, the officer gives himself over to the apparatus. He removes the criminal, puts himself on the bed, inserts a new design, which reads 'Be Just', and waits for his righteous death. The apparatus, however, begins to fall apart, the mechanism fails, the spike is driven into the officer's head, and the apparatus grinds to a halt before he can be thrown into the pit. The apparatus cannot inscribe this particular design because there can be no justice in this violation. In an insightful passage from his book on the narration of bodies, Peter Brooks takes this twist in Kafka's tale to indicate the failure of the law in its attempt to sublimate the body from its criminality to the realm of culture and meaning.

> It is as if the promise of a body recovered for the law and for meaning by writing were untenable, false. To the extent that the writing project is imposed by a totalitarian ideology, one may see in the officer's untranscendent death an affirmation of the body's resistance to claims of correction, ennoblement, and conversion asserted upon it. (Brooks, 1993: 285)

'In the Penal Colony', then, shows both the violence of the law but also its injustice. In order, then, to show how the body might be considered as both criminal and resistant, it is necessary to discuss some current theorizing of the body in order to situate the argument.

The Criminal Body

A social or anthropological view of the body is given by Pasi Falk, who understands the body to be passive, as 'a canvas to be painted or a lump of clay to be moulded . . . as a material object (form and surface) to be intentionally elaborated' (Falk, 1995: 95). Here, it is cultural codes that paradoxically complete 'the "natural" mode of bodily existence for that particular culture' (1995: 95). Where these codings are not practised by being written on or in the flesh, the body is still regulated visually via dress codes, and physically choreographed when eating, walking, dancing, etc.

Although Elizabeth Grosz still speaks of the body as pliable flesh, she moves away from theorizing the body as passive. In her article 'Bodies and Knowledges: Feminism and the Crisis of Reason', she writes of the body as 'a kind of *hinge* or threshold: . . . placed between a psychic or lived interiority and a more socio-political exteriority that produces interiority through the *inscription* of the body's outer surface' (Grosz, 1995: 33). This creation of subjectivity through the cultural inscription of codes is the operation by which bodies are narrativized, given a history, an identity and a meaning, and an operation through which the law, as norms and rules, is actualized. Returning to the point made by Falk, that bodily inscription is a process of cultural completion, the operation by which the body succumbs to the law is at once the dedication of a particular body to an ideal and the materialization of that ideal on, and in, a particular body, something I will pick up on later in relation to the VHP. While this reiterates some of Falk's observations, the analogy of the 'hinge' intimates a radical shift from the dualism implied in a passive body, to what, in a slightly different context, Grosz calls 'the body's positive contribution to the text' (1995: 35). Through this reciprocity, or co-dependency, the law is enacted upon the body. To phrase this mutuality in a slightly more explicit way, the law presupposes the necessity of its embodiment. This dependency on the part of the law, however, is always denied. The denial, Grosz argues, comes from the fact that the law, being abstract and general, is threatened by the particularity in which it is embodied each time. The singular instance of each body is a potential threat, a disturbance and a disruption, to the realm of a universalized legislation. This is the crisis in the title of her article and points towards the way in which I wish to conceive of the law's violence in this article: in order to maintain itself the universal must deny the particular, and yet to embody itself it must inscribe itself on something heterogeneous, reducing that heterogeneity in the process.

This simple deconstruction of a binary hierarchy is highly effective. However, in order to consider how the body might be conceived as heterogeneous to the discursive practices inscribed upon it, I am more concerned with what Lyotard would call the differend between the bodily modes 'before' and 'after' inscription. In 'Prescription', Lyotard offers the formulation that the body, rather than being deficient, is in fact in excess with regard to the law. It exceeds the law in the sense that it is not reducible to the organization the law prescribes and which inscription executes. For Lyotard the body is intractable, that is, unmanageable and uncontrollable; it is 'that which resists all law' (Lyotard, 1993b: 170) because it remains non-totalizable, incommensurate to the law's realm. The body resists in two senses. First, the law is prescriptive, that is, an address directed at an addressee, but the body is not of this order of addressees and addressers, and consequently cannot be subject to a command. As Lyotard points out in an interview, the body is never the 'you' the law is addressed to, the 'you' refers to an inscribed interiority or subjectivity (Lyotard and Larochelle, 1992: 412). This offers some indication of the law's originary violence in that it must cut this subjectivity into the body, it must commandeer the body in order to be both announced and obeyed, as Lyotard puts it, and all modificatory practices and discursive inscriptions of the body contain this commandeering element. Second, the body is intractable with regard to the law because it is exposed to something in advance of the law that can only be regarded in terms of aesthetics. This is not the aesthetics of a style or a 'look', but a more archaic use of the term. In 'Prescription' Lyotard argues that:

> ... [t]o be, aesthetically ... is to be-there, here and now, exposed ... before any concept or representation. This *before* is not known.... It is something like birth and infancy – there before we are. The *there* in question is the body. It is not 'I' who am born, who is given birth to. 'I' will be born afterwards, with language, precisely upon leaving infancy ... when the law comes to me, with the ego and language, it is too late. Things will have already taken a turn. And the turn of the law will not manage to efface the first turn, this first touch: the one that touched me when I was not there. (Lyotard, 1993b: 179)

This bodily mode of exposure, which (after Lyotard) I will refer to as aesthesis, is not an aesthetic of representation, but a bodily mode regarded as primitive, savage and alien by the law. It is a 'sinful peregrination' (1993b: 179) that remains a potentiality of the body. It is this bodily mode that specifically sets up the body as always already an outlaw. '[G]uilt is always beyond question', because in aesthesis the body is always open to an other freedom.

This other freedom Lyotard discusses in relation to the blood-letting of Kafka's text in which he identifies two definitions of blood. Latin gives us *cruor* which is blood that runs from a wound and is part of the 'blood debt' integral to many forms of bodily inscription. This draws on the founding cruelty of the law, exposed in the mnemotechniques of Nietzsche's *Genealogy of Morals*, where, '[f]or an unconscionably long time culprits were not punished because they were felt to be responsible for their actions ... rather, they were punished ... out of rage at some damage suffered, which the doer must pay for' (Nietzsche, 1956: 195). There is no legal or moral subject prior to this trade of pain for damage, much as there is no interiority prior to the exchange of the second 'touch' for the first. The second definition of blood is that of *sanguis*, which counter to cruor, is the life blood that flows around the body. According to Lyotard sanguis is what 'nourishes the flesh. It gives it its hue of blueness, its pinkness, its pallor, its sallowness, its early-morning freshness, the infinite juxtaposition of nuances that drive the painter and the philosopher crazy ...' (Lyotard, 1993b: 180).

Cruor is found in all methods of scarification which subsume bodies within laws, reminding the subject of its inscription. In the context of Lyotard's essay, I believe cruor refers specifically to circumcision, which in turn, is already a substitution for sacrifice.[1] The incision of circumcision is a mark of differentiation and identity for the Jewish people, but it also acts as a reminder that the body is given over to the law. Within Christianity the cruor no longer flows in actuality, only symbolically. Lyotard argues that Christians have given up the practice of circumcision because Christ spilled blood once and for all, an eternal cruor. This violence, however, is still repeated through the ingestion of Christ's broken and bleeding body. Another reminder of the authority of the law. But why such brutality? Apart from the necessity of erasing the first 'touch', Lyotard suggests, almost flippantly, that the law is jealous. The law regards itself to be the realm of rights and obligations, and hence the realm of freedom – indeed this is the power of the ingested Messiah as emancipator and saviour – but the law is jealous precisely because the sanguis of the body circulated 'freely' before the law arrived. The body is always an outlaw because it has the potential for an other freedom that is in excess of the realm of law.

Aesthesis and Candour

There are a number of issues that need to be examined here. First I need to devote a few words to this aesthetic. The use of the term 'aesthesis' to speak of this first 'touch' of sensibility needs to be developed, as Lyotard is clearly not talking about an exposure to the intuitions of space and time, for this would create something of a contradiction. The sensible intuitions of space and time, are intrinsic to the faculty of representation and pertain, therefore, to an interiority called the 'I think'. If this 'savage space-time' is to be conceived, then it needs to be approached in a different manner, something more akin to the Deleuzian *spatium*, a primal or groundless space prior to the passive synthesis performed by the 'I think', a depth Deleuze referred to as the 'intensity of being' (1994: 231).

In a discussion of the work of painter Valerio Adami, entitled 'Anamnesis of the Visible, or Candour', Lyotard bears witness to this exposure as a receptiveness to presence, that is, a receptiveness to the field from which all representations spring, where before the present is re-presented as a concept, as a 'what', 'there is no boundary to be crossed between an object and a subject existing in a mode of respective closure, but an instantaneous openness' (Lyotard, 1989: 235). But this presence to which we are exposed in the infancy of aesthesis still needs elaboration. In an article which discusses Lyotard's interpretation of Adami, Jacob Rogozinski provides an excellent synopsis of what Lyotard is trying to think. Presence:

> ... is the perceptible event, the advent of the perceptible, which gives rise to painting, music, and writing. That which they [artists, etc.] try to render present is *presence* itself. Not *Gegenwärtigkeit*, the maintaining of a subsisting-being, but *Anwesen*, the giving which delivers, which *makes present* its offering. (Rogozinski, 1991: 117)

Continuing, and quoting Lyotard, Rogozinski reminds the reader that it is this presence which signification and meaning is always too late for. To situate this a little, the presence being discussed here is not that which gives something its aura (Benjamin, 1992), 'which pierces us with the sense of the uniqueness, the unrepeatableness of the occasion' (Josipovici, 1996: 10). Although evoking the advent of a singular presence, as discussed above, this is not the presence which Lyotard is attempting to think for, as Benjamin stresses, aura is intrinsically bound up with the authority and authenticity of an object, which can only come after one has learned the generic rules concerning its origin. Neither is it the presence of an 'incarnate subjectivity' which, for Merleau-Ponty, is the relation of the pre-personal living body to the phenomenal field (although comparisons with Merleau-Ponty's analysis of 'the invisible' would certainly be fruitful for this was no doubt influential on Lyotard's contemplation of presence). While Merleau-Ponty's attempt to break the dualistic thinking of mind and body is relevant to what Lyotard is attempting to work through here, the presence of 'incarnate subjectivity', as Merleau-Ponty discusses it in *The Phenomenology of Perception* (1962), is bound up with the generation of signification and meaning. What Lyotard turns us towards is the non-signifying, non-intelligible remainder of a sensible presence to which we are exposed, prior to any conceptual or linguistic organization. The bodily mode of this exposure is an abandonment or a 'free conformity' (Lyotard, 1989: 236), and corresponds to the mode of 'donation' (1989: 235) in the sensible field. For Kant the sensible is divisible into the *form* and *matter* of a sensation, with form being given and registered as a feeling before the understanding begins to conceive the matter or appearance of the sensation, or 'what' it is that is being sensed. While form and matter are a priori features of experience for Kant, Lyotard designates form as the 'childhood of the visible' or the 'childhood of what will be represented' (1989: 228). Aesthesis, then, is an exposure, an openness, a candour; the susceptibility of a bodily mode not pre-pared.[2]

Aesthesis and Infancy

To understand a little more about the priority of this exposure and to develop further the modality of the non-discursive body being offered here, it is necessary to say a few words about its 'infancy'. To suggest that infancy is prior to the law is instantly problematic because it seemingly avoids the observation that infancy will already have been the referent of discourses which position it in relation to the law. The most notable example of this is that before the infant is born, it is already inscribed according to the rules of its prospective gender, for example, and to refuse this would be to omit some rather evident functionings of ideology. Infancy, then, must be considered as the moment when the child is already situated as a referent but is not aware of it yet, and is consequently open to the first 'touch' of aesthesis. Indeed, the title of Lyotard's collection of correspondence: *The Postmodern Explained to Children* (1992), comes precisely from this notion of an openness. In order to receive the experimental moment of the 'post', one must divest oneself of rules, accepted discourses and ideologies, in order that something as yet indeterminable might give itself. Countering this earlier 'touch' of aesthesis, the law makes itself known to the body by a second 'touch' through which the infant becomes conscious of it. Returning to Kafka's story, perhaps this is the reason for the embellishment in the inscription of the law; as Lyotard suggests, it signifies that aesthesis has been brought into the service of the law; that the law has its own aesthetic, its own 'look', and it is this aesthetic that must dominate. The force of the second 'touch' is designed to make the body relinquish the former. Again it is possible to make a general point about the complementar-ity of aesthetics and the law in body modificatory practices, as the alterations and embellishments of the body are an overwriting of one 'touch' in favour of another, with each new 'touch' repeating the subsumption of aesthesis. This reiterates Lyotard's point concerning a 'criminal birth'. The body has already been touched in the exposure to aesthesis, and the 'touch' of the law must be a re-touch that is peremptory; this means that '[o]nly the sacrifice of the body maintains the law' (1993b: 181).[3]

If the bodily mode Lyotard calls infancy is not its mode as referent, neither is infancy the object, that is, the immature body of the child, for that is already something textualized and represented. Judith Butler has done much to interrogate and upset the assumed inside/outside binary of culture and nature, and has shown that what is called matter, and therefore presumed to be extra-discursive, is already meaningful. In her book entitled *Bodies that Matter* (1993) she argues that matter is always materialized, that is, it always has a history, is always narrativized. Any reference to matter will always be a particular formation of materiality that has been discursively set. Matter, nature or the body is never an absolute outside but is rather a constitutive outside that generates the significance of an interiority, culture or law. It is an outside that gives the inside its meaning and is, therefore, already textualized and incorporated within the oppositional space in which signification takes place. For Butler, the suggestion that the body is the valueless matter on which inscription takes place hides the inscription already there. The assumption that gender is the moment of inscription covers over, or naturalizes, the prior inscription of the material/biological body as heterosexual. Bringing matter back into the fold of inscription increases the manoeuvrability of political activism as it is no longer anchored by an unquestionable reality, the fixity of which is only secured by continual iteration of the norms attributed to it. 'I would propose', Butler argues, 'a return to the notion of matter as *a process of materialization that stabilizes over time to produce the effect of boundary, fixity, and surface we call matter*' (Butler, 1993: 9).

A useful analogy for this lack of fixity might be the reconceptualization of both space and matter within the new sciences, especially quantum mechanics, where matter, even that which we perceive as rigid or solid, is shown to be permanently in motion, and where the space which gives form to seemingly individual and autonomous objects is now understood to be a less dense area of matter itself. The analogy is doubly useful for it not only aids the visualization of the fluid boundaries of which Butler speaks, but it also illustrates how matter is both discursively regulated and conceptually categorized in order that it might be intelligible. This is not an argument in favour of the thesis which claims the world to be an illusion, it is rather an observation whereby '[r]eality is not what is "given" to this or that "subject", it is a state of the referent ... which results from the effectuation of establishment procedures defined by a unanimously agreed-upon protocol' (Lyotard, 1988a: 4). Matter, manifested as individual and voluminous objects/bodies, is the referent of classical science. Matter as the 'fluid' movement of atoms is the 'reality' established through the protocol and procedures of quantum mechanics. The body, as it is perceived is clearly not external to this discursive ordering.

But it is necessary to remain with this use of analogy, for that is how the 'infancy' of this bodily mode of exposure to sensible presence is to be conceived. This bodily mode of exposure is neither the referent of familial discourses, nor the organic/voluminous body of the actual child. 'Infant' or 'infancy' is rather an analogy for a bodily mode, or relation to the sensible that is not representable. This is Lyotard using the analogical reasoning most fully explored in Kant's third *Critique* (1951).[4] The 'infancy' of this bodily mode is an analogy for an exposure that cannot be directly presented to the mind as it has no object in experience. 'Infancy' is rather the Idea of a primitive relation to the sensible field symbolized.

Having considered the field to which aesthesis is exposed, and the 'infancy' of this exposure, what is needed now is a conception of the body where '[t]here is no boundary to be crossed between an object and a subject existing in a mode of respective closure', that is to think how the free circulation of sanguis and the 'being-there' of aesthesis, might offer another way of thinking the body otherwise to the law without naively assuming an outside to signification and discourse.

Aesthesis and Co-Presence

In order to approach this and to move away from the technical difficulty of an inconsistency in Lyotard's work, whereby the law has elsewhere been considered immemorial (1990), precluding the possibility of anything prior to it,[5] I propose a return to Lyotard's earlier work *Discourse/Figure* (1971), in order to consider this bodily mode as other than, and not prior to, the law. This also helps to think the 'sinful peregrination' as the body's continuing potential and not a mode that can be completely overwritten. The figural, for Lyotard, is that thing which is resistant to the rule of signification. As Bill Readings explains:

> If the rule of discourse is primarily the rule of representation by conceptual oppositions, the figural cannot simply be opposed to the discursive. Rather the figural opens discourse to a radical heterogeneity, a singularity, a difference which cannot be rationalized or subsumed within the rule of representation. (Readings, 1991: 4)

The bodily mode of aesthesis, then, is the 'touch' of an exposure to irreducible singularities; the 'touch' of sensible events understood as irreducible occurrences. In this mode the body is always susceptible to the advent of an immanence that disturbs and disrupts the domain of inscription and law. It is a condition, Lyotard remarks, in which Cézanne remained at the foot of 'Montagne St. Victoire, waiting for the emergence of what he called "small sensations" which are the pure occurrences of unexpected colour' (1988b: 18). This specular example should not indicate a heliocentrism within this conception of the bodily mode, despite its concern with light. For this example indicates how even this sense which is so bound up with distance and separation reveals the 'touch' of sensible presence.

The eyes are filled with light in their exposure to chromatic events; filled to flooding.

Such flooding and bodily fluidity have been used by many writers to express a poetic/erotic intensity where, as Amos Oz has written, 'the toucher is the touched and also the touch' (1988: 118). The following lines from Jeanette Winterson also begin to approach this first 'touch' of aesthesis. In *Written on the Body* she explores perception in terms of the co-presence of zones and planes. The androgynous narrator tells us:

> I am living in a red bubble made up of Louise's hair. It's the sunset time of year but it's not the dropping disc of light that holds me in the shadows of the yard. It's the colour I crave, floodings of you running down the edges of the sky on to the brown earth on to the grey stone. On to me. (Winterson, 1992: 138)

And with regard to taste, on eating an olive

> ... [t]he sun is in your mouth. The burst of an olive is breaking of a bright sky. The hot days when the rains come. Eat the day where the sand burned the soles of your feet before the thunderstorm brought up your skin in bubbles of rain. (1992: 137)

In the work of Elizabeth Grosz there is a conception of the body similar to the extended and polymorphous body first touched in aesthesis. The body, she argues, is a 'receptive surface' and as such:

> ... its boundaries and zones are constituted in conjunctions and through linkages with other surfaces and planes: the lips connected with the breast in orality, possibly accompanied by the hand in conjunction with an ear, each system in perpetual motion and interrelation with the other; toes in connection with sand. ... These linkages are assemblages that harness and produce the body as a surface of interchangeable and substitutable elements. (Grosz, 1995: 34)

This is very similar to Lyotard's discussion of the libidinal body which, unlike the organic body, is not simply a volume in Euclidean space. This body has no limits because various things such as books, food, images, as well as words, machines and even sounds can be charged with libidinal investment and therefore become areas of the body.

While 'Prescription' is not concerned with desire but with the priority of aesthesis, the libidinal body does bear a resemblance to the extended body of sensibility. Lyotard is right to call this aesthesis, this raw sensibility, a 'touch', as if joining. Both the referential and the voluminous-organic body are effects of discursive inscription, yet there remains a bodily mode otherwise to the law, representation and discourse. When I lie under the sky, my space is that which discourses of materiality and spatial organization delimit, this is the voluminous body. When I lie under the sky I do it at certain times dictated by discourses of work and leisure, and the amount of my skin exposed is determined by class, gender, history and ecology. The presentation of my body, how I lie there, to what extent and in what style it is clothed, are discursive practices. My body is completely inscribed and textualized – *and yet my hand touches the grass and the sun touches my face.*

This bodily mode of exposure, then, does not come 'before' the law as conceptual and discursive organization, but must be conceived as co-present and incommensurate. It is not the inside and outside of mind and matter, law and body, but the figure of heterogeneity, ever present. Although it shares features with the polymorphous and libidinal body, it is not simply a question of the extension and investment of spatial organization, it is rather a condition of primordial receptivity. Not tied to a beginning, it is a continual affinity in the multiple advent of sensibility.

Because this figure of sensible presence cannot be accounted for, it is precisely what the law must repress and forget in order to maintain itself, for, as was mentioned earlier, it is an opening to a freedom that is not part of the law's jurisdiction. If the bodily mode of aesthesis is understood in terms of an exposure to events, to the 'touch' of sensibility that is different every time, it is precisely the project of discursive practices, driven by the ends of accountability and the optimizing of performance, to eradicate these moments that might disrupt an otherwise secure realm of intelligibility. It is also the point at which a consideration of aesthesis becomes implicated in a politics and an ethics that bears witness to the indeterminate which must always be removed for the closed interiority of a discursive system (be that technical or political) to function. And it is in this manner that I wish to consider the VHP.

Representing the Body

In its representation of the body of a 39-year-old convicted murderer named Joseph Jernigan, who had donated his body to science before being executed by lethal injection in Texas,[6] the VHP reproduces not a 'complete' body as it would have us believe, but the body as perceived by the particular discourse of which it is a product. In this techno-medical re-creation of the body (by using the prefix 'techno' I follow Lyotard's lead in describing the procedures of technological performativity designed to produce the increased efficiency and effectiveness of a system) cruor and blood-letting are a strong feature. What is curious about first gaining access to the VHP, particularly the 'animated trip through Visible Human male cryosections' [at http: //www.nlm.nih.gov/research/visible/visible_gallery. html], is that the view appears upside down. The slab on which Jernigan lies is at the top of the screen, with Jernigan hanging from it as if, in Kafka's words, 'the apparatus' has done with him and 'the bed' has turned in order to cast him into the pit. He has been inscribed, 'the apparatus' has done its job, but he is somehow interminably suspended over the pit. This sense of suspense is heightened by the cruor which is exposed in each slice of the criminal body; the blood does not run from the wound and the cruor does not pass. It is rather displayed like cuts of meat; signifying the complete domination of techno-science over the body; a cruor without end.

This sense of Jernigan being displayed is very significant for it is the public display of the law that facilitates the comparison between the National Library of Medicine's representation and Kafka's. In the VHP the criminal does not experience the inscription but in the latter it is precisely the experience of the inscription that draws the reader into the pain and cruelty of its execution. Pain, however, is only one aspect of Kafka's story, for in many respects the story is more concerned with the wonders of 'the apparatus' and the majesty of the law it serves. The cruelty is derived from a primary concern to ensure that the traveller sees the intricate workings of the process of inscription. Indeed the execution is a public affair, it is a time (or there was a time) when the valley was full of spectators 'standing on tiptoe right up to the top of the slopes' and 'every high official was required to attend' (Kafka, 1992: 140). But, as I mentioned in the introduction, while I am not suggesting that the VHP has its analogue in 'In the Penal Colony', I do suggest that it is the *demonstration* of the law as techno-scientific or juridical inscription that is, literally, the significant moment of each narrative. Both representations reinforce the submission of the body to the law.

Each time the VHP animation is downloaded, the violent force of techno-scientific inscription is given for all to see. What is so revolutionary about the VHP is not simply the digital reconstruction of the body but that the 'atlas' leaves no tube, passage, vein, fibre, sinew, muscle or cavity of the body hidden, there is nothing which it cannot present. Due to the sheer number of scans completed, the body and each of its component parts can be reconstructed, rotated in three dimensions and analysed from every conceivable angle. The project is so impressed that this is a 'complete' model of a real body that it loses sight of the fact that it is simply the materialization of a discursive ideal. This extreme modificatory practice, rather than reproducing a 'complete' body, has produced a representation whereby the body has been reduced to causes, effects, inputs, outputs, volumes, connections, components and information, while physically it has been converted into the following:

The MRI images are 256 pixel by 256 resolution. Each pixel has 12 bits of grey tone resolution. The CT data consists of axial CT scans of the entire body taken at 1mm intervals at a resolution of 512 pixels by 512 pixels where each pixel is made up of 12 bits of grey tone. The axial anatomical images are 2048 pixels by 1216 pixels where each pixel is defined by 24 bits of colour, about 7.5 megabytes. (US National Library of Medicine, 1997: 1)

To return briefly to Judith Butler's critique, which suggests that 'there is no reference to a pure body which is not at the same time a further formation of the body' (Butler, 1993: 10), the metaphysics of the VHP is its citation and reproduction of a certain configuration of the body, not only as a complex machine, but as the enclosed volume we call the organic body. However, in these 'scans of the entire body' of a 'complete, normal' and 'representative male', there is no sanguis; no life. This, of course, does not concern the techno-scientific law, after all, its procedures can return a form of life to the body. I say a 'form of life', for life here is still determined by the ends of the techno-scientific and techno-medical discourse of which it is part. These techniques can reanimate the body and rebirth it, but can life be reduced to a simple reconstruction of motility? Clearly not.[7]

With regard to the differend silenced in the VHP, the body is judged according to the rule of one specific discourse of bodily inscription, namely the techno-scientific, to the omission of other possible discourses. But most importantly for this article, it completely denies the non-inscribed bodily mode of an exposure to sensible presence. The VHP does not, and cannot, recreate this bodily mode, instead it represents the body as the materialization of a techno-scientific ideal. The body's death is no obstacle to its reanimation in the likeness of techno-scientific law. And this is my difficulty with the VHP in its confusion of a 'complete' body with an *anatomically* complete body. It seeks to make this ideal present (re-presented and fully rendered) while silencing the presence of aesthesis which, as a means of access to singularities, threatens both the universalism and determinism of such a discourse.

Concluding Remarks

While a study of aesthesis cannot be concluded in a short article such as this, certain things can be highlighted in order to reiterate what is at stake. What I have shown is that the body might be understood as incommensurate to the law if it is understood in terms of the 'infancy' of aesthesis which does not assume a fundamental or 'natural' body external to the law and discourse, but a mode of openness otherwise to this realm. As a consequence a wrong is instituted each time the law is inscribed upon the body and this first 'touch' of aesthesis effaced. However, as aesthesis is a continuing potentiality of the body, offering the possibility of another freedom, the body is constantly managed and organized in order that the law might police the possibility of such a 'sinful peregrination'. The VHP is an example of such a policing, and is announced as a breakthrough precisely because it allows no fold, no layer, no depth in which such a peregrination might secrete itself.

In Kafka's novel *The Trial* (1994), the proper name Joseph K. came to stand for the anonymous force of juridical law. Perhaps the proper name of Joseph J. will come to signify the anonymous domination of techno-scientific law. The bodily mode of exposure, which techno-science can neither contain nor render intelligible, brings this law up against its limits and disturbs its claim to a complete knowledge of the body. The voluminous-organic body might be captured but not the bodily mode of aesthesis, instead, through inscription, aesthesis is subsumed within the law's aesthetic. What is written over in the operation of bodily inscription, is the double 'touch' of aesthesis, as the irredudicible occurrences of sensory events and the free conformity to the sensible field. This is not technophobia but a challenge to the technophilia which, ordered by the logic of performativity, is one more instance of the silencing of indeterminacy.

The particularity of each body and its consequent antagonism to the universal and determinate realm of law was mentioned earlier in relation to Elizabeth Grosz's theorizing of the body, and the consideration of aesthesis outlined here develops this antagonism. If indeterminacy threatens the determinate world of conceptual and discursive organization, ordered and maintained by the rules of particular communities and practices, then the 'being-there' of aesthesis, the condition of openness as the source of material for reflection and the creation of new rules, needs to be refused if the determinate is to maintain itself. It is not simply the body in its singularity, but the body as open to singularities that disturbs the realm of law. In its exposure it is not only open to an other freedom in the irreducible vitality of sanguis, but is also the source of feelings which provoke reflective experimentation in representation and thought. This, clearly, goes beyond the maintenance of the techno-scientific or techno-medical discourse evident in the VHP. However, taken as an analogy, the VHP symbolizes the general domination of models organized by the ends of optimum performance which increasingly legitimize research in all fields. As such it is important to bear witness to this differend and to this wrong, and to remain questioned by the indeterminacy of aesthesis.

Notes

Thank you to the anonymous referees for their advice, the editors for requesting more revisions, and especially to Sigal Gooldin for her careful reading and encouragement.

1. This is how one might read the *Akedah*, Genesis 22 and 23. For many Judaic commentators the story of the binding of Isaac is significant not because God commanded Abraham to kill his only son,

but because God intervenes to prevent the sacrifice. The story proscribes murder in order to separate the Jewish people from the barbarous ritual of child sacrifice, which many neighbouring tribes practised at the time.

2. I am using an etymology deployed by Lacan when discussing the alienation and engendering of the subject. 'Separare, to separate – I would point out at once the equivocation of the se parare, in all the fluctuating meanings it has in French. It means not only to dress oneself, but also to defend oneself, to provide oneself with what one needs to be on one's guard, and I will go further still ... to the se parare, the s'engendrer, the to be engendered, which is involved here' (Lacan, 1977: 214).

3. Whether the law is socio-political, juridical or (and especially) moral, this violence is highly disturbing for Lyotard. In the 1970s he tried to think the bodily without the law, but found that the proposition that libidinal intensities should be released without any regulation, might itself lead to all manner of violence and terror. To this extent Lyotard has been trying to think a regulatory Idea of justice that maintains the law while bearing witness to the differend between it and the body. To this effect 'Prescription' sets out this difficulty.

4. In a discussion of the limits of cognition, Kant (1951) argues that there are concepts of the understanding for which there exist corresponding objects, intuitions of which can be directly presented to the mind. However, there are also concepts, or Ideas of reason, for which there are no objects and for which intuitions can only be indirectly presented to the mind, via the imagination which must provide an intuition that symbolically corresponds with the concept.

5. In Heidegger and "the jews" (1990), Lyotard talks of the moral Law in terms of an immemorial obligation, or debt, prior to the constitution of a subject with the capacity to think its freedom.

6. It is possible to make much of this seeming reversal of the procedures inscription/injection, injection/inscription but this ascribes too much weight to the function of the injection in Kafka's story. Execution is carried out by the inscription of the crime on the body over a period of 12 hours, the puncturing of the head by a large metal needle is simply a punctuation that marks the end of that period of time and ensures death in the unlikely event that the prisoner has not already bled to death.

7. An excellent analysis of these quasi-mystical and regenerative narratives can be found in Catherine Waldby's discussion of what she calls the 'digital Eden' (1997) implicit in the project.

References

Benjamin, Walter (1992) 'The Work of Art in the Age of Mechanical Reproduction', in Illuminations. London: Fontana Press.
Brooks, Peter (1993) Body Work: Objects of Desire in Modern Narrative. Cambridge, MA: Harvard University Press.
Butler, Judith (1993) Bodies that Matter: On the Discursive Limits of 'Sex'. London: Routledge.
Deleuze, Gilles (1994) Difference and Repetition. London: Athlone.
Falk, Pasi (1995) 'Written in the Flesh', Body & Society 1(1): 95–106.
Grosz, Elizabeth (1995) Space, Time and Perversion: Essays on the Politics of Bodies. New York: Routledge.
Josipovici, Gabriel (1996) Touch. New Haven, CT: Yale University Press.
Kafka, Franz (1992) The Transformation and Other Stories. London: Penguin.
Kafka, Franz (1994) The Trial. London: Penguin.
Kant, Immanuel (1951) Critique of Judgement. New York: Hafner Press.
Lacan, Jacques (1977) The Four Fundamental Concepts of Psycho-Analysis. London: Penguin.
Lorensen, Bill (1997) 'Marching Through the Visible Man', hypertext document: http://www.crd.ge.com/esl/cgsp/projects/vm/#thevisibleman
Lyotard, Jean-François (1971) Discours/figure. Collection d'esthétique no. 7. Paris: Klincksieck.

Lyotard, Jean-François (1988a) *The Differend: Phrases in Dispute*. Manchester: Manchester University Press.

Lyotard, Jean-François (1988b) *Peregrinations: Law, Form, Event*. New York: Columbia University Press.

Lyotard, Jean-François (1989) 'Anamnesis of the Visible, or Candour', *The Lyotard Reader*, ed. Andrew Benjamin. Oxford: Blackwell.

Lyotard, Jean-François (1990) *Heidegger and "the jews"*. Minneapolis: University of Minnesota Press.

Lyotard, Jean-François (1992) *The Postmodern Explained to Children*. London: Turnaround.

Lyotard, Jean-François (1993a) *Libidinal Economy*. London: Athlone.

Lyotard, Jean-François (1993b) 'Prescription', *Toward the Postmodern*, ed. R. Harvey and M.S. Roberts. New Jersey/London: Humanities Press.

Lyotard, Jean-François (1993c) *Political Writings*. London: UCL Press.

Lyotard, Jean-François and Gilbert Larochelle (1992) 'That Which Resists: After All', *Philosophy Today* 36(4): 402–17.

Merleau-Ponty, Maurice (1962) *The Phenomenology of Perception*. London: Routledge.

Nietzsche, Friedrich (1956) *The Birth of Tragedy* and *The Genealogy of Morals*. New York: Anchor Books.

Oz, Amos (1988) *Black Box*. London: Vintage.

Readings, Bill (1991) *Introducing Lyotard: Art and Politics*. London: Routledge.

Rogozinski, Jacob (1991) 'Lyotard, Difference, Presence', *L'Esprit Createur* 31(1): 107–21.

US National Library of Medicine (1997) Fact Sheet: The Visible Human Project: http://www.nlm.nih.gov/pubs/factsheets/visiblehuman.html

Waldby, Catherine (1997) 'Revenants: The Visible Human Project and the Digital Uncanny', *Body & Society* 3(1): 1–16.

Winterson, Jeanette (1992) *Written on the Body*. London: Jonathan Cape.

Neal Curtis is Research Fellow in the Department of English and Media Studies at Nottingham Trent University, and is the editorial assistant for *Theory, Culture & Society* and *Body & Society*. His research interests include issues of community, judgement and action.

Creating 'The Perfect Body': A Variable Project

LEE MONAGHAN

Dear friend, you and I are quite likely different in many ways, but there's one thing we definitely have in common – we both want to gain muscle size and strength and build a lean, muscular physique. (Article in a bodybuilding magazine; Phillips, 1997: 10)

My reason for training [with weights] was to obtain what I considered to be the perfect physique, and in my opinion the perfect physique is when you look in the mirror and you see what you want to see, whatever that may be. (Interview extract, Respondent 007)

Heterogeneity, Embodiment and Bodybuilding Ethnophysiology

Several articles in *Body & Society* highlight the significance of bodily display and modification among bodybuilders (Aoki, 1996; St Martin and Gavey, 1996; Wacquant, 1995a). Primarily concerned with the social construction and signification of gender, current work notes how 'bodybuilding' is a social activity which takes the physique (body) and its development (building) as central (similarly, see Gillett and White, 1992; Klein, 1993; Mitchell, 1987). However, the sociology of bodybuilding remains underdeveloped. Couched largely within 'constructivist' frameworks, current work pays scant attention to the *diverse* ways in which bodybuilding as a specific social world is constituted by the embodied agents constituting that world. (Similarly, see Wacquant, 1995b, on boxing.) Correspondingly, precious little is learnt about the phenomenological body which is simultaneously an objective signifier in the social world and a 'lived body' of action, intention and emergent disposition (Turner, 1992).

As a singular (sub)cultural phenomenon, bodybuilding lends itself to various different academic readings or *'outsiders' accounts'* (Widdicombe and Wooffitt,

Body & Society © 1999 SAGE Publications (London, Thousand Oaks and New Delhi),
Vol. 5(2–3): 267–290
[1357–034X(199906/09)5:2–3;267–290;008870]

1995: 139, their emphasis). While 'there are in principle always an indefinite number of theories that fit the facts more or less adequately' (Hesse, 1980: viii), I feel existing readings may be criticized for (among other things) homogenizing the variable project of bodybuilding. Adopting a psychoanalytic stance, Klein states in his ethnography that 'bodybuilding is, at the very least, a subculture whose [male and female] practitioners suffer from large doses of insecurity; hence, compensation through self-presentation of power to the outside world' (1993: 174). Allegedly caused by antecedent personal and/or gender inadequacy and a masculinity-in-crisis within the larger society, bodybuilding represents an 'atavistic' strategy for concealing self-perceived flaws. In particular, the erosion of men's traditional occupationally derived privileges in a post-industrial order prompts some to compensate for their feelings of powerlessness by embodying the physical trappings of 'hegemonic masculinity'. Accordingly, 'the muscular body' becomes synonymous with the culturally idealized masculine/powerful/self-assured body (Klein, 1993: 242).

Muscle-building may be linked not only to gender anxieties, but also to ontological and class insecurity (Wacquant, 1995a), the constitution of 'docile' bodies through discourse (Foucault, 1980), and a culture of narcissism (Lasch, 1980). More positively, the unitary act of bodybuilding may be theorized in terms of the reflexivity of the self and a proliferation of 'bodily regimes' in late modernity (Giddens, 1991), or the representational significance of the (homogenized) exercised and dieted fe/male body within postmodernity (Glassner, 1990), consumer culture (Featherstone, 1991) or somatic culture (Wachter, 1984). And, in following Shilling's (1993) extension of Bourdieu's analysis of cultural and embodied capital to the sociology of the body, there is the manner in which sport renders the unfinished object of the human body a social project and bearer of symbolic value (Shilling, 1993: 128).[1]

While existing sociological theory is noteworthy, and may be invoked to explain bodybuilding at various different levels of abstraction, it rarely takes as its starting point the embodied experiences of individuals within their own social worlds (Watson et al., 1995). Using qualitative data obtained from ethnography, depth semi-structured interviews and secondary sources, this article helps redress the disembodied nature of the sociology of the body in general (Scott and Morgan, 1993; Wacquant, 1995b), and the sociology of bodybuilding in particular. Employing an interpretive sociological perspective, it considers male[2] bodybuilders' shared 'in-order-to motive' (Schutz, 1967). While many different, overlapping and often contradictory reasons *may* be invoked for the (sub)cultural phenomenon of bodybuilding and individual predilections for accruing muscle, what is certain is that all bodybuilders are united in the ongoing project of enhancing bodily aesthetics. In short, bodybuilding is undertaken by embodied social agents – within a carnal version of what Bourdieu (1984, 1992a, 1992b) would term the 'habitus' (Crossley, 1995: 56) – 'in-order-to' create 'the perfect body'.

If the body is the point at which all muscle enthusiasts converge, then this is also their point of departure. Building a lean muscular body is a project which unifies bodybuilders (Phillips, 1997), but also a source of contrast given many different visions of physical perfection. In this highly individualized domain, 'bodybuilder' (a less than satisfactory referent according to some members) is a heterogeneous category. Participants may even set their own muscle agenda independent of the dynamic and frequently contested 'objective' criteria dictated by their various different competition federations. (Similarly, see Guthrie and Castelnuovo, 1992: 406, on female bodybuilding.) Conceptions of 'physical perfection' are spatially and temporally contingent, varying from one individual to the next and also for the same individual during the course of their bodybuilding career.

This article argues that, at least for 'hard-core' (i.e. dedicated) bodybuilders (Mansfield and McGinn, 1993), conceptions of 'the perfect body' are dependent upon a subculturally informed 'ethnophysiological' (Manning and Fabrega, 1973: 257) appreciation of 'excessive' muscularity. Grounded in data (Glaser and Strauss, 1967), this article 'grapples with theoretical issues' (Frank, 1995: 187) by questioning the critical feminist claim that bodybuilding is a 'knee-jerk' response to psychosocial forces and a wish to embody hegemonic masculinity. Stigmatized rather than idealized by the mainstream public, 1990s physique bodybuilding (at least at regional and national level competitions and beyond) is analogous with various non-Western ethnophysiological practices, e.g. neck-stretching, cranial deformation, ornamentation of the earlobes and insertion of lip discs (see Brain, 1979; Polhemus, 1978). Shaping members' socially acquired 'ways of looking', bodybuilding ethnophysiology also enables subcultural aesthetes to differentiate and evaluate different bodies and parts of bodies, as well as providing a knowledge of what is required to achieve a certain body type (e.g. ascetic training and dietetic regimens, drug-taking). Correspondingly, bodybuilders' learnt ways of looking *at* bodies informs *their* decision to approximate the look of a particular soma type and thus *their willingness* to commit themselves to bodybuilding over time.

Becoming and remaining a bodybuilder, it will be argued, is only possible if the individual has arrived at a conception of the meaning of the activity and perceptions and judgements of types of muscular body which make ongoing physical development possible and desirable (similarly, see Becker, 1953). In discussing the importance of acquired ethnophysiology in the *transmogrification* of the physical body, a critique is levelled not only against feminist analyses (Gillett and White, 1992; Klein, 1993; White and Gillett, 1994), but also other critical work on this topic (e.g. Day, 1990). In short, it highlights the limitations and blind spots of existing approaches which treat 'bodybuilder' as a singular category, and which explain bodybuilding in terms of the dual interplay of the masculinist imagery of 'the muscular body' and antecedent sociocultural forces perceived to be beyond individual control (Gillett and White, 1992: 366).

Viewed through the lens of social phenomenology and symbolic interactionism, motives and dispositions (not *predispositions*) for bodybuilding emerge during the course of the individual's experience. Ongoing practical involvement in the bodybuilding habitus in time produces motivations for accruing 'excessive' muscularity (the *sine qua non* of the dedicated bodybuilder) rather than the other way round. Vague impulses and desires – in this case, most frequently a wish to 'tone up' and look athletic, fit, young and sexually attractive (see Monaghan et al., 1998) – are transformed into definite patterns of action through the subcultural interpretation or 'artistic deciphering' (Bourdieu et al., 1991) of what non-participants consider a homogeneous entity. This argument, which recognizes the body is social and the social is embodied (Crossley, 1995), is advanced by pluralizing 'the muscular body' and highlighting the importance of social process.

Methods and Epistemology

The study is based on seven years participant observation which enabled me to submit my personality, social situation and, most importantly, my body, to the set of contingencies that play upon individuals comprising the bodybuilding collectivity. (See Goffman, 1989: 125, on the importance of this in ethnography.) However, while my hermeneutic understandings of bodybuilding are derived from participation in gym culture (and collecting data from various other indigenous media, including bodybuilding magazines and published insider accounts), most of the materials presented here were generated during an Economic and Social Research Council funded project on bodybuilding, steroids and violence (see Bloor et al., 1998). Based in South Wales, a two-year project (1994 to 1996) was conducted embracing ethnography and semi-structured depth interviews. Given critical feminist arguments on bodybuilding, the study's geographic location is noteworthy. According to Harris (1987), mining and steel production have been powerful determinants of masculinity and gender relations in South Wales. In the past two decades this part of Britain has experienced a shrinking manufacturing base, a diminution of traditional male working patterns of employment and a marginal, though socially significant, increase in the employment opportunities for women (Cooke, 1987).

Pilot work was undertaken at a range of different possible fieldwork sites in 12 towns located across South Wales (15 gyms, 12 leisure centres, 3 needle exchanges and a 'Well Steroid User Clinic'). After gauging the suitability of various sites, the ethnography was anchored in four 'hard-core' bodybuilding gyms on a time-sampling basis (see Mansfield and McGinn, 1993, on types of gym). In obtaining a theoretically representative sample – which is necessary in the generation of theory and a wider understanding of social processes (Glaser and Strauss, 1967) – a range of bodybuilders and weight trainers[3] (67 in total) were formally interviewed. Most were recruited through ethnographic contacts, though others were contacted including a group of men who worked out with weights in a prison. Posters were also placed in three needle exchange facilities, and an advertisement was featured in two issues of *Bodybuilding Monthly*. All the interviews were audio recorded and transcribed. Transcripts and ethnographic field notes were then indexed using coding software: 'Ethnograph' (Seidel and Clark, 1984). This facilitated systematic data analysis, developing analytical propositions which apply to the entire universe of data carrying particular indexed codes. This approach is variously termed 'analytic induction' or 'deviant case analysis' (Bloor, 1978).

With respect to epistemology, there are clearly various ways of approaching members' accounts. If viewed as a topic of analysis rather than a resource in research, much can be made of members' talk as 'situated narratives' where participants produce demonstrably 'morally adequate' accounts (Silverman, 1993: 110). Certainly, viewing bodybuilders' accounts as displays of perspectives or moral forms (Silverman, 1993: 107) enables us to appreciate the enormous amount of complex 'identity work' members engage in when eschewing negative stereotypes (Monaghan, 1997). However, while recognizing that accounts cannot be read as literal descriptions of an external reality, by adopting a position of 'subtle' as opposed to 'naive' realism (Hammersley, 1992), I am still concerned with obtaining information about social worlds. In seeking to contribute knowledge that can be beneficial in expanding understanding, I share Miller and Glassner's (1997) conviction that researchers may tap into, explore and learn about social realities outside of any particular interview situation engaged in by the researcher. This, I feel, does not undermine the value of other approaches since 'perspective' and 'information' analyses occupy a complementary role in ethnographic research (Hammersley and Atkinson, 1995: 126).

Pluralizing 'The Muscular Body' or 'Ways of Looking'

In critically engaging a particular strand of feminist literature (Gillett and White, 1992; Klein, 1993; White and Gillett, 1994), a caveat is required. Documenting bodybuilding ethnophysiology and members' heterogeneous body-projects does not, by itself, place a question mark against existing knowledge claims. The following could merely be taken to suggest that academics should be more sensitive to differences in the bodybuilding community. However, if the types of muscular bodies to which 1990s bodybuilders (not weight-trainers) orient themselves are not culturally prescribed but are instead stigmatized, then bodybuilding cannot be theorized adequately in terms of an antecedent culturally endorsed image, i.e. 'the muscular (masculine) body'. Of course, a general masculine will-to-be-muscular may figure in the genesis of body-work, but then again it may not (Glassner, 1990). In accounting for the ongoing variable project of bodybuilding, I feel a more satisfactory account – which is attentive to the diversity of members' meanings – must recognize that in the sport and art[4] of bodybuilding, 'aesthetic pleasure presupposes learning and, in any particular case, learning by habit and *exercise*' (Bourdieu et al., 1991: 109, my emphasis).

In contrast to other types of weight-trainer (see Bednarek, 1985), bodybuilders typically pluralize 'the muscular body'. The individual bodybuilder's desire to emulate or approximate the 'look' *of* a particular soma type is therefore intimately tied to the lived body's socially acquired 'ways of looking' *at* physical bodies. This statement, which differentiates between the body as *Korper* and *Leib* (Turner, 1992), is concordant with Merleau-Ponty's (1962) phenomenology of embodiment. According to Merleau-Ponty the body-subject's primary relation to the environment consists in practical competence. In short, there is a primacy of practical over theoretical or abstract ways of being-in-the-world (Crossley, 1995: 53). Within bodybuilding subculture, members' practical purposes at hand render 'the muscular body' (*Korper*) a variegated and thus heterogeneous entity rather than an undifferentiated object which supposedly signifies hegemonic masculinity to the outside world. Academic writings on bodybuilding, offering a reading of the singular 'muscular body' at the level of cultural signification, therefore ride roughshod over complex social reality.

Consider the following extract. Various issues and themes emerge, including Soccer's and Al's shared ability to differentiate and evaluate *different types of muscular body*. These 'ethnophysiological' understandings enable bodybuilders to discern between various types of physique which are, for all practical purposes, homogeneous to non-initiates but more or less aesthetically pleasing from their acquired viewpoints:

> Soccer was talking about some of the physiques displayed on posters in the gym reception. There was a picture of Dorian Yates [current professional world champion].
>
> *Soccer*: My friend saw him at a seminar. I think he was about 23 stone. . . . I suppose it's a bit difficult to gauge how big he is from that picture since there's nothing there to put it into scale. I suppose you'd get a good idea if you put Linford Christie there. I mean,

Christie isn't a small man. If he was stood next to that [Dorian] though, he'd be dwarfed.... I wouldn't want to look like that [Dorian]. Then again, I would for a year so I could earn loads of money, get the prestige, give seminars, but I wouldn't be happy with the way I looked. I'd slim down to that after a year [pointing to a picture of a less well-known professional bodybuilder who was not as muscular as Dorian Yates, but who was still extremely muscular by anybody's standards]. More of a natural physique as opposed to that [Dorian]. Obviously that [smaller bodybuilder] isn't natural [i.e. he uses steroids] but it's more pleasing to the eye in my opinion...

Al, the gym owner and competitor of world amateur standard, walked in.

Soccer: I was just talking to Lee, saying how I'd prefer to look like that [smaller bodybuilder] than that [Dorian]. At least with this physique [smaller bodybuilder] you could still wear clothes and not look fucking ridiculous [in your day-to-day interactions with the public]. I'd like to be more like him there, Bob Paris. He's very symmetrical, not a lump like Dorian Yates.... Paris has got a good physique, not massive [by today's competition standards] but very symmetrical.

Al: Yeah, in the Mr Olympia in the 1980s when he competed it was said he was gonna be the new face of bodybuilding.

Al went on to talk about the issue of size in bodybuilding:

Al: No doubt, Dorian Yates is the best there is, but for me bodybuilding is not about getting as big as you can get. I'm not a big guy anyway. Then again, because of my height [he's 5' 6"] I'd look like a wardrobe if I was carrying a load of mass. I create the illusion that I'm big on stage though. Bodybuilding is all about illusion. Sculpting your body, carving out a shape which looks impressive but which, in reality, isn't that big. (Field-diary extract, 24/2/95: Al's Gym)

As well as rejecting the idea that sheer size is the primary goal of bodybuilding (see Klein, 1993: 246), the national physique champion quoted below also pluralized 'the muscular body'. And, given sensitivity to the objective attitudes of generalized others (Mead, 1934) viz. the mainstream public's disparagement, this narrator attempted to reconcile competing definitions of 'the body beautiful':

I've never actually seen Dorian Yates in the flesh but I think, to be honest, I don't think the [name of bodybuilding entrepreneurs] are realizing the image they're putting on bodybuilding and the way that they're starting to frighten the public off. If they had somebody like sort of Flex Wheeler who has a nice shape and had him as a winner of [name of professional competition]. He had nice genetics [natural predisposition to accruing muscle] before he started, you know, and a lovely shape. You know, like Shawn Ray as well. He enters [competitions] at about 14 stone. And then you've got Dorian Yates who enters at like 20 stone and he walks on stage and scares the shit out of everybody! ... I think a classic physique is like Francis Benfatto, the French one. There's superb quality. He'll enter at about 13 stone and he had beautiful genetics and yet he wouldn't get a look in [rank highly in the competitions]. It's got to be like this mass of muscle, flesh and veins, you know, nothing beautiful about it like. It's just basically like a big fuck-off body like! And the [name of bodybuilding entrepreneurs] who've brought bodybuilding into the public eye over the last say, 40 years, have turned round and spoilt it all by doing this now. Like with Arnold Schwarzenegger, everybody accepted that he was sort of big ... but bloody Dorian Yates [is absolutely massive]. You get Dorian Yates and you're talking holy shit! It's like seeing two lots of Shawn Ray! (Interview extract, Respondent 018)

Sam Fussell's bodybuilding narrative (1991: 102–4) similarly highlights the heterogeneity of bodybuilders' body-projects ('muscular bodies') and variable subcultural perceptions. Not only does the protagonist refer to different types of muscular body, this member's specific value-orientation means that from his perspective *'Mass'* (i.e. sheer size) is prioritized over *'Class'* (i.e. typically smaller, more 'elegant' and defined musculature). At a time when the championship standard male physique veered towards the chiselled or cut look, this man was not happy:

> 'Now, you look at these shrunken poodles that pass for Mr Universe these days', he [Macon] said, showing me a well-thumbed magazine with a particularly emaciated specimen in green posing trunks on its cover . . . 'I'll tell you somethin': You just give me one of them starvin' Biafrans, and I'll show you muscle striations. I mean have you seen the abs and intercostals on some of them guys? . . .' Macon continued. 'It's just like I told you yesterday son, these things go in cycles. All you got to do is open a book and examine history. Now, son, the late 1960s and early 1970s were a time when size ruled, with them Arnold and Serge Olivas and Lou Ferrignos. Then – kind of like what the good book says – a darkness fell over the land, 'cause the mid-1970s came and those Frank Zanes and sunken-cheeked foreigners ruled the stage. I mean, why would anybody in their right mind pay to see some guy with a Chippendale's physique? But now, thanks to Lee Haney, we might be coming back to good times, Arnold times. . .'

For the iron cognoscenti, particular bodies displayed by specific individuals (e.g. Frank Zane, Lee Haney), or more generalized figures of popular culture (e.g. 'the Chippendales'), are of one ethnophysiological type or another. Such categorization or typification entails (among other things) an acquired knowledge of the properties of body parts and somatic features. In focusing upon various physical characteristics, participants talk about *'Abs'*, *'Intercostals'*, *'Quads'*, *'Lats'*, *'Muscle Striations'*, *'Symmetry'*, *'Mass'*, *'Vascularity'*, etc. Foucault's analysis of the 'disciplining' of bodies, and the significance of technologies of power in the institutional elaboration of (gendered) bodily practices, could be considered particularly relevant in this sporting context (cf. Connell, 1987: 49–50). However, the important (compatible and complementary) point being made here is that these indigenous terms – employed by the 'pictorially competent' (Bourdieu et al., 1991) when looking *at* muscular bodies – are meaningful to members but foreign to out-groups (cf. Aoki, 1996: 60).

In distinguishing between different bodies and parts of bodies, participants describe the features of various physiques displayed at bodybuilding competitions, in the gyms, magazines, etc. During interactions with significant others, neophytes also arrive at an acquired appreciation of types of muscular body in terms of their overall visual impact. In short, they learn to define different types of muscular body exhibited by contemporaries and predecessors as more or less aesthetically pleasing.[5] As might be anticipated from Crossley's (1995) extension of Bordieu's (1984, 1992a, 1992b) concept of the habitus to a 'carnal sociology of the body', types of muscular body *may* then be consciously set as projects for the self. The bodybuilding habitus effectively becomes 'the basis of choice [and] a structure of preferences' (Crossley, 1995: 56). These choices are, however, made within limits of practicability (Schutz, 1967: 73). Experienced gym members claim that types of bodybuilding physique – though shaped by training, diet and (often) drug-taking – are ultimately dependent upon genetics.[6] If every*body* is different, the look an individual bodybuilder is able to achieve will always be an approximation of any idealized image selected from the plethora of bodies mediately and immediately displayed:

> You look at bodybuilders in magazines and I think I wouldn't mind having a body like that, but then every body type is different so it's really hard to picture yourself what you're going to look like. I suppose everyone does sort of picture what they'd like to look like, but what you'd like to look like and what you do look like is completely different. (Interview extract, Respondent 042)

> I want to look like this, you know, him. Or, yeah, I want to be like that. But you've no idea how it's going to turn out. It never turns out the way you think it's going to turn out. Unless you're progressing through bodybuilding, you don't tend to realize this. Each bodybuilder is an individual. You know? (Interview extract, Respondent 029)

Clearly, each bodybuilder is an individual. Contrary to the common assumption in subcultural analyses, participation does not entail a transitory loss of self or individuality (see Widdicombe and Wooffitt, 1995: 139). Rather, as noted among bodybuilding ethnopharmacologists, 'individuality' is championed (Bloor et al., 1998). Of course, the heterogeneity implied by this individuality does not obviate shared meaning; it is possible to clarify what is meant by 'the muscular body' among bodybuilders. Here reference should be made to Table 1. This typology of different male muscular bodies includes the names of specific figures or individuals exemplifying particular soma types (including types of muscular bodies which differ from bodybuilding physiques and against which bodybuilders contrast and thus define themselves). The typology not only highlights the limitations of critical feminist work on bodybuilding, but also other academic readings where it is claimed bodybuilding emphasizes one ideal body type and exhibits a trend towards uniformity and sameness (Day, 1990: 50–1).

Cultural analysts, who typically view the body as a target and object, or 'effect', of discourse (Wacquant, 1995a: 173), would perhaps consider these category differences irrelevant. While significant for participants, cannot the whole panoply of types have the same, or similar social psychological underpinnings (just as, say, bulimia and anorexia may have similar psychosocial determinants)? Certainly,

Table 1 A Typology of Male Muscular Bodies

1. Competition Standard Bodybuilding Physiques (Sizeably Muscular and Exceptionally Lean):
    Ripped, Awesome Mass Monster (e.g. Dorian Yates)
    Ripped, Extremely Vascular Mass Monster (e.g. Paul Dillett)
    Ripped, Massive and Classy (e.g. Kevin Levrone)
    Ultra Ripped/Cut/Striated and Big (e.g. Andreas Muntzer)
    Class with Perfect Symmetry (e.g. Bob Paris, Shawn Ray, Flex Wheeler)
    Class from the Past (e.g. Frank Zane)
    Mass from the Past (e.g. Arnold Schwarzenegger)

2. Powerful-Looking Bodies (Sizeably Muscular but Lacking Definition)
    Smooth-Looking Physique Competitors in the Off-Season
    Strength Athletes, e.g. Power-Lifters, Olympic Weight-Lifters, *World's Strongest Man*
    Competitors, Wrestlers or Rugby Players

3. Athletically Muscular/Toned Bodies (Moderately Muscular and Typically Fairly Lean):
    Natural or Non-Drug Enhanced Competition Bodybuilders
    Champion Bodybuilders in the 1950s
    Neophyte Bodybuilders
    Fitness-Oriented Weight-Trainers
    The Sprinter (e.g. Linford Christie) or the Chippendale
    The Long-Distance Runner or the Swimmer
    Olympic Gymnast
    Naturally Lean Men

body-work could be considered the 'psychopathological' crystallization of culture, where bodies are constrained and trained in docility and obedience (Bordo, 1993). However, such theorizing must presuppose some notion of a body-subject and communicative intersubjectivity which is facilitated through symbolic processes (Crossley, 1996: 110). Phenomenologically speaking, the body is not simply an object in the social world but 'a sentient being whose primary relation to its environment should be understood in terms of this meaningful sentience' (Crossley, 1995: 47). If the body's being-in-the-world is mediated through perceptual meaning, and meanings are subject to re-definitions, re-locations and re-alignments (Blumer, 1969), social theorists should concern themselves with the concrete practices through which real bodies are produced. Bodybuilders, it would seem, are not 'cultural dopes' (Garfinkel, 1967) whose actions are 'caused' in a mechanical way by an external force (though they could, in 'bad faith' [Sartre, 1958], view themselves and others as determined objects through a retrospective glance). Rather, they are embodied social agents who are communicative, practical and intelligent beings, drawing upon a common habitus (Shilling, 1993: 129) which is amenable to sociological study (Crossley, 1995: 60–1).

Contrary to theories explaining bodybuilding in terms of the masculinist imagery of 'the muscular body' and psychosocial forces perceived to be beyond individual control, the following considers the importance of social process and acquired ethnophysiology in the creation and re-creation of 'Sizeably Muscular and Exceptionally Lean Bodybuilding Physiques'.

The Importance of Social Process

Various contributors assert the agency of bodies in social processes (Connell, 1995; Gatens, 1996), arguing for a theoretical position in which bodies are seen as sharing in social agency, in generating and shaping courses of conduct (Watson, 1998: 177). My ethnographic observations strongly suggest that bodybuilders' ways of looking at bodies, rendering ongoing muscular enhancement possible and desirable, are acquired over time in the bodybuilding habitus. Social process and subcultural affiliation are therefore important. In claiming that bodybuilders *qua* social agents possess a subculturally learnt system of cognitive and motivating structures (Shilling, 1993), the following notes the extent to which their 'indigenous' perceptions contrast with non-members' (and marginal members') ethnocentric evaluations.

Divided into two, the first subsection highlights the significance of social process when arriving at a conception of 'physical perfection' which is stigmatizing in non-participants' eyes. It shows that bodybuilding and mainstream evaluations of bodily perfection digress, and that 'extreme' muscularity is denigrated outside the subculture (Aoki, 1996: 67). Since muscles are typically equated with masculinity, this issue is well documented for female physique bodybuilders who transgress the sex/gender system (e.g. Bolin, 1992; Mansfield and McGinn, 1993; Schulze, 1990). However, male bodybuilders may also transcend normative (i.e. widely accepted) limits to the extent that they evoke feelings of repulsion and disgust (St Martin and Gavey, 1996: 47). Consequently, since the *types of* 'muscular body' to which 'hard-core' bodybuilders orient themselves and the types of 'muscular body' tolerated by non-participants are different, commitment to the subculture entails a social process of becoming. During this process the individual learns to define 'Sizeably Muscular and Exceptionally Lean Bodybuilding Physiques' as aesthetically pleasing.

This aspect of bodybuilding ethnophysiology is less important for individuals striving to create 'Moderately Muscular and Typically Fairly Lean Bodies'. Following the 1980s fitness boom, these 'Athletically Muscular/Toned Bodies' are widely endorsed outside bodybuilding subculture (see Glassner, 1990, on the representational significance of the ·fit-looking' body). While social process therefore seems unimportant, this does not invalidate the general argument for two main reasons.

First, the exercised and dieted body is prescribed and valorized within our larger society *only up to a certain point*. As muscle mass increases and body-fat decreases, the more outlandish it becomes and thus (depending upon the individual's previous contact with bodybuilding subculture) the greater the significance of acquiring an appreciation. Second, bodybuilding ethnophysiology entails more than simply admiring the superficiality of the specular body. In shaping members' perceptions, this schema provides an understanding of the ascetic commitment necessary to accrue substantial muscularity. In accord with the *Protestant Ethic and the Spirit of Capitalism* (Weber, 1976), this quasi-religious awareness renders types of bodybuilding physique more or less impressive to subcultural aesthetes.

After establishing that indigenous and non-bodybuilding conceptions of physical perfection digress (at some juncture), the process of *acquiring an ethnophysiological appreciation* is underscored. Since favourable perceptions of the 'abnormal, extreme and unattractive bodybuilding body' (Aoki, 1996: 67) are temporally contingent and are learnt in the subcultural context, individual commitment to bodybuilding (as opposed to weight-training) *could* be independent of antecedent predispositions, viz. a masculinity-in-crisis within the larger society, feelings of inadequacy and a wish to embody hegemonic masculinity.

Finally, bodybuilders – who are both in and of the larger society – recognize 'Sizeably Muscular Bodies' may be the focus of 'incivil attention' (Smith, 1997). Although participants learn to view 'outlandish' bodies as more or less 'impressive', sensitivity to actual or potential negativity may check their wish to attain or maintain 'excessive' muscularity. This recognition of culturally dominant aesthetic codes is particularly relevant and is broached in both subsections.

From Frog to Impressive Bodybuilding Physiques

Bodybuilding physiques and 'fit-looking' bodies are not radically dissimilar. The former are an extension and exaggeration of the latter. However, while bodybuilders' normative standards interpenetrate with larger societal values, if one sufficiently extends and accentuates any values then at some juncture they must become different values (Taylor et al., 1973: 187). Certainly for the out-group (non-bodybuilders), 'marginal members' (fitness-oriented weight-trainers) and 'bodybuilders' sharing an affinity for body-sculpting as opposed to building, the aesthetic criteria of 'successful' physique bodybuilding are different from their own. One trainer interested in 'body-sculpting', for example, told me that the accomplished bodybuilder's physique (understood here as a singular concept) is not aesthetically pleasing from his perspective:

> *Noel*: If you take the bodybuilding too far you can look like a frog, and who wants to look like a frog?
> *LM*: What do you mean, 'a frog'?
> *Noel*: Mmmm, well, if you can imagine getting hold of a frog by its front legs and holding it up, and looking at it from behind. You've got the big back like the bodybuilder spreading his lats [latissimus dorsi], the small waist and the big thighs. (Field-diary extract, 27/8/94)

While interviewing Noel I asked him to elaborate this remark after he claimed it is possible to become 'too muscular'. The extract is noteworthy for three main reasons. First, it highlights how social process renders many gym members willing and able to accrue 'excessive' muscularity. Second, it suggests that perceptions of muscular bodies are relative and context bound. And, third, the unflattering similes employed to describe the type of physique displayed by accomplished male bodybuilders are particularly colourful and are indicative of his value-orientation:

> *003*: That's where you've gone to the extreme. I mean, once they've got to that size it's competition within the gym. They go into it to be bigger than the next bodybuilder next to them, as much or more than him ... and before they know it with the years of bodybuilding they've increased and the comparison in the gym is not as great [i.e. the differences between the levels of muscularity are subtle in this context as judged by non-bodybuilders] because they're all the same size and they're competing to get bigger all the time. They're feeling good in that gym: 'Sure I feel great, look good'. When they put their clothes on they're not too bad. When they walk into a pub then, they just know that they're big lads, and it looks good in clothes, big lads. But as soon as it comes to the beach they get a shock I think. I've seen it many a time. They go on to that beach and they look bloody big and all of a sudden they realize that all eyes on them are not swooning ... you can see some girls going 'ugh!' You do see it, 'ugh!' They wouldn't say it to your face, but you know that's what the expressions are on people's faces. You only have to walk past and in the corner of your eye you can see someone going 'ugh!' And that's a typical person who's not got a body like that that says that. At the end of the day that [look] has gone too far and they don't look athletic anymore. You put Linford Christie walking past, and they'll all swoon, and Linford Christie's a fine physique of what a male. . .
> *LM*: The body-beautiful yeah?
> *003*: Yeah, you know, it's muscular, it's lean, it's a tiger isn't it? A puma, compared to a rhinoceros.
> *LM*: So you would compare a bodybuilder to a rhino then? ... I know you've compared them to a frog.
> *003*: A frog or a rhino and Linford Christie is a puma. [003 went on to talk about how height is an intervening variable. For him, tall bodybuilders carry muscle better.] You normally find the average height of a bodybuilder is five foot six, seven, eight ... so they go on to the beach with a physique like bloody that wide as well, they're like an Oxo cube. Do you know what I mean?

What is impressive according to one aesthetic code is not necessarily appealing from another. This point is also evidenced below where indigenous and ethnocentric evaluations are counterbalanced by the same individual. Soccer offered a particularly graphic description of a fellow bodybuilder who was 'probably awesome from a bodybuilding point of view' but who would be considered 'ridiculous' by the mainstream public. While such ambivalence and oscillation of identification are important considerations in relation to stigma and its management (Goffman, 1968: 130), the analogy Soccer draws between non-Western body-modification practices and ethnophysiological perceptions of physical beauty is particularly relevant in the context of this article (similarly, see Brain, 1979):

> Soccer told me about Grim Reaper whom he recently saw in the supermarket.
>
> *Soccer*: He's fucking massive. When I say massive I mean he's taken it to the point where it's fucking ridiculous. He was just a one-man freak show. You know where you can take the bodybuilding to the point where it's not seen as acceptable? Well, he'd taken it one stage beyond that. He couldn't even walk properly, he walked like this [hunching his shoulders up and waddling], like a fucking clockwork toy. If you asked 99 percent of the population what they thought about the way he looked then they'd say ridiculous. He probably thinks he looks attractive but I bet no one else does. Like, you get these African tribes where they put these discs in their mouth and ears. They do that because they think it looks attractive and in their eyes it is. Well, I'd say it was the same with this bloke. He thinks he looks good but he doesn't. I suppose to the average person on the street there's no difference between him and a 30-stone Mr Blobby fat man. If you asked them which they preferred then they'd probably have to flick a coin to decide.
>
> *LM*: It's unusual in that you've trained for years and yet you describe him in this way. I thought that you'd be more likely to say he looked impressive rather than ridiculous.
>
> *Soccer*: Don't get me wrong. From a bodybuilding point of view he's probably awesome. I don't know for sure though as he was fully dressed. He might be bloated [suffering oedema due to excessive steroid use] or he might actually have a very impressive physique. If he took his top off then I might change my mind about how he looked, and I'd be the first to say he's got a good physique. He might look like Dorian Yates with his top off. I don't know. But in clothes, and to the average person on the street he looks fucking stupid. No different than a big fat man. (Field-diary extract, 11/3/95: Olympia Gym)

Despite (or in spite of) their sheer size, bodybuilders may be ridiculed when interacting with 'normals'. The following extract, solicited from an elite physique competitor, is illustrative. It is recognized, of course, that these accounts lend themselves to the type of conversation analysis undertaken by Widdicombe and Wooffitt (1995: 116–36). Similar to punks, bodybuilders do 'being ordinary' (Sacks, 1984; cited by Widdicombe and Wooffit, 1995: 119) when complaining about negative assessments. However, such data also inform us that accomplished bodybuilders – though personally satisfied with their bodies – may use clothing as a technique of information control (Goffman, 1968) in public settings sanctioning partial nudity.

This, in turn, serves as a strategy for deflecting the unappreciative attention of non-participants:

> Al: I am satisfied with the way my body looks, it's just that I don't think other people [the public] appreciate it. They don't appreciate the work that I put into it. OK I've taken steroids – they say 'Yeah, you're a steroid freak.' But they don't realize the work I've also had to put in to develop it. The prime example is, we went to the beach a couple of years back and it was just before I did the [Mr] Universe, and I was in a pair of shorts and there were five young women, if you like, around the 20 mark, four of them reasonable – one of them really, really grossly overweight. She was the one that passed the comment! We were with friends, with family and friends – she made comments loud enough for everybody to hear, that she thought I was grossly-overdeveloped, I looked sick, disgusting, you know. . . . Normally I just shut myself off to it, but now I won't even put a pair of shorts on or whatever. I'll go on the beach and I'll be like this [wearing clothes]. And it's not that I'm not satisfied with my own body, it's the fact that I don't feel I'm appreciated. I think in a lot of people's eyes outside of bodybuilding I'm a bit of a freak.
>
> LM: I'd have thought such a reaction would have been strange today. I mean you have the ideal of what the body should look like – low fat and muscular.
>
> Al: Yeah, I think it's more the athletic type of physique though. Bodybuilding takes the athletic physique one stage further, and for some people that's too freaky. (Field-diary extract, 26/1/95: Al's Gym)

The mesomorph may be a masculinist cultural ideal (Klein, 1993: 242), provided this body-image equals 'Moderately Muscular and Typically Fairly Lean Bodies'. However, the aesthetics of 'Sizeably Muscular and Exceptionally Lean Bodies' must be learnt in the subcultural context if the individual is to 'embrace this profane religion of physicality that is bodybuilding' (Wacquant, 1995a: 163). As stated by Becker (1963: 56): 'what was once frightening and distasteful becomes, after a taste for it is built up, pleasant, desired, and sought after'. Respondent 018, who developed his physique to the extent that it secured him a national title, had the following to say (though as a qualification, while this body-builder *thought* he wanted to display his 'new' body at the beach, this was something he had not yet done):

> Now I've been using a bit of gear [steroids] I know what's going to happen this year. I'll walk on to the beach and they'll go 'Jesus Christ, he's a bodybuilder!' And I never would have got that without steroids, and to be honest, *a lot of people would say 'Well, I really don't want to look like that, I don't want to be like that'*, and in one sense I never used to, but once you start seeing yourself in the mirror and you start seeing the body take shape, you think you can't wait to get down to that bloody beach and rip your top off and say 'Look at this!' (Interview extract, Respondent 018, my emphasis)

Acquiring an Ethnophysiological Appreciation

Undoubtedly the functionality of talk is of important analytic concern: the following excerpts, for example, may be considered 'techniques of neutralization' (Sykes and Matza, 1957) or rhetorical devices which negate the questionable features of bodybuilding (see also Edwards and Potter, 1992, on the rhetorical use of language). However, these accounts – voiced by bodybuilders who had competed at the local level – also inform us about their subcultural perceptions which serve to structure and maintain their 'deviant' activities over time. In short, they highlight what is, in effect, a necessary condition for ongoing muscular enhancement, viz an acquired ethnophysiological appreciation:

> My legs, you put them next to a normal person, and they wouldn't even know what they were. And it's only since I've been a bodybuilder I've realized how different a set of legs can look from a bodybuilder to a normal person. You know, bloody hell, there's nothing to a normal person's legs! I've got tear drops [muscle located on the inside leg just above the knee], I've got splits [separation between muscles], I've got lines everywhere in my legs and it's a hell of a difference, like. You know? (Interview extract, Respondent 043)

> The World's Strongest Man, you can see the different types of muscle mass. I can look at their muscle mass and say 'Yeah, that's for that purpose.' The same with weight-lifters. The same with bodybuilders. You can identify between, you know, different types of muscle mass. Watch The World's Strongest Man. People say 'Oh, he's a big bugger isn't he? Huge, big arms.' But no definition. You know? It's all there for strength and power. We can identify what it's there for and the people who don't train can't. 'Why isn't he a bodybuilder? Look at him, why isn't he?' But we can tell the difference, because we're involved in it. (Interview extract, Respondent 029)

Similarly, consider the following exchange. Again this points towards the temporal nature of social action and the importance of acquired ethnophysiology during the career of the bodybuilder:

> LM: Is this [body] image [which you have in mind and which you aspire to build] any different from the one you initially had when beginning weight-training?
> 004: Oh yes, it has changed. If I was to imagine if I was to look like I do now when I was doing it [in the beginning] I would have probably thought I would have been happy. But you obviously want to get bigger all the time. When I first started off I really didn't know much about body types as I do now. You know? What would be lacking. Things like rear delts, rear delts missing. . . . To the ordinary person they don't really notice. If you see someone who has got a bit of muscle, a big chest you just think he is muscular. They [non-bodybuilders] don't notice a big chest, more shoulder, they don't notice that.

These narrators' self-reflexive awareness that their aesthetic taste has been cultivated in the bodybuilding habitus is unsurprising given mainstream negativity, and is an interesting contrast to Bourdieu et al.'s (1991: 108) claim that 'the love of art is loath to acknowledge its origins'. More importantly, such data support Wacquant's observation that participation in bodybuilding progressively transforms 'the mental and corporeal schemata through which the individual perceives reality and endows it with meaning and value' (1995a: 173). For non-affiliative members perception is increasingly indeterminate and is proportionately related to the social distance between the individual and bodybuilding subculture. In the absence of bodybuilding ethnophysiology, onlookers may mistake muscle for fat. Soccer, whose body-fat composition was measured using skin-fold callipers at around 10 percent, and who was thus not fat by non-body-building standards (see McArdle et al., 1986), said:

> ... my flat mate, Wayne, had arranged to meet these two women opposite the night-club where I was working [as a doorman]. One of the women who passed the night-club said to Wayne 'Was that your mate on the doors, the big fat one?' Wayne goes 'He's on the doors, yeah, but he's not fat, there's not an ounce of fat on him, he's a bodybuilder.' She just said 'Well, he looks fat to me.' ... It's strange but if you don't know what you're looking for I suppose as a body-builder you can look fat to ordinary people. I was on the beach once and there was this body-builder walking along. I overheard two women talking behind me. They said 'Oooow, look at him. Is that muscle or fat?' And the thing is, this bloke had a terrific physique, he wasn't fat at all. (Soccer, in Field-diary extract, 8/10/94: Pumping-Iron Gym)

Although, as indicated above, accomplished (stigmatized) bodybuilders may feel uncomfortable when subjected to the public gaze, it is not contradictory to exhibit the physique in contexts occupied by those who have acquired an ethno-physiological appreciation. Bodybuilding competitions, for example, are social fields where developed bodies are seen to possess symbolic value and are posi-tively acknowledged (see Shilling, 1993: 127):

> 017: I wouldn't go to a swimming baths and things like that, you know, because I didn't want people looking and all that. I used to be covered and you know. . . . I trained to get on well in bodybuilding. . . . I just didn't want to sort of show it off like, only in the right place.
> LM: You didn't want to be *looked* at?
> 017: Yes, I get embarrassed everybody stopping and having a look, and I didn't want all that.
> LM: I suppose on stage when you're competing everyone's still looking at you.
> 017: Yeah, but that's the reason you do it. You do it for that day, for that competition, you want to win that competition, you know, that's your goal isn't it?

Displaying 'excessive' muscularity outside the subculture, and the attendant risk of being subject to breaches of the 'civil inattention' rule (Goffman, 1963), often entails adopting an air of defiance or indifference. Again, several of my informants were aware that muscle read according to acquired ethnophysiologi-cal criteria differs from non-members' evaluations:

> Soccer: Because I'm out of shape at the moment I feel I can walk around without a shirt [on a sunny day like today] because I'm more like a normal person now. I'm not to the extreme where people look and, from their expressions, are saying 'That muscle is just too much. He's gone too far.'
> Mike (a national junior champion): I was like that. I'd wear sweatshirts and stuff in the summer. I don't give a shit now.
> Soccer: Yeah, well, I think I need to adopt that attitude. Unfortunately I don't like it when I get that reaction 'What the fuck?' At the moment it's OK as I look less freaky to people on the street. I should have the same attitude as you though Mike. I should say 'This is my body, this is the way I want to look, so if you don't like it then fuck it. I don't give a shit.' I do give a shit though. (Field-diary extract, 2/8/95: Pumping-Iron Gym)

Social process, variable definitions of 'the perfect body', and the balancing of indigenous and mainstream perspectives during the career of the bodybuilder are themes clearly illustrated by Soccer. This bodybuilder for over 20 years, who remarked that he initially started training 'to sort of build up my physique a little bit' experienced ongoing conflict vis-a-vis what he had learnt to see as impressive from an insiders' perspective and what he believed outsiders' considered a 'body beautiful'. After peaking at a muscular body weight of $16^1/_2$ stone, Soccer felt he transgressed mainstream limits during a summer holiday; here 'I read from people's eyes that they thought I'd taken it too far. That I'd ruined a good physique by going overboard with the bodybuilding' (Field-diary, 19/9/94). Of course, developed muscularity is similar to primitive body decoration, painting and masking in that it represents a reversible form of body-marking (Falk, 1995: 98). Less than one year later, and twelve pounds lighter, Soccer believed he had 'put things into perspective' and settled for a type of physique which he previously considered inferior from a bodybuilding point of view:

> Soccer: At the end of the day I just want a body beautiful which is impressive to the average person on the street. To someone like Al, who has a trained eye, there'll be flaws in my physique. A bodybuilding judge may say to me: 'Yeah, you've got a good foundation but you need to work on this, this and that.' Well, I couldn't give a fuck what a bodybuilding judge would say. If I was good in his eyes I'm pretty sure the average woman on the street would think I'm fucking disgusting because to be good in a bodybuilding judge's eyes you have to look like a freak, especially today in the 1990s. I don't want to look like a competitive bodybuilder, I'm not gonna compete. No, I want what is considered a sexy physique like a Chippendale. Now, if a Chippendale entered a bodybuilding show they'd get pissed all over [beaten]. A Chippendale wouldn't really stand a chance. Even so, I bet 98 percent of the population would agree that a Chippendale physique is far more pleasing to the eye than Dorian Yates. Whereas bodybuilders who are no more than 2 percent of the population would rate Dorian Yates. Now, you have to decide what you want to aim for, but personally I'll go with 98 percent who say the Chippendale has got the best physique. (Soccer in Field-diary extract, 19/3/95: Olympia Gym)

In sum, there are different evaluations of 'the muscular body (bodies)' which is itself a variable project. Individuals wishing to create a type of 'Sizeably Muscular' physique – and who thus risk being ostracized in non-bodybuilding settings – must adopt a certain perspective which is *acquired through a social process of becoming*. Participants sensitive to actual or potential negativity may readjust their ethnophysiologically informed preferences and aim to develop or maintain a type of muscular body which is a closer approximation to hegemonic masculinity or normative standards of beauty (but which is unlikely to win a high level physique championship).[7] Body-projects are variable: they are spatially and temporally contingent, and are increasingly dependent upon bodybuilding ethnophysiology the further muscle transgresses mainstream normative limits.

Concluding Comments

Bodybuilding lends itself to various different readings, both within and outside the academe. Although questioning the generality of existing knowledge claims I am not therefore dismissing existing studies of bodybuilding.[8] In the theoretical attitude 'the muscular body' may be abstracted from embodied culture and recast as a singular concept which is, among many other things, the literal embodiment of patriarchal power (White and Gillett, 1994). Bodybuilders, who are capable of homogenizing body-projects through a process of 'carnal reflexivity' (Crossley, 1995), may themselves lend credence to the claim that 'the muscular body' valorizes a dominance-based notion of masculinity which naturalizes male privilege. For *some* individuals this *may partly* contribute to the attraction of bodybuilding. At the level of abstracted affinities 'muscle' signifies potentially violent masculinity (Mansfield and McGinn, 1993: 50) rendering *some* willing to *try* the style of the bodybuilder (see Matza, 1969). However, this article has argued that theories ascribing bodybuilding to antecedent predispositions (the 'masculinist imagery' of 'the muscular body' alongside feelings of gender and personal insecurity) are not sufficient when accounting for the ongoing variable project of bodybuilding. From those data reported here, it appears that in the sport and art of bodybuilding, commitment is dependent upon a 'pictorial competence' learnt through habit and exercise (Bourdieu et al., 1991: 109). Correspondingly, personal involvement in 1990s physique bodybuilding could be independent of *antecedent* anxieties caused by a masculinity-in-crisis within the larger society.

Before finishing, three points. First, additional data support this article's central argument. Documenting spatial variations in perception, where male respondents assess photographs of different types of muscular body, underscores the importance of acquired ethnophysiology among today's bodybuilders. In contrast to hard-core bodybuilders (and other affiliative members, e.g. bodybuilding judges), weight-trainers on the 'margins' of the group could not offer an 'artistic deciphering' of 'Sizeably Muscular and Exceptionally Lean Competition Standard Bodybuilding Physiques'. In the absence of bodybuilding ethnophysiology, they set more moderately muscular bodies as projects for the self (Monaghan, 1998).

Second, in focusing upon bodybuilding ethnophysiology I am not appealing to a single element as an explanation (Silverman, 1993). Within postmodernity or visually oriented consumer culture, reasons for exercising and dieting are manifold and are well understood (Featherstone, 1991; Glassner, 1990). In making their activities 'visibly-rational-and-reportable-for-all-practical-purposes' (Garfinkel, 1967: vii), bodybuilders themselves may invoke the importance of 'the look' and position themselves within culturally 'familiar discursive and representational space' (Schulze, 1990; see also Crossley, 1995: 51, on how we can study 'the body as a being which constructs representations of itself – or of other bodies'). Through a retrospective glance, 'because motives' (Schutz, 1967) may be voiced by participants, including their wish to signify (gender-wide) attributes; viz health, youth, social status and sexual attractiveness. Paradoxically, 'excessively' muscular bodybuilders – who know, and can articulate upon, the fact that there exists a common negative reaction to them – may even do this without experiencing any ideological inconsistencies in their belief systems (similarly, see Converse, 1964). These understandings, which are independent of a masculinity-in-crisis, will be addressed in future publications.

Finally, it is worth stressing that the body exists both as a sentient and a sensible being (Crossley, 1995: 46). Accordingly, the sensuous experiences associated with training, for example, (the so-called 'erotics of the gym', Mansfield and McGinn, 1993: 66), which bodybuilders 'learn to enjoy', further contribute to the attraction of body-work. Inscription accounts of bodybuilding, focusing on the social construction and signification of gender, should therefore recognize the central precept of what Crossley (1995) would term a 'carnal sociology of the body'. The body is not simply an objective signifier in the social world but an active, embodied sentient being, subject to the contingencies of space and time.

Notes

I would like to thank all my ethnographic contacts, Soccer in particular. Many thanks also go to Michael Bloor for his guidance when drafting an earlier version of this paper for a PhD thesis, and Russell and Rebecca Dobash for their help while working on a cognate Economic and Social Research Council project ('Bodybuilding, Steroids and Violence'). Finally, I am grateful to Sara Delamont and the anonymous referees for commenting on earlier drafts.

1. The significance of adequate finances in bodybuilding is worth noting here given the class dimension in Bourdieu's analyses, and the view that muscular bodies equal working-class male bodies (Shilling, 1993). Certainly, bodybuilding – like many other sports – is male dominated (Klein, 1993: 6). However, the idea that bodybuilding (not weight-training or Olympic and Power-Lifting) is a pursuit largely favoured by unemployed or working-class men, searching for a secure masculine identity, is not supported empirically. The majority of bodybuilders have to work to support their training, and are employed in occupations ranging from unskilled manual labour to the professions. Contrary to the 'grim post-industrial scenario', bodybuilders are more akin to 'gainfully employed semi-bourgeois hobbyists' (Kane, 1994: 2).

2. This article's argument also extends to female participants. However their views will be considered in future work given space constraints.

3. The views of individuals affiliated to bodybuilding subculture are of central concern in this article. However, weight-trainers' perceptions are noteworthy. These individuals typically homogenize and denigrate accomplished bodybuilders' physiques despite their ecological proximity to the subculture (Monaghan, 1998).

4. For many participants bodybuilding is a sporting and artistic enterprise (Gaines and Butler, 1974). As stated by one indigenous author: 'bodybuilding is as much art as sport, if not more. In fact, Arnold [Schwarzenegger] felt the same way – he surmised that bodybuilders were akin to sculptors, that the physique is a work of art' (Phillips, 1997: 12).

5. Bodybuilding ethnophysiology is framed in terms of identification rather than homo-erotic desire, though clearly this does not negate the possibility of a sexualized reading of muscle.

6. Genetic potential, or 'choosing the right parents' (Kennedy, 1983: 7) is considered requisite in successful bodybuilding. Importantly, a phenomenological approach to the body – with its focus on lived-embodiment – is able to take into account these ethnoscientific beliefs without reducing human behaviour to an unchanging pre-social/naturalistic body (cf. Leder, 1990: 6).

7. Although a body*builder* for many years, Soccer eventually came to see himself as a body-*sculptor*. He had no intention of accruing more muscle; instead, he was more concerned with 'polishing' and 'refining' his physique.

8. Although Klein's (1993) work may be seriously questioned (cf. Monaghan, 1997), he makes some important substantive contributions to the sociology of bodybuilding. For instance, he notes body-builders' argot and symbolic style, the importance of training partnerships, cultural relations with the larger society (particularly the public's disrespect of bodybuilding), the political-economy of elite competition bodybuilding in southern California, etc.

References

Aoki, D. (1996) 'Sex and Muscle: The Female Bodybuilder Meets Lacan', *Body & Society* 2(4): 59–74.

Becker, H. (1953) 'Becoming a Marihuana User', *American Journal of Sociology* 59: 235–42.

Becker, H. (1963) *Outsiders: Studies in the Sociology of Deviance.* New York: Free Press.

Bednarek, J. (1985) 'Pumping Iron or Pulling Strings: Different Ways of Working Out and Getting Involved in Body-Building', *International Review for the Sociology of Sport* 20(4): 239–58.

Bloor, M. (1978) 'On the Analysis of Observational Data: A Discussion of the Worth and Uses of Inductive Techniques and Respondent Validation', *Sociology* 12: 545–52.

Bloor, M., L. Monaghan, R.P. Dobash and R.E. Dobash (1998) 'The Body as a Chemistry Experiment: Steroid Use among South Wales Bodybuilders', in S. Nettleton and J. Watson (eds) *The Body in Everyday Life.* London: Routledge.

Blumer, H. (1969) *Symbolic Interactionism: Perspective and Method.* Englewood Cliffs, NJ: Prentice-Hall.

Bolin, A. (1992) 'Vandalized Vanity: Feminine Physiques Betrayed and Portrayed', in F. Mascia-Lees and P. Sharpe (eds) *Tattoo, Torture, Mutilation, and Adornment: The Denaturalization of the Body in Culture and Text.* Albany: State University of New York Press.

Bordo, S. (1993) *Unbearable Weight: Feminism, Western Culture and the Body.* Berkeley: University of California Press.

Bourdieu, P. (1984) *Distinction.* London: Routledge.

Bourdieu, P. (1992a) *The Logic of Practice.* Cambridge: Polity Press.

Bourdieu, P. (1992b) *Language and Symbolic Power.* Cambridge: Polity Press.

Bourdieu, P., A. Darbell and D. Schnapper (1991) *The Love of Art: European Art Museums and their Public.* Cambridge: Polity Press.

Brain, R. (1979) *The Decorated Body.* New York: Harper and Row.

Connell, R. (1987) *Gender and Power.* Cambridge: Polity Press.

Connell, R. (1995) *Masculinities.* London: Polity Press.

Converse, P. (1964) 'The Nature of Belief Systems in Mass Publics', in D. Apter (ed.) *Ideology and Discontent.* New York: Free Press.

Cooke, P. (1987) 'Wales', in P. Damesick and P. Wood (eds) *Regional Problems, Problem Regions and Public Policy in the UK.* Oxford: Oxford University Press.

Crossley, N. (1995) 'Merleau-Ponty, the Elusive Body and Carnal Sociology', *Body & Society* 1(1): 43–63.

Crossley, N. (1996) 'Body-Subject/Body-Power: Agency, Inscription and Control in Foucault and Merleau-Ponty', *Body & Society* 2(2): 99–116.

Day, G. (1990) 'Pose for Thought: Bodybuilding and Other Matters', in G. Day (ed.) *Readings in Popular Culture: Trivial Pursuits.* New York: St Martins Press.

Edwards, D. and J. Potter (1992) *Discursive Psychology.* London: Sage.

Falk, P. (1995) 'Written in the Flesh', *Body & Society* 1(1): 95–105.

Featherstone, M. (1991) 'The Body in Consumer Culture', in M. Featherstone, M. Hepworth and B. Turner (eds) *The Body: Social Process and Cultural Theory.* London: Sage.

Foucault, M. (1980) 'Body-Power', in C. Gordon (ed.) *Power/Knowledge.* Brighton: Harvester.

Frank, A. (1995) 'Review Symposium: As Much as Theory Can Say About Bodies', *Body & Society* 1(1): 184–7.

Fussell, S. (1991) *Muscle: Confessions of an Unlikely Bodybuilder.* New York: Avon Books.

Gaines, C. and G. Butler (1974) *Pumping Iron: The Art and Sport of Bodybuilding.* New York: Simon and Schuster.

Garfinkel, H. (1967) *Studies in Ethnomethodology.* New York: Prentice-Hall.

Gatens, M. (1996) *Imaginary Bodies: Ethics, Power and Corporeality.* London: Routledge.

Giddens, A. (1991) *Modernity and Self-Identity: Self and Society in the Late Modern Age.* Cambridge: Polity Press.

Gillett, J. and P. White (1992) 'Male Bodybuilding and the Reassertion of Hegemonic Masculinity: A Critical Feminist Perspective', *Play and Culture* 5: 358 – 69.

Glaser, B. and A. Strauss (1967) *The Discovery of Grounded Theory.* Chicago: Aldine.

Glassner, B. (1990) 'Fit For Postmodern Selfhood', in H. Becker and M. McCall (eds) *Symbolic Interaction and Cultural Studies.* Chicago: University of Chicago Press.

Goffman, E. (1963) *Behavior in Public Places: Notes on the Social Organization of Gatherings.* New York: Free Press.

Goffman, E. (1968) *Stigma: Notes on the Management of a Spoiled Identity.* Middlesex: Penguin Books.

Goffman, E. (1989) 'On Fieldwork', *Journal of Contemporary Ethnography* 18(2): 123–32.

Guthrie, S. and S. Castelnuovo (1992) 'Elite Women Bodybuilders: Models of Resistance or Compliance?', *Play and Culture* 5: 401–8.

Hammersley, M. (1992) *What's Wrong with Ethnography?* London: Routledge.

Hammersley, M. and P. Atkinson (1995) *Ethnography: Principles in Practice,* 2nd edn. London: Routledge.

Harris, C. (1987) *Redundancy and Recession in South Wales.* Oxford: Blackwell.

Hesse, M. (1980) *Revolutions and Reconstructions in the Philosophy of Science.* Brighton: Harvester Wheatsheaf.

Kane, P. (1994) 'New Men in the Making', *Guardian* 12 Sept.: 2.

Kennedy, R. (1983) *Hard-Core Bodybuilding: The Blood, Sweat and Tears of Pumping Iron.* New York: Sterling.

Klein, A. (1993) *Little Big Men: Bodybuilding Subculture and Gender Construction.* Albany: State University of New York Press.

Lasch, C. (1980) *The Culture of Narcissism: American Life in an Age of Diminishing Expectations.* London: Abacus.

Leder, D. (1990) *The Absent Body.* Chicago: University of Chicago Press.

Manning, K. and H. Fabrega (1973) 'The Experience of Self and Body: Health and Illness in the Chiapas Highlands', in G. Psathas (ed.) *Phenomenological Sociology.* London: Wiley and Sons.

Mansfield, A. and B. McGinn (1993) 'Pumping Irony: The Muscular and the Feminine', in S. Scott and D. Morgan (eds) *Body Matters*. London: Falmer Press.

Matza, D. (1969) *Becoming Deviant*. Englewood Cliffs, NJ: Prentice-Hall.

McArdle, W., K. Fank and V. Katch (1986) *Exercise Physiology: Energy, Nutrition and Human Performance*, 2nd edn. Philadelphia: Lea and Febiger.

Mead, G.H. (1934) *Mind, Self and Society*. Chicago: University of Chicago Press.

Merleau-Ponty, M. (1962) *The Phenomenology of Perception*. London: Routledge.

Miller, J. and B. Glassner (1997) 'The 'Inside' and the 'Outside': Finding Realities in Interviews', in D. Silverman (ed.) *Qualitative Research: Theory, Method and Practice*. London: Sage.

Mitchell, J. (1987) ' "Going for the Burn" and "Pumping Iron": What's Healthy about the Current Fitness Boom?', in M. Lawrence (ed.) *Fed Up and Hungry: Women, Oppression and Food*. London: The Women's Press.

Monaghan, L. (1997) ' "We're Not Druggies, We're Athletes": Bodybuilding, Polypharmacology and Self-Identity', unpublished PhD thesis, University of Wales, Cardiff.

Monaghan, L. (1998) 'The Bodybuilding Ethnophysiology Thesis', paper presented at the BSA Annual Conference, *Making Sense of the Body: Theory, Research and Practice*, 6–9 April, University of Edinburgh.

Monaghan, L., M. Bloor, R.P. Dobash and R.E. Dobash (1998) 'Bodybuilding and Sexual Attractiveness', in J. Richardson and A. Shaw (eds) *The Body in Qualitative Research*. Aldershot: Ashgate.

Phillips, B. (1997) 'No Holds Barred', *Muscle Media* July: 10–13.

Polhemus, T. (1978) *Social Aspects of the Human Body*. Middlesex: Penguin Books.

St Martin, L. and N. Gavey (1996) 'Women's Bodybuilding: Feminist Resistance and/or Femininity's Recuperation?' *Body & Society* 2(4): 45–57.

Sartre, J. (1958) *Being and Nothingness*. London: Methuen and Co.

Scott, S. and D. Morgan (1993) *Body Matters: Essays in the Sociology of the Body*. London: Falmer Press.

Schulze, L. (1990) 'On the Muscle', in J. Gaines and C. Herzog (eds) *Fabrications: Costume and the Female Body*. London: Routledge.

Schutz, A. (1967) *Collected Papers I: The Problem of Social Reality*. The Hague: Martinus Nijhoff.

Seidel, J. and J. Clark (1984) 'The Ethnograph: A Computer Program for the Analysis of Qualitative Data', *Qualitative Sociology* 7: 110–25.

Shilling, C. (1993) *The Body and Social Theory*. London: Sage.

Silverman, D. (1993) *Interpreting Qualitative Data: Methods for Analysing Talk, Text and Interaction*. London: Sage.

Smith, G. (1997) 'Incivil Attention and Everyday Intolerance: Vicissitudes of Exercising in Public Places', *Perspectives on Social Problems* 9: 59–79.

Sykes, G. and D. Matza (1957) 'Techniques of Neutralization: A Theory of Delinquency', *American Sociological Review* 22: 664–70.

Taylor, I., P. Walton and J. Young (1973) *The New Criminology: For a Social Theory of Deviance*. London: Routledge.

Turner, B. (1992) *Regulating Bodies: Essays in Medical Sociology*. London: Routledge.

Wachter, F. (1984) 'The Symbolism of the Healthy Body: A Philosophical Analysis of the Sportive Imagery of Health', *Journal of the Philosophy of Sport* 11: 56–62.

Wacquant, L. (1995a) 'Review Article: Why Men Desire Muscles', *Body & Society* 1(1): 163–79.

Wacquant, L. (1995b) 'Pugs at Work: Bodily Capital and Bodily Labour Among Professional Boxers', *Body & Society* 1(1): 65–93.

Watson, J. (1998) 'Running Around Like a Lunatic', in S. Nettleton and J. Warson (eds) *The Body in Everyday Life*. London: Routledge.

Watson, J., S. Cunningham Burley and N. Watson (1995) 'Lay Theorising About the Body and Health', paper presented to the British Sociological Association Medical Sociology Group 27th Annual Conference, University of York, 22–4 September.

Weber, M. (1976) *The Protestant Ethic and the Spirit of Capitalism*. London: Allen and Unwin. (Orig. 1905.)

White, P. and J. Gillett (1994) 'Reading the Muscular Body: A Critical Decoding of Advertisements in Flex Magazine', *Sociology of Sport Journal* 11: 19–39.

Widdicombe, S. and R. Wooffitt (1995) *The Language of Youth Subcultures: Social Identity in Action*. Hertfordshire: Harvester Wheatsheaf.

Lee Monaghan is a Lecturer in Sociology at the Cardiff School of Social Sciences, Cardiff University. He has a forthcoming book titled *Bodybuilding, Drugs and Risk* (Routledge).

Body Modification, Self-Mutilation and Agency in Media Accounts of a Subculture

VICTORIA PITTS

Claims and Making News

The body modification subculture has become increasingly newsworthy in this decade as an emotionally provocative topic. Non-mainstream or radical body modification, which has origins in the West Coast sexual underground of the 1970s and 1980s, has spread in this decade as a subcultural movement advocating body adornment, rituals and performances which borrow from a mix of indigenous practices, s/m styles and performance art. Body modifiers have created spectacular body styles which deviate from Western or 'classical' bodily norms (Mascia-Lees and Sharpe, 1996) and often involve pain, bleeding and healing. While certain forms of body modification have become popularized or fashionalized (Polhemus, 1995; Steele, 1996), its more invasive, permanent or nonnormative forms of adornment such as scarification and branding have become socially problematized. My study of a sample of 35 newspaper articles[1] on body modification published between 1993 and 1998 found that most articles on the topic are concerned with its controversial or shock value, and that a significant number of them present body modification as a social problem. Moreover, the most recurrent issue raised is that body modifiers may be engaging in self-mutilation and thus may be mentally ill. The 'mutilation debate', as it is referred to in news accounts, is advanced in nearly half of the articles I analyzed (17 of 35),[2] and, as MacKendrick (1998: 6) also suggests, is 'more readily indulged where body modifications are less mainstream', including scars and brands. As I describe

Body & Society © 1999 SAGE Publications (London, Thousand Oaks and New Delhi),
Vol. 5(2–3): 291–303
[1357–034X(199906/09)5:2–3;291–303;008857]

below, the self-mutilation issue presents body modifiers as 'horror stories' (Johnson, 1989), likely to provoke fear, repugnance or alarm.

News media, powerful mediators of social understandings of events (Tuchman, 1978; Gans, 1979), present and 'frame' cultural phenomena, a process through which 'issues are problematized and definitions of situations are advanced' (Mulcahy, 1995: 450; see also Spector and Kitsuse, 1977; Best, 1989). Framing, which draws on news media's ideological and organizational resources, includes the promotion of 'certain issues as problematic, certain outcomes as desirable, and certain strategies as appropriate' (Mulcahy, 1995: 451; see also Hall, 1977; Tuchman, 1978). The news media, as constructionists have argued, have a power-ful role in spurring the problematization of social events through typifying an event or phenomenon. Sensational, dramatic and provocative coverage can effect social problems claims, which 'want to convince others that X is a social problem or that Y offers the solution' (Best, 1989: 1).[3] Often, media report claims which 'present fresh aspects of familiar social problems', but occasionally, they present claims of discoveries of brand-new problems (Best, 1989: 250), as is the case with body modification, as an emerging (and alarming) subculture. The employment of a particular news frame 'may advance or impede a group's ability to secure legitimacy', which is constructed through the 'grounding of perceived phenom-enon in valid and culturally accepted claims' (Mulcahy, 1995: 451).

The claims of 'new' problems often depend upon the testimony of official or professional claims-makers. Medical and mental health experts in particular are prominent in claims-making, because they lend the 'authority of their [influen-tial] disciplines' to their claims (Best, 1989: 75). The claims-making of such experts has resulted in the medicalization or pathologization of a number of phenomena (Conrad and Schneider, 1980).[4] In the construction of body modification as a problem of mutilation, the 'demand made by one party to another that something has to be done about some putative situation', Spector and Kitsuse's definition of a claim (1977: 78), is presented as a demand made by mental health professionals that attention be drawn to body modification as a mental health problem. As Miller (1993) argues, these kinds of claims are highly 'readable', because they benefit from official or institutional speakers, use authoritative discourses, engage discernible partisan interests and operate in the public sphere.

Other claims are less readable or immediately visible and are often 'discredited by dominant discourses and practices', as Miller (1993: 156) argues from a post-structuralist perspective.[5]

> Talk that is grounded in fragmented or marginal discourses (or ones unavailable to the community of speakers) cannot be formulated as a recognizable stance or position and is [often] read as idiosyncratic or personal comment, having no political force. (Miller, 1993: 163)

The knowledges of subcultural members, for instance, are often expressed in bodily experience, marginalized social contexts, and alternative discourses and styles which are less easily recognizable by the broader group than dominant discourses. A subculture's mode or style of communicating, expressing problems or articulating knowledge can take forms outside of established practices and institutions. Body modifiers' knowledge about body modification is not only affective (Sweetman, 1999), but expresses new, alternative and recirculated attitudes toward technology, pleasure, sexuality, cultural membership, gender, spirituality, aesthetics and beauty (Boyd, 1996; Mellor, 1996; Hewitt, 1997; Rosenblatt, 1997; MacKendrick, 1998; Pitts, 1998). Outside accounts of subcultures, such as those of the news media, have the potential to 'reinstate inaudible or marginalized speakers as claimants', in Miller's words (1993: 156), or present their knowledges to a broader group. To some extent news accounts of body modification have operated as a medium for these knowledges to reach a broader 'community of speakers'. However, as I show below, in their reliance on mental health discourse to raise body modification as an emotionally provocative social problem, news accounts discredit body modifiers' competing knowledges by calling into question the possibility of the actors' agency.

Body Modification as Self-Mutilation

Body modification's newsworthiness seems to depend in part upon the ability of journalists to describe it in what Johnson (1989) calls 'horror story' terms. Body modifiers are depicted not only as members of a subculture who have created their own defiant, deviant or shocking bodily adornments, but also as potential self-mutilators – self-hating, ill and out of control.[6] In nearly half of the articles I examined, body modification is constructed as a potential mental health problem, in which body modifiers are presented as engaging in self-mutilation. While body piercing may seem relatively innocuous to readers, the notion that body modifiers may be self-mutilating raises the prospects of more normatively extreme practices and of escalation. Many articles that raise the issue of self-mutilation begin with some version of the question, 'Where does body modification end and self-mutilation begin?' (Brown, 1997). From the Latin *mutilus*, the term has a negative connotation – to maim, cut off a limb, create dysfunction or to make imperfect through excision. Moreover, in the mental health use of the term, the 'self-mutilated' body expresses a suffering self.

The construction of mutilation discourse begins with the presentation of mental health practitioners as experts on body modification. While some accounts use professional body piercers or scarifiers, performance artists, body modification enthusiasts, and publishers of body modification magazines and books as sources, those which pose the question of mutilation generally associate the practices with the expertise of mental health practitioners, ask mental health practitioners to comment on the phenomenon, and describe the qualifications of such practitioners in relation to their scholarship, employment and/or education. The qualifications of these 'experts' sometimes include their experience treating body-related disorders like anorexia, bulimia or delicate self-harm syndrome, which is an addictive, repetitive, non-decorative and usually hidden cutting of the skin.[7] The practitioners are presented to answer the question of whether or not body modification constitutes self-mutilation as it is understood medically, as self-injurious behavior which is symptomatic of mental illness.[8]

Comparing within and across newspaper accounts, mental health professionals are presented as unified in their condemnation of body modification as pathological. Although the intensity of the condemnation varied somewhat among mental health professionals, not one of them cited in the accounts I analyzed gave body modifiers a clean bill of health. The very least pathologizing statement made by a mental health practitioner is that while body modification is self-injurious, 'that doesn't mean that *every* person who goes in for piercing is mentally ill' (Beaubien, 1995, emphasis mine). The absence of a healthy diagnosis by any mental health professional cited in these accounts does not of course mean that mental health workers as a whole are necessarily willing to pathologize the practices or are even concerned about them. This absence, however, does seem to indicate that in press accounts, the experts are employed to constitute one side of a conflict and to raise body modification as a mental health issue. Psychiatrists and psychologists are described, for example, as the 'mental-health camp' in the mutilation debate (Beaubien, 1995).

The message of the mental health argument as it is presented in the media is that body modifiers, like other sufferers of disorders, do not choose their practices but are driven by pathological impulses. The mental-health camp condemns body modification as self-mutilation largely through questioning the intent behind the practices. Body modification is depicted as an expression of self-loathing and one which is directed by reasons which body modifiers do not themselves understand. Body modifiers are depicted as more psychopathological than other groups (also see Favazza, 1996) and body modification is explicitly described as deliberate self-injury and compared to body related disorders such as anorexia and delicate self-harm syndrome. For example:

> Two psychologists who have worked with anorectics readily see the connections between all these forms of body modification. For Susie Orbach, 'there is a projecting onto your body of an absolute hatred'. . . . To psychologist Corinee Sweet, it's all just self-mutilation. 'From my

experience as a counselor, what we do on the surface nearly always has some deep structure behind it. The expression of anger may be impossible, so we turn it in on ourselves'. (Grant, 1995)

This account contains explicit assertions that body modifiers are self-mutilators, that they are driven by need or desire to express anger or self-hatred, that the body is victimized through body modification, and that body modification constitutes a body-oriented disorder. In another example, body modification is associated with 'internal stuff' which suggests pathology. The article cites:

> Wendy Lader, a clinical psychologist at Hartgrove Hospital, a private psychiatric facility on Chicago's West Side. Lader works with women who habitually slice their arms with razor blades as a means of alleviating overwhelming anxiety. Lader suggests that many forms of body modification derive from similar psychological impulses. 'There are some obvious differences – self-injury tends to be very private', she says . . . [but body modifiers find] 'a socially acceptable venue for this kind of internal stuff'. (Beaubien, 1995)

The reader is given little information here as to precisely what psychological impulse is behind burning, scarring and piercing, or whether or not body modifiers fit into the same psychological category as women who suffer from anxiety. Yet, body modification is tethered to unidentified 'internal stuff' which, the reader must guess, may or may not include 'overwhelming anxiety' or something potentially worse, and body modification is compared to other forms of self-injury like habitual slicing of the arms (what is sometimes called delicate self-harm syndrome, see Walsh and Rosen, 1988). Later in the article, the journalist claims that because of its 'habit-forming nature, Lader sees a strong link between body modification and deliberate self-injury'. From this perspective, body modification is equated to *mutilus* not simply because the body is rendered imperfect, ugly, dysfunctional or physically unhealthy, but because the imperfect body expresses an imperfect, out of control and suffering self which might need to be treated.

The use of mental health workers as experts on body modification establishes a pathology lexicon in relation to body modifiers. In the passages above, terms like anorectics, (self-) hatred, self-mutilation, anger, counsel(ing), psychologists, overwhelming anxiety, clinic, psychiatric facility, habitual (arm) slicing, psychological impulses, self-injury, suffering, (bad) home lives and internal motivations are presented as relevant to discussions of body modification. While experts pathologize body modification directly, this lexicon also pathologizes body modification connotatively. In the example below, a text by Armando Favazza, a psychiatrist who studies self-mutilation, is cited to elaborate the 'chilling detail[s]' of self-mutilation even though the journalist writes that Favazza considers branding in the same category as ear piercing.

> Psychiatrist Armando Favazza calls most body art – from ear piercing to ritualistic branding – culturally sanctioned self-mutilation. In his book 'Bodies Under Siege', Favazza describes in

> chilling detail pathological self-mutilation – the nonsuicidal, repetitive episodes of self-inflicted
> injury, more often in women than men, through head banging, skin cutting, and burning.
> (Leonard, 1998)

One effect of this tactic is that branding is semantically placed near disorders – 'nonsuicidal' 'episodes' of 'head banging' and so on – despite it being categorized with body art and ear piercing. The journalist goes on to point out that 'Favazza estimates that 2 to 3 million Americans are afflicted with a self-mutilation pathology'. The use of this statistic in the context of an article on the spread of body modification implicitly links the pervasiveness of body modification to the pervasiveness of mental illness. The elaboration of 'chilling' forms of self-injury imbues body modification with horrifying possibility, even indirectly raising the spectre of suicide. In another example, the *Independent* merges the words 'abuse' and 'use' in an assessment of the branding practices of an s/m lesbian couple: 'Couples like Kate and Mandy feel that, as consenting adults, they should be free to (ab)use their bodies as they wish' (Brown, 1997). The terms 'use' and 'abuse' differ in their acknowledgment of agency. Here, the prospect of 'use' is posed by Kate and Mandy, but their agency is challenged even as their perspective is (re)presented. This deliberate word play endorses the pathologizing remarks of mental health workers which were cited earlier in this article and casts doubt on Kate and Mandy's status as 'consenting' actors free to make intentional choices.

The framing of body modification as mutilation makes the prospect of agency dubious or theoretically impossible. Given the equation of body modification with mutilation and mental illness, it is not surprising that in accounts which use mutilation discourse, the practices of tattooing, scarification, piercing and branding are generally associated with other social problems, especially those which express a lack of control, such as drug addiction, bulimia and crime. In a *Washington Post* column, body modification is listed among the 'methods of ruining' one's life:

> There is alcohol, of course, but also marijuana and hashish and heroin and cocaine and LSD;
> amphetamines and methamphetamines, barbiturates and airplane glue, and animal tranquilizer
> and Ecstasy. There are the aesthetic means of self-harm: tattooing, body piercing, scarification,
> anorexia, bulimia. There is the outlaw life: gangs, guns, crimes, prison. (Kelly, 1998)

The comparison with anorexia and bulimia underscores not only the way body modification is socially problematized, but also the way mutilation discourse explicitly and implicitly denies agency to subcultural actors. Even though body modification is undertaken to change appearance, and for self-definition, it turns out that self-definition is not a choice, but a desire, addiction, need or urge:

> Though every generation seeks ever more dramatic ways to define itself, Amy is part of a
> growing subculture that is exploring the line between fashion and mutilation, design and
> destruction, choice and compulsion. (Ryan, 1997)

The depiction of body modification as a potentially addictive, harmful and escalating mental health problem which reveals inner sufferings is only furthered by the thematization of gender in mutilation discourse. While not a single article I surveyed suggested that there are more female body modifiers than male body modifiers, body modification is nonetheless depicted in a number of accounts as especially problematic for women and girls. One empirical reason for this is that delicate self-harm syndrome and anorexia, with which body modification is often compared, are much more prevalent among girls and women than their male counterparts.[9] To the extent that body modification is equated with or situated in proximity to these disorders, they are considered gendered. Moreover, though, the use of delicate self-harm syndrome and anorexia as models furthers the notion that body modification shares their attributes – obsessive-compulsion or addiction, victimization, escalation and uncontrollability.[10] For instance, in the *Boston Globe*:

> '[W]omen particularly are pushing the envelope of body decoration, and the question is why – is it body enhancement or body dissatisfaction?' asks Hesse-Biber, author of 'Am I Thin Enough Yet?' 'Maybe they are making a political statement with their bodies, or maybe this is just one more tool, like plastic surgery, in the box of being beautiful'. (Leonard, 1998)

Without ever asserting that females use body modification more than males, this expert is presented as claiming that women are '*particularly* pushing the envelope'. Neither the expert nor the journalist offers an explanation for why this is so. Are they especially 'pushing the envelope' because they are doing so more often, because their body modifications are more extreme or because, as women, their use of body modification is somehow more problematic than that of men? Given the other social problems raised in the passage – anorexia, cosmetic surgery and social pressures on female beauty – and that Hesse-Biber herself is an expert on anorexia, it is possible for the reader to interpret that female body modification is an inherently more treacherous problem than male body modification.[11] Interestingly, the 'political statements' to which Hesse-Biber alludes are never elaborated for readers, and thus body modification's discourse of self-empowerment – an explanation for why women might be 'particularly pushing the envelope' – is left muted. The image Hesse-Biber depicts is instead presented as evidence for the suggestion that body modifiers are victims, answering the question posed at the beginning of this article, 'Where does body modification end and self-mutilation begin?' In this and other accounts, the image of the suffering body modifier is added to other figures of escalated female victimization, such as the anorectic, the 'delicate self-harm' cutter and the objectified teenager. Another article even compared body modifiers to Princess Diana, who is reported to have had episodes of repeatedly throwing herself against glass cabinets (Leonard, 1998).[12] No image more clearly epitomizes the out-of-control (female) victim of suffering and self-hatred who is greatly in need of help.

Agency and Claims-Making from the Underside

News accounts do not generally deny body modifiers the chance to self-interpret their practices, and mutilation is not the only theme surrounding body modification in the media. Many articles suggest that body modifiers interpret their practices as assertions of self-control over their bodies and that they take offense at suggestions that they are mentally ill. These marginal discourses find representation in 'mutilation' accounts as the other side of the debate. For instance, body modifiers' embrace of the 'rush' of pain, interpreted from the mutilation perspective as pathological, is also described in other terms by the *Independent*:

> For Deacon, body modification is a way of expressing himself and taking control of his body. It is also his way of exploring the body's limits. . . . 'I am interested in the experience, what you can do to your body'. (Brown, 1997)

In another *Independent* article, a female body modifier argues, 'It's about being able to define yourself' (Beaubien, 1995). Similarly, the *Guardian* summarizes the perspectives of body modifiers: '[Body modifiers] tell the world, I can do what I like with my body' (Grant, 1995).

These kinds of claims by body modifiers, which suggest that they may use body modification as a 'vehicle for staging cultural identities' (Balsamo, 1996: 78), have been articulated elsewhere. Body modification practices are presented in subcultural texts as appealing for 'whole groups of people [who] socially, are alienated' (Musafar, 1996), who want to 're-empower' themselves through asserting 'control over [their] bod[ies] and [their] beliefs' (Musafar, 1995). Women body modifiers in particular have articulated that they are 'redefining beauty' and 'reclaiming' their bodies from patriarchal culture.[13] In the words of the women's underground body modification film *Stigmata*, women's body modification resists the way 'men impose their will and their ideas about how women should look' (Gladsjo, 1991).

Body modifiers can be considered speakers 'negotiating the order of things' (Miller, 1993: 142). They enact new forms of embodiment and invent new knowledges. They are enjoying new, transgressive pleasures (Sweetman, 1999), and inventing new body technologies (MacKendrick, 1998). They are claiming an interest in self-control and bodily self-ownership (Pitts, 1998). These features of body modification find articulation in newspaper accounts, which bring them to a broader community of speakers. News accounts suggest that body modifiers may express an interest in redefining beauty, or 'making political statements with their bodies', as the *Boston Globe* article put it. The articles I have cited report that a subculture might be interested in identity, 'seeking ... dramatic ways to define itself' or that body modifiers like Kate and Mandy might be expressing a 'right' to choose what to do with their bodies. Yet unofficial or marginalized knowledges like these are already less likely to be 'read' in public discourse as discernible or legitimate positions. A female body modifier's interest in establishing self-control over the body, for instance, may be expressed in a kind of talk (or performance, fashion statement, phenomenological experience or subcultural jargon) which is fragmented and understood idiosyncratically.

In many mainstream news accounts, moreover, the self-interpretations or insider discourses of the subculture are juxtaposed with the interpretations of mental health experts, who discount them on the basis of body modification's pathological nature. For example, one account describes the neo-tribal thesis of the book *Modern Primitives*, which argues that body modifiers, like the indigenous 'primitives' before them, can use pain to create self-reflection and self-awareness and a sense of bodily self-ownership. In response to this perspective, the journalist poses the question, 'What do the psychologists make of this?' The answer:

> 'Sickening tosh', says Dorothy Rowe. 'To write about pain as if it is some kind of cosmetic activity shows that they don't know what life is about and don't wish to. If you have to resort to using your body to express things, you haven't got much to draw on. If suffering improves character, we would all be living in a perfect world. What it does to most people is to harden them.' (Grant, 1995)

In another article, a clinical psychologist is asked to react to the idea of body modification as a matter of redefining beauty:

> They may think it's adornment, and I'm sure they think it's OK, but I would be really interested to find out about their home lives. It's my belief they're running from something. (Beaubien, 1995)

The notion that body modifiers are 'running from something' suggests that whatever reasons actors express for modifying themselves, they are simply 'justifications' (Grant, 1995).

Since the mental health literature understands self-mutilators as 'deeply disturbed individuals' motivated by 'various psychopathological reasons' (Myers, 1992: 296; see also Walsh and Rosen, 1988; Herman, 1992; Rubenstein, 1995; Favazza, 1996), the framing of body modification as mutilation has a particularly powerful ability to impede the legitimacy of body modifiers' own claims in media accounts. Because, from this perspective, self-mutilators are 'quite out of control' (Leonard, 1998) and do not understand or cannot manage the motivations for their practices, this frame lends to body modifiers a powerful stigma, rendering them 'discredited person[s]' (Goffman, 1995). The claim of mental illness situates body modifiers outside of a legitimate social sphere; mental health discourse has a capacity for muting competing claims and silencing other knowledges. In the mutilation debate, claims of agency are rendered as rationalizations of self-harming desires. If body modifiers are sick, after all, then their reasons are modes of denial, the therapeutic version of false consciousness, as some radical feminists have argued (see Jeffries, 1994).[14]

Media accounts, while amplifying marginal discourses for a broader audience, also have a tendency to reinforce dominant discourses. As I have shown, the construction of the mutilation debate in mainstream accounts pits already marginal discourses against speakers who benefit from the authority of their professions, and stand to gain from advancing their claims (Best, 1989: 76). The presentation of body modification as a new entity to be treated by the mental health profession expands the authority of disciplinary institutions into new realms, renders body modifiers' agency illegitimate and subjugates their already less 'readable' knowledges.

Notes

The author would like to thank the anonymous reviewers for their helpful comments.

1. In this article I rely on a content analysis study of mainstream newspaper articles. I analyzed 35 articles from mainstream newspapers registered with an electronic database. I analyzed the first 35 articles listed, which were published in reverse chronological order over the last five years in the US and the UK. The limitation of this sample is that the articles include only those which are from newspapers registered with the database used, and only those articles which were registered with 'body modification' as one of their topics. Newspapers registered with this database are generally those from large cities with large circulations. The articles are from the following newspapers: the *Atlanta Constitution*, the *Boston Globe*, the *Chicago Tribune*, the *Courier-Journal* (Louisville, KY), the *Denver Post*, the *Guardian* (London), the *Independent* (London), the *New York Times*, the *Los Angeles Times*, the *San Francisco Chronicle*, the *Seattle Times*, the *Star Tribune* (Minneapolis), the *Sunday Telegraph*, and the *Washington Post*. The articles tended to be published in the feature sections of newspapers, with the exception of editorials. A number of them were run as cover stories for the sections in which they were published (*Weekender*, *Life & Style*, etc.).

2. The 'mutilation debate' is addressed in 17 of the 35 articles I analyzed. While nearly all of the articles discussed the shocking, disturbing nature of body modification, not all of them addressed the issue of body modification as pathological self-mutilation. The 17 I found to be 'mutilation' articles: (1) posed body modification as mutilation, or posed the question of body modification as mutilation, through use of terms like 'mutilation', 'self-mutilation', 'self-harm' and 'self-injury'; (2) discussed the meaning of this mutilation – for example, whether or not this mutilation is pathological, self-injurious, self-damaging and indicative of a social problem. The other 17 articles dealt with the shocking aspects of body modification in a number of ways. For example, some focused on the censorship of sexuality implied by public outcries against performance artists who use scarification. Others focused on the meaning of shock for parents, jobs, lifestyles, fashion. Still others asserted that body modification is an assertion of individuality by actors.

3. Social problems claims are the stuff of the human interest stories which are 'increasingly important' to the interests of the mass media (Johnson, 1989: 15).

4. Pathologization of body modification is effected at 'conceptual level' in which a psychiatric vocabulary is used to 'order or define a problem at hand' (Conrad, 1992: 211).

5. Poststructuralists and feminist poststructuralists, while representing a diverse array of approaches, share an interest in subjugated knowledges (Miller, 1993: 156).

6. Until recently, psychiatrists generally considered suicide the ultimate possible result of pathological, escalating self-mutilation, a theory which is now disputed (Walsh and Rosen, 1988).

7. Delicate self-harm syndrome, a widely publicized disorder, afflicts mostly females and is associated with sexual abuse and a wide array of illnesses, including depression, borderline personality disorder and psychosis. This form of cutting is indiscriminate and uncontrolled, promoting pain and endorphins to alleviate dissociation, sometimes resulting in a mass of scars across the limbs. It is associated with shame and thus is usually hidden from others, except in 'contagion' syndrome where institutionalized individuals tend to copy each other's mutilations. As a response to sexual trauma, cutting has also been associated with Post-Traumatic Stress Disorder (Herman, 1992).

8. For examples of the medical/psychiatric model, see Walsh and Rosen (1988) and Favazza (1996).

9. Both are also related to sexual abuse (Hewitt, 1997).

10. As we have seen from sad experience, anorexia can be deadly, and while the notion of delicate self-harm as a precursor to suicide has recently been discredited, for many years mental health professionals made this link (Walsh and Rosen, 1988; Favazza, 1996).

11. Compare, for example, the pathologizing description of female body modification above with a non-pathologizing one of college fraternity body modification which appeared in the same article: ' "It seems barbaric to me," says Joel Wade, an associate professor of social psychology at Bucknell University, "but it is meant to show loyalty and prove you're a real man." ' Interestingly, while male body modifiers are depicted here as virile and brave, as tough men, I did not find a single example of female body modifiers described as tough women (even though I did find reports of brandings among sororities).

12. In contrast, male fraternity members who have incorporated branding into their hazing practices might be called 'barbaric', but also interested in proving that they're 'loyal' and 'a real man'. (And, nowhere in the articles I studied were these mainstream body modifiers used to exemplify the notion of the victim of conformity and social pressure.)

13. For interview-based studies and academic arguments, see MacKendrick (1998), Pitts (1998), Hewitt (1997), Boyd (1996).

14. This point is raised in a letter published in the *Guardian*, whose author, a 'pierced, tattooed, corseted, make-up wearing active member of Feminists Against Censorship', took issue with the presentation of psychologist Corinee Sweet as an expert on body modification without mentioning her political convictions: 'I feel that psychologist Corinee Sweet – a well-known anti-pornography campaigner – is one of the last people Linda Grant should have commenting on a subject such as modifying the human body. In pointing out that any body modification is self-mutilation, Sweet is constantly looking for an underlying message of horror and dread. Instead, we should rejoice the fact that people, especially women, are finding ways of celebrating their bodies with self-beautification. Ms. Sweet herself is in the psychotherapists' favourite mode of deep denial – denial that anyone can enjoy flesh by decorating it or by viewing the erotic photographs of the human body that Ms Sweet campaigns to have censored' ('Weekend Letter', *Guardian*, 1 April 1995).

References

Balsamo, Anne (1996) *Technologies of the Gendered Body: Reading Cyborg Women*. Durham, NC: Duke University Press.

Beaubien, Greg (1995) 'Burning Question: Branding Makes its Mark as the Latest Fad in Body Modification, but is it Art or Self-Mutilation?', *Chicago Tribune* 17 Feb.

Best, Joel (ed.) (1989) *Images of Issues: Typifying Contemporary Social Problems*. New York: Aldine de Gruyter.

Boyd, Kelly (1996) 'Women's Stories Around Their Experiences with Body Art', thesis for Brock University, reprinted in *Body Modification Ezine*: http://www.bme.freeq.com/culture/wb/wb/wb000.html-wb014.htm

Brown, Hero (1997) 'The Human Condition: The First Cut is the Deepest: Scarring and Branding is the Body Modifier's Way of Saying I Love You', *Independent* (London) 5 Oct.

Conrad, Peter (1992) 'Medicalization and Social Control', *Annual Review of Sociology* 18: 209–32.

Conrad, Peter and Joseph Schneider (1980) *Deviance and Medicalization*. St Louis: Mosby.

Favazza, Armando (1996) *The Body Under Siege: Self-Mutilation and Body Modification in Culture and Psychiatry*. Baltimore, MD: Johns Hopkins University Press.

Gans, Herbert (1979) *Deciding What's News*. New York: Pantheon.

Gladsjo, Leslie Asako (director) (1991) *Stigmata: The Transfigured Body*. Video.

Goffman, Erving (1995) *Asylums: Essays on the Social Situation of Mental Patients and Other Inmates*. Chicago, IL: Aldine. (Orig. pub. 1962.)

Grant, Linda (1995) 'Written on the Body: Piercing, Tattooing, Body-Building, Cosmetic Surgery, Trans-Sexualism, Anorexia, Scarring and a Range of Lesser-Known "Body Modifications" are Increasingly Common. Why Do So Many People Feel the Need to Alter Their Flesh?', *Guardian* 1 April.

Hall, Stuart (1977) 'Culture, the Media, and the Ideological Effect', pp. 314–48 in J. Curran, M. Gurevitch and J. Woollacott (eds) *Mass Communication in Society*. London: Edward Arnold.

Herman, Judith Lewis (1992) *Trauma and Recovery*. New York: HarperCollins.

Hewitt, Kim (1997) *Mutilating the Body: Identity in Blood and Ink*. Bowling Green, OH: Bowling Green State University Popular Press.

Jeffries, Sheila (1994) 'Sadomasochism, Art and the Lesbian Sexual Revolution', *Artlink* 14: 1.

Johnson, John M. (1989) 'Horror Stories and the Construction of Child Abuse', pp. 5–20 in Joel Best (ed.) *Images of Issues*. New York: Aldine de Gruyter.

Kelly, Michael (1998) 'Reviving the Lure of the Evil Weed', *Washington Post* 22 April.

Leonard, Mary (1998) 'Making a Mark on Culture: Body Piercing, Tattoos, and Scarification Push the Cutting Edge', *Boston Sunday Globe* 16 Feb.

MacKendrick, Karmen (1998) 'Technoflesh, or "Didn't That Hurt?"', *Fashion Theory* 2(1): 3–24.

Mascia-Lees, Frances and Patricia Sharpe (eds) (1996) *Tattoo, Torture, Mutilation, and Adornment: The Denaturalization of the Body in Culture and Text*. Albany, NY: SUNY Press.

Mellor, David Allan (1996) 'The Chameleon Body', pp. 10–15 in *The Chameleon Body: Photographs of Contemporary Fetishism by Nicholas Sinclair*. London: Lund Humphries.

Miller, Leslie J. (1993) 'Claims-Making from the Underside: Marginalization and Social Problems Analysis', pp. 153–80 in Gayle Miller and James Holstein (eds) *Constructivist Controversies*. New York: Aldine de Gruyter.

Mulcahy, Aogan (1995) 'Claims-Making and the Construction of Legitimacy: Press Coverage of the 1981 Northern Irish Hunger Strike', *Social Problems* 42(4): 449–67.

Musafar, Fakir (ed.) (1995) 'Editorial', *In the Flesh* 1(1): 3.

Musafar, Fakir (ed.) (1996) 'Editorial', *In the Flesh* 1(2): 3.

Myers, James (1992) 'Nonmainstream Body Modification', *Journal of Contemporary Ethnography* 21: 267–307.

Pitts, Victoria (1998) '"Reclaiming" the Female Body: Embodied Identity Work, Resistance, and the Grotesque', *Body & Society* 4(3): 67–84.

Polhemus, Ted (1995) *Streetstyle: From Sidewalk to Catwalk*. London: Thames and Hudson.

Rosenblatt, Daniel (1997) 'The Antisocial Skin: Structure, Resistance, and "Modern Primitive" Adornment in the United States', *Cultural Anthropology* 12(3): 287–334.

Body Modification ■ 303

Rubenstein, Ruth (1995) *Dress Codes*. Boulder, CO: Westview Press.
Ryan, Joan (1997) 'A Painful Statement of Self-Identity: "Body Modification" is S.F. Subculture's Rite of Passage', *San Francisco Chronicle* 30 Oct.
Spector, Malcolm and John Kitsuse (1977) *Constructing Social Problems*. Menlo Park, CA: Benjamin/ Cummings.
Steele, Valerie (1996) *Fetish: Fashion, Sex and Power*. New York: Oxford University Press.
Sweetman, Paul (1999) 'Only Skin Deep? Tattooing, Piercing, and the Transgressive Body', in M. Aaron (ed.) *The Body's Perilous Pleasures: Dangerous Desires and Contemporary Culture*. Edinburgh: Edinburgh University Press.
Tuchman, Gaye (1978) *Making News: A Study in the Construction of Reality*. London: Collier Macmillan.
Walsh, Barent and Paul Rosen (1988) *Self-Mutilation: Theory, Research, and Treatment*. New York: The Guilford Press.

Victoria L. Pitts is Assistant Professor of Sociology at Queen's College, City University of New York. Her interests include agency, identity and the body in culture and subculture. She has published numerous articles, including a study of women's body modification in *Body & Society*.

Tattoos and Heroin:
A Literary Approach

KEVIN McCARRON

After smoking, the body thinks. It is not a question of the *confused thinking* of Descartes.
The body thinks, the body dreams, the body becomes soft and flaky, the body flies. (Cocteau,
1990: 87)

In their essay 'Pain and the Mind–Body Dualism: A Sociological Approach',
Gillian Bendelow and Simon Williams suggest: 'At the hermeneutical level, pain
and suffering give rise to the quest for interpretation, understanding and meaning
…' (1995: 87). In Angela Carter's post-apocalyptic novel *Heroes and Villains*,
Marianne looks at her new husband's tattoo:

> She parted the black curtains of his mane and drew her hands incredulously down the orna-
> mented length of his spine. He wore the figure of a man on the right side, a woman on the left
> and, tattooed the length of his spine, a tree with a snake curled round and round the trunk.
> This elaborate design was executed in blue, red, black, and green. The woman offered the man
> a red apple and more red apples grew among green leaves at the top of the tree, spreading
> across his shoulders, and the black roots of the tree twisted and ended at the top of his
> buttocks. The figures were both stiff and lifelike: Eve wore a perfidious smile. The lines of
> colour were etched with obsessive precision on the shining, close-pored skin which rose and
> fell with Jewel's breathing, so it seemed the snake's forked tongue darted in and out and the
> leaves on the tree moved in a small wind, an effect the designer must have foreseen and allowed
> for. (1969: 85)

Marianne has no interest in interpreting the tattoo; it is the act of being tattooed
that engages her. She asks her husband 'Was it very painful?' and follows this with
'Why did you let him mutilate you so?' (1969: 86). In Herman Melville's *Moby-
Dick*, however, Ishmael has no interest in the pain that the heavily tattooed Quee-
queg must have suffered. His interest lies elsewhere:

Body & Society © 1999 SAGE Publications (London, Thousand Oaks and New Delhi),
Vol. 5(2–3): 305–315
[1357–034X(199906/09)5:2–3;305–315;008868]

> And this tattooing had been the work of a departed prophet and seer of his island, who, by those hieroglyphic marks, had written out on his body a complete theory of the heavens and the earth, and a mystical treatise on the art of attaining truth; so that Queequeg in his own proper person was a riddle to unfold; a wondrous work in one volume. (1988: 480)

Ishmael is interested only in the meaning of the tattoos, what it is they might signify. Carter's protagonist focuses on the act of tattooing and ignores meaning, while Ishmael focuses on hermeneutics at the expense of the physical act of tattooing. Both, of course, are thoroughly artificial distinctions.

Although Marianne has no interest in hermeneutics, this is not the case for the reader, who recognizes the conventionally misogynistic interpretation of the Biblical narrative and integrates this depiction into their overall response to the novel. Generally, however, readers of literary texts endorse Ishmael's perspective: they interpret tattoos, or attempt to, and construct thereby an artificial distinction between the act of being tattooed, which is negated, and the meaning of the tattoo, which is privileged. This artificial dualism, between act and meaning, rarely replicated in life, is replicated in the equally artificial distinction between mind and body within the texts I now wish to discuss: William Burroughs's *Junky* (1977), Irvine Welsh's *Trainspotting* (1996), Jerry Stahl's *Permanent Midnight* (1995) and David Foster Wallace's *Infinite Jest* (1996). In these books, act and meaning, as in life, are inseparable: tattoos can be interpreted, but that they are tattoos, that they have been indelibly inscribed into the flesh, is also stressed. In these books tattoos are represented as, in addition to whatever specific interpretive significance can be attached to them, visible markers of the hatred junkies feel for their own bodies. I will suggest throughout this article that the body in these texts is always a source of shame and horror. Tattoos in these novels do not decorate a body, rather they visibly emphasize its pathetic corporeality: no flesh, no image. The central dynamic of these texts is toward the transcendence of the body by the injection of heroin, a use of the needle which mimics the practice of tattooing and stresses the subservient, inessential nature of the body.

Cartesian Dualism and Heroin

In 'Merleau-Ponty, the Elusive Body and Carnal Sociology', Nick Crossley writes: 'The chief obstacle to the formation of a carnal sociology of the body is the Cartesian ontology which many writers, from quite distinct perspectives, have identified as being inherent in and even foundational to much sociology ...' (1995: 44). Crossley notes the limitations of Cartesian ontology before suggesting that the work of Maurice Merleau-Ponty productively rethinks the Cartesian position:

Merleau-Ponty challenges the mechanistic, Cartesian view of the body. He argues for an under-standing of the body as an effective agent and, thereby, as the very basis of human subjectivity. Moreover, he understands embodied subjectivity to be intersubjective and he understands inter-subjectivity to be an institutional and historical order. His 'body-subject' is always-already situated and decentred in relation to a historical world. (1995: 44)

Similarly, in his article 'Justice in the Flesh', David Levin writes: 'we belong to a matrix of flesh; so much so that we can achieve an "interior life" only by grace of our intercorporeality' (1990: 41). Both of these views seem truer to life as it is experienced than does Descartes' artificial and mechanistic dualism, but 'Junk Narratives' are incapable of perceiving body and mind as anything but totally separate: the body is material, the mind is a thinking substance. In her study of 19th-century American slave narratives, Katherine Fishburn suggests that because of the slave writers' emphasis upon the body they:

... challenge the disembodied rationalism of Western liberalism even as they employ its demo-cratic ideals in order to define themselves as equal to – if not indistinguishable from – white subjects. That is to say, I will argue that the slave narrators offered one of the most effective, if heretofore overlooked, pre-Heideggerian critiques of humanism and metaphysics ever attempted in the West. (1997: 1)

Junk narratives, however, thoroughly support the 'disembodied rationalism of Western Liberalism'; politically and philosophically one of the most striking features of these texts is their conservatism. Fishburn argues of slave narratives that they offer 'a counter-hegemonic discourse that challenged the dominant thinking of the time' (1997: 10). Junk narratives, however, appearances to the contrary, endorse the philosophical and political positions which the slave narra-tives reject. The books I wish to discuss are remarkable precisely because of their combination of seedy, contemporary glamour and their strikingly anachronistic endorsement of Cartesian dualism. Literary texts, particularly those as extraordi-narily popular as *Trainspotting*, are objects-in-the-world; the ideologies they promote, the philosophical positions they adopt, offer provocative insights into pervasive contemporary beliefs.

Ink, the Body, and the Book

'It's hideous. It's unnatural.'
But she was lying again; the tattoo seemed to her a perilous and irrestible landscape, a terra incognita or the back of the moon. (Carter, 1969: 86)

Marianne describes Jewel's tattoo as 'unnatural' and while the omniscient narra-tor observes that she is lying it is noticeable that the succession of images that the tattoo evokes for Marianne are not represented as unequivocally 'natural'. I want to suggest that in literature, if not necessarily in life, the tattoo is always represented as unnatural. George Burchett, one of England's best-known tattooists for more than 50 years, writes in the opening pages of *Memoirs of a Tattooist*:

> Only heaven knows exactly when the first man, or half man, first added some natural ornament to his body, or a woman to hers. Not long after, I feel sure, the first primitive attempt was made at putting a permanent decoration, or magic sign, on the skin. If so, it would be a proud claim for tattooing that it was one of man's first conscious acts which distinguished him from the rest of the animal kingdom. (1960: 10)

Similarly, Pasi Falk, in a recent issue of *Body & Society*, writes of tattooing:

> The irreversible reshaping of the body and its permanent marking manifests the stable and static character of relations in society. It also indicates a specific relation to the body as raw material – clay to be moulded and a surface to draw on. This does not imply contempt for the body nor does it express particular adoration of the 'natural' body image. The body is an unfinished piece of art to be completed. It must be transformed from nature to culture. (1995: 99)

While any division between nature and culture needs to be distinguished from the idea of 'naturalness', in which 'nature' is turned into a cultural, artificial, construction, it is interesting to note that both Burchett, who left school at 12, and Falk, a professional sociologist, agree on the essential 'unnaturalness' of tattooing – its orientation toward the cultural rather than the natural, its fundamental disdain for 'naturalness'. In literary texts the tattoo is always used to depict a (Western) character's movement away from the natural toward the cultural, or from the real to the artificial. The literary depiction of heroin injection signals a similar shift from the natural to the cultural. Falk notes that the human body is man's first worked on object and goes on to suggest: 'This is difficult to comprehend from a Western perspective which is dominated by a reified conception of the relationship between subject and object...' (1995: 99). It is noticeable that tattoos are always represented as a priori; no character is ever described getting a tattoo, but many characters are depicted injecting heroin. The act of injecting heroin is invariably represented as a violation of the body, which has become a clearly apprehended Other in the mind of the junkie.

Junk and Ink

Junky opens with the narrator entering an apartment full of drug addicts: 'the door was opened by a large, flabby, middle-aged queer, with tattooing on his forearms and even on the backs of his hands' (Burroughs, 1977: 5). In *Permanent Midnight*, Jerry Stahl notes of another testee at the methadone clinic: 'He laid his head on the desk, crying, so that the tattooed angel on the back of his neck spread her wings for the ceiling' (1995: 146). After the methadone has proved ineffectual

Stahl writes of his new dealer, a junkie himself: 'He had more ink than Satan: calves, neck, and arms a near solid catalog of tattooed Aryan brotherhood icons: Swastikas, Iron Crosses, barbed wire, doe-eyed naked beauties astride S.S. lightning bolts' (1995: 165). In Will Self's *My Idea of Fun*, John, a long-term junkie, is described as chopping the air 'with his thin, blue-tattooed forearms' (1993: 175). In *Infinite Jest*, set for the most part in a rehabilitation clinic, so many of the resident junkies are tattooed that one character, Tiny Ewell, is driven to construct what he refers to as a 'dermo-taxonomy' of tattooing.[1] Tiny's appraisal of the specific genre of 'jailhouse tattoo', interestingly, rejects Falk's suggestion, cited above, that tattooing 'does not imply contempt for the body'. Wallace writes:

> Ewell's personal feeling is that jailhouse tatoos aren't poignant so much as grotesque, that they seem like they weren't a matter of impulsive decoration or self-presentation so much as simple self-mutilation arising out of simple boredom and general disregard for one's own body and the aesthetics of decoration. (1996: 210)

Welsh's *Trainspotting* depicts another environment full of heroin and ink; one in which the body is first disfigured by tattoos, in a proleptic manner:

> He looked seedy and menacing done up in a suit, the wey draftpaks do, indian ink spilling oot from under cuffs and collar onto neck and hands. Ah'm sure Beggar's tattoos move intae the light, resentful at being covered up. (1996: 77)

Later, the body is abandoned completely: 'A mosaic shell ay scar tissue and indian ink, ah presume there's some cunt inside it, is screaming...' (1996: 77).

Tattooing is not, clearly, a purely symbolic utterance in such texts; pragmatic issues need to be considered. In *Permanent Midnight*, Stahl's first visit to a methadone clinic prompts this observation: 'Right off, what you noticed about the people waiting were their tattoos and their eyes. The green jailhouse ink and the hard dead stare of the majorly incarcerated' (1995: 144). Another dealer has a junkie friend called Felix: 'a lumbering, jug-eared tattoo victim he knew from the joint' (1995: 266). Most of the junkies in such narratives are routinely in and out of jail, where tattooing is a pervasive cultural practice. Indeed, I can think of no more compelling evidence to support the theory that tattooing represents a movement away from the natural towards the artificial than to note the prevalence of tattooing in prisons. One need not have read Foucault's *Discipline and Punish* to recognize the extraordinary unnaturalness of prison life. In the fiction of Jean Genet, much of whose work is set in prisons, the symbolic and the pragmatic are intertwined. Genet's male narrators are often transfixed by desire for heavily tattooed criminals, but their colourful flesh merely encases an essential criminality – and it is this essence which Genet's narrators really wish to possess; the heavily inscribed flesh is the only available conduit.

Falk writes of modernity and tattooing: 'irreversible body-marking became closely associated with stigmatization' (1995: 102). In junk narratives the body becomes a surface upon which, socially, the junkie announces his marginalization, and, philosophically, one upon which he utters his contempt for the flesh. The junkie's attitude to his body is effectively Cartesian. Tattooing neatly parallels the junkie's principal non-custodial activity: the injection of heroin, the piercing of the flesh with needles. Conflated, indeed paradoxical, issues emerge here. The junkie, constantly threatened with imprisonment, voluntarily surrenders his freedom immediately upon release from prison, this time to heroin. The needles of the prison tattooist or, more usually, the prisoner's safety pin and ink, are exchanged for the junkie's own needle; in the former case the body is used as a declarative surface, and in the latter case the body is again used – this time to service the mind.

Not only is the addict physically enslaved to heroin, but he is, it can be argued, enslaved to drugs because of an extravagant belief in the mind/body dichotomy. The junkie typically treats his own body as though it were a slave to his consciousness. The mind is the master in junk narratives, the body is the slave. It is true that the disdain shown by the junkie for the body could also be shown to be true of the 'will', a common feature of Western intoxication discourse, and that, therefore, contrasting body denial to the privileging of the mind is problematic. It is equally true that in the case of the junkie there is not a simple constellation of the body serving the mind because mind here has not actually a position of being the 'master' of the body – or anything else. From this perspective, mind is primarily a name for a experiential state which is first and foremost a bodily state. Thus leaving and deserting the body, as a spirit or as 'pure' mind, is actually the same thing as dissolving one's conscious self and regressing to a 'purely' bodily state of being, a movement which eventually dissolves also the body.[2] However, these arguments are similar to those advanced above regarding the flaws in Cartesian dualism; they are considerably more plausible than the philosophical positions which they critique, but these novels actually promote an artificial and anachronistic dualism which is in itself worth tracking. Burroughs's description of the heroin addicted Jack in *Junky* makes this point quite emphatically:

> You would see him one time a fresh-faced kid. A week or so later he would turn up so thin, sallow and old-looking, you would have to look twice to recognize him. His face was lined with suffering in which his eyes did not participate. It was a suffering of the cells alone. He himself – the conscious ego that looked out of the glazed, alert-calm hoodlum eyes – would have nothing to do with this suffering of his rejected other self, a suffering of the nervous system, of flesh and viscera and cells. (1977: 3)

What is particularly striking here is the way in which the 'self' is disconnected from the body; it is defined solely as the 'conscious ego'. Jack rejects his own body

– he simply inhabits it, like a seedy hotel room he periodically leaves to buy drugs. His body is absolutely necessary to him, but it has a purely subservient status. Again and again throughout his book Burroughs stresses a mind/body dichotomy which is represented as inseparable from the junkie's view of life. Writing of an old junkie and thief, Bill Gains, Burroughs notes: 'He smiled, listening down into himself as if attending to something there that pleased him.... His veins were mostly gone, retreated back to the bone to escape the probing needle' (1977: 42). Just as Welsh's narrator in *Trainspotting* imagines Begbie's tattoos consciously moving into the light, resentful at being covered up, so here Burroughs anthropomorphizes Gains's veins, utilizing a martial image to depict them as 'retreating'. Later, he writes of a sick junkie: 'Doolie sick was an unnerving sight. The envelope of personality was gone, dissolved by his junk-hungry cells' (1977: 58). When he is withdrawing the narrator says: 'I was too weak to get out of bed. I could not lie still. In junk sickness, any conceivable line of action or inaction seems intolerable. A man might die simply because he could not stand to stay in his body' (1977: 97). In each of these extracts the body is clearly represented as something quite separate from mind, as an instrument, a conduit, a vehicle, and subservient to the mind.

Metonymy and Metaphor

Metonymy is a ubiquitous device in *Trainspotting*. Renton's opening comments on Sick Boy: 'There's nothing in his eyes but need' (1996: 4), eliminates everything physical about his friend except the eyes, because, of course, conventionally only the eyes can depict the workings of the mind. Tattoos and eyes, of course, are what Stahl first notices in the methadone clinic. Overall, while Burroughs employs a dry, restrained narrative style, to give his account a realistic 'documentary' tone, Welsh's book is driven by an exuberant comic hyperbole. In one scene Spud wakes up in his girlfriend's bed, feeling rather uncomfortable: 'I had pissed the bed. I had puked up in the bed. I had shat myself in the bed' (1996: 92). There is here a hierarchy of befoulment; each transgression is more disgusting than its predecessor. Then we learn about the relationship Spud is having with the owner of the bed:

> Gail and I have been going out together for five weeks but have not yet had sex. Gail had said that she didn't want our relationship to start off on a physical basis, as that would be how it would principally be defined from then on in. She'd read this in *Cosmopolitan*, and wanted to test the theory. So five weeks on, I've got a pair of bollocks like watermelons. There's probably a fair bit of spunk alongside that pish, shite and puke. (1996: 93)

The scene actually mocks Gail's disinclination for a physical relationship: the grossness of the body, and all its numerous excretions, when the mind is no longer in control, is the point of the scene. The grossness of the body, and a concomitant loathing for it, are essential aspects of junk narratives. Tattoos are one manifestation of this distaste for the flesh, but their depiction is proleptic in that inscription announces a desire to transcend the flesh; ultimately, to abandon it. Stahl's most striking depictions of a heroin high focus on disembodiment: 'At last, my grateful spirit eased out of the fetid bag of humanity crumpled in that Japanese car, eased out and drifted overhead, until it floated high over the San Fernando Valley. . .' (1995: 250). It is noticeable here that Stahl's preoccupation is with the spirit which floats above the valley, not the body which is left behind in the car.

Welsh is particularly graphic in his depictions of the body's physicality. Much was made of the infamous 'suppository scene' in *Trainspotting*, by reviewers of both the novel and the film, and when this episode was treated seriously it was usually read as powerful evidence of Welsh as a grittily, uncompromising, 'realistic' writer. But he isn't, as indeed this sequence in the film stresses. Throughout his book, but particularly here, Welsh focuses on the imperfections of the body, its fundament/tal grossness, so as to offer a tacit explanation of the junkie desire to transcend it. In the suppository scene, Renton, who is junk sick, has been sold two opium suppositories and has inserted them. The suppositories actually loosen his bowels, but, luckily, he finds the most disgusting toilet in the whole of Scotland:

> Ah whip oaf ma keks and sit oan the cold wet porcelain shunky. Ah empty ma guts, feeling as if everything; bowel, stomach, intestines, spleen, liver, kidneys, heart, lungs and fucking brains are aw falling through ma arsehole intae the bowl. As ah shit, flies batter oaf ma face, sending shivers through my body. (1996: 25)

The flies, although plausibly present in such unsanitary surroundings, simultaneously point to human decay and the eventual carrion status of all flesh. Renton catches one of the flies:

> Ah smear it against the wall opposite; tracing out an 'H' then an 'I' then a 'B' wi ma index finger, using its guts, tissue and blood as ink. Ah start on the 'S' but ma supply runs thin. Nae problem. Ah borrow from the 'H', which has a thick surplus, and complete the 'S'. (1996: 25)

The reader assumes Renton is writing 'HIBS' to stand for Hibernians Football Club, but running out of 'ink' he uses blood, borrowing, significantly, from the H, itself the letter that stands for Heroin, the reason he is there in the first place. A brilliant, self-reflexive metaphor, I would argue, for the act of writing the book itself. This is not a 'realistic' scene, although its major referents are familiar enough. What animates the incident, and the several others like it in the book, is a distaste for the body, not an amused tolerance of its gross physicality. This is Swiftian in its loathing for the body and its unsavoury productions. The mind, throughout all these books, regards the body with distaste, condescension and even hatred.

Heroin and the Penis

The mastery of the mind over the body in junk narratives is most graphically depicted in scenes which describe characters injecting heroin into the penis. In junk narratives the act of injecting often stresses the violation that is occurring. In Robert O'Connor's novel *Buffalo Soldiers*, for example, the narrator is injecting a friend with heroin but cannot find a vein: ' "Nothing left to hit," you say, but you want to raise the flag of blood. Coming up empty means you've missed the vein and hit meat' (1993: 6). The carnality, the 'fleshness' of the body is clearly emphasized here. The injecting user does, of course, actually pierce the flesh; he stabs himself, mutilates himself, violates his own body. A contempt for the body, even a hatred of it, is indeed, I would argue, a pervasive topos of junk narratives. However, while on the one hand junk narratives seem to advance a simple mind/body dichotomy, it is also possible to suggest that it is not simply the body which is being assaulted. In 'Flesh and Otherness', Gary Madison writes: 'The flesh is the trace of the other, the inscription of the other, in the subject's own self-hood – in its very flesh. What flesh means is that *the subject is for itself an other*' (1990: 31). It might actually be more accurate to suggest that the junkie's real hatred is not so much for the body as for the flesh itself, which can be perceived in some sense as preceding the body. Fishburn writes: 'In Merleau-Ponty's usage, the flesh is neither mind nor matter. Instead one might think of it as similar to the ancient elements of earth, wind, and fire – that is, as "an element of Being" ' (1997: 32) Fishburn goes on to note:

> Hortense Spillers makes a different distinction between body and flesh, claiming that 'before the "body" there is the "flesh," that zero degree of social conceptualization that does not escape concealment under the brush of discourse, or the reflexes of iconography'. (1997: 47)

The junkie's lack of interest in sex is a feature of all these books, but in terms of drama it is only figured as an absence. It isn't symbolic enough to depict the junkie's absolute contempt for the body. Only accounts of penis injection can adequately demonstrate the mastery of the consciousness over the mutilated vessel so essential for the transportation of pleasure. Stahl's doctor in the detoxi-fication clinic tells him: 'I used to shoot Dilaudid in my penis' (1995: 205). In *Trainspotting*, in a chapter called 'Cock Problems', Renton begins by saying:

> I had to shoot into my cock, where the most prominent vein in my body is.... Ah shoot into my knob for the second consecutive day. As the needle goes in it looks like a horrible experi-ment being conducted on an ugly sea snake. (1996: 86)

In an even more horrifying scene, near the end of the book, Renton goes to see Johnny Swann, who has just had his leg amputated: 'Johnny ran out of veins and started shooting into his arteries. It only took a few ay they shots to give him gangrene. Then the leg had to go' (1996: 311). Again, although the scene is depicted 'realistically', the episode is strikingly symbolic. Bendelow and Williams quote Ivan Illich: 'increasingly painkilling turns people into unfeeling spectators of their own decaying selves' (1995: 99). Renton expresses surprise at Johnny's high spirits: 'To my surprise the cunt was exuberant for somebody that had recently lost a leg' (1996: 310). But Renton's surprise is misplaced. Johnny can now 'lose' entire sections of his body without distress. His body has become increasingly irrelevant to him as his addiction gains total mastery. In *Infinite Jest*, a legless Swiss character informs a bar full of people: 'I am in early twenty years, without the legs. Many of my friends also; without legs' (1996: 776). Burroughs's book, too, refers on a number of occasions to amputations and prosthetics. One woman tells the narrator: 'You see, my system can't absorb calcium and the bones are slowly dissolving. My legs will have to be amputated eventually, then the arms' (1977: 13). Later, the narrator notes that heroin can always be bought, in any city, near 'Stores selling artificial limbs, wig-makers, dental mechanics. . .' (1977: 111).

Tattoos in junk narratives mark out bodies which, paradoxically, are constantly attempting to deny their own physicality and transcend their corporeality. In junk narratives, the writing on a junkie's body is like writing as understood by Deconstruction – constantly under the threat of erasure.

Notes

1. I am grateful to Paul Sweetman for reminding me just how much ink there is in *Infinite Jest*.
2. I am indebted to my referees not only for both of these provocative arguments but also for several other helpful suggestions.

References

Bendelow, Gillian and Simon Williams (1995) 'Pain and the Mind–Body Dualism', *Body & Society* 1(2): 83–103.
Burchett, George (1960) *Memoirs of a Tattooist*. London: Pan.
Burroughs, William (1977) *Junky*. Harmondsworth: Penguin. (Orig. 1953.)
Carter, Angela (1969) *Heroes and Villains*. Harmondsworth: Penguin.
Cocteau, Jean (1990) *Opium*, trans. Margaret Crosland. London: Peter Owen.
Crossley, Nick (1995) 'Merleau-Ponty, the Elusive Body and Carnal Sociology', *Body & Society* 1(1): 43–63.
Falk, Pasi (1995) 'Written in the Flesh', *Body & Society* 1(1): 95–105.
Fishburn, Katherine (1997) *The Problem of Embodiment in Early African American Narrative*. Westport, CT: Greenwood Press.

Levin, David (1990) 'Justice in the Flesh', in G. Johnson and Michael Smith (eds) *Ontology and Alterity in Merleau-Ponty*. Evanston, IL: Northwestern University Press
Madison, Gary (1990) 'Flesh as Otherness', in G. Johnson and Michael Smith (eds) *Ontology and Alterity in Merleau-Ponty*. Evanston, IL: Northwestern University Press.
Melville, Herman (1988) *Moby Dick*. Evanston, IL: Northwestern University Press.
O'Connor, Robert (1993) *Buffalo Soldiers*. London: Flamingo.
Self, Will (1993) *My Idea of Fun*. Harmondsworth: Penguin.
Stahl, Jerry (1995) *Permanent Midnight*. London: Abacus.
Wallace, David Foster (1996) *Infinite Jest*. New York: Little, Brown and Co.
Welsh, Irvine (1996) *Trainspotting*. London: Minerva. (Orig. 1993.)

Kevin McCarron is a Senior Lecturer in American Literature at Roehampton Institute, London. He has published widely in a variety of academic journals and books. His most recent full-length publications include *William Golding* (The British Council and Northcote House, 1995) and *The Coincidence of Opposites* (Sheffield Academic Press, 1996). He is currently writing a book, to be published by Macmillan, provisionally entitled *Alcoholism, Drug Addiction and the 'Recovery Narrative'*.

Performing the Technoscientific Body: RealVideo Surgery and the Anatomy Theater

EUGENE THACKER

Dr. Benway is operating in an auditorium filled with students: 'Now, boys, you won't see this operation performed very often and there's a reason for that. . . . You see it has absolutely no medical value. No one knows what the purpose of it originally was or if it had a purpose at all. Personally I think it was a pure artistic creation from the beginning.

'Just as a bull fighter with his skill and knowledge extricates himself from danger he has himself invoked, so in this operation the surgeon deliberately endangers his patient, and then, with incredible speed and celerity rescues him from death at the last possible split second. . . . Did any of you ever see Dr. Tetrazzini perform? I say perform advisedly because his operations were performances. He would start by throwing a scalpel across the room into the patient and then make his entrance like a ballet dancer.' (Burroughs, 1990: 60–1)

The Anatomical Performative

In looking over current news and bio-science resources (from the 'Science Times' section of the *New York Times*, to the magazines *Science* and *Nature*, to the online network BioSpace.com), one notices a curious absence. There is no shortage of information concerning contemporary biotechnology and genetics (e.g. debates over human embryonic cloning or human gene patenting) and, indeed, these rapidly developing biological technosciences seem to be, in many ways, the defining sciences of the body in the West, speaking a complex language of genetic codes, DNA chips and genomic databases. To speak of anatomy in this context seems disturbingly anachronistic, as if the modern narrative of scientific progress had already substituted biotech for anatomy as the coming scientific paradigm of

Body & Society © 1999 SAGE Publications (London, Thousand Oaks and New Delhi), Vol. 5(2–3): 317–336
[1357–034X(199906/09)5:2–3;317–336;008867]

the body. What follows here is an attempt to show how modern anatomical science is currently engaged with digital and networking technologies, and the ways in which this engagement is transforming anatomical science's production of bio-medical normativity.

I would like to begin with a juxtaposition of two genealogically related event-scenes, which will form the main objects of inquiry in this article. They are significantly different in a variety of respects (historically, scientifically, as disciplines, politically), but are also linked as instances of technological embodiment in scientific and medical practice.

The first example occurred in cyberspace, over the Web, in mid-August of 1998. It was the first instance of 'live' surgery transmitted over the Web (using digital video), and its subject was a 57-year-old woman undergoing open heart surgery at Providence Hospital in Seattle. The event, co-presented by the hospital and a media-health website called America's Health Network (AHN), is the first of a series of such operations which will be broadcast live over the Web, and it also follows a few months after the first live webcast of a birth on the Internet. The broadcast lasted nearly three hours, and included pre-surgery segments of interviews with the surgeons, as well as a 'pre-surgery prayer' between the head surgeon and the patient. The technology utilized for the webcast included a head-mounted digital video camera worn by the head surgeon, accompanied by an ongoing voice-over during the operation from the surgeons. The signal was then sent over the Internet using a software application called 'RealVideo', designed in part for live broadcasts of events over the Web. RealVideo is a product of Real-Media Networks, which also produces RealAudio.

These applications use a networking technology called 'streaming media'. Usually, when a computer user wants to view a movie clip or hear a sound file over the Web, that file is completely downloaded prior to its being viewed or listened to, a process which, depending on file sizes, can be extremely time-consuming. With streaming media applications such as RealVideo, a 'buffer' is created which creates a lag-distance between information downloaded and viewable information. The streaming media applications are able to distinguish and allocate information so that, for example, the beginning of a movie clip will be downloaded first – that is, in the way in which the information would be viewed by the computer user (something which is not implied in data transfers). Thus, when a computer user wishes to see a movie clip, the RealVideo application will begin downloading the beginning of the clip first. Once this buffer is established, the RealVideo application will immediately begin playing the beginning of the movie clip, and this will create a continuous streaming of information – information will be viewed as soon as it is downloaded. This continual, real-time innovation in data transfer technology also means that streaming media is applicable not only to archived movie clips (or news segments, interviews, etc.), but to 'live' webcasts of events as well (sex shows and popular music concerts being the most common use of live streaming media).

Providence Hospital, as well as several other US hospitals and medical centers, have planned further webcasts of medical events as well. A statement released by the staff at Providence supports the utilization of networking technologies for educational purposes (both in terms of a general, non-specialist public and in terms of the medical community), remote advising or pedagogy (where, in future webcast operations, medical students at remote locations will be able to pose questions to the surgeon during the operation), and for the future of what many in the technical-medical community are calling 'virtual surgery' (where trial operations can be performed on virtual patients prior to the actual surgery).

The second event-scene is located in the early part of the 16th century in several European metropolitan areas, such as Padua, Bologna and Leiden (Persaud, 1997; Rupp, 1990; Sawday, 1995). In these contexts one finds the intersection of advances in anatomical science, changing structures of institutional and university accommodation, and a political investment in the developing sciences as a sign of cultural prosperity. These forces are found condensed in the space of the numerous 'anatomy theaters', many of which were constructed during the mid–16th century, and intended to be used exclusively for anatomical presentations. Though the first 'public' human dissections have been dated back to the 13th century, such demonstrations were usually presented to a specialized audience of anatomists, physicians and students of anatomy and medicine (and, throughout its history, a majority of such presentations were closely affiliated with educational institutions).[1]

Yet the anatomy theaters, as they developed during the 16th century, became public spectacles which attracted a range of audience members, from physicians to nobility to state officials (thus 'public' has a certain meaning in these contexts – see Ferrari, 1987; Knight, 1980; Rupp, 1990). Many presentations opened with elaborate processions, some had musical accompaniment and there are stories of banquets being held after the dissections performed at the Leiden anatomy theater. At the center of these presentations was, of course, the public dissection of a human corpse, usually a (male) criminal body executed in public. The anatomist would sometimes perform the actual dissection himself, and sometimes the actual labor of dissection would be performed by orderlies or students. Next to the dissected corpse was an anatomical text, usually a canonic text by Galen, from which the anatomist would read while revealing the corresponding materialization in the corpse (a kind of self-fulfilling, scientific show-and-tell). As may be guessed, the main attraction of the anatomy theaters lay in a certain type of voyeurism associated with a sense of real-time discovery before one's very eyes, a universalized glimpse into one's own interior. Added to this was, in the tradition of Renaissance humanism, the performative display of the metaphysical homologies between the (universal, male) body, the (mechanistic) cosmos, and a rationalized political and governing order: centralized, hierarchical and functional parts and wholes (Sawday, 1995; Stafford, 1997).

The cultural excitement which surrounded the anatomical sciences, rooted for the most part in Italian scientific culture, and which also spread to northern Europe, was a product of multiple forces, primary among them being the interest in which the state and various other political bodies took in this emerging modern science as cultural currency. Padua and Bologna were as renowned for their anatomy theaters as for their universities specializing in the arts and sciences. As both Sawday (1995) and Tierney (1998) suggest, while human dissection prior to the early modern period was heavily beset by various taboos, the rise of the anatomy theaters constituted part of a larger technology of social production, where the regulation of corpses for dissection was made possible, in part, by the complex relationships between penal law and medical educational support. The anatomy theaters were linked to the juridical and penal system by the economy of bodies which circulated between them (usually in semi-legal or illegal forms – see Persaud, 1997, and Tierney, 1998), the most common arrangement (as exemplified by the example of Leiden) being the transition of the executed, criminal body from the executioner/state to the anatomist/university. Various readings have been proposed here in this transition, the most prevalent being the shift from the cathartic extinguishing of the transgressive in the carnivalesque scene of public execution, towards the more rigidly organized, rationalized and civil demonstration of the scientific, political, and cosmological implications of the body's secret order (Ferrari, 1987; Sawday, 1995; Stafford, 1997).

These examples form significant, historically situated intersection points, where the body and technology are both configured through the mediating legitimation practices of medical science. Though the issues concerning the shifting roles of human dissection, and the complex relationships between institutional structures and the economy of bodies are interwoven in both of these instances, what I would like to highlight in particular is how both of these moments constitute particular, performative spectacularizations of the anatomico-medical body – spectacles which are concurrent with organizational and epistemological structures. Here the technological plays a crucial role, both in terms of facilitating anatomical science's will to visualize the non-visible (in public demonstration), and in a mobilizing of this visualization process into new image-bodies (through the medium of performance, texts and strategic representation). However, 'body' and 'technology', and the objects they appear to signify, might benefit here from a brief conceptual elaboration on the way to inquiring further into the techno-bodies of the anatomy theater and RealVideo surgery.

The Body of Technology/Technology of the Body

In the critical 'genealogies' of Michel Foucault (especially *Discipline and Punish* and the first volume of *The History of Sexuality*), to discuss the body is to discuss technologies of corporeal production in discourses and in practices, just as to discuss technology is to discuss their contextualized inscriptions into patterns of corporeal docility and normativity. This is, of course, not to relativize the efficacy of 'body' and 'technology' as distinct terms, but rather to begin to suggest that what Foucault offers is a theory of discourse, power and the body which obligates a consideration of the epistemologies, practices, techniques and discursive reiterations which contribute to the articulation of bodies in specific contexts. For our purposes here, those discourses and practices have to do with the complex history of modern anatomical and medical science (while also underscoring its connections to educational, national-political and juridical contexts), as well as its contemporary configurations through networking technologies such as the Web.

Though Foucault rarely discussed particular technologies in his analyses of the prison, sexuality or the hospital, a notion of the technological is implicit in all his writings. Foucault's usage of the term 'technology', as well as tropes referencing mechanistic philosophies, 'machinic' power relations and techniques of rationalization, classification and 'tables', all recur in a variety of ways describing the particular manifestations of discursive-institutional networks as they productively and 'somatically' render subjects and bodies. In *Discipline and Punish*, Foucault briefly comments on the relationship of power to his notion of technology:

> That is to say, there may be a 'knowledge' of the body that is not exactly the science of its functioning, and a mastery of its forces that is more than the ability to conquer them: this knowledge and this mastery constitute what might be called the political technology of the body. (Foucault, 1979: 26)

In his analyses of subjects and bodies within penal and juridical networks, Foucault's notion of technology places an emphasis on the legitimized and legitimizing production and utilization of an institutional and discursive apparatus applied towards the formation of bodily practices, habits and exercises conducive to normativity. As Foucault states in the first volume of *The History of Sexuality*, 'a normalizing society is the historical outcome of a technology of power centered on life' (1978: 144). This conception of a 'bio-power' whose main task is the establishment of patterns of social regulation, applies equally to the population – a 'bio-politics of the population' – as well as to the individual subject – an 'anatomico-politics of the human body' (Foucault, 1978). Thus, the situated implementation of these technologies of the body also means that bio-power is never monolithic in its effects; rather, the specificity of a given context, and the specificity of the technologies which constitute that context, produce a multiplicity of normative constraints and models of normativity. This distribution of docility can occur across disciplines and discourses (as Foucault's analyses of the asylum, the hospital, the prison and medicine demonstrate), as well as within them (for example the differences between the anatomical body in a medical textbook and the specific, individualized body of the patient undergoing surgery).

However, this is also more than a metaphoric appropriation of the term 'technology', displaced from its quotidian connotation of technological objects, and grafted onto the space of social and political formations. While Foucault's concern in his analyses places less emphasis on discrete technological objects, his notion of technology suggests that, prior to the consideration of the social and cultural effects of a given technology or technological object, there is the complex social and cultural backdrop within which the emergence of certain technologies and objects becomes possible (in enframed research programs and institutions, and through some form of intervening social necessity):

> The classical age discovered the body as object and target of power. It is easy enough to find signs of the attention then paid to the body – to the body that is manipulated, shaped, trained, which obeys, responds, becomes skillful and increases its forces. The great book of Man-the-Machine was written simultaneously on two registers: the anatomico-metaphysical register, of which Descartes wrote the first pages and which the physicians and philosophers continued, and the technical-political register, which was constituted by a whole set of regulations and by empirical and calculated methods relating to the army, the school and the hospital, for controlling or correcting the operation of the body. (Foucault, 1979: 136)

In this narrative involving the emergence of new forms of science, politics and governmentality, nature had to be reinterpreted, in the light of Cartesianism's objectification, as a clockwork machine in which parts and whole, the visible and not-yet-visible, the knowable and not-yet-knowable, all constituted mechanisms in a continuing inquiry into the human body. When the body natural was also considered a mechanistic body, the facticity of nature coincided with new knowledge paradigms to enframe a 'technological' docility that would be explored extensively in anatomy and medicine.

That is, Foucault's notion of technology as a productive and regulatory logic is helpful in suggesting that technologies and technological objects are not sole causes, but rather the endpoints of an entire social and political process whose underlying assumptions concerning the transformation of the object-world inform the possibility of emergence of those same technologies. It is precisely for this reason, however, that it will also be of interest to consider the particularity of the technologies utilized in a given context – their specific uses, effects, linkages, and performative/constitutive instances of the technologies themselves, as they are embedded in particular practices (e.g. anatomical dissection, anatomy theater presentation, medical surgery, live webcasting). This will be a point of connection between the historically specific instances of the anatomy theater and RealVideo surgery, but because these are also different technological instances, it will also be a point of differentiation between the types of bodies produced in each context.

In considering early modern anatomy and RealVideo surgery, Foucault's particular configurations of the body–technology relationship suggest three main things. One is that, while distinct terms, 'body' and 'technology' will always necessitate their interdependent consideration as a relationship. Second, if 'the body' is articulated through a range of contextualized discourses and practices, it will have a distributed character which will contribute to a multiplicity of normative sites, both across and within disciplines. And, finally, a consideration of the body–technology relationship (in our case, within anatomical and medical science) will also be a consideration of the discrete techniques and methodologies through which bodies are strategically made visible and knowable as objects of knowledge.

Hans Bellmer[2] in Med School: Producing the Body in the Anatomy Theater

In *The Body Emblazoned*, Jonathan Sawday highlights several features which characterize the emergence of the anatomical sciences during the early modern period. These include a renewed interest in the value of observation and the visible within the development of a 'modern' science, the increasing use of tables, charts, diagrams and 'keying mechanisms' accompanying new strategies in representation and, finally, a resultant objectification of the body simultaneously informed by philosophy and specific to modern science (Sawday, 1995). For the practices of dissection in the anatomy theaters, these general issues of early modern anatomy become, respectively: (1) emphasis on direct and unmediated 'ocular evidence', through the authority of the performative and the figure of the anatomist, with the aid of the anatomical text (the rhetorical 'see-for-yourself' approach); (2) the proof (and, in the case of Vesalius, the problematizing – see Cunningham, 1997) of the early modern anatomical text through its actual, physical demonstration on a real body (the performance-anxiety of pointing to the wrong body part); and (3) an objectification particular to modern science, through the spectacularizing and theatricalizing of the corpse as the universal sign of 'Man' in an articulated architectural space.

What the anatomy theaters as well as early modern practices of anatomical dissection make clear, is that the objectification and 'making visible' of the body is coextensive with a range of shifting techniques for producing an anatomical body. The basis of this renewed functionality is evident in the numerous anatomical treatises of the early modern period, when the role of dissection in research, pedagogy and public demonstration gained a more centralized role, in part due to the emphasis placed upon the direct evidence of dissected bodies by anatomists such as Jacobus Sylvius and Andreas Vesalius (Cunningham, 1997; Persaud, 1997; Sawday, 1995). In this sense, it is helpful to distinguish several elements at work in the emergence of modern anatomy dissection practices. Contrary to what may seem to be the case – that is, what is presented – there is not simply a single body dissected within the anatomy theater. Indeed the primary accomplishment of early modern anatomy was its ability to performatively discern organizational structures and forms; to 'technologically' articulate the very structures and forms it claimed to be describing. The anatomy theater provides an instance where the ways in which anatomical science multiply produces certain bodies is put into a performative, material and 'scientific' practice, based, above all, on the assumption of the natural facticity of the human body and the testimony of public demonstration. This is, then, to suggest that anatomical science during the early modern period does not simply produce a single, normative 'body', but that the normative elements of anatomical science are productively distributed through a range of techniques, processes and performative gestures, which in no way deny the efficacy of normativity. Within the context of the early modern anatomy theater, we might say that its teleology – the clear and enunciative demonstration of a paradigmatic 'anatomical body' – comprises only one aspect in the self-legitimation process within anatomical practice. Thus, prior to the completed dissection we also find the 'corpse', and in the complex and messy zone of the dissection process itself we also find the 'dissected body'.

To begin with, we can distinguish the pre-dissection 'corpse' from the 'anatomical body'. In one sense, the whole point of dissection, and of anatomical science generally, is that the truth of the body's organization, function and larger metaphysical meaning, is not self-evident in the social, political, professional, domestic and cultural spheres of everyday life. From the anatomist's perspective, anatomy – as a science, as a body of knowledge, as a discourse – is thus somehow necessitated in its participation in what will come to be accepted as a body and a subject in spheres outside of the sciences. In the anatomy theater there is a complex, ritualistic morphology which takes place, from the acquisition of the corpse for dissection, to the completed demonstration in the anatomy theater, or to a completed anatomical text.[3] This process is both linear and, despite its being enframed within scientific investigation, also only partially closed off. The 'corpse' is the medium for this transformation, and it is always understood as a pre-dissection – that is, pre-discursive – entity (in the sense that it is prior to the discourse of science).

Of course, such corpses were not simply natural objects but, depending on their contexts, variously situated by the social taboos surrounding bodily exhumation, capital punishment, hospitalization or poverty and vagrancy (Ferrari, 1987; Rupp, 1990). The corpse is enframed by the natural markers of death, but this death only delegitimizes it as a body according to the equally natural markers of decay. Though emptied of life, the corpse is thus still a thick signifier of the natural world, and its processes of decay have a great deal to do with the development of dissection techniques – that is, with how, exactly, the corpse will be methodically deconstructed while it slips away in the process of decay as a normal body. Coextensive with anatomical education was the education of dissection techniques which, especially when anatomy theater presentations lasted several days, paid particular attention to the markers of decay in the corpse. Thus, upon entering the anatomy theater, these excavated and extracted bodies became 'corpses', a flesh-and-blood morphology before the discourse of anatomy.

This morphology of the corpse meant that, as a universal instance of 'Man', it contained a potential linkage to what might be called the 'anatomical body', the job of the anatomist being to clarify in the messiness of things this furtive, secret order.[4] Historically, the anatomical body is a thoroughly textual and theoretical body, obtained through a variety of elements which oscillated around the body like homologous satellites – comparative anatomies based on animal dissection, rudimentary physical observation and analysis, practices in classical medicine, interrelations with theology, physics and philosophy (Cosans, 1995, 1997; Park, 1995; Siraisi, 1997). As a discursive product, the anatomical body's main locus finds itself in the early modern period in the anatomical treatise. In the anatomy theaters and in dissection generally, the anatomical body devolves around the text, though it is not bound to it, especially in Vesalian anatomy. The differences between the numerous anatomical treatises of Galen, and Vesalius' famous *De Humani Corporis Fabrica* ('On the Fabric of the Human Body') reveal important shifts in the anatomical body. As Sawday (1995), Cunningham (1997) and others point out, Vesalius' rigorous engagement with contemporary modes of visual representation placed great emphasis on the visual (that is, the observable) as the anatomist's primary mode of investigation. The innovations which Vesalius developed for the *De Humani* . . . , including diagrams, tables and keying mechanisms, marks a move away from a purely linguistic-descriptive mode of anatomy (found in Hippocrates, Avicenna or Galen), and towards an informational, taxonomic and classificatory mode grafted upon a highly ornate and graphic sensibility.

More than anything else, the anatomical body is a model, articulated through the specific discourses and discipline of anatomical science: its ontology is an object only produced through its strategic dismantling. With Vesalian anatomy the body becomes a partially translucent image, waiting to be filled with the thickness and density of performative dissection. In a practical sense this is how the anatomical text was most often utilized in dissection and in the anatomy theaters – as a guidebook, or reference book, to both the techniques and the discursively based structures of the interior of the body. Performative enunciation and textual dissemination created a space for material demonstration. There are numerous instances in early modern dissection practices where disagreements between text and body are ascribed to an error of nature in the corpse, in its failure to coincide with the anatomical text, and Jacobus Sylvius – an ardent Galenist and teacher of Vesalius – would often attribute differences between (Galenic) text and dissected corpse to changes which had supposedly naturally occurred within the body since the time of Galen (Persaud, 1997).

But anatomical practice is not simply this straight line from the pre-discursive corpse to the thoroughly textualized anatomical body. Along the way one finds numerous ambiguous sites where the task of clarifying the body's structures is enframed by a visceral, abject lack of clarity. If the corpse signified the body prior to the discourse of anatomy, marked by the natural processes of death and decomposition, the actual practice of dissection constitutes a different, more ambivalent phase in the production of the anatomical body. One of the primary characteristics of the anatomy theater which cultural historians note is the disturbing juxtaposition between the messy corpse and the ordered anatomical text (Cunningham, 1997; Hillman and Mazzio, 1997; Sawday, 1995). Dissection is a practice, informed by anatomy and medicine, and as such it is composed of a range of techniques, tools, subjects, texts and modes of objectification. Though there was not necessarily one single mode of dissection during the early modern period, their commonality lies in the ways in which the various techniques of dissection contributed to the formation of an anatomical body as their primary goal. Every cut is strategic here, as an art of making the interior visible to both anatomical science and (in the anatomy theaters) to the naked eye of the spectator. *The process of dissection is thus a constant negotiation between a potentially disarticulated corpse and the scientific rigor of the anatomy text.* The body that develops during this phase – the 'dissected body' – is constantly being incorporated into the anatomical frame, though as a literally opened, unbounded and grotesquely visceral form, it may also threaten the coherence of that same framework. Again, there is a unique type of distance or space articulated here within the dissected body, situated between the corpse and the anatomical text or, more specifically, between the technical implementation of anatomical discourse and anatomical discourse itself. Despite the range of ritualistic, spectacular ornaments in many anatomy theaters (ornate processions, entrance fees and refreshments, post-dissection banquets), it was difficult for anyone present to deny a disturbing, extremely visceral experience in relation to the dissected body – a body that, through its being read as a universal signifier of the human body, was made doubly strange for the observer as a moment of auto-voyeurism (for some references to and accounts of public dissections see Eriksson, 1959; Ferrari, 1987; Rupp, 1990).

The key point here is that anatomical science does not sublimate or repress this visceral aspect of the dissected body; rather, it discursively aligns that visceral body – a body made visible and manifest through a technological apparatus – with anatomical science's articulation of the natural order, granting it a kind of ontology which significantly de-emphasizes its thoroughly mediated state. This explicit alignment of the grotesque, visceral body of dissection with a notion of the universal body 'as it really is', is one of the major discursive and technical strategies of early modern anatomy. The experiential impact and indeed necessity of seeing the visceral, dissected body – *presented within and articulated through the discourse of anatomical science* – forms an instance where the body may be understood as unmediated, natural and, above all, anatomical.

There is thus a political economy at work in the dissection practices of early modern anatomy. If, for early modern medicine and science, seeing was knowing, knowing was also thoroughly mediated through discourse and organizational-performative instances. In developing a 'modern' anatomical science, figures such as Vesalius, Realdo Colombo, Gabriele Fallopio and Hieronymous Fabricius were involved in the very gradual instantiation of experiment and observation as the primary methodological tools of a science of the body. The body undergoing anatomical dissection is put into a liminal space (the visceral, messy body of dissection) specifically so that it may be reincorporated into another discursive-material framework (the realization of the text of/on the anatomical body). But, as suggested above, the dissected body is not simply recuperated or sublimated into anatomical discourse *en masse*. It is, however, articulated through a complex discursive alignment, wherein the dissected body and anatomical discourse are constantly regulated with respect to each other. But, if the viscerality of the dissected body is in some way necessary for the success of anatomical discourse, we might also ask whether there are zones of slippage within anatomical discourse and practice, which in some way are also self-critical moments within the organizational and visual episteme of anatomical discourse and practice.

Georges Bataille's term 'formless' is useful here in describing this excessive portion of the dissected body (Bataille, 1985); it describes an instance of materialization whose function is to articulate the regions of slippage within discursive structures enframing that materialization. Bataille originally situates the term 'formless' as a dictionary entry (in the 'Critical Dictionary' compiled with dissident Surrealists during the 1930s) whose purpose is to undo the fixing of meaning characteristic of the dictionary (see Bataille et al., 1995). We are back again to the tension between body and text – both variously enframed as natural and naturalized elements made visible through the transparency of anatomical knowledge and demonstration. The excess portion of the dissected body – an 'anatomy of formlessness' – thus remains to be diffused in this economy through spectacularization (into image, text or inert, empty object), or through the accommodations of the formless by anatomical science's neutral objectivity within a heavily rationalized framework (the rational acceptance of the grotesque as natural). One of the key points in understanding the pragmatics of 'formless' as a(n anti-) concept is that it is not reducible to an object that might be located exterior to a given norm – rather the formless arises intimately from within the thick contingency of a specific set of discourses and practices. For Bataille, its attractiveness lay in its potential ability to reveal epistemological limits, or points of slippage, within such frameworks, thus leading to a kind of alternative, critical epistemology (as the 'Critical Dictionary' was meant to propose).

So then, within the dissected body, one finds a bodily economy structured so that a constant discursive and technical regulation may be maintained. This regulatory apparatus operates in two ways: it simultaneously opens the boundaries of the body while also incorporating it into the discourse of anatomical science (the strain of the anatomist to discern the interior structures of the body), and it also articulates and re-routes the excessive, formless elements of the dissected body through a rigorous scientific objectification proposed as natural. This process is further characterized by a renewed notion of the natural concurrent with the knowable – both in the body outside of the anatomy theater (the truth of bodies as they appear in everyday contexts) and inside it as well (the truth of the body's inner workings universalized beyond the individual subject).

'Up to and Including her Limits':[5] RealVideo Surgery

Perhaps one of the most significant aspects of these early anatomical treatises (treatises where body, text and diverse representational strategies all intersected) was not so much an articulated knowledge pertaining to the total functioning of the body, but rather an arsenal of organizing practices – dissecting techniques –

which contributed in different ways to knowledge of the anatomical body. That is, behind the seemingly trivial enumerations of dissecting techniques outlined in the anatomical texts of the early modern period, there is a complex organizational logic at work which approaches the body as raw material. Whether this raw material was viewed vitalistically (in the appropriations of humoral or pneumatic science) or mechanistically (under the 17th-century influence of materialism and Descartes), the body became in these instances a repository of a range of techniques which seemed merely practical, but which reveal a whole set of assumptions and logics concerning the scientific ontology of the body. The increasing prevalence of dissection was chief among the mediating practices which materialized in practice the speculative theories of earlier anatomists such as Galen.

In the technologically-advanced cultures of the First World, the live 'cybercasting' of events (from music concerts to news events), gradual integration of computer-mediated communication (CMC) into everyday life and the increasing habituation with which bodies are seen on screens, are all contributing to novel conditions in which the presence of event and audience are being significantly redefined. The world of medicine is certainly no exception here, for, along with a dense history of technological incorporation (e.g. the standardization of medical technologies such as x-rays and CT scans – see Howell, 1995; Kevles, 1997), the instance of RealVideo surgery is one of many examples where the practice of medicine is spectacularized (e.g. the recent Discovery Channel TV show *Operation*, and the popularity of videotaping births). Thus, RealVideo surgery combines, first, the increasingly pervasive implementation of computer and networking media in privileged transnational social sectors (e.g. MUDs, email, IRC, CU-SeeMe, the Web), and second, a range of bio-medical technologies involved in surgical and medical procedure (from biomonitoring equipment to surgical technologies such as the endoscope).[6]

In considering RealVideo surgery, it is important to note that, as a practice or event, it is not dependent upon Internet and Web technologies in the same way that medical surgery depends on an array of life-support and biomonitoring technologies (surgeries are quite capable of carrying on without being cybercast); nor is its mode of spectacular presentation necessary to its context in the way that it was for the anatomy theaters (at least not yet). RealVideo surgery is, first and foremost, a case of technology-as-supplement, whose projected use does include contexts where a greater dependence on the Internet and Web will play an important role (e.g. education, remote advising, virtual surgery, etc.). What RealVideo surgery does do is to combine the physically and institutionally located context of modern medical surgery with the public and mediated context of the early modern anatomy theaters. The main significance of RealVideo surgery is the ways in which the non-transparency of the medium of the Web and streaming media will affect habits of looking, recognizing and representing bodies. The body of RealVideo surgery is multiply marked through technologies of medical and biological knowledge: by anatomical knowledge generally, by hospitalization and health-related data, by modern diagnoses of anatomical/physiological disorder and/or disease, by the procedures and techniques of surgery, by operating-room technologies and, finally, by the mediation and digitization of the patient-body over the Web.

The strange oscillation of attraction–repulsion of the anatomy theater's spectacularizing of the body is paralleled in RealVideo surgery in two primary ways. These are not so much intended mediations, but rather the data transmission errors that are part and parcel of the Internet as a medium. As many a Web user will testify, these inadvertent moments of deconstruction can occur when an image does not get transmitted properly, and appears either in fragments or in unfocused, large pixels.[7] It can also occur when viewing movie clips which are by turns too fast, too slow, or unpredictable and jittery. So then, an instance such as RealVideo surgery, functioning as the transmission of surgical bodies, is likewise undone by the pixellation or digitizing of the surgical body, and second, through the unpredictable streaming of visceral, grotesque anatomical imagery over the Internet.

However, whereas the anatomy theaters dealt with a certain horror of death, an always looming *memento mori*, RealVideo surgery deals with the 'hyperreality' of mediation – with a certain loss of a notion of reality as the coextension of real-time occurrence and physical presence (the most direct, explicit imagery simultaneously registered as nothing but ones and zeros transmitted through fiber optic cable). The body of RealVideo surgery thus approaches Jean Baudrillard's (1988) notion of the hyperreal as manifested in the shift from the real, physical space of the stage or the 'scene', towards the simulational, superficial space of the 'screen'. Here 'obscenity' and 'transparency' work together to produce the effects of unmediated bodies made doubly explicit or immediate by their scientific obscenity (surgical technique – even when 'minimally invasive') and by their technological obscenity (real-time public webcasting of bodily interiors and cavities).

However, in contrast to Baudrillard's techno-gothic proposals concerning the disappearance of the body (something which is both an exaggeration and which presupposes a pre-mediated, 'real' body), what is happening with something like RealVideo surgery is the production of specifically legitimized bodies (legitimized through science and medicine), transformed through networking technologies of digital visualization. Extending Bataille's notion of the 'formless' in relation to the dissected body of early modern anatomy, we can also outline a possible 'critical anatomy' in the case of RealVideo surgery. Though the basic mechanism is the same (the mediation of the visceral body as unmediated), the issues are significantly different. While early modern anatomy enframes the dissected body (through a range of dissection techniques), RealVideo surgery more explicitly highlights the mediation of the visceral body as both image and data (as both streaming information and as the digital image which that information encodes for). At issue in both contexts is the discursive and technical training or docility involved in outlining and recognizing the (anatomical) body. However, what RealVideo surgery presents us with is an instance where a novel regime of bodily representation – that of computer and networking technologies – is strategically incorporated into the anatomical paradigm of modern medical science. Most often the products of this type of mediation (as illustrated by the example of digital image pixellation above) are understood as either manifest distortion or error (when the video transmission breaks up or is not continuous) or simply as unmediated invisibility (the acceptance of the 'live' cybercast event without any extraneous disturbances). What this incorporation of digital technology amounts to is that the event, and the bodies, are only understood as mediated when there is an excess of information (causing informational 'noise' in the transmission). The effects of such technologies on these particular types of 'embodiment' are of several types, which we might briefly list (in a dictionary or encyclopedia-like fashion) here:

The Pixellated Abject: The uncanny tension between a recognition of opened, visceral, grotesque bodies of/in medical surgery, and their imperfect, unpredictable renderings via a digital medium, most often resulting in fragmented, accidentally deconstructed digital images of the body. Here a question arises in a distance between (visceral) materiality and (terminal) data; when viewers see, through a RealVideo window, a close-up of a surgically opened chest, an extreme push occurs towards the dream of the unmediated, as framed within codes of digital imaging and data transfer.

Streaming Kinesthetics: Along with the former, spatialized quality is also the particular technological eccentricities of live-networking or 'streaming media', which transpose networking and communicational activities on the Internet (such as website surfing, email and so forth) into real-time media (such as CU-SeeMe, IRCs, MUDs and Java programming). The effect with such media generally is an unpredictable data-transmission rhythm, made more explicit when the material being transmitted is the 'real' body-in-movement (a beating heart, flowing blood, movement of the surgeon's hand or head-cam). A reading process – or better yet, a decoding process – occurs here in the viewer, not as a specialist in medicine of course, but as a specialist within a mediated society. One primary question here, as in the category above, relates to the processes, signs and modes of decoding whereby the unpredictable streams of digital images are read or decoded as their real, physically-located referent.

Voyeuristic Exhibitionism: Events webcasted live such as RealVideo surgery (or, similarly, live sex shows or pornography) harbor a strange indeterminate place between public spectacle and private voyeurism. On the one hand, as live events broadcast live over the Web, they present themselves as public media(ted) spectacle, yet on the other this is only registered via physically isolated, individual computer users. On the broadcasting end, or from a more broad, conceptualized perspective, events such as RealVideo surgery are 'public' networking events which actively constitute both spectacle/event and audience. On the viewing and/or participatory end (in CU-SeeMe, IRC or MUDs), mediated collectivity is either reconfigured and reflected onto the user's interface (as in CU-SeeMe), or the collectivity associated with spectacle is dispersed along lines of technological mediation and reification. Though much discussion of 'virtual communities' has focused on this troubling need to redefine mediation, what is also at issue here is the way that ephemeral, event-based, virtual collectivities are constantly produced through networked media events such as RealVideo concerts.

A Histology of the Digital Screen

At issue with RealVideo surgery is a range of techniques for articulating bodies, for producing them as legible forms mediated by contemporary medical science – the production of new corporeal-legibility structures. RealVideo surgery is situated by its intimate conjunction of networking and computer-based technologies transparently applied to the specific techniques and technologies of contemporary surgery. While one question does have to do with the ways in which the incorporation of technologies such as the Internet and Web will contribute to the progress of medical science another, more pertinent, question is how new modes of reading and recognizing different types of bodies are in the process of being formed in such medical and scientific contexts. There is here a kind of networking, data-transmission legibility of the 'truth' or 'ocular evidence' of scientific bodies conjoined and infused with digital technology. What is ostensibly given to the viewer of a webcast surgery – or indeed a videotape or televised program of a surgical operation – is a body reconfigured through the techniques of surgical procedure but, simultaneously, due to medicine's general social claim upon matters of the natural and the biological, the most 'real' body possible, inside and out, living and undead. Following the nexus of desire, knowledge and scientific inquiry which marks much of the history of anatomical science, the relationship of the visible to scientific truth still persists in RealVideo surgery, as well as other contemporary technoscientific projects such as the Visible Human Project and the Human Genome Program. In the case of RealVideo surgery, of primary concern is how this shift from the physical space of the theater to the digitized mediated space of the screen is linked to a complex reconfiguration of what will come to be recognized, in a given context, as a medical and anatomical body.

Through a combination of computer and networking media, and contemporary biomedicine, RealVideo surgery is an instance where the anatomical-medical body is productively articulated as a complex visceral–digital hybrid, enframed by medical discourse and practice. As with the anatomy theater, such a performative instance, in renegotiating what will come to constitute the (scientific) body, must form a coherent political economy so that (medical) body, (surgical) event and (distributed) media may converge in communicating transparency and the truth of bodies. As alternatives to positions which either necessitate a conservative preservation of the body outside of medical and scientific discourses, or which obsessively see the body continually disappearing behind a technological semiosis, this article suggests that one of the more interesting spaces to occupy might be these instances of formlessness and embodiment, technoscientific slippages within the discursive apparatuses of anatomy and medicine. Such instances do not posit themselves outside of or in strict opposition to normative anatomical and medical models, but rather (as in Bataille's texts) work from within, asking whether a critical epistemology may be formed by starting with those excess elements which form the limits of anatomical and medical discourse.

Notes

1. Most histories of anatomy mention that there were instances of furtive and not-so-furtive human dissection prior to the early modern period (particularly in classical medicine), but its gradual introduction in a pedagogical and scientific context during the Renaissance constitutes an example where legitimizing institutions (universities, physicians' guilds) intersect with emerging sciences vying for respectability. The early instances of non-human dissection (comparative anatomical dissection of animals) can be traced back to Aristotle, among others, and the Alexandrian anatomist Herophilus, along with his contemporary Erasistratus, are said to have performed the first public human dissections. They were also accused in their time of having practiced human vivisection, though no evidence exists for such claims. For more on pre - and early modern dissection, see the articles by Cosans (1995, 1997), Park (1995) and Siraisi (1994, 1995, 1997).

2. Hans Bellmer was a German artist, photographer and sculptor associated with the Surrealist movement during the 1930s and 1940s. He became known for a series of photographs of rearranged doll and mannequin parts called, simply, 'La Poupée'.

3. As Persaud, Sawday, Tierney and others mention, the acquisition of corpses for dissection during

the early modern period was most often achieved through surreptitious means of grave-robbing, trans-actions between the executioner and the anatomist or, when juridical structures were established and actually implemented, corpses were regulated and circulated to medical universities (see Tierney, 1998). O'Malley and others tell of a famous story of Vesalius, as a student at Padua, coming across the corpse of a recently executed criminal just outside the city's limits. Vesalius is reported to have stayed the night outside the city, and to have smuggled the body in, piece by piece, under his coat during the next night, for use in his own dissection experiments (see O'Malley, 1964; Sawday, 1995).

4. Studies on the historical relationship between gender and science in the West have highlighted the implicit inscribing of gender in the very language and habits of vision of modern science. For example, most representations of the uterus (especially in Vesalius) depicted it as an inverted penis; a model of a female skeleton did not appear until the 19th century; throughout the 18th and 19th centuries the numerous debates concerning the female genitals, hermaphroditism and homosexuality reached a complex state as they were embedded in social-scientific disciplines and juridical practices (see Hillman and Mazzio, 1997; Laqueur, 1990).

5. This is the title of a performance piece by the controversial performance and body artist Carolee Schneeman, who, during the 1960s, explored issues of sexuality, gender, the abject and performativity from within and upon her own body.

6. MUDs (Multi-User Dungeons) are a popular, text-based, community environment on the Internet. MUDs often have themes (from role-playing sword-and-sorcery scenarios to virtual cafes) and users often take on virtual identities. IRC (Internet Relay Chat) is also popular, but more for general, non-themed 'chat' or discussion online. Both MUDs and IRC have a great number of virtual cross-dressers and cybersexual encounters as well. CU-SeeMe is a video-conferencing application to be used with a video camera. Users can log on to a 'reflector site' and see and chat with each other in real-time. CU-SeeMe was originally developed at Cornell University in New York State, but has subsequently been bought by White Pine Software and is being marketed for business and educational contexts.

7. Digital images are basically composed of large numbers of tiny squares – 'pixels' – each with a certain color-value which, in a mosaic-like fashion, compose an image. The greater number of pixels means greater color range and detail, and thus greater accuracy of reproduction. Because the Web is limited by bandwidth requirements (only so much information can be squeezed through a phone line at a time), image resolution tends to be much lower than it is for, say, print publishing.

Bibliography

America's Health Network (AHN): http://www.ahn.com

Bataille, Georges (1985)*Visions of Excess, Selected Writings, 1927–1939*, ed. Allan Stoekl. Minneapolis: University of Minnesota Press.

Bataille, Georges, Michel Leiris, Marcel Griaule, Carl Einstein and Robert Desnos (1995) *Encyclopedia Acephalica*. London: Atlas.

Baudrillard, Jean (1988) *The Ecstasy of Communication*, trans. Bernard Schutze and Caroline Schutze. New York: Semiotext(e).

BBC News Online (1998) 'Internet Heart Surgery First', *BBC Online Network* (18 August): http://news.bbc.co.uk: 80/hi/english/sci/tech/newsid_153000/153819.stm

Biospace: http://www.biospace.com

Burroughs, William (1990) *Naked Lunch*. New York: Grove.

Butler, Judith (1993) *Bodies That Matter*. New York: Routledge.

Cartwright, Lisa (1995) *Screening the Body: Tracing Medicine's Visual Culture*. Minneapolis: University of Minnesota Press.

Cosans, Christopher (1995) 'The Platonic Origins of Anatomy', *Perspectives in Biology and Medicine* 38(4): 581–96.

Cosans, Christopher (1997) 'Galen's Critique of Rationalist and Empiricist Anatomy', *Journal of the History of Biology* 30(1): 35–54.

Cunningham, Andrew (1997) *The Anatomical Renaissance: The Resurrection of the Anatomical Projects of the Ancients*. Brookfield, VT: Scolar.

Daston, Lorraine (1998) 'The Nature of Nature in Early Modern Europe', *Configurations* 6(2): 149–72.

de C.M. Saunders, J.B. and Charles O'Malley (1950) *The Illustrations from the Works of Andreas Vesalius*. New York: Dover.

Eriksson, Ruben (1959) *Andreas Vesalius' First Public Anatomy at Bologna, 1540: An Eyewitness Report by Baldasar Heseler*. Stockholm: Almqvist and Wiksells.

Ferrari, Giovanna (1987) 'Public Anatomy Lessons and the Carnival: The Anatomy Theatre of Bologna', *Past and Present* 117: 50–106.

Foss, Laurence and Kenneth Rothenberg (1987) *The Second Medical Revolution: From Biomedicine to Infomedicine*. Boston, MA: New Science Library.

Foucault, Michel (1973a) *The Birth of the Clinic*. New York: Vintage.

Foucault, Michel (1973b) *The Order of Things*. New York: Vintage.

Foucault, Michel (1978) *The History of Sexuality, Vol. I*. New York: Vintage.

Foucault, Michel (1979) *Discipline & Punish*. New York: Vintage.

Foucault, Michel (1994) *Ethics, Subjectivity and Truth: The Essential Works of Michel Foucault, 1954–1984, Vol. I*, ed. Paul Rabinow. New York: The New Press.

Foucault, Michel (1996) *Foucault Live: Selected Interviews 1961–1984*, ed. Sylvère Lotringer. New York: Semiotext(e).

Gallagher, Catherine and Thomas Laqueur (eds) (1991) *The Making of the Modern Body: Sexuality and Society in the Nineteenth Century*. Berkeley: University of California Press.

Hafner, Katie and Matthew Lyon (1988) *Where Wizards Stay Up Late: The Origins of the Internet*. New York: Touchstone.

Haraway, Donna (1991) *Simians, Cyborgs, and Women*. New York: Routledge.

Hayles, N. Katherine (1999) *How We Became Posthuman: Virtual Bodies in Cybernetics, Literature, and Informatics*. Chicago, IL: University of Chicago Press.

Hillman, David and Carla Mazzio (eds) (1997) *The Body in Parts: Fantasies of Corpoeality in Early Modern Europe*. New York: Routledge.

Hirschauer, Stefan (1991) 'The Manufacture of Bodies in Surgery', *Social Studies of Science* 21: 279–319.

Howell, Joel (1995) *Technology in the Hospital: Transforming Patient Care in the Early Twentieth Century*. Baltimore, MD: Johns Hopkins University Press.

Jones, Colin and Roy Porter (eds) (1998) *Reassessing Foucault: Power, Medicine and the Body*. New York: Routledge.

Jordanova, Ludmilla and Deanna Petherbridge (1997) *The Quick and the Dead: Artists and Anatomy*. Berkeley: University of California Press.

Kemp, Martin (1993) ' "The Mark of Truth": Looking and Learning in Some Anatomical Illustrations from the Renaissance and Eighteenth Century', in W.F. Bynum and Roy Porter (eds) *Medicine and the Five Senses*. Cambridge: Cambridge University Press.

Kemp, Martin (1996) 'Temples of the Body and Temples of the Cosmos: Vision and Visualization in the Vesalian and Copernican Revolutions', in Brian S. Baigrie (ed.) *Picturing Knowledge: Historical and Philosophical Problems Concerning the Use of Art in Science*. Toronto: University of Toronto Press.

Kevles, Bettyann Holtzmann (1997) *Naked to the Bone: Medical Imaging in the Twentieth Century*. Reading, MA: Addison-Wesley.

Knight, Bernard (1980) *Discovering the Human Body*. New York: Lippincott and Crowell.

Laqueur, Thomas (1990) *Making Sex: Body and Gender from the Greeks to Freud*. Cambridge, MA: Harvard University Press.

Lawrence, Christopher (ed.) (1992) *Medical Theory, Surgical Practice: Studies in the History of Surgery*. London: Routledge.

Levin, David Michael (1990) 'The Discursive Formation of the Body in the History of Medicine', *The Journal of Medicine and Philosophy* 15(5): 515–38.

Lind, L.R. (1975) *Studies in Pre-Vesalian Anatomy: Biography, Translations, Documents*. Philadelphia, PA: The American Philosophical Society.

Lock, Margaret (1997) 'Decentering the Natural Body: Making Difference Matter', *Configurations* 5(2): 267–92.

O'Malley, Charles (1964) *Andreas Vesalius of Brussels*. Los Angeles: University of California Press.

Park, Katherine (1995) 'The Life of the Corpse: Division and Dissection in Late Medieval Europe', *Journal of the History of Medicine and Allied Sciences* 50: 111–32.

Persaud, T.V.N. (1997) *A History of Anatomy: The Post-Vesalian Era*. Springfield, IL: Charles C. Thomas.

Pouchelle, Marie-Christine (1990) *The Body and Surgery in the Middle Ages*. Cambridge: Polity Press.

RealAudio: http://www.realaudio.com

Roberts, K.B. (1992) *The Fabric of the Body: European Traditions of Anatomical Illustrations*. Oxford: Clarendon Press.

Rupp, Jan C.C. (1990) 'Matters of Life and Death: The Social and Cultural Conditions of the Rise of Anatomical Theaters, with Special Reference to Seventeenth Century Holland', *History of Science* 28: 263–87.

Rupp, Jan C.C. (1992) 'Michel Foucault, Body Politics and the Rise and Expansion of Modern Anatomy', *Journal of Historical Sociology* 5(1): 31–60.

Sawday, Jonathan (1995) *The Body Emblazoned: Dissection and the Human Body in Renaissance Culture*. New York: Routledge.

Schultz, Bernard (1985) *Art and Anatomy in Renaissance Italy*. Ann Arbor, MI: UMI Research Press.

Singer, Charles (1957) *A Short History of Anatomy from the Greeks to Harvey*. New York: Dover.

Siraisi, Nancy (1994) 'Vesalius and Human Diversity in *De Humani Corporis Fabrica*', *Journal of the Warburg and Courtauld Institutes* 57: 60–88.

Siraisi, Nancy (1995) 'Early Anatomy in Comparative Perspective: An Introduction', *Journal of the History of Medicine and Allied Sciences* 50: 3–10.

Siraisi, Nancy (1997) 'Vesalius and the Reading of Galen's Teleology', *Renaissance Quarterly* 50: 1–37.

Stafford, Barbara Maria (1997) *Body Criticism: Imaging the Unseen in Enlightenment Art and Medicine*. Cambridge, MA: MIT Press.

Tierney, Thomas F. (1998) 'Anatomy and Governmentality: A Foucauldian Perspective on Death and Medicine in Modernity', *Theory & Event* 2(1): http://calliope.jhu.edu:80/journals/theory_&_event

Tsiaras, Alexander (1997) *Body Voyage: A Three-Dimensional Tour of a Real Human Body*. New York: Time-Warner.

Eugene Thacker [maldoror@eden.rutgers.edu] teaches at Rutgers University and directs [techne] New Media + Digital Art. His essays and net.art projects have recently been shown at Alt-X, CTHEORY, frAme, Leonardo Electronic Almanac, and The Thing.

Index

Index Compiled by
Jackie McDermott